A FOOD LOVER'S GALLERY OF PURE
TEN

SHELLFISH STEW

Clams, mussels, shrimp, and scallops are cooked together in a fennel- and tarragon-scented tomato sauce and spiked with Pernod, see page 162.

LOBSTER MASHED POTATOES

Combining coziness and luxury—mashed potatoes with large chunks of lobster, enhanced with lemon zest and chives, see page 329.

BARBECUED BABY BACKS
with Sheila's Raucous BBQ Sauce

A rich and tangy Texas-style sauce slathered over great grilled ribs, see page 122

THE GREAT LOBSTER BAKE

Succulent lobsters accompanied by clams, mussels, and shrimp accented by Parsley-Garlic Butter—the combination makes a splendid party dish, see page 197.

COLOMBE D'OR CRUDITÉS

A decorative basket of vegetables and eggs,
accompanied by a robust Anchoïade—an
unfussy appetizer that transports you to the
South of France, see page 12.

SALMON CAVIAR–STUFFED EGGS

In these deviled eggs, always the first hors d'oeuvre
to disappear, the yolk is mixed with smoked salmon,
capers, chives, and créme fraîche, and garnished
with salmon caviar, see page 17.

RED SNAPPER
with Citrus Salsa

Grapefruit and oranges combine with
jalapeño and honey in a salsa that tops a
delicate red snapper fillet, see page 190.

BACON SWISS BURGERS
with Tomato and Avocado

Ripe tomatoes and avocados
elevate a classic Bacon Swiss Burger
to new heights, see page 109.

MY FAVORITE BEACH PASTA

A dish to be made when local tomatoes
and basil are at their prime, perfect for
casual summer entertaining, see page 342.

LEMON SCALLOPS
with Grapefruit, Orange, and Watercress Salad

A citrus salad offset with peppery watercress brings the flavor of the grilled scallops to life, see page 174.

THAI PORK CHOPS
with a Spicy Vegetable Salad

Thick pork chops get plenty of heat from jalapeño peppers, see page 102.

ROASTED CARROT GINGER SOUP

Roasting turns ordinary vegetables into extraordinary ones in this soup made of caramelized carrots and parsnips, flavored with ginger, and finished with a garnish of créme fraîche and chives, see page 43.

SHRIMP TACOS

Delicious—with a little heat
from ancho chile powder, plus
fresh corn salsa and a minty
yogurt topping, see page 220.

ASPARAGUS AND SNAP PEA SALAD

An ideal springtime salad:
two seasonal vegetables tossed
with a lemony dressing,
topped with chopped eggs
and dill, see page 281.

CROWN ROAST OF LAMB
with Bright Green Tabouleh

A sprightly Bright Green Tabouleh
stuffing—redolent of parsley and
mint—transforms a Crown Roast of
Lamb into an enticing warm-
weather main course, see page 56.

SPARKLING LIMONCELLO

A combination of lemon liqueur, fresh lime juice, and sparkling water, see page 8.

FLORADORA

Gin sparked with a raspberry syrup, see page 6.

VODKA ROSE

Icy vodka colored with fresh pink grapefruit juice, see page 9.

SPAGHETTINI
with Clams and Tomato Herb Sauce

A refined version of spaghetti with clam sauce, including ripe tomatoes and garden-fresh basil and tarragon, see page 236.

BRAISED OSSO BUCO
with Gremolata

A tradition worth preserving: braised veal shanks in the classic Italian style with a sprinkling of parsley, lemon zest, and garlic served over Golden Orzo, see page 84.

GRILLED CORN
with Chipotle Butter and
Parmesan Cheese

Chipotle chile powder adds a
smoky kick to fresh grilled corn
on the cob, and a sprinkling of
Parmesan cheese provides a
smooth finish, see page 311.

BILL GROSS'S
BURNT ORANGE ICE CREAM

Caramelized sugar and
orange peel flavor an unusual
ice cream, see page 422.

SINFUL CHOCOLATE TART

A rich and fudgy chocolate ganache fills an almond-scented tart crust for a truly indulgent dessert, see page 386.

BIG STRAWBERRY SHORTCAKE

A buttery cake, freshly whipped cream, and ripe red strawberries add up to an American seasonal classic, see page 392.

RASPBERRY CASSIS SORBET

A little black currant liqueur brings out the best in a Raspberry Cassis Sorbet, see page 427.

RIB EYE WITH WILD MUSHROOM RAGOUT

Fresh shiitake, cremini, and porcini mushrooms, cooked with shallots, garlic, parsley, and butter to bring out their flavors, top a tender rib eye for a perfect company dinner, see page 69.

WHEAT BERRY SALAD
with Pineapple and Cranberries

The wonderfully chewy texture of wheat berries, combined with ripe pineapple, cucumbers, and dried cranberries, add up to a hearty, healthy salad, see page 317.

PEACH BLUEBERRY PIE

Two of summer's sweetest fruits
join together in a lattice-topped pie
best served warm with a scoop
of vanilla ice cream, see page 416.

Ten

all your favorite foods...

Sheila

...and ten recipes for each

Lukins

CREATIVE ASSISTANT: LAURIE GRIFFITH

WORKMAN PUBLISHING · NEW YORK

FOR
BAILEY & MATTHEW
TWO PERFECT 10S

Library of Congress Cataloging-in-Publication Data
Lukins, Sheila.
Ten : all the foods we love and ten perfect recipes for each / by Sheila Lukins. —1st ed.
p. cm.
Includes index.
ISBN 978-0-7611-3982-9 (pb. : alk. paper)—ISBN 978-0-7611-5125-8 (hb : alk. paper)
1. Cookery. I Title.
TX714.L8354 2008
641—dc22   2008035530

Cover design: Paul Hanson
Book design: Lisa Hollander and Katherine Tomkinson
Cover and interior food photographs: Ben Fink
Author photograph: Francesco Scavullo
Glassware used in the Cocktails photograph and the bowl and saucer used in the Roasted Carrot Ginger Soup
photograph are all courtesy of Clio, 92 Thompson Street, New York, NY 10012, www.clio-home.com.

The author thanks the following for the use of their recipes:
Balthazar's Steak Tartare and Beet and Endive Salad. Adapted from *The Balthazar Cookbook* by Keith McNally, Riad Nasr, and Lee Hanson. Copyright © 2003. Reprinted by permission of Clarkson Potter/Publishers, a division of Random House, Inc.; Velvety Black Bean Soup and Jeremiah Tower's Black Truffled Hamburger. Adapted from *Jeremiah Tower's New American Classics* by Jeremiah Tower. Copyright © 1986. Harper & Row. Used by permission of the author; Choucroute Garni. Adapted from *Anthony Bourdain's "Les Halles" Cookbook* by Anthony Bourdain. Copyright © 2004. HarperCollins. Used by permission of the author; Daniel Boulud's Chicken Grand-Mere Francine. Adapted from *Daniel Boulud's Café Boulud Cookbook* by Daniel Boulud and Dorie Greenspan. Copyright © 1999 by Daniel Boulud. Scribner. Used by permission of the author; Zuni Roast Chicken with Savory Bread. Adapted from *The Zuni Café Cookbook* by Judy Rodgers and Gerald Asher. Copyright © 2002 by Judy Rodgers. Norton. Used by permission of the author; Smoked Pork Chops with Cherry Brandy Sauce and Filipino Pork Adobo. Adapted from *Bruce Aidells's Complete Book of Pork* by Bruce Aidells. Copyright © 2004 by Bruce Aidells. Reprinted by permission of HarperCollins Publishers; Tom Valenti's Braised Duck in Red Wine and Tomatoes. Adapted from *Soups, Stews, and One-Pot Meals* by Tom Valenti and Andrew Friedman. Copyright © 2003 by Tom Valenti. Reprinted by permission of Scribner; Joan Nathan's Cooked Tomato and Pepper Salad. Adapted from *The Foods of Israel Today* by Joan Nathan. Copyright © 2001 by Joan Nathan. Used by permission of the author; Pink Lentil Dal with Fresh Ginger. Adapted from *Indian Home Cooking* by Suvir Saran and Stephanie Lyness. Copyright © 2004. Clarkson Potter/Publishers, a division of Random House, Inc. Used by permission of the author; Banana Upside-Down Cake. Adapted from *Craft of Cooking* by Tom Colicchio. Copyright © 2003 by TC Enterprises. Clarkson Potter/Publishers, a division of Random House, Inc.; Schrafft's Hot Fudge Sauce. Adapted from *Classic Home Desserts* by Richard Sax. Copyright © 1994 by Richard Sax. Reprinted by permission of Houghton Mifflin Harcourt Publishing Co. All rights reserved.

Workman books are available at special discounts when purchased in bulk for premiums and sales promotions as well as for fund-raising or educational use. Special editions or book excerpts can be created to specification. For details, contact the Special Sales Director at the address below.

Workman Publishing Company, Inc.
225 Varick Street
New York, NY 10014-4381

Manufactured in the United States of America

First printing October 2008
10 9 8 7 6 5 4 3 2 1

ACKNOWLEDGMENTS

O

I find writing cookbooks thrilling, and after having written six books I was looking for the seventh thrill. When the wheels start turning, I always hope for an epiphany—a lot to ask for—but I was blessed with a great idea by my one-in-a-million publisher, Peter Workman, when he suggested the concept for *Ten*. As always, I think he is a perfect 10, and I thank him dearly for all his support and caring over our 25-year relationship.

None of my books would have been possible without my exceptional editor, Suzanne Rafer. She, too, played a significant roll in conceiving *Ten*. She is a dear friend and an extraordinary person to work with. It's sheer joy to do a book with her and I could not imagine writing one without her guidance.

Then of course there's the wonderful Laurie Griffith, who I have the great pleasure of working with in my kitchen. We have been working together for so long that I can barely picture doing a book without her—a million thanks!

I'd be lost without Arthur Klebanoff, my great friend and agent, who is always there helping and guiding me, and turning the ordinary into the extraordinary with our special conversations. Those are the best and the funniest.

Happily, I am a longtime member of the *Parade* magazine family, watched over by Walter Anderson, who has always been supportive of my publishing efforts. I am so thankful for this. I thank everyone at *Parade*, especially editor Janice Kaplan.

Many thanks to Laura Donnelly, who has helped to sweeten up *Ten*.

With great thanks to Marc Reyes, my excellent butcher; Fernando Alcoser, for his fresh fish; and Ammo Manbodh, who helps me daily with my food, all from Eli's Manhattan.

Great thanks to all the fine chefs who shared their recipes with me: Tom Valenti, Tom Colicchio, Daniel Boulud, Anthony Bourdain, Andrew Engle, Keith McNally, Lee Hanson, Riad Nasr, Karen DeMasco, Jason Epstein, Jeremiah Tower, Bill Yosses, Jim Botsacos, Judy Rodgers, and Bruce Aidells.

Big hugs and cheers to: Paul Hanson for his gorgeous cover design, which I loved at first sight; Lisa Hollander, thank you for a delightful book design; and publicist Ron Longe, who I love dearly and who does a fabulous job of putting me on the map. Thanks, too, to the rest of the Workman family, including: Walter Weintz, David Schiller, Ann ffolliott, Jenny Mandel, Katherine Tomkinson, Barbara Peragine, Julie Primavera, and Peggy Gannon.

For making the food looks so delicious, thanks go to photographer Ben Fink, food stylist Jamie Kimm, and prop stylist Sarah Abalan.

Love and kisses to my daughters Molly and Annabel, who keep me happy every day. And a big hug to my sister Elaine Yanell. ❧

TABLE OF CONTENTS

INTRODUCTION:
A REPERTOIRE OF
PURE CRAVE

We all have foods we crave, foods we rate a perfect "10." A well-grilled steak, tender and juicy; a roast chicken, its skin beautifully crisp, its meat moist and flavorful; lobsters, steaming hot with a small bowl of melted butter for dipping; chocolate, deep and dark or milky sweet; I can go on and on. And, in fact, I did do just that. And this book is the result.

What spurred me on was a dinner I had with my publisher Peter Workman and editor Suzanne Rafer during which we talked about our favorite foods. Foods we love to eat every chance we get. Dishes we hope are on the menu when we go out for dinner. Wouldn't it be wonderful to have a book that not only featured these foods, but also featured them in the best recipes possible, we wondered. Peter and Suzanne looked at me. Well, why not, I thought. What a splendid challenge!

Needless to say, I couldn't wait to get started and by the next day, I had a list of the foods I knew were beloved countrywide. Some were seasonal ingredients—corn, tomatoes, asparagus, berries. Some were classic types of dishes—large important roasts, vegetable soups, seafood salads. Some were just all-out passions—chocolate, ice cream, burgers, ribs. By the time I was finished, there were 32 foods on my list.

But how best to present these foods in all their glory? When I thought about it, I realized that I couldn't name just one favorite recipe for each. Thirty-two recipes didn't add up to a cookbook, and besides, the best roast chicken I'd make for a cold winter night is different than the best roast chicken I'd take to a summer picnic. And the same holds true for a family gathering celebrating a special occasion, where I might serve a Big Fancy Rib Roast of Beef. But on a quiet Sunday night in January, I'm more likely to serve an aromatic, tender, slow-cooked brisket. In a eureka moment, I realized that I could probably name ten favorites for each food, covering different moods, seasons, combinations of flavors, cooking methods, or serving occasions. Ten best steak recipes. Ten best recipes for ribs, for shrimp, for chocolate. Ten recipes for each of my 32 chapters and each a perfect "10." That's it!

When creating the recipes, I focused on bringing a lot of fresh ideas to some of our favorites: Steamed clams had to be included in the Clams chapter, but wait until you taste them steamed in white wine that's been infused with fresh lemongrass. A chapter on Mashed Potatoes made sense—they're so classic and comforting, but here they're out of this world and unexpected in versions like Lobster Mashed Potatoes and

Caramelized-Apple Mashed Potatoes. A rib eye steak (one of ten Sizzling Steaks), tender to the knife, is sensational buried under a ragoût of wild mushrooms. All had to go in the book, along with fresh ideas for new favorites: Salsas made with pineapple, mango, and papaya; quinoa blended with chimichurri herbs; lobster in an updated Cobb salad; pork shoulder braised with Chinese spices and homemade preserved kumquats.

While I was cooking up a storm in my kitchen, I knew I also wanted to include recipes from chefs whose food I admire and whose recipes are a "10" in anybody's book. To name some: Daniel Boulud's Chicken Grand-Mere Francine; Tom Valenti's Braised Duck in Red Wine and Tomatoes; Anthony Bourdain's Choucroute Garni; Tom Colicchio's Roasted Rack of Pork; Judy Rodgers's Zuni Roast Chicken with Savory Bread Salad; Bruce Aidells's Smoked Pork Chop with Sour Cherry Brandy Sauce; and others. These recipes enrich the chapters they're in and I'm delighted to be able to share them with you.

A book like this is hard to organize in the traditional way. Although it contains all the types of dishes that make up a meal, leading off with a chapter of Cocktails (Honeydew Daiquiri, Floradora, Vodka Rose—just three of the perfect beginnings to an evening!) and closing with Ice Creams and Sorbets (Key Lime Ice Cream, Raspberry Cassis Sorbet, and Pineapple Sorbet—all perfect endings), recipes are placed in the chapters that best suit them. So, while the Vegetable Soups chapter features a range of notable hot and cold soups, the Fresh Tomato Soup is a highlight of the Tomato chapter and the Creamy White Asparagus Soup headlines the Springtime Asparagus chapter. Chicken—Roasted and Baked contains ten terrific recipes for, unsurprisingly, roasted and baked chicken. But, if you're looking to make chicken stew, you'll find a couple of great recipes in the Stews chapter. It's a little quirky, but it adds to the energy and enjoyment of each chapter. Plus, the index groups recipes of a kind together, so you shouldn't have a problem locating your current crave.

Having been a caterer and also a cooking school teacher, I understand the importance of creative menu planning. Scattered throughout are menu boxes of suggested meals for special occasions. I hope you cook them up, but mostly I hope they inspire you to use the chapters to prepare the dishes you crave the most. Of course, if it's spring and asparagus are piled high in the market, I say cook through the entire asparagus chapter. In the height of summer, don't pass up any of the tomato or corn recipes. And while you're at it, fire up the grill and lay on the steaks and kebabs (the Pickup Sticks chapter). In the cooler months, Vegetable Soups give you what you need, as do the flavorful braised meats in Sunday Suppers. To finish off the meal, check out the Ice Cream and Sorbet chapter and the Fruit Desserts. Of course, if dessert in your house is spelled c-h-o-c-o-l-a-t-e, that chapter starts on page 375.

My best advice to you—don't spend another minute on this introduction. There are too many great recipes to follow, so get in there and start cooking. You're in for the best of the best. ❧

"NEW AND REFRESHING, THESE ARE DELIGHTFUL UPDATES."

COCKTAILS

There are no rules any more when it comes to cocktails—just make them playful and creative and sip them at a leisurely pace. While I haven't gone overboard on exotic mixers, there are always new ingredients available that add excitement to even the most traditional drinks. Pomegranate juice revives the predictable Kir Royale, and cranberry juice wakes up a tired margarita. I've frozen grapes to re-create a Gin Fizz garnish I enjoyed in Marrakech—a top-off of champagne does the trick! A Floradora, made with gin and fresh lime juice, blushes from a dab of raspberry syrup—very sexy, like its namesake, the leggy dancing girls of the turn of the twentieth century. I've put a fresh spin on all these inviting drinks.

There's always room for a classic dry bourbon Manhattan to add a little weight to the mix. If you serve it in an old-fashioned glass, try to find a stylish glass swizzle stick to serve with it. I particularly like clear glass with one or two colors added. Another grounded drink, fizzy none the less, is the Ginger Snap: dark rum, lime, and for fun, ginger beer. Stir with a cinnamon stick—the longer, the better! Serve this drink on a small silver tray for a very elegant presentation. And if you're enjoying it near the water or on the veranda—perfect.

BLUSHING SANGRIA

SERVES 6

americans have adopted Spain's traditional sangria—made with red wine, oranges, lemon, and sparkling water—as their own. My choice for a beautiful, refreshing warm-weather drink is this lively riff on the classic: a rich rosé, peaches, melon, strawberries, a splash of Cointreau, and sparkling water. If you wish, substitute 7-Up for the sparkling water. Place a garnish of fresh mint in each glass.

4 ripe white or golden peaches, peeled, pitted, and cut into ¼-inch dice

2 cups diced ripe cantaloupe (¼-inch dice)

1 cup diced hulled ripe strawberries (¼-inch dice)

1 bottle (750 ml) rosé or dry white wine

¼ cup fresh grapefruit juice

2 tablespoons Cointreau

2 cups sparkling water or 7-Up

Ice cubes, for serving

6 mint sprigs, for garnish

1. Combine all the fruit in a large glass pitcher. Pour in the wine, grapefruit juice, and Cointreau, and stir. Let rest at room temperature for 1 to 2 hours for the flavors to blend.

2. Just before serving, stir in the sparkling water. Pour the sangria over ice in each wineglass, and garnish with a mint sprig.

GINGER SNAP

SERVES 1

ginger beer is a lively carbonated beverage flavored primarily with ginger, lemon, and sugar. It has a much more pronounced flavor than ginger ale and is a great mixer for dark rum. I add a squeeze of fresh lime juice to perk up the flavors and stir the drink with a long cinnamon stick, for fun.

Ice cubes, for serving

1½ ounces (3 tablespoons) dark rum

1 lime wedge (¼ lime)

4 ounces (½ cup) chilled ginger beer

1 long cinnamon stick, for garnish

1 lime slice, for garnish

Fill a tall glass with ice cubes. Pour the rum over the ice and squeeze the lime wedge over it. Top with the ginger beer and stir with the cinnamon stick. Garnish with the lime slice, and serve.

HONEYDEW DAIQUIRI

SERVES 2

O

In the heat of summer, there is no cocktail quite as splendid as a fruity daiquiri with just enough rum to let us know the party has started. While I put honeydew melon at the top of my list, watermelon and strawberries are also up to the task. Mixed with lime juice and crushed ice, this Cuban original is on its way up the ladder. Don't forget the paper parasols for the full effect (if you can't find any, try a decorative pick or skewer for the melon balls.)

1 cup cubed ripe honeydew melon, plus
    4 small melon balls for garnish (see Note)
1½ ounces (3 tablespoons) white rum,
    preferably Bacardi
3 tablespoons fresh lime juice
1 tablespoon Sugar Syrup (page 8)
1½ cups cracked ice

Place the cubed melon, rum, lime juice, sugar syrup, and cracked ice in a blender. Blend on high speed until foamy and well mixed. Pour into two martini glasses. Garnish each glass with 2 melon balls, speared with a hot-pink or turquoise paper parasol.

NOTE: If you'd like to make your daiquiris using either watermelon or strawberries, just substitute a like amount of either for the honeydew. Remove the seeds from the watermelon (of course!) and hull the strawberries before blending. 🌿

HOW TO CHOOSE A RIPE MELON

There are no guarantees when it comes to selecting a melon, but here are a couple of tips that should help you choose a ripe one.

First use your thumbs to feel the stem end. If it has a slight give, you're on the right track. Then use your nose. The sniff test will help confirm your melon is ripe. If there's a nice, sweet melony smell, you're in business.

FLORADORA

SERVES 1

I've loved Floradoras from my first sip at one of New York City's one-time trendy restaurants, Aix, and have been serving them out at the beach ever since. Just offering a drink with the name Floradora gives me great pleasure. I recommend Tanqueray gin for its smoothness. Raspberry syrup completes the picture for a quintessential summer drink.

1½ ounces (3 tablespoons) gin,
preferably Tanqueray

1 ounce (2 tablespoons) fresh lime juice

½ ounce (1 tablespoon) raspberry syrup

Ice cubes, for serving

4 ounces (½ cup) ginger ale

3 fresh raspberries, for garnish

1 sprig mint, for garnish

Pour the gin, lime juice, and raspberry syrup over ice in a tall glass. Stir, and then top with the ginger ale. Garnish with the raspberries and mint, and serve.

MY MANHATTAN

SERVES 1

Living in Manhattan, I feel I should tip my hat to my hometown drink and include it made with the best bourbon available. For me, it's Maker's Mark and dry vermouth, garnished with a lemon twist ... or sometimes sweet vermouth and a maraschino cherry. It all depends on my mood.

Ice cubes

1½ ounces (3 tablespoons) best-quality bourbon

½ ounce (1 tablespoon) dry vermouth

2 dashes Angostura bitters

1 lemon twist, for garnish

1. Place an old-fashioned or Manhattan glass in the refrigerator or freezer to chill.

2. When you are ready to serve the drink, fill a mixing glass or pitcher with ice cubes. Pour the bourbon, vermouth, and bitters over the ice, and stir.

3. Strain into the chilled glass, garnish with the lemon twist, and serve.

POMEGRANATE COUPE DE CHAMPAGNE

SERVES 1

New and refreshing, this is a delightful update on the Kir Royale. Made with natural pomegranate juice, chilled sparkling champagne, and a twist of lemon, this aperitif is an instant winner. It's not too sweet, because the juice is light and flavorful, yet it's not tart either—just right.

1 ounce (2 tablespoons) pomegranate juice
(see Sources, page 439)

5 ounces (10 tablespoons) chilled champagne

1 thin lemon twist, for garnish

Pour the pomegranate juice into a champagne flute and fill it slowly with the champagne. Float the lemon twist on top. ❧

CRANBERRY MARGARITA

SERVES 1

Margaritas are so popular that some restaurants list all their variations on a separate menu. Whether you prefer yours as a frozen slushie, on the rocks, or straight up, once the margaritas are poured, the party begins. There are many stories about the cocktail's origins, but whether it comes from Texas or south of the border in Mexico, it's a great drink. I go for mine over ice and enhanced by cranberry juice, which gives it a rosy glow.

About ¼ cup coarse (kosher) salt, for the glass

1 lime wedge

Ice cubes

1½ ounces (3 tablespoons) best-quality tequila

1½ ounces (3 tablespoons) cranberry juice

1 ounce (2 tablespoons) triple sec

½ ounce (1 tablespoon) fresh lime juice

1. Place the salt on a small plate. Moisten the rim of a cocktail glass by running the lime wedge around it. Dip the rim in the salt, making sure it is well coated.

2. Fill a mixing glass or a small pitcher with ice cubes.

3. Pour the tequila, cranberry juice, triple sec, and lime juice over the ice and shake well.

4. Strain into the salt-rimmed glass, and serve.

SPARKLING LIMONCELLO

SERVES 1

With its radiant lemon color and sunny, sweet flavor, limoncello has almost beat out Campari as the national drink of Italy. I love it mixed with a little fresh lime juice and sparkling water, to create a long, refreshing drink so perfect for the warmer months. Garnish it with a sprig of lemon verbena or mint.

Ice cubes

1½ ounces (3 tablespoons) limoncello

1½ ounces (3 tablespoons) fresh lime juice

2 to 3 tablespoons Sugar Syrup (recipe follows), to taste

4 ounces (½ cup) sparkling water

1 sprig lemon verbena or mint, for garnish (optional)

1. Fill a mixing glass or pitcher with ice cubes.

2. Pour the limoncello, lime juice, and syrup over the ice, and stir.

3. Strain into a tall glass filled with ice. Add the sparkling water and garnish with the lemon verbena.

SUGAR SYRUP

MAKES ABOUT 6 CUPS

Sugar syrup is excellent to have on hand when making certain cocktails and for sorbets. Once you cook some up, it lasts indefinitely.

4 cups sugar

4 cups water

Combine the sugar and water in a saucepan, and bring to a boil. Reduce the heat and simmer gently, stirring occasionally, until the sugar has dissolved, about 5 minutes. Cool to room temperature. The syrup can be used immediately or stored indefinitely in a covered container in the refrigerator.

VODKA ROSE

SERVES 1

I'm a fan of pink grapefruit juice, and it complements vodka to a tee. In a particularly rose-colored mood one day, I simply added rose water and a garnish of hot-pink rose petals for a most refreshing drink, with a bit more bite than the expected orange juice.

Ice cubes, for serving

1½ ounces (3 tablespoons) vodka

2 teaspoons rose water (see Sources, page 439)

4 ounces (½ cup) fresh pink grapefruit juice

2 hot-pink edible rose petals from unsprayed garden
    roses, lightly rinsed and patted dry, for garnish

Fill a tall glass with ice. Pour in the vodka, rose water, and grapefruit juice. Stir, garnish with the rose petals, and serve. 🌸

WHITE GRAPE FIZZ

SERVES 1

this is fizzy, fun, and very unusual. The mandarin vodka adds just the right hint of orange, champagne always adds buzz, and the frozen grapes make an unforgettable garnish.

¼ cup seedless white grapes, halved crosswise

Ice cubes

1½ ounces (3 tablespoons) mandarin vodka

¼ cup white grape juice

6 ounces (¾ cup) chilled champagne

1. Several hours before you plan to serve the drink, freeze the grapes in a single layer on a small sheet pan.

2. When ready to serve, fill a mixing glass or pitcher with ice cubes. Pour the vodka and grape juice over the ice and shake well.

3. Place the frozen grapes in a champagne flute. Strain the vodka mixture into the flute, fill the glass with the champagne, and serve. 🌸

"THE RESULTS ARE MAGICAL."

SPREADS, DIPS & FINGER FOODS are the

mainstays of any get-together where drinks are served. They can appear before

dinner or be stand-alone sustenance at cocktail parties. These tidbits and spreads

need to be full-flavored and luscious, while still being delicate enough to enjoy with a

drink. My ten favorite recipes in this category take a modern stance; they are unusual

versions of their kind and easy to prepare, while still being perfectly delicious.

No party should be without everyone's favorite: stuffed eggs. Here they are

gussied up with salmon caviar, which makes them a welcome addition to the most

elegant of parties.

The next hors d'oeuvre to disappear is the guacamole. Who can resist this

unctuous mixture of avocado, onion, and tomato seasoned with chile, cilantro, and

lime juice?

Sometimes simplicity is the key. Green picholine olives become sublime

when marinated in a mixture of fresh chile, garlic, rosemary, thyme, and—for an

unusual flavor note—tangerine zest. And how about Salmon Tartare, made from

the very highest quality salmon seasoned with a little lemon zest, Tabasco, and

chives, and served with Ficelle Toasts. Yum ...

COLOMBE D'OR
CRUDITES

SERVES 4

At the Colombe d'Or in St. Paul de Vence, France, they serve decorative baskets of vegetables and eggs on the table for everyone to pass around and enjoy. There's very little, if any, prep work done to the vegetables—and the eggs are even left unshelled. It's up to the diners to break off a piece of celery, pluck an artichoke leaf, select a radish, slice off a bite of cucumber, or shell a hard-cooked egg, and dip the selection in a dollop of Anchoiade. The results are magical and might even transport you to the South of France.

1 small inner celery rib

1 artichoke, cooked (see page 438)

4 to 6 scallions (white bulbs and 5 inches green)

1 small Belgian endive, trimmed, outer leaves removed

1 small fennel bulb, trimmed and halved lengthwise

½ hothouse (seedless) cucumber, halved crosswise

1 small red onion, peeled

6 to 8 radishes, preferably the long red and white variety

4 hard-cooked eggs, unpeeled

Anchoiade (recipe follows), for serving

Arrange the vegetables and eggs decoratively in a basket. Offer a sharp knife and small plates so everyone can help themselves to a serving of the vegetables. Place the anchoiade in a small bowl and serve it alongside for dipping. 🌿

ANCHOIADE

MAKES ABOUT 2 CUPS

Anchoiade is a robust anchovy sauce, bursting with garlic and brightened with a hint of red wine vinegar. It takes only a little to add pizzazz to a favorite crudité. Fresh parsley and extra-virgin olive oil help mellow the flavors and meld them together. Don't shy away from this because of the salt in anchovies—rinsing them in water makes much of the salt disappear.

1½ jars anchovy fillets packed in olive oil (23 fillets)

5 cloves garlic, coarsely chopped

1 cup fresh flat-leaf parsley leaves

2½ tablespoons red wine vinegar

1½ teaspoons Dijon mustard

1 cup extra-virgin olive oil

1. Drain the anchovies, reserving the oil. Rinse them well in cold water to remove the salt. Pat dry on paper towels. Coarsely chop the anchovies and place them in a food processor along with the garlic, parsley, vinegar, and mustard. Process until the mixture is just pureed, scraping down the sides of the bowl as needed.

2. With the motor running, drizzle the olive oil and 2 tablespoons of the reserved anchovy oil through the feed tube, and process until smooth. Transfer the mixture to a small decorative bowl, and serve. (The anchoiade will keep, covered, in the refrigerator overnight. Before serving it, add about 2 tablespoons hot water to thin it slightly.) 🌿

SUGAR-AND-SPICE NUTS

MAKES 2¼ CUPS

although they are marvelous all winter long, I save these nuts for Christmas—if I don't pack them up quickly and give them away, I'll eat them all! It's the egg white that holds the spices to the nuts. Once they bake and the egg white dries and hardens, the spices coat the nuts beautifully. If you use salted nuts, eliminate the salt in the recipe.

½ cup sugar

½ teaspoon ground cinnamon

½ teaspoon ground nutmeg

½ teaspoon ground cloves

¼ teaspoon salt

8 ounces mixed nuts

1 large egg white, lightly beaten

1. Preheat the oven to 350°F.

2. Combine the sugar, spices, and salt in a bowl. Stir well and set aside.

3. In a separate bowl, toss the nuts with the egg white to coat them. Then add the sugar-and-spice mixture and mix well.

4. Spread the coated nuts in a single layer on a baking sheet. You may need to use your fingers to separate the nuts as much as possible. Bake for 15 minutes. Remove the baking sheet from the oven and use a metal spatula to scrape up the nuts and break them apart. Return the nuts to the oven for 5 minutes more to dry them thoroughly.

5. Remove the baking sheet from the oven and shake it to break up the nuts. Let the nuts sit on the baking sheet in a cool dry place for 1 hour to cool and harden. (Stored in a tin in a cool dry place, the nuts will keep for up to 2 weeks.) 🌿

ROSA MEXICANO
GUACAMOLE

SERVES 2

◯

Josephina Howard was the genius behind the hugely popular Rosa Mexicano restaurants. When she established her first outpost on Manhattan's East Side, Josephina's food was ethereal—different from the food typical of Mexican restaurants on the East Coast. There are now Rosa Mexicanos in cities around the United States, but Josephina's guacamole is still made tableside, in a *molcajete*, a traditional lava-stone bowl used for grinding and mixing. You can achieve the same results using a mortar and pestle. If you don't own either of those things, use a chef's knife for mincing and flattening.

3 tablespoons chopped onion

1 teaspoon chopped seeded jalapeño chile

1½ teaspoons chopped fresh cilantro leaves

½ teaspoon salt, plus more to taste

1 ripe Hass avocado

2 tablespoons chopped tomato
   (discard juice and seeds)

Tortilla chips, for serving (a mix of blue and
   white tortilla chips is fun)

1. Place 1 tablespoon of the chopped onion, ½ teaspoon each of the jalapeño and cilantro, and the ½ teaspoon salt in a mortar or a *molcajete*. Pound with the pestle until the mixture resembles a juicy paste. (Or, combine the ingredients in a little pile on a cutting board and finely mince them, using the side of a wide knife to smash and crush them as you mince.) Place the mixture in a bowl.

2. Halve the avocado and remove the pit. Holding an avocado half in the cup of your hand and using a small knife, slice it in ⅛-inch strips lengthwise and crosswise, without cutting through the skin. Use a spoon to scoop the avocado out of the skin, dropping the pieces into the bowl. Mix the ingredients together, mashing the avocado slightly—but don't let it get mushy.

3. Add the remaining 2 tablespoons chopped onion, ½ teaspoon chopped jalapeño, 1 teaspoon chopped cilantro, and the chopped tomato. Season to taste with salt. Fold the ingredients together gently. Serve immediately with tortilla chips. ☙

OLIVADA

MAKES ¾ CUP

france, Spain, and Italy all have their versions of olivada. This one is an assertive blend of green Spanish Manzanilla olives and Greek Kalamata olives—a delicious deep purple slather mellowed with olive oil and lemon juice. It's marvelous spread on small round toasts and served with a chilled Provençal rosé or a glass of pastis.

> ½ cup pitted green Manzanilla olives
>
> ½ cup pitted Kalamata or Niçoise olives
>
> 1 teaspoon finely minced garlic
>
> 2 tablespoons fresh lemon juice
>
> 1 tablespoon extra-virgin olive oil
>
> 3 tablespoons coarsely chopped fresh
>   cilantro leaves
>
> Freshly ground black pepper, to taste
>
> Ficelle Toasts (recipe follows), for serving

1. Combine the olives, garlic, lemon juice, olive oil, 2 tablespoons of the cilantro, and the pepper in a food processor. Pulse the machine on and off until the mixture is just pureed but retains a bit of texture. If necessary, stop the food processor halfway through and scrape down the sides of the bowl with a spatula.

2. Transfer the mixture to a small decorative bowl and garnish with the remaining tablespoon of cilantro. Serve at room temperature, spread on the toasts. (The puree will keep, covered, in the refrigerator for up to 1 week.) ❧

FICELLE TOASTS

MAKES 75 TOASTS

thinly sliced toasts are perfect for different slathers, cheeses, sausages, and fish tartares. You bite into the ideal portion of crisp toast—no big slice of chewy bread. If you use a baguette, look for the narrowest one possible and slice it as thin as you can before toasting it.

> 1 ficelle (long thin French bread) or baguette
>
> ¼ cup olive oil

1. Preheat the oven to 350°F.

2. Cut the ficelle into ⅛-inch-thick slices and arrange them in a single layer on two baking sheets. Lightly brush the top sides of the slices with the olive oil. Bake until lightly toasted, about 15 minutes. (Once they have cooled completely, the toasts will keep in a metal container for 2 to 3 days.) ❧

MARINATED
PICHOLINE OLIVES

MAKES 1½ CUPS

These marvelous green French olives are fresh tasting, crisp, and tender at the same time. With those qualities, they are ripe candidates for a delicate marinade. Serve them with almonds, country pâté and toasts, hard-cooked eggs, and mixed nuts. (They're also wonderful pitted and cooked in stews.)

1½ cups (8 ounces) picholine olives, drained
　　and rinsed
1 long fresh red chile, such as a serrano or
　　red jalapeño, thinly sliced crosswise
2 cloves garlic, quartered lengthwise
2 teaspoons chopped fresh rosemary
2 teaspoons finely grated tangerine or orange zest
1 large thyme sprig
2 very thin lemon slices, pitted and cut into
　　small pieces

3 tablespoons fresh lemon juice
3 tablespoons extra-virgin olive oil

Combine all the ingredients in a bowl and toss them together gently. Let sit at room temperature, tossing the mixture occasionally, for 6 hours. Then cover and refrigerate overnight. Let the olives come to room temperature before serving. ❧

SALMON TARTARE

MAKES 12 BITES

Salmon tartare is a very modern bite. You must be sure to buy the freshest and best-quality fish, which means that you don't want to serve this on a Monday because fish markets usually don't bring in their fresh new stock until Tuesday. The wait is worth it. I use lemon zest to flavor the salmon and Tabasco to give it an extra kick. Sometimes I set out a small bowl of crème fraîche to dollop on the tartare.

1 pound center-cut king salmon fillet,
　　wild or farmed, skin removed,
　　cut into ¼-inch dice
2 generous dashes Tabasco sauce

Finely grated zest of 1 lemon
Coarse salt, to taste
1½ teaspoons finely snipped fresh chives
12 Ficelle Toasts (page 15), for serving

Place the salmon in a bowl and add the Tabasco sauce, lemon zest, salt (not too much), and chives. Toss gently. Transfer the mixture to a decorative bowl, cover, and refrigerate for up to 2 hours. Serve with a basket of toasts and a small spoon for scooping. 🥢

SALMON CAVIAR– STUFFED EGGS

MAKES 12 DEVILED EGGS

No matter how many hors d'oeuvres you put out on the table, the one that is absolutely sure to disappear entirely is the deviled eggs. I've fancied up this favorite finger food with smoked salmon, capers, lemon zest, chives, salmon caviar, and a few dollops of crème fraîche. You won't be able to stop at one, either!

6 large eggs

1 ounce Nova Scotia salmon (about 1½ slices),
    finely shredded into small pieces

2 teaspoons drained tiny capers

3 teaspoons snipped fresh chives

Finely grated zest of ½ lemon

Salt and freshly ground black pepper, to taste

2 generous teaspoons salmon caviar
    (from a jar is fine)

2 tablespoons crème fraîche

2 tablespoons prepared mayonnaise,
    preferably Hellmann's

1. Rinse the eggs with warm water and place them in a saucepan. Cover with warm salted water. Bring to a boil, reduce the heat, and simmer for 13 minutes. Drain the eggs and run them under cold water until they are cool.

2. When the eggs are cool, peel them and then halve them lengthwise. Carefully scoop out the yolks and place them in a bowl. Set the whites aside.

3. Lightly mash the yolks with a fork. Add the smoked salmon, capers, 2 teaspoons of the chives, the lemon zest, and salt and pepper, and stir with a fork. Still using the fork, carefully stir in the caviar.

4. Mix the crème fraîche and mayonnaise together in a small bowl, and add this to the yolk mixture to bind it. Fill the egg whites with the salmon mixture, mounding it attractively. Sprinkle the remaining 1 teaspoon snipped chives over the eggs, arrange them in a spoke fashion on a small decorative plate, and watch them disappear. 🥢

GRILLED SMOKED ROSY SHRIMP

MAKES 24 SHRIMP

Smoked paprika hit the market like a ball of fire. Imported from Spain, *pimenton de La Vera* is made from peppers roasted over an oak fire. It comes in both hot and sweet varieties, and here it's the sweet that enhances the shrimp for an easy, surprising bite. The touch of brown sugar helps bind all the flavors. Grill or broil the shrimp on 12-inch metal skewers. I often include some thinly sliced dry chorizo on wooden picks to complement my shrimp on the cocktail tray.

24 large shrimp (about 1 pound), peeled and
    deveined along the curve of the back,
    tails left on
2 tablespoons extra-virgin olive oil
1 tablespoon dark brown sugar
2 teaspoons sweet smoked paprika
1 clove garlic, peeled and grated

1. Preheat a barbecue grill to high, or preheat the broiler.

2. Rinse the shrimp in cold water and pat them dry.

3. Combine the olive oil, brown sugar, paprika, and garlic in a bowl. Add the shrimp and toss to coat them well.

4. Thread the shrimp on six long, thin metal skewers, leaving a ½-inch space between them. Grill or broil for 2 minutes per side.

5. Remove the shrimp from the skewers and arrange them on a small cocktail tray or in a basket so that the tails can be used as handles. Set a small bowl alongside for the discarded tails. ❦

SPICED GOAT CHEESE SLATHER

MAKES 1½ CUPS

I call my spreads "slathers" because you'll want to cover the toasts with a generous amount—that's how good they are! In this one, soft goat cheese blends with crème fraîche, which brightens the tang of the cheese and smooths out its texture a bit. A little extra-virgin olive oil adds finesse, and the garlic and lemon zest provide the touch of spice you look for in a cocktail bite.

1 log (14 ounces) fresh goat cheese,
    such as Montrachet (without ash),
    at room temperature
¼ cup crème fraîche
2 teaspoons finely minced garlic
Finely grated zest of 1 lemon
1 tablespoon extra-virgin olive oil

Salt and freshly ground black pepper,
    to taste
Ficelle Toasts (page 15), for serving

1. Combine all of the ingredients, except the toasts, in a bowl and stir thoroughly. Transfer the slather to a decorative bowl and let it rest at room temperature for 2 hours for the flavors to develop.

2. Place the toasts on a pretty platter to serve with the slather. Or cover the slather and refrigerate until serving time.

FRESH RICOTTA SLATHER

MAKES 1 CUP

fresh ricotta cheese, with its lush consistency and large curds, makes a wonderful slather, lightly drizzled with a fruity extra-virgin olive oil seasoned with freshly ground black pepper. I recommend serving it with a robust olive or rosemary bread. When drizzled with honey, it's lovely with pears and walnut raisin bread for dessert.

1 cup (8 ounces) fresh whole-milk ricotta
    cheese
Maldon (flaky) sea salt (see Notes, page 66) or
    coarse sea salt, to taste
1 teaspoon extra-virgin olive oil,
    plus more for serving (optional)
Coarsely ground black pepper
Six slices (½ inch thick) olive or rosemary bread,
    lightly toasted, for serving

1. Place the ricotta in a bowl, sprinkle it lightly with salt, and mix gently with a fork. Place in a small serving bowl. Drizzle the olive oil and grind some pepper over the ricotta.

2. Cut the toasts in half crosswise and serve them with the ricotta, with some extra olive oil and pepper alongside to sprinkle over the slathered toasts, if desired.

"ONE FLAVOR PLAYS BEAUTIFULLY OFF ANOTHER."

SMALL PLATES can hold

big flavors and a variety of tastes and textures, making them the best kinds of meals. In the United States, we have been reveling in this culinary style since small plates took over the hip restaurant scene a decade ago. But I have adored them since I enjoyed my first tapas in Spain and mezes in Greece and Turkey.

Recently the small plates revolution has moved from restaurant fare to home cooking and now we are embracing them at home as an antidote to super-sizing. Eating this way, sharing small plates with friends, is fun and leads to evenings where great conversations seem to come naturally. It makes for a more relaxed social occasion.

The recipes in this chapter are for my ten favorite small plates. Taken together, they create the menu for an excellent party. The dishes can all be prepared ahead, and when it's time for the party you can just set everything out on a table buffet-style accompanied by a stack of small plates. There is nothing left for you to do other than to make a grand entrance and then be the life of the party, not slaving away behind the scenes in the kitchen.

ROASTED BEETS
WITH TANGERINE VINAIGRETTE

SERVES 8

Roasted beets, with their luscious gem tones and caramelized sugars, make the most divine salad, especially when tossed in a tangerine vinaigrette thickened with honey mustard. One sweet flavor plays beautifully off another, making the beets ideal to serve as a starter followed by roasted meats, or on a buffet in combination with White Beans Vinaigrette, Marinated Picholine Olives, Paella Rice, and Sweet-and-Sour Onions.

6 beets

1½ tablespoons honey mustard

Salt and freshly ground black pepper, to taste

Finely grated zest of 1 tangerine

3 tablespoons fresh tangerine juice

1 tablespoon red wine vinegar

⅓ cup extra-virgin olive oil

1. Preheat the oven to 350°F.

2. Scrub the beets well, and trim the stems and roots, leaving 1 inch of each. Wrap the beets individually in aluminum foil. Place them on a baking sheet and bake until tender, 1 to 1½ hours, depending on their size.

3. While the beets are roasting, prepare the vinaigrette: Whisk the mustard, salt and pepper, tangerine zest and juice, and vinegar together in a small bowl. Whisking constantly, slowly drizzle in the olive oil, and continue whisking until the dressing is slightly thickened. Adjust the seasonings as needed, and set aside.

4. Remove the beets from the oven and unwrap them. When they are cool enough to handle (but still warm), slip off the skins.

5. Cut the roasted beets into ½-inch cubes and place them in a bowl. Toss with the vinaigrette, and serve at room temperature.

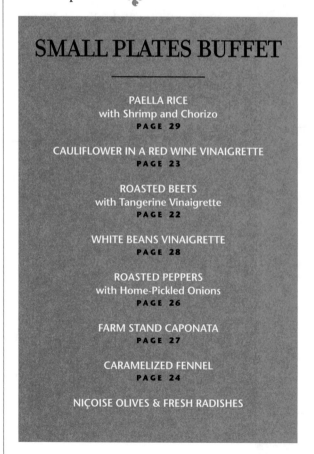

SMALL PLATES BUFFET

PAELLA RICE
with Shrimp and Chorizo
PAGE 29

CAULIFLOWER IN A RED WINE VINAIGRETTE
PAGE 23

ROASTED BEETS
with Tangerine Vinaigrette
PAGE 22

WHITE BEANS VINAIGRETTE
PAGE 28

ROASTED PEPPERS
with Home-Pickled Onions
PAGE 26

FARM STAND CAPONATA
PAGE 27

CARAMELIZED FENNEL
PAGE 24

NIÇOISE OLIVES & FRESH RADISHES

CAULIFLOWER
IN A RED WINE VINAIGRETTE

SERVES 8

Cauliflower combined with briny Niçoise olives, tiny capers, fresh parsley, and a well-balanced vinaigrette fits beautifully on the Small Plates Buffet (see facing page). Look for a firm, tight head and be sure to break the florets into very small pieces for the most delicate eating.

> 1 medium-size head cauliflower, trimmed
>   and cut into marble-size florets
> ½ cup Red Wine Vinaigrette (recipe follows)
> ½ cup Niçoise olives, preferably pitted
> 2 tablespoons drained tiny capers
> 2 tablespoons chopped fresh flat-leaf parsley

1. Bring a pot of salted water to a boil. Add the cauliflower florets and cook until just tender, 2 to 3 minutes. Do not overcook. Drain well and transfer to a bowl.

2. While the cauliflower is still hot, toss it with the vinaigrette (this allows the flavors to be absorbed). Add the olives, capers, and parsley, and toss well. Serve at room temperature. (This will keep in the refrigerator, covered, for up to 1 day. Let it come back to room temperature before serving.) 🌺

RED WINE
VINAIGRETTE

MAKES 1 CUP

This is an excellent all-purpose vinaigrette which is easily doubled and kept in the refrigerator. For heightened flavor, let the garlic flavor the vinaigrette overnight and then remove it before serving.

> 2 tablespoons Dijon mustard
> 6 tablespoons red wine vinegar
> 1 teaspoon sugar
> Salt and freshly ground black pepper, to taste
> ½ cup extra-virgin olive oil
> 2 cloves garlic, peeled and smashed (optional)

Whisk the mustard, vinegar, sugar, and salt and pepper together in a small bowl. Slowly drizzle in the olive oil, whisking constantly until thickened. If desired, add the garlic clove and let it flavor the vinaigrette overnight.

NOTE: This vinaigrette can be made 2 to 3 days in advance. Store it, covered, in the refrigerator. Bring to room temperature before using. 🌺

CELERI REMOULADE

MAKES ABOUT 3 CUPS; SERVES 6

Céleri rémoulade is a classic French hors d'oeuvre. My rémoulade is a bit simpler than the traditional French mustard sauce. I begin with a good-quality prepared mayonnaise and enrich it with some complementary additions. It coats the celery root beautifully.

FOR THE CELERY ROOT:

1 celery root (1 pound)

Juice of ½ lemon

Salt, to taste

FOR THE DRESSING:

½ cup prepared mayonnaise, preferably Hellmann's

2 tablespoons Dijon mustard

1 tablespoon olive oil

1 tablespoon fresh lemon juice

Salt and freshly ground black pepper, to taste

2 tablespoons chopped fresh flat-leaf parsley, for garnish

1. Trim and peel the celery root, and cut it into matchstick pieces (you should have 3 to 3½ cups). Place them in a bowl and toss with the lemon juice and salt. Let rest until slightly softened, 30 minutes. Then drain, rinse under cold water, drain again, and pat dry.

2. In another bowl, whisk together the mayonnaise and mustard. Whisking constantly, slowly drizzle in the olive oil and then the lemon juice. Season with salt and pepper.

3. Toss the dressing with the celery root to coat it well. Transfer to a decorative bowl and sprinkle with the chopped parsley.

CARAMELIZED FENNEL

SERVES 6

Fennel, with its delicate anise flavor, becomes all the more scrumptious when caramelized. Its natural sugars make the vegetable ideal for combining with other small plates. Its flavor both blends in and stands out. On its own, caramelized fennel is delicious served with roasted venison or a roasted chicken.

4 medium-size fennel bulbs (about 12 ounces each)

4 tablespoons (½ stick) unsalted butter

2 tablespoons extra-virgin olive oil

3 tablespoons sugar

3 tablespoons fresh lemon juice

Salt and freshly ground black pepper, to taste

2 tablespoons chopped fresh flat-leaf parsley

1. Cut the stalks (if any) off the fennel bulbs. Halve the fennel lengthwise and remove the core. Sliver the bulbs lengthwise into ¼-inch-thick strips.

2. Melt the butter in the oil in a very large saucepan over medium-low heat. Add the fennel and sugar, and toss to coat. Cook, stirring occasionally, until the fennel begins to wilt and brown, 15 minutes.

3. Add the lemon juice and salt and pepper, and toss well. Raise the heat to medium and cook, stirring, until the fennel is nicely caramelized and tender, 3 to 5 minutes. Toss with the parsley and transfer to a serving dish. Serve hot or at room temperature. ❧

SWEET-AND-SOUR ONIONS

MAKES 3 CUPS

these slowly cooked sweet-and-sour onions are as delectable with foie gras as they are with roasted duck. Use the cooked onions as a filling for a puff pastry tart or individual puff pastry hors d'oeuvres. They're also delicious on a grilled cheese sandwich or on the truffle burger (page 110). They fit well as a selection on a Small Plates Buffet (page 22). Serve them at room temperature to appreciate the full flavors.

12 tablespoons (1½ sticks) unsalted butter

8 medium-size onions, cut into thin rings

¾ cup dry red wine

¾ cup red wine vinegar

¾ cup (packed) dark brown sugar

Coarse (kosher) salt and freshly ground black
    pepper, to taste

1. Melt the butter in a large heavy saucepan over low heat. Add the onions, wine, vinegar, brown sugar, and salt and pepper. Cover and cook slowly over low heat, stirring occasionally, for 1 hour. Then remove the cover and continue cooking over low heat, stirring occasionally, until most of the liquid has evaporated, another 1½ to 2 hours.

2. Cool to room temperature, then refrigerate, covered, for up to 3 days. Serve at room temperature. ❧

ROASTED PEPPERS
WITH HOME-PICKLED ONIONS

SERVES 4

the inspiration for this unusual dish came from a starter at a marvelous pizza restaurant, Franny's, on Flatbush Avenue in Brooklyn. All the food there is wonderfully original, but the pickled onion pizza topper is the best, and it inspired me to make my own. I serve it on home-roasted bell peppers, but the pickled onions are also great atop thick slices of summer tomatoes or grilled steaks and burgers. Serve this with slices of toasted peasant bread on the side, and you're in for a treat.

FOR THE PICKLED ONIONS:

1½ cups cider vinegar

1 cup sugar

2 tablespoons pickling spices, wrapped in a
    cheesecloth bag

Pinch of salt

2 red onions, thinly sliced and separated into rings

FOR ASSEMBLING:

2 green bell peppers, cut in half, seeded, and
    roasted (see page 438)

4 canned or bottled anchovies, rinsed and
    patted dry

2 tablespoons extra-virgin olive oil

Freshly ground black pepper, to taste

¼ cup pine nuts, lightly toasted (see box, this page)

2 tablespoons chopped fresh flat-leaf parsley,
    for garnish

1. A day ahead, prepare the pickled onions: Combine the vinegar, sugar, bag of pickling spices, salt, and ½ cup water in a small saucepan. Bring to a boil, stirring until the sugar dissolves. Reduce the heat to medium and simmer for 5 minutes.

2. Place the onion rings in a bowl and cover with the hot pickling brine. Let sit at room temperature for 8 hours. Then pack the onions with their liquid in an airtight container and refrigerate overnight.

3. To assemble, place a roasted pepper half in the center of each of four large salad plates. Arrange an anchovy diagonally on top of the pepper. Drizzle the olive oil over the peppers, and season with black pepper. Place 2 tablespoons of the onions in the center of each pepper. Sprinkle with the pine nuts and chopped parsley. Serve immediately. ❧

TOASTING PINE NUTS

To toast pine nuts, spread them in a single layer on a baking sheet and toast in a preheated 350°F oven until golden and fragrant, 3 to 5 minutes. Check them after 3 minutes, as pine nuts burn easily.

FARM STAND CAPONATA

SERVES 6 TO 8 AS A SPREAD

Whether served as an appetizer or spread on crostini, this southern Italian specialty is rich and delicious, with its typical sweet-and-sour flavors. Golden raisins and balsamic vinegar bring out the best of the classic combination of eggplant, tomato, and celery.

2 eggplants, cut into ½-inch cubes

2 tablespoons coarse (kosher) salt, plus more to taste

5 tablespoons olive oil

2 red onions, cut into ¼-inch dice

2 tablespoons minced garlic

3 pounds diced ripe plum tomatoes (½-inch dice)

2 tablespoons tomato paste

1 cup diced celery hearts and leaves (¼-inch dice)

⅓ cup pitted green olives, halved lengthwise

⅓ cup balsamic vinegar

⅓ cup golden raisins

2 tablespoons drained tiny capers

Freshly ground black pepper, to taste

1. Toss the eggplant in a large colander with the 2 tablespoons coarse salt. Let rest for 1 hour.

2. Rinse the eggplant lightly and press on it with paper towels to remove the excess water. Then squeeze it in a kitchen towel. Set aside.

3. Heat 2 tablespoons of the olive oil in a large heavy pot over low heat. Add the onions and cook, stirring occasionally, until almost softened, about 7 minutes. Add the garlic and cook for another 3 minutes.

4. Add the tomatoes, tomato paste, and salt to taste, and simmer over low heat, stirring occasionally, for 20 minutes. Add the celery and simmer for 10 minutes longer.

5. Meanwhile, line the bottom of a bowl with paper towels. In another heavy pot, heat the remaining 3 tablespoons olive oil over medium heat. Add the eggplant, in batches, and cook until it is browned, 3 to 5 minutes per batch. As the batches are cooked, transfer them to the paper-towel-lined bowl to drain.

6. Stir the browned eggplant into the tomato sauce, and add the olives, vinegar, raisins, capers, and pepper. Simmer (do not boil), partially covered, over low heat for the flavors to blend, 5 minutes. Uncover and simmer for 5 minutes longer. Adjust the seasonings as needed. Cool to room temperature. Serve immediately or refrigerate, covered, for up to 4 days; let the caponata return to room temperature before serving. ❧

WHITE BEANS VINAIGRETTE

MAKES 3 CUPS; SERVES 8

While this dish may not seem unusual, the cooking water is flavored just right and the beans are cooked just long enough to be tender but not mushy. Tossed with the vinaigrette while they're still warm, the beans absorb all the flavor. The scallions and celery add just the right texture and color.

FOR THE BEANS:

8 ounces dried white kidney beans

1 onion, halved

1 carrot, halved

1 rib celery, with extra leaves, halved

1 clove garlic, bruised (see box, page 82)

1 bay leaf

FOR THE SALAD:

⅓ cup Red Wine Vinaigrette (page 23)

4 scallions (white bulb and 3 inches green),
    thinly sliced

2 ribs celery, trimmed and cut into ¼-inch dice

2 tablespoons chopped fresh flat-leaf parsley

Salt and freshly ground black pepper, to taste

1. Pick over the beans, discarding any debris. Place them in a bowl, add cold water to cover by 2 inches, and soak overnight.

2. Drain and rinse the beans, and place them in a large pot with the onion, carrot, celery, garlic, bay leaf, and 8 cups of water. Bring to a boil over high heat, skimming off any foam that rises to the surface.

Reduce the heat to medium-low and simmer until the beans are tender but not mushy, about 40 minutes.

3. Drain the beans, discarding the flavoring vegetables and bay leaf. While they are still warm, toss the beans with the vinaigrette (this allows them to absorb the flavors). Stir in the scallions, celery, and parsley, and season generously with salt and pepper. Serve at room temperature. 🌿

WHITE BEANS FOR PASTA

To serve 4, you'll need only half the amount of cooked beans. Add them plus 2 chopped plum tomatoes, 1 cup chicken broth, and 2 sprigs fresh sage to lightly sautéed garlic. Cook over low heat to blend the flavors, add salt and pepper and serve over cooked pasta.

PAELLA RICE
WITH SHRIMP AND CHORIZO

SERVES 12

When served with an assortment of vegetable small plates, this rice dish from Spain adds substance—especially at a time of the evening when people are really hungry. The colors and flavors are appealing, and the fact that you can serve it hot or at room temperature makes it a convenient party dish to serve as the centerpiece of a buffet. To turn this into a dinner entrée, simply add more shrimp.

4 tablespoons extra-virgin olive oil

1 onion, cut into ¼-inch dice

Salt and freshly ground black pepper,
   to taste

½ cup long-grain white rice

¼ teaspoon saffron threads, crumbled

1⅓ cups low-sodium chicken broth, preferably
   homemade (see page 434)

1 red bell pepper, stemmed, seeded, and
   cut into ¼-inch dice

1 green bell pepper, stemmed, seeded, and
   cut into ¼-inch dice

16 medium-size shrimp, peeled, deveined,
   and halved crosswise

½ cup diced hard chorizo (¼-inch dice)

3 tablespoons chopped fresh flat-leaf parsley

1. Place 2 tablespoons of the oil in a heavy saucepan over low heat. Add the onion and cook until tender, about 10 minutes. Season with salt and pepper. Add the rice and cook, stirring, to coat all the grains with the oil, 1 minute.

2. In a small bowl, mix the saffron with 2 tablespoons water. Stir this into the rice, and add the broth. Bring to a boil, stir, reduce the heat to medium, and cover. Simmer until the water has been absorbed, 20 minutes. Fluff the rice with a fork.

3. Heat the remaining 2 tablespoons oil in a non-stick skillet over medium heat. Add the red and green bell peppers and cook, stirring occasionally, until wilted, about 5 minutes. Add the shrimp and cook, stirring, for 3 minutes. Season with salt and pepper. Stir this mixture into the rice, and add the chorizo and 2 tablespoons of the chopped parsley. Serve hot or at room temperature, sprinkled with the remaining 1 tablespoon of parsley.

NOTE: This recipe can be halved.

JIM BOTSACOS' BAKED GIGANTES, FENNEL, ONIONS, AND TOMATOES

MAKES 4 CUPS; SERVES 6

his luscious dish, created by Jim Botsacos, chef of Molyvos and Abbocato in New York City, makes a stunning small plate when the beans are allowed to rest overnight so that all the flavors meld. The sweet and sour tastes—thanks to the honey and vinegar—create a terrific balance of flavors. While the beans bake, their creamy, buttery character flowers. The dill tops it off. Serve this with pita toasts, Olivada (page 15), and chilled ouzo or a chilled rosé.

8 ounces dried Greek gigantes or dried giant lima
    beans

1 onion, halved

4 cloves garlic, halved

4 sprigs flat-leaf parsley

4 black peppercorns

1 bay leaf

2 tablespoons extra-virgin olive oil

¼ cup diced onion (¼-inch dice)

Coarse (kosher) salt

¼ cup diced fennel bulb (¼-inch dice)

¼ cup diced celery (¼-inch dice)

¼ cup diced carrot (¼-inch dice)

Freshly ground black pepper, to taste

⅓ cup honey

¼ cup dry white wine

¼ cup plus 1 teaspoon red wine vinegar

¾ cup diced, peeled, seeded plum tomatoes
    (¼-inch dice)

1½ cups vegetable or chicken broth, preferably
    homemade (see pages 436 and 434)

2 tablespoons chopped fresh dill

1. Place the dried beans in a large bowl, add cold water to cover by 3 inches, and set aside to soak for 8 hours or overnight.

2. Drain and rinse the beans and place them in a large saucepan.

3. Cut a piece of cheesecloth about 6 inches square, and place the onion and garlic halves, parsley sprigs, peppercorns, and bay leaf on it. Gather up the corners, and using kitchen string, tie the bag closed. Add the sachet to the beans, and fill the saucepan with enough cold water to cover the beans by 3 inches.

4. Place the saucepan over medium-high heat and bring to a boil. Reduce the heat and simmer, stirring occasionally, skimming frequently with a metal spoon, until the beans are tender, about 40 minutes. Drain the beans, discarding the flavor sachet, and set them aside.

5. Preheat the oven to 400°F.

6. Heat 1 tablespoon of the olive oil in a large ovenproof sauté pan over medium heat. Add the diced onion along with a pinch of salt and cook, stirring occasionally, until the onion is soft and translucent, about 5 minutes. Stir in the fennel, celery, and carrot, and season with salt and pepper. Stir in the honey, wine, and the ¼ cup vinegar. Raise the heat and bring the mixture to a boil. Then reduce the heat and simmer until the vegetables are just tender, about 6 minutes.

7. Stir in the tomatoes, the reserved beans, and the broth, and season to taste. Simmer for 5 minutes.

8. Cover the pan with a tight-fitting lid, transfer it to the oven, and bake until the beans are very soft and creamy, about 1 hour. Remove the pan from the oven and set it aside to cool. Refrigerate, covered, overnight.

9. Before serving, stir in the dill, the remaining 1 tablespoon olive oil, and the remaining 1 teaspoon vinegar. Serve at room temperature.

"VEGETABLES COME TO LIFE WHEN EXPOSED TO THE MAGIC OF THE SOUP POT."

VEGETABLE SOUPS

There is nothing quite like a bowl of vegetable soup. Whether it's heartiness on a cold night or refreshment on a warm afternoon, soup always gives us exactly what we need.

The recipes here—there are 11 (it was too hard to decide!)—run the full spectrum of vegetable flavors, taking advantage of ingredients when they're at their seasonal peaks. Creamy Minted Sweet Pea Soup, silky and brightly flavored, embodies the essence of springtime. For fall, Mixed-Up Mushroom Barley Soup elevates that classic to something truly special. And of course for summer, there is nothing better than Gingery Summer Squash Soup garnished with a liberal dose of scallion slices.

I've always been a fan of roasting winter vegetables, and the method is used to intensify the carrots' sweetness in Carrot Ginger Soup.

On the hottest days of the year, nothing could be more elegant than a bowl of White Gazpacho, with its garlicky bite tempered by the cooling flavors of cucumber, grape, and apple.

Whatever the season, be sure to use only the best ingredients—don't ever skimp on quality and flavor when it comes to your fine pots of soup. ❧

WHITE GAZPACHO

SERVES 6

Most of us are familiar with tomato-based gazpacho, a summer favorite—a chilled soup easily blended with vegetables fresh from the farm stand or garden. When you're ready for a change, try this sublime white gazpacho: cucumber and cream with the surprise of white grapes, Granny Smith apples, coarsely chopped salted almonds, and a little fresh dill. Inspired by the Málaga-style gazpacho served in southern Spain, this is *some* cold summer soup!

2 hothouse (seedless) cucumbers, peeled, seeded,
    and coarsely chopped (see Note)

2 teaspoons finely minced garlic

4 cups half-and-half

2 dashes Tabasco sauce

Coarse (kosher) salt and freshly ground black
    pepper, to taste

1½ cups diced Granny Smith apples
    (¼-inch dice), for garnish

1½ cups seedless white grapes, halved crosswise,
    for garnish

½ cup coarsely chopped salted almonds, for garnish

3 tablespoons chopped fresh dill leaves,
    for garnish (optional)

1. Combine the cucumbers, garlic, half-and-half, and Tabasco in a bowl. Puree the mixture, in batches, in a food processor or blender. Season with salt and pepper. Chill for 6 hours, or until very cold.

2. To serve, place ¼ cup of the apples and ¼ cup of the grapes in each of six soup bowls. Ladle 1 cup of the chilled soup into each bowl. Sprinkle each serving with the almonds and dill.

NOTE: Hothouse cucumbers do have seeds—they're smaller and softer than those found in regular cucumbers, but they are there. For this elegant gazpacho, we want to eliminate all traces of seeds.

BREAD SOUP

While there are many versions of gazpacho, most of us think of it as a refreshing summer classic chock-full of tomatoes, peppers, cucumbers, and garlic. In fact, gazpacho first gained popularity in Andalusia, Spain, as a poor man's soup based on stale bread, water, olive oil, and vinegar. Tomatoes and peppers were added when Spanish explorers brought these ingredients back from the Americas.

APPLE VICHYSSOISE

SERVES 12

○

I have always been snapped to attention by a cold vichyssoise. Yet a warm version of this potato soup is so comforting—same soup, different moods. This is lovely to serve in the autumn, when apples are in season. Try it at a dinner featuring roast pheasant or turkey, or a rack of pork. The milk and the tang of lemon juice brighten up the flavors.

4 leeks, white bulbs only, trimmed

2 tablespoons distilled white vinegar

2 Granny Smith apples, peeled, cored,
    and sliced

3 tablespoons fresh lemon juice
    (from 1 large lemon)

3 tablespoons unsalted butter

3 tablespoons olive oil

1 onion, thinly sliced

7 cups vegetable or chicken broth, preferably
    homemade (see box, page 38)

4 russet potatoes, peeled and thinly sliced

1 cup half-and-half

1½ cups whole milk

Salt and freshly ground black pepper,
    to taste

⅓ cup snipped fresh chives, for garnish

1. Halve the leeks lengthwise, place them in a bowl, and cover with water. Add the vinegar and soak for 15 minutes. Then rinse, pat dry, and thinly slice.

2. Toss the apples with 1 tablespoon of the lemon juice in another bowl, and set aside.

3. Melt the butter with the olive oil in a heavy pot over low heat. Add the leeks, apples, and onion and sauté until tender, about 15 minutes.

4. Add the broth, potatoes, and remaining 2 tablespoons lemon juice. Bring to a boil. Then reduce the heat to medium-low and simmer, partially covered, for 30 minutes. Remove from the heat and let cool slightly.

5. Puree the soup, in batches, in a food processor or blender. Do not overprocess; the texture should be slightly coarse. Return the soup to the pot and stir in the half-and-half and milk. Season with salt and pepper. Heat it through, but do not let it boil.

6. Garnish the soup with the snipped chives just before serving.

NOTE: If you plan to serve this vichyssoise cold, make it ahead of time, let it cool to room temperature, and then refrigerate it, covered, for at least 6 hours or, even better, overnight. ❧

BEET AND APPLE SOUP

SERVES 8

his is a very different sweet and sour version of borscht. Do use the crème fraîche if you can: the sour tang plays beautifully off the sweet sautéed apples. Although delicious served hot with Roasted Rack of Pork (page 50), this soup reaches its full potential when served cold—try it with Maple Bourbon Baked Virginia Ham (page 54).

6 beets, trimmed (leave 2 inches of stems and
    roots) and scrubbed
8 cups vegetable or chicken broth, preferably
    homemade (see box, page 38)
2 cups apple juice
3 tablespoons unsalted butter
3 Granny Smith apples, peeled, cored, and sliced
3 tablespoons fresh lemon juice
    (from 1 large lemon), or to taste
Salt and freshly ground black pepper, to taste
Crème fraîche, for garnish (optional)

1. Place the beets in a large heavy pot, add the broth and apple juice, and bring to a boil. Then reduce the heat and simmer, partially covered, until tender, about 45 minutes. Using a slotted spoon, transfer the beets to a bowl, reserving the broth. When they are cool enough to handle, slip off the skins and cut the beets into pieces. Set them aside.

2. Line a fine-mesh sieve with a double layer of paper towels, and strain the reserved broth through it into a large bowl.

3. Melt the butter in a large skillet over medium-low heat. Add the apples and sauté until just caramelized, 10 to 15 minutes.

4. Combine the cooked beets and sautéed apples, in batches, in a food processor, and puree, adding some of the broth through the feed tube. Return the puree and reserved broth to the pot. Stir in the lemon juice, and season with salt and pepper. If you'd like the soup to be extra-fine, pass it through a strainer. (Alternatively, add a little more broth or apple juice to thin it slightly.)

5. Serve the soup hot or cold, dolloped with crème fraîche.

CREAM OF CAULIFLOWER SOUP

SERVES 8

the rich flavors of cauliflower, curry powder, and cream blend beautifully with the surprise of crystallized ginger, creating a rich soup that is ideal to serve with simple roast poultry or pork. Cooking the spices along with the vegetables brings out the flavors of the fabulous seasoning.

2 leeks (white bulbs and 2 inches green), trimmed

2 tablespoons olive oil

2 tablespoons unsalted butter

1 celery rib, with extra leaves, coarsely chopped

2 tablespoons finely minced garlic

2 teaspoons curry powder

1 teaspoon ground ginger

6 cups chicken or vegetable broth, preferably
    homemade (see box, page 38),
    or more if needed

Juice of ½ lemon

1 head cauliflower, cored and broken into florets
    (discard the heavy stems)

1 cup half-and-half

Salt and freshly ground black pepper, to taste

3 tablespoons finely chopped crystallized ginger,
    for garnish

1. Cut the leeks in half lengthwise. Wash them well to remove the dirt. Pat dry and thinly slice crosswise.

2. Melt the butter in the oil in a heavy pot over low heat. Add the leeks and celery and cook for 5 minutes. Add the garlic and cook until the leeks and celery are soft, another 5 minutes.

3. Stir in the curry powder and ground ginger, and cook over very low heat until the spices permeate the vegetables, 1 minute.

4. Add the broth, lemon juice, and cauliflower florets. Raise the heat to high and bring to a boil. Then reduce the heat and simmer, partially covered, until the cauliflower is very tender, 15 minutes. Allow the soup to cool slightly.

5. Puree the soup in a food processor, in batches if necessary, until very smooth. Then add the half-and-half through the feed tube. If the soup seems too thick, add some extra broth. Season with salt and pepper.

6. If you will be serving it right away, reheat the soup. If serving it chilled, cool the soup completely and refrigerate it, covered, for at least 4 hours.

7. Garnish the center of each portion of soup with a teaspoon of crystallized ginger before serving.

GINGERY SUMMER SQUASH SOUP

SERVES 6

because yellow squash has a rather mild flavor, it needs a rich broth and the bite of fresh ginger to wake it up. The results are delicious, with the scallion garnish adding the final punch. The soup is good served hot, but for the best effect, serve it thoroughly chilled.

2 tablespoons olive oil

1 onion, slivered

4 yellow summer squash (about 1¾ pounds total), trimmed and chopped

1 pound Yukon Gold potatoes, peeled and cut into 1-inch cubes

5 cups vegetable or chicken broth, preferably homemade, or more if needed (see box)

1 piece (1 inch) fresh ginger, peeled and thinly sliced

Salt and freshly ground black pepper, to taste

3 scallions (white bulbs and 3 inches green), thinly sliced, for garnish

1. Heat the olive oil in a large heavy pot over low heat. Add the onions, squash, and potatoes, and cook, stirring occasionally, for 15 minutes.

2. Add the broth and the ginger, and bring to a boil. Then reduce the heat and simmer, partially covered, until the vegetables are tender, about 20 minutes. Remove from the heat and season generously with salt and pepper. Let the soup cool to room temperature.

3. Puree the soup, in batches if necessary, in a blender or food processor. If you prefer a thinner soup, add a

little more broth. Adjust the seasoning as needed. If you are serving the soup hot, return it to the pot and heat through. Or chill it, covered, in the refrigerator for 4 to 6 hours to serve it cold.

4. Garnish the soup with the scallions before serving. 🌿

DOCTORING BROTH

If you'd rather not start from scratch (pages 434 and 436), you can doctor a canned broth. Enrich 5 to 6 cups of canned chicken broth by adding 3 chicken wings and simmering the broth, covered, for 15 minutes. For canned vegetable broth, add 4 parsley sprigs, ½ small onion (unpeeled), 2 garlic cloves, smashed, and 2 mushrooms; simmer, covered, for 15 minutes. Up the ingredients slightly for larger amounts of canned broth. Strain either broth before continuing with the recipe.

KITCHEN TOMATO SOUP

SERVES 8

there is nothing like a bowl of tomato soup and a grilled cheese sandwich for lunch on a chilly Sunday. Nowadays a snazzy cheese panini updates the meal, but any way you look at it, there are certain foods you'll never want to do without. Even during the cruelest winter weather, a pinch of allspice blends with canned tomatoes and fragrant dill to set everything to rights (when summer comes, look to the Fresh Tomato Soup on page 354). Now, if only *I Love Lucy* were still on TV!

2 tablespoons unsalted butter

2 tablespoons extra-virgin olive oil

2 cups diced onions (¼-inch dice)

1 tablespoon finely minced garlic

½ teaspoon ground allspice

6 tablespoons chopped fresh dill leaves

Salt and freshly ground black pepper, to taste

6 cups chicken or vegetable broth
    (see box, facing page)

2 cans (28 ounces each) peeled plum tomatoes,
    drained and chopped

1 teaspoon sugar

Sour cream or crème fraîche, for garnish

Fresh dill sprigs, for garnish

1. Melt the butter in the olive oil in a heavy pot over low heat. Add the onions and cook, stirring occasionally, until softened, about 10 minutes. Add the garlic and cook, stirring, for 3 minutes. Sprinkle the allspice over the onion mixture and cook for 1 minute longer.

2. Add 4 tablespoons of the dill, season with salt and pepper, and cook over low heat, stirring, for 5 minutes. Add the broth, tomatoes, and sugar.

3. Bring to a boil, reduce the heat to medium-low, and simmer, partially covered, for 20 minutes. Remove from the heat and let cool slightly.

4. Puree the soup, in batches, in a blender or food processor. Return the soup to the pot and stir in the remaining 2 tablespoons dill. Taste, and correct the seasonings if necessary.

5. Serve hot, or let cool and then refrigerate for 4 to 6 hours to serve cold. Serve garnished with a generous dollop of sour cream and a sprig of dill.

NOTE: If you like your tomato soup creamy, stir in the sour cream and then top it with the dill sprig. ❧

GARDEN GREENS SOUP

SERVES 6

back in the 1970s and '80s, watercress was at the top of the greens hit parade. Since then, so many other exciting greens have been introduced to the marketplace—from baby arugula to red mustard greens to mizuna—that we've focused on them instead. I'm voting for a watercress renaissance! Its peppery bite adds a great kick to this mellow broccoli soup.

2 leeks (white bulbs only), trimmed

1 tablespoon white distilled vinegar

1 tablespoon unsalted butter

2 tablespoons olive oil

1 onion, chopped

6 cups vegetable or chicken broth, preferably homemade (see box, page 38)

1 russet potato, peeled and sliced

1 bunch broccoli (1¼ to 1½ pounds)

1 medium-size bunch watercress, stems removed, well rinsed

⅓ cup heavy (whipping) cream

Crème fraîche, for garnish

Small watercress sprigs, for garnish

1. Cut the leeks in half lengthwise and place them in a bowl. Add water to cover, stir in the vinegar, and let soak for 15 minutes. Carefully lift the leeks out of the water without disturbing any sediment that has settled on the bottom of the bowl. Rinse and pat dry. Chop coarsely.

2. Melt the butter in the oil in a large pot over low heat. Add the leeks and onions and cook, stirring occasionally, for 15 minutes.

3. Add the broth and potato, and bring to a boil. Then reduce the heat to a simmer and cook, partially covered, for 20 minutes.

4. Trim off and discard the heavy broccoli stalks. Divide the broccoli into florets and thinly slice the remaining smaller stalks. Reserve 1 cup of the florets for the garnish. Add the remaining broccoli to the soup and simmer for 15 minutes. Remove the pot from the heat, stir in the watercress leaves, and let the soup stand for 3 minutes.

5. Meanwhile, bring a small pot of water to a boil. Cook the reserved 1 cup broccoli florets for 1 minute. Drain, rinse under cold water, and set aside.

6. Process the soup, in batches, in a blender or food processor, pulsing the machine on and off so that the soup is not completely smooth. Leave a slight bit of texture. If it's too textured, however, strain the soup. Transfer the soup to a pot, stir in the cream, and reheat over low heat. Serve each bowl of soup garnished with a dollop of crème fraîche, a small sprig of watercress, and a few broccoli florets. 🌿

MIXED-UP MUSHROOM BARLEY SOUP

SERVES 8

While the traditional mushroom-barley soup serves up hearty bowls of comfort, I've added finesse with fresh shiitakes, tarragon, and a little sherry. These touches elevate the pot to dinner-party status. Of course, if it's just the two of you, a hot bowlful still evokes that all's-right-with-the-world feeling.

8 cups chicken or vegetable broth, preferably homemade (see box, page 38)

½ cup pearl barley, rinsed and drained

½ cup diced carrot (¼-inch dice)

1 tablespoon chopped fresh tarragon; or 1 teaspoon dried, crumbled

10 ounces white mushrooms

6 ounces fresh shiitake mushrooms (see Note)

3 tablespoons olive oil

1 cup diced onion (¼-inch dice)

2 teaspoons finely minced garlic

Salt and freshly ground black pepper, to taste

3 tablespoons medium-dry sherry

¼ cup chopped fresh flat-leaf parsley

1. In a large heavy pot, combine the broth, barley, carrot, and tarragon, and bring to a boil. Reduce the heat to medium-low and simmer, partially covered, until the barley is just tender but not mushy, about 30 minutes.

2. Meanwhile, remove and discard the stems from the white and the shiitake mushrooms. Wipe the caps clean with a damp paper towel. Cut the white mushrooms into quarters and the shiitakes into 1-inch pieces. Set them aside.

3. Heat the oil in a nonstick skillet over medium heat. Add the onion and cook, stirring occasionally, until wilted, about 10 minutes. Add the garlic and cook for 3 minutes longer. Add the mushrooms, raise the heat to medium-high, and cook, stirring, until the mushrooms are nicely browned, about 10 minutes.

4. Stir the mushroom mixture into the soup pot. Season with salt and pepper and cook to blend the flavors, about 20 minutes.

5. Add the sherry, adjust the seasonings as needed, and stir in the parsley. Serve hot.

NOTE: Cremini mushrooms are a good alternative to the shiitakes. They are a little rounder and larger, with brown or tan caps. Remove the stems, wipe the caps clean, and quarter them.

CREAMY MINTED SWEET PEA SOUP

SERVES 6 TO 8

○

I'm a fool for cold sweet pea soup, and in the spring, when fresh peas are in season, you can bet this soup is a mealtime favorite. But, truth be told, frozen peas work beautifully too. They hold their color and have great flavor, making me a big fan. What adds special interest to this version is the Mint Pesto garnish softened with a dab of crème fraîche. If you're lucky enough to find pea tendrils at your market, top each bowl with one.

FOR THE MINT PESTO:

2 cups fresh mint leaves

2 cloves garlic, bruised (see box, page 82)

¼ cup olive oil

1 tablespoon chicken broth, preferably homemade (see page 434), heated

FOR THE SOUP:

2 leeks (white bulbs and 2 inches green), trimmed

1 tablespoon white distilled vinegar

2 tablespoons unsalted butter

2 tablespoons olive oil

7 cups shelled fresh peas (about 7 pounds pods), or 4 packages (10 ounces each) frozen peas, thawed

8 cups chicken broth, preferably homemade (see box, page 38)

1 cup loosly packed fresh mint leaves

1 cup heavy (whipping) cream

Salt and freshly ground black pepper, to taste

Crème fraîche, for garnish

1. Prepare the Mint Pesto: Place the mint leaves and crushed garlic in a food processor and process until chopped. With the motor running, slowly drizzle in the olive oil and the hot broth, stopping the motor to scrape down the sides of the bowl as necessary. Transfer the pesto to a bowl and set it aside.

2. Prepare the soup: Cut the leeks in half lengthwise. Place them in a bowl and add water to cover. Stir in the vinegar and soak for 30 minutes to remove the dirt. Carefully lift the leeks out of the water without disturbing any sediment that has settled on the bottom of the bowl. Rinse and pat dry. Chop the leeks coarsely.

3. Melt the butter in the oil in a large heavy pot over medium-low heat. Add the leeks and cook, stirring occasionally, until softened, about 12 minutes.

4. Add the peas and the broth and bring to a boil. Reduce the heat to medium-low and simmer, partially covered, for 15 minutes. Add the mint, remove from the heat, and allow to cool slightly.

5. Puree the soup, in batches, in a food processor or blender until completely smooth. Pour the soup through a fine-mesh strainer into a pot, using the back

of a spoon to mash the solids and extract as much liquid as possible.

6. Add the cream to the soup and season with salt and pepper. If serving cold, cover and chill the soup in the refrigerator for at least 6 hours. If serving hot, reheat it gently, stirring, without letting it boil.

7. Garnish each portion with a dollop of the reserved Mint Pesto and a small dollop of crème fraîche.

NOTE: Do not freeze the Mint Pesto or it may turn black. It will keep for a day or two in the refrigerator, but it's best used right away. ✿

ROASTED CARROT GINGER SOUP

SERVES 10

there is nothing like roasting to make the ordinary extraordinary. The humble carrot and parsnip become stars when popped in the oven, where the flavors caramelize beautifully.

1½ pounds carrots, peeled and halved lengthwise

1 pound parsnips, peeled and quartered lengthwise

1 large onion, sliced

1 piece (3 inches) fresh ginger, peeled and chopped

6 tablespoons (¾ stick) unsalted butter

3 tablespoons (packed) dark brown sugar

8 cups chicken broth, preferably homemade
     (see box, page 38), or more if needed

Salt, to taste

Pinch of cayenne pepper

¼ cup crème fraîche, for garnish

Snipped fresh chives, for garnish

1. Preheat the oven to 350°F.

2. Combine the carrots, parsnips, onion, and ginger in a shallow roasting pan. Dot with the butter and sprinkle with the brown sugar.

3. Pour 2 cups of the broth into the pan, cover tightly with aluminum foil, and bake until the vegetables are very tender, 2 hours.

4. Transfer the vegetables and broth to a large soup pot, and add the remaining 6 cups of broth. Season to taste with salt and cayenne pepper, and bring to a boil. Then reduce the heat and simmer, partially covered, for 10 minutes.

5. Puree the soup, in batches, in a blender or food processor until smooth, adding more broth if needed. Return the soup to the pot, adjust the seasonings if necessary, and heat through. Serve each portion dolloped with a teaspoon of crème fraîche and sprinkled with chives. ✿

CREAM OF
CELERY ROOT SOUP

SERVES 8

○

In times past I've added celery root to my vichyssoise, but because I adore the flavor of celery root, I decided to feature it and to push the flavor even further with fresh celery leaves. The result is stunning, especially because of the maple syrup garnish—the little touch that makes magic. (You'll have some leftover Spiced Maple Swirl—drizzle it over your oatmeal or pancakes for an extra-special breakfast.)

FOR THE SPICED MAPLE SWIRL:

¾ cup pure maple syrup

¼ teaspoon ground nutmeg

⅛ teaspoon ground cloves

⅛ teaspoon ground allspice

FOR THE SOUP:

1 lemon, halved

1 celery root (about 1½ pounds)

1 tablespoon distilled white vinegar

2 leeks (white bulbs and 2 inches green),
    trimmed and cut in half lengthwise

2 tablespoons unsalted butter

2 tablespoons olive oil

1 onion, chopped

1 celery rib, plus about a third of the pale
    leaves from the inner celery heart, chopped

Salt and freshly ground black pepper, to taste

2 teaspoons minced garlic

7 cups chicken or vegetable broth, preferably
    homemade (see box, page 38)

1 cup heavy (whipping) cream, or half-and-half

1. Prepare the Spiced Maple Swirl: Whisk the maple syrup and the spices together in a small saucepan. Bring to a boil over medium heat, whisking occasionally. Reduce the heat to medium-low and simmer (do not boil) until the syrup thickens and is reduced to ½ cup, about 25 minutes. Remove from the heat and allow to cool.

2. Prepare the soup: Squeeze one of the lemon halves into a medium-size bowl and fill the bowl halfway with water. Peel the celery root with a small sharp paring knife. Cut it into 1- to 2-inch pieces and place them in the bowl of lemon water to prevent discoloration.

3. Stir the vinegar into a bowl of water, add the leeks, and soak for 30 minutes to remove the sand and dirt. Carefully lift the leeks out of the water without disturbing any sediment that has settled on the bottom of the bowl. Then rinse, drain, and dice the leeks.

4. Melt the butter in the oil in a large heavy pot over low heat. Add the leeks, onion, and celery, and season with salt and pepper. Cook until the vegetables are tender, about 10 minutes. Add the garlic and cook to soften, stirring occasionally, for 3 minutes longer.

5. Drain the celery root. Add the broth, the juice of the remaining lemon half, and the drained celery root to the pot and bring to a boil over medium-high heat. Reduce the heat to medium and simmer, partially covered, until the celery root is very tender, about 30 minutes. Remove from the heat and let cool slightly.

6. Puree the soup, in batches if necessary, in a food processor or blender until it is very smooth. Strain the soup through a fine-mesh sieve into a pot, pressing on the solids with the back of a wooden spoon. Stir in the cream and adjust the seasonings.

7. Reheat the soup, and ladle it into eight bowls. Swirl 1 teaspoon of the Spiced Maple Swirl into the center of each bowl of soup.

NOTE: The Spiced Maple Swirl will keep, covered and refrigerated, for up to 5 days. Remove it from the refrigerator 30 minutes before using it.

"THEY'RE WORTH THE SPLURGE."

LARGE IMPORTANT ROASTS

Special family occasions and fancy dinner parties call for an elegant roast. What better reason to serve a majestic bird such as a turkey, or a standing rib roast, a tenderloin of beef, a crown roast of pork, or a leg of lamb? These showstoppers are actually quite easy to prepare, and here you'll find ten of my favorite recipes, which include surprising ingredients that coax the meaty fragrances from these luscious cuts of meat. I've filled a crown roast of lamb with bright green tabouleh, slathered a fresh ham with Cuban-style mojo sauce, and glazed a turkey with spiced orange sauce. Loin of venison makes a bold and beautiful roast. Roasted rack of pork is another brilliant cut, not often prepared by home cooks. After trying chef Tom Colicchio's recipe, you will surely add it to your collection of entertaining staples.

When you're planning an elegant dinner for two, a *small* important roast is called for. What could be better than a rack of lamb, here marinated in a sauce with Chinese accents—my favorite version.

BIG FANCY STANDING
RIB ROAST OF BEEF

SERVES 8

during the winter holidays, there is no more festive a meal than one featuring a well-marbled standing rib roast. It's a splurge, but worth it for a special occasion. I begin planning the menu the week after Thanksgiving and put an order in with my butcher well in advance of the big night. My 9-pound roast includes four ribs and serves eight. To garnish your platter for the holidays, create a garland of fresh bay leaves or look for fresh kumquats with the leaves attached.

1 standing rib roast of beef (4 ribs, 9 pounds),
  top fatted (see Note)

Salt and freshly ground black pepper,
  to taste

1 head Roasted Garlic (page 433), or 6 cloves
  garlic, slivered

2 or 3 rosemary sprigs (7 to 8 inches long),
  tough woody ends cut off

3 to 4 fresh thyme sprigs (7 to 8 inches long)

Fresh bay leaves, rosemary sprigs, and/or
  kumquats with leaves, for garnish

1. Position a rack in the center of the oven and preheat the oven to 450°F.

2. If your meat is fatted on top, gently lift the top sheet of fatting off the roast (it may be necessary to snip the ties and then re-tie it afterward) and season the meat well with salt and pepper. Spread the Roasted Garlic all over the top of the meat. Lay the rosemary and thyme sprigs on the meat, and then replace the top fatting and, if necessary, re-tie the roast with kitchen string. If the meat is not fatted, simply season it with salt and pepper, poke ½-inch-deep holes all over the meat side of the beef and insert the garlic slivers in the holes, and arrange the rosemary and thyme sprigs on top.

3. Place the roast, rib side down, on a rack in a shallow roasting pan, and roast for 25 minutes. Then reduce the heat to 350°F and roast for another 2 hours and 20 minutes for medium-rare meat (135° to 140°F on an instant-read thermometer inserted in the thickest part of the meat).

4. Remove the roast from the oven, tent it loosely with aluminum foil, and let it rest for 20 minutes. Then place the roast on a platter, garnish it generously, and present it to your guests.

5. In the kitchen, transfer the roast to a cutting board for carving, removing the string and any tough herbs. Cut it into 1-inch-thick slices, and serve immediately.

NOTE: Some top-grade butchers will supply you with a fatted roast, in which the meat side of the rib roast is covered with a thin layer of fat to protect the meat while it cooks. But others do not believe in this practice because they think the roast's own fat should get crisp and browned. 🌿

WHOLE BEEF TENDERLOIN
WITH MUSTARD HORSERADISH CREAM SAUCE

SERVES 10 TO 12

tenderloin of beef is an irresistible party favorite. It was popular when I was growing up, and it has never lost its cachet. Here peppercorns and thyme create a savory crust that enhances the delicate flavor of the meat. Starting the tenderloin in a hot oven seals in the juices; finishing it off at a slightly lower temperature makes for a perfectly cooked roast.

1 beef tenderloin (about 3¾ pounds)

2 cloves garlic, slivered

1 tablespoon olive oil

1½ to 2 tablespoons whole black peppercorns, crushed (see box, page 54)

1 tablespoon chopped fresh thyme leaves, or 1 teaspoon dried

Coarse (kosher) salt, to taste

Mustard Horseradish Cream Sauce (recipe follows), for serving

1. Position a rack in the center of the oven and preheat the oven to 425°F.

2. Using the tip of a sharp knife, cut small slits all over the tenderloin. Insert the garlic slivers into the slits.

3. Brush the tenderloin with the olive oil, and press the crushed peppercorns and thyme into the surface. Sprinkle with salt.

4. Place the tenderloin on a rack in a shallow roasting pan, and roast it for 15 minutes. Then reduce the oven temperature to 350°F and roast for another 20 minutes for medium-rare meat (130° to 140°F on an instant-read thermometer), or 25 minutes for medium (140° to 145°F). Let the tenderloin rest for 15 minutes before carving it.

5. Cut the tenderloin into ½-inch-thick slices and arrange them on a platter. Serve with the Mustard Horseradish Cream Sauce. 🌿

MUSTARD HORSERADISH CREAM SAUCE

MAKES ABOUT 1¼ CUPS

there are certain sauces that suit a roast to a tee, and in the case of the tenderloin, each element of this sauce hits the nail on the head. Both mustard and horseradish complement the meat, and the sour cream ties it all together.

⅓ cup Dijon mustard

⅓ cup sour cream

¼ cup prepared mayonnaise, preferably Hellmann's

¼ cup well-drained prepared white horseradish

Combine all the ingredients in a small bowl and stir well. Cover, and refrigerate until ready to use.

ROASTED RACK OF PORK

SERVES 8

tom Colicchio, noted chef and owner of the family of the Craft restaurants, was kind enough to share this marvelous recipe with me. Cooked to perfection, the chops exemplify his style of modern eating!

¼ cup Dijon mustard

6 sprigs fresh rosemary, leaves chopped

2 tablespoons fennel seeds

1 rack of pork (8 chops; about 4 pounds, frenched (see Note)

1 tablespoon vegetable oil

Coarse (kosher) salt and freshly ground black pepper

Several long rosemary sprigs, for garnish

1. The one day before serving the roast, combine the mustard, chopped rosemary, and fennel seeds in a small bowl. Spread this marinade over the meat, wrap it in plastic wrap, and refrigerate it overnight.

2. Thirty minutes before roasting time, remove the pork from the refrigerator. Scrape the marinade off the pork with a small rubber spatula, and reserve it.

3. While the pork is coming to room temperature, preheat the oven to 400°F. Position a rack in the center of the oven.

4. Pour the oil into a large shallow roasting pan and heat it in the oven for a few minutes.

5. Season the pork with salt and pepper and set in the hot roasting pan, meat side up. Place the pan in the oven, and roast until the pork is browned, 7 minutes. Then turn it over and brown the rib side, another 7 minutes.

6. Turn the pork over again, lower the oven temperature to 250°F, and continue to roast the pork, meat side up, until the meat is just cooked through and an instant-read thermometer registers 150°F, about 1¼ hours. During the last 5 minutes, brush the reserved mustard marinade over the pork to form a light crust.

7. Remove the roast from the oven and let it rest for 10 to 15 minutes before carving it.

8. Transfer the rack of pork to a platter, garnish it with the rosemary sprigs, and because it looks so good, show it off to your guests. Then return it to the kitchen and carve it between the bones to serve.

NOTE: If you'd like to try your hand at frenching the rib bones, follow the instructions for How to French a Rack of Lamb on page 56. Otherwise, ask your butcher to french the bones when you order the meat.

BAKED FRESH HAM
WITH MOJO SAUCE

SERVES 20 TO 25

Just as a reminder: A fresh ham is not ham at all, but rather a whole pork leg. Also called an uncured ham, it is perfect for serving a crowd, with its beautiful moist white meat. The combination of the pork's rich flavor and the pungent Cuban Mojo Sauce is a match made in heaven. (You will need two batches of the sauce: one for cooking the ham and one for serving with the ham. I prefer to make it in two batches rather than doubling the recipe.)

This is not a difficult party dish, but it's not quick to prepare. Once you've made the sauce, there's little to do—except to stay at home. You'll want to baste the roast every half hour for the almost 6 hours of cooking time. You'll see that it's well worth the wait.

FOR THE HAM:

1 fresh ham (16 to 18 pounds; have the
    butcher remove the skin of the ham just
    down to the shank)

2 cups Mojo Sauce (recipe follows)

1½ cups dry white wine

FOR THE GRAVY:

4 tablespoons (½ stick) unsalted butter

¼ cup all-purpose flour

½ teaspoon dried oregano

Salt and freshly ground black pepper,
    to taste

1¼ cups chicken broth, preferably homemade
    (see page 434), if needed

1 tablespoon chopped fresh flat-leaf
    parsley leaves

FOR GARNISHING AND SERVING:

Large bunches of fresh sage

2 cups Mojo Sauce (recipe follows)

1. Position a rack in the center of the oven and preheat the oven to 425°F.

2. Prepare the ham: Carefully score the surface of the ham in a diamond pattern, making the cuts about 1 inch deep (this allows the meat to absorb the sauce). Place the ham in a large shallow roasting pan, and pour 1 cup of the Mojo Sauce all over the meat. Roast for 30 minutes.

3. Reduce the oven temperature to 325°F and baste the ham with ¼ cup of the wine. Continue roasting, basting every 30 minutes: alternating basting with ¼-cup portions of the remaining Mojo Sauce and ¼-cup portions of the remaining wine, and eventually with the pan juices. Cook until an instant-read thermometer registers 160°F in the thickest part of the meat, 5 to 5½ hours. (Do not overcook the ham; it will continue to cook after it comes out of the oven.)

4. Place the ham on a large decorative platter and tent it with aluminum foil. Let it rest for 15 minutes.

5. Meanwhile, pour the pan juices through a strainer into a gravy separator, discarding any solids. There should be 4 cups of defatted pan juices.

6. Prepare the gravy: Melt the butter in a medium-size heavy saucepan over medium-low heat. Gradually add the flour, whisking constantly, and cook until it browns slightly, 2 to 3 minutes. Continue whisking as you slowly pour in 2 cups of the reserved pan juices, whisking until smooth. Raise the heat to medium and add the oregano and salt and pepper. Simmer, whisking, until the gravy has thickened. If you prefer a thinner gravy, whisk in some of the chicken broth, ¼ cup at a time, until the gravy is to your liking. Taste, and adjust the seasonings as needed; then stir in the parsley.

7. Garnish the ham with the bunches of sage and present it to your guests. Then return it to the kitchen, transfer it to a cutting board, and carve the meat. As you carve, cover the slices with aluminum foil to keep them warm. Serve with the Mojo Sauce and the pan gravy. ❧

MOJO SAUCE

MAKES 2 CUPS (TO DOUBLE THIS RECIPE, MAKE IT IN TWO BATCHES FOR THE BEST RESULTS.)

Mojo sauces are a very important component of many roasted Latino dishes. Made with fresh citrus juices, garlic, and often herbs, their bright flavors easily complement fish, meat, and poultry. The sauce is usually made with the tart juice from Seville oranges. I've combined fresh lime juice and fresh orange juice to achieve the same effect.

> 8 cloves garlic, thinly sliced lengthwise
>
> ½ cup slivered onion
>
> ½ teaspoon ground cumin
>
> Salt and freshly ground black pepper, to taste
>
> ½ cup extra-virgin olive oil
>
> 1 cup fresh orange juice (from 1 to 2 oranges)
>
> ¼ cup fresh lime juice (from 1 to 2 limes)
>
> 1 tablespoon white wine vinegar

1. Combine the garlic, onion, cumin, and salt and pepper in a small bowl.

2. Heat the olive oil in a small heavy saucepan over low heat. Add the onion mixture and cook, stirring, until wilted, about 10 minutes. Then add the orange juice, lime juice, and vinegar, and cook for another 5 minutes for the flavors to blend.

3. Let the sauce cool to room temperature, and serve. (You can store the sauce, covered, for up to 1 day in the refrigerator.)

IN PRAISE OF CUMIN

The beguiling flavor of cumin makes this spice one of our most ubiquitous. Its warm, earthy tones are as at home in the tagines of Morocco as they are in a rich Indian curry or a Texas-style barbecue sauce. The more dishes I create, the more I find that I reach for cumin to enrich other flavors.

We can date the use of cumin to over 4,000 years ago in the Nile River valley, where Egyptians harvested and then bartered with the seeds, traveling by camel along the trading routes across North Africa to the west and Asia to the east. Eventually cumin reached the New World with the Spaniards in Mexico. At each port the locals created ways to add the spice to their foods. New recipes were born and cumin became a global spice.

Much of the cumin seed crop today is cultivated in northwest India. It has its best growth spurt during the mild winter months, when the moisture and cool temperatures are ideal. The harvest takes place from March to May, when the air is dry. (The weather must be dry for the harvest or the cumin seeds, resembling caraway seeds, will be washed away by the rain.) The plant is a fast-growing, delicate-looking annual reaching up to 3 feet. Its small white flowers remind me of dill flowers.

It's best to toast the seeds in a dry skillet and grind them into a powder yourself, but nowadays, the ground cumin and the whole cumin seeds available in our markets are generally of high quality.

MAPLE BOURBON
BAKED VIRGINIA HAM

SERVES 20 TO 25

here is something about the down-home flavor of Kentucky bourbon that mixes well with the sweetness of Vermont maple syrup. And something sumptuous happens when the North and South blend so well on top of a fully cooked ham! This ham looks and tastes spectacular and it dazzles at Christmas and Eastertime.

FOR THE GLAZE:

1 cup bourbon

⅔ cup pure maple syrup

⅔ cup ketchup

⅓ cup soy sauce

2 tablespoons finely minced fresh ginger

2 tablespoons (packed) dark brown sugar

FOR THE HAM:

1 bone-in smoked Virginia ham (15 pounds)

About 28 whole cloves

2 tablespoons Dijon mustard

1. Prepare the glaze: Combine all the glaze ingredients in a bowl. Stir well, and set aside.

2. Position a rack in the center of the oven and preheat the oven to 350°F.

3. Prepare the ham: Carefully trim off the thick rind and all but ¼ inch of the fat from the surface of the ham. Use a sharp knife to score a diamond pattern in the surface of the ham, making the cuts about ¼ inch deep, and insert the cloves at the crossed points of the diamonds.

4. Set the ham in a shallow baking pan. Brush the mustard all over the top, and pour 1 cup of the glaze over the ham.

5. Bake, basting generously with the remaining glaze every 15 minutes, for 1½ hours.

6. Place the ham on a large decorative platter, and let it rest for 15 minutes. Present the ham to your guests, and then return it to the kitchen and thinly slice it for serving. ❦

CRUSHING PEPPERCORNS

To crush peppercorns, place them on a sheet of wax paper and crush them with the side of a wide chef's knife. Don't pound on the knife—the peppercorns will jump all over the place. Simply press down hard on the flat side of the knife until the peppercorns break into very small pieces.

ROASTED LEG OF LAMB
RUBBED WITH LEMON AND ZESTY SPICES

SERVES 8

Chiles, cumin, and ginger work their magic on lamb when they get to sit together overnight, which is the best way to prepare this meat. I enjoy my lamb medium-rare because the meat is so succulent and I am able to taste all its great flavors.

FOR THE RUB:

2 tablespoons finely minced garlic

2 tablespoons finely minced fresh ginger

2 small dried red chiles, crushed; or

½ teaspoon crushed red pepper flakes

1 tablespoon ground cumin

¼ cup extra-virgin olive oil

Finely grated zest of 2 lemons

Salt and freshly ground black pepper,

to taste

FOR THE LAMB:

1 bone-in leg of lamb (6 to 7 pounds)

½ cup fresh lemon juice (from 2 large lemons)

½ cup chicken broth, preferably homemade

(see page 434)

1. Combine all the rub ingredients except the salt and pepper in a small bowl, and rub the mixture into the lamb. Sprinkle all over with salt and pepper. Cover the lamb loosely with aluminum foil and let it rest at room temperature for 4 hours, or overnight in the refrigerator.

2. Position a rack in the center of the oven and preheat the oven to 400°F.

3. Place the lamb in a shallow roasting pan. Pour the lemon juice and chicken broth into the pan.

4. Put the pan in the oven and immediately reduce the heat to 350°F. Roast, basting occasionally with the pan juices, for 1 hour and 40 minutes for medium-rare meat (an instant-read thermometer inserted into the thickest part of the leg should register 140°F). If you prefer the lamb cooked to medium, roast it for 10 minutes more (160°F on an instant-read thermometer). Let the lamb rest for 10 minutes before carving it.

5. Carve the lamb, arrange the slices on an attractive platter, and serve. ❧

CROWN ROAST OF LAMB
WITH BRIGHT GREEN TABOULEH

SERVES 8

Crown roasts of lamb are often stuffed with wild rice and served at Christmas, but I thought that in warmer weather a Bright Green Tabouleh stuffing, festooned with fresh mint, would be perfect. The parsley-laden tabouleh, the mint, and the watercress bring a springtime freshness to this cold-weather standard.

1 crown roast of lamb (two 8-chop racks tied
    together), bones frenched (see box)
2 teaspoons dried thyme leaves
Coarse (kosher) salt and freshly ground black
    pepper, to taste
4 cups Bright Green Tabouleh (page 319)
4 large bunches fresh mint, for garnish
4 large bunches fresh watercress, for garnish

1. Position a rack in the center of the oven and preheat the oven to 450°F.

2. Season the crown roast with the thyme and with generous amounts of salt and pepper, pressing the seasonings into the meat. Cover the tips of the bones with aluminum foil to prevent burning, and place the roast in a shallow roasting pan.

3. Roast for 30 minutes for perfectly cooked medium-rare meat. If you like your lamb cooked to medium, add another 5 minutes of cooking time.

4. Place the roast on a decorative round serving platter, and let it rest for 10 minutes. Then fill the center with the tabouleh, and garnish the tabouleh with a full, leafy mint sprig. Arrange the watercress and the remaining mint sprigs around the roast.

5. To serve, spoon the tabouleh from the center of the roast onto plates; then carve the roast between the bones into chops.

HOW TO FRENCH A RACK OF LAMB

To french the rib bones of a rack of lamb, place the rack, fat side (meat side) up, on a flat surface. Using a very sharp knife (a boning knife works well), make a cut across the rack, down to the bone, about 2 inches from the tip of the ribs. From this point, cut out all the meat and fat from between the ends of the bones; then scrape them clean. If you are making a crown roast, once the bones are cleaned, stand the racks up meat facing in and tie the end chops together with kitchen string.

CHINESE-SCENTED RACK OF LAMB

SERVES 2

his is a *small* important roast, something to serve at a very special dinner for two. A rack somehow is much more elegant than a few lamb chops. When we think of rack of lamb, Chinese flavorings rarely come to mind, but the creativity of American cooking sets us free to travel the globe in our kitchens. The succulence of the meat matches beautifully with the delectable sweetness of hoisin sauce. A splash of rice vinegar tames and balances the flavors. If you'd rather not french the bones, ask your butcher to do it for you.

FOR THE MARINADE:

3 tablespoons dry sherry

2 tablespoons soy sauce

2 tablespoons hoisin sauce

1 tablespoon rice vinegar

1 tablespoon finely minced fresh ginger

1 tablespoon finely minced garlic

1 teaspoon toasted sesame oil

FOR THE LAMB:

1 rack of rib lamb chops (8 chops, about
    2½ pounds), frenched (see box, facing page)

Salt and freshly ground black pepper to taste

1. The day before you plan to cook the lamb, combine all the marinade ingredients in a bowl and stir well. Place the rack of lamb, curved (meaty) side down, in a large, shallow ovenproof dish and coat it with the marinade. Cover with plastic wrap or aluminum foil, and marinate in the refrigerator overnight.

2. Thirty minutes before you plan to roast the lamb, remove the dish from the refrigerator.

3. Position a rack in the center of the oven and preheat the oven to 400°F.

4. Transfer the lamb to a plate, brushing off any bits of garlic and ginger, and set it aside. Pour the marinade through a fine-mesh strainer into a bowl or a spouted measuring cup. Return the lamb, curved side up, to the baking dish and brush the strained marinade over it. Season the meat with salt and pepper. Roast until it is medium-rare (140°F on an instant-read thermometer), 25 minutes. If you prefer your meat cooked to medium, add another 5 minutes of cooking time. Let the lamb rest for 5 minutes before slicing it into individual chops.

5. Decorate the bones with paper frills before serving, if desired. 🌿

ROASTED
LOIN OF VENISON

SERVES 8

When looking for a particularly elegant roast to serve in the autumn and winter, it's hard to match venison, with its rich flavor. There's skill involved since the meat has so little fat: venison must be roasted at a high heat and served with a luscious sauce. In this recipe I've chosen ruby port enriched with shallot butter, which complements the flavors of the meat. No flour thickens the sauce; I've kept it as natural as possible. Curry Butternut Mash (page 334) is a perfect accompaniment.

FOR THE VENISON:

1 boneless loin of venison (about 6 pounds)

3 tablespoons unsalted butter, at room temperature

Coarse (kosher) salt and freshly ground black
        pepper, to taste

FOR THE SAUCE:

4 tablespoons (½ stick) unsalted butter

2 shallots, finely chopped

1 teaspoon finely minced fresh ginger

1 cup chicken broth, preferably homemade (page 434)

1 cup ruby port

1 tablespoon chopped fresh thyme leaves

Salt and freshly ground black pepper, to taste

4 tablespoons chopped fresh flat-leaf parsley leaves

1. Position a rack in the center of the oven and preheat the oven to 450°F.

2. Prepare the venison: Place the venison loin on a large rimmed baking sheet, and pat it dry with paper towels. Spread the butter all over the meat. Sprinkle the meat generously with salt and pepper.

3. Roast the venison until it is medium-rare (about 135°F on an instant-read thermometer inserted in the thickest part of the meat), about 20 minutes. Transfer the meat to a cutting board and let it rest for 15 minutes.

4. Slice the meat into sixteen 1-inch-thick slices, and cover them loosely with aluminum foil to keep them warm.

5. Prepare the sauce: Melt 2 tablespoons of the butter in a medium-size saucepan over low heat. Add the shallots and ginger and cook, stirring, until softened, about 5 minutes. Add the broth, port, and thyme and bring to a boil. Then reduce the heat and simmer for 10 minutes. Season with salt and pepper. Swirl in the remaining 2 tablespoons butter, and stir in 2 tablespoons of the parsley.

6. To serve, arrange 2 slices of the roast on each of eight dinner plates. Spoon the sauce over the top, and sprinkle with the remaining 2 tablespoons parsley. ❧

ORANGE SPICE ROASTED TURKEY WITH YUM GRAVY AND HARVEST CORN BREAD STUFFING

SERVES 16

There's nothing quite as intoxicating as the aromas of Thanksgiving, and every year, a perfectly festooned roasted turkey steals the show. Let paprika, thyme, sage, and fresh orange juice spice your bird this year, with a little Grand Marnier punching up the gravy. All in all, it adds a little new without going over the top—after all, this is a holiday where families crave the familiar.

Be sure to have a game plan for preparing your Thanksgiving dinner. Make the stuffing and the giblet broth the day before, and you'll be in very good shape to cook the bird on the day of. Just follow the timing exactly for juicy white meat and well-cooked dark meat.

FOR THE GIBLET BROTH
(make 1 day ahead):

Giblets and neck from turkey, rinsed
(do not use the liver)

2 cans (14 ounces each) chicken broth

2 ribs celery, with leaves

2 onions, unpeeled, cut in half

2 cloves garlic, lightly crushed

4 sprigs fresh parsley, thyme, or sage

3 whole cloves

3 whole black peppercorns

Salt, to taste

FOR THE TURKEY AND GRAVY
(make on Thanksgiving Day):

1 fresh turkey (18 pounds) with giblets and neck

1 orange, halved

Paprika, to taste

Salt and freshly ground black pepper, to taste

10 to 12 cups Harvest Corn Bread Stuffing
(recipe follows)

10 tablespoons (1¼ sticks) unsalted butter,
at room temperature

1 cup fresh orange juice

4 tablespoons (½ stick) unsalted butter

¼ cup all-purpose flour

2 tablespoons Grand Marnier or Triple Sec

1½ teaspoons dried thyme leaves, or
1 tablespoon fresh (see Note)

FOR GARNISH:

2 to 3 large bunches fresh sage

1. One day ahead, prepare the giblet broth: Place all the broth ingredients in a heavy saucepan, add 2 cups water, and bring to a boil. Then reduce the heat and simmer, skimming off any foam that rises to the surface, until the giblets are tender, about 1 hour. Strain the broth into a bowl, reserving the giblets and neck and discarding the vegetables. Cover and refrigerate the strained broth.

2. When it is cool enough to handle, shred the meat from the neck. Finely chop the giblets and mix the meats together. Cover and refrigerate.

3. On Thanksgiving day, preheat the oven to 325°F.

4. Prepare the turkey: Rinse the turkey well inside and out, removing any excess fat. Pat it dry with paper towels.

5. Squeeze the juice from the orange halves into the body and neck cavities. Sprinkle the cavities with paprika, salt, and pepper. Fill the cavities loosely with the stuffing, using about 3 cups for the neck and 8 cups for the body. (If you have extra stuffing, bake it alongside the turkey in an ovenproof casserole at 350°F for 20 minutes.) Close the cavities with turkey lacers, or sew them closed with a large needle and heavy thread. Tie the legs together with kitchen string.

6. Rub the turkey with 6 tablespoons of the butter, and sprinkle it with paprika, salt, and pepper.

7. Place a rack in a large roasting pan. Tear off two long pieces of heavy-duty aluminum foil, and place them on the rack—one piece lengthwise and one piece crosswise. Set the turkey, breast side up, on the foil-covered rack. Pour the orange juice and 2 cups of the giblet broth into the bottom of the pan, and cover the turkey loosely with the foil. Place the turkey in the oven and roast for 1½ hours.

8. Open up the foil and roast the turkey, basting it with the pan juices every 30 minutes, for another 2½ hours. If the turkey gets too brown, tent it loosely with the foil.

9. Raise the oven temperature to 350°F and cook the turkey for 1 hour, or until an instant-read thermometer inserted into the thickest part of the thigh (without touching the bone) reads 170°F and the juices run clear when the thigh is pricked with a small sharp knife. (The temperature in the breast should read 160°F.)

10. Transfer the turkey to a platter. Remove the stuffing from the body and neck cavities, place it in a serving dish, and cover it with aluminum foil to keep warm. Let the turkey rest, loosely covered with foil, for 20 minutes before carving.

11. While the turkey is resting, prepare the yum gravy: Carefully pour the pan juices into a measuring cup. There should be about 2 cups. Pour these juices back into the roasting pan and warm them over low heat, scraping up the brown bits in the pan. Strain the liquid into a gravy separator to remove any fat.

12. Melt the remaining 4 tablespoons butter in a heavy saucepan over low heat. Gradually whisk in the flour and continue whisking until it browns slightly, 2 to 3 minutes. Whisking constantly, slowly pour in the 2 cups of the strained, defatted pan juices and continue whisking until smooth. Slowly bring the gravy to a boil. Then reduce the heat to medium-low and add the Grand Marnier, thyme, salt and pepper, and reserved meat/giblet mixture. Simmer, stirring, until the gravy has thickened, about 10 minutes. If the gravy is too thick, thin it with some of the remaining giblet broth. Taste, and adjust the seasonings if necessary.

13. Garnish the turkey with the bunches of sage, and present it to your guests before carving it on a cutting board in the kitchen. Arrange the carved meat on a large decorative platter, and serve with the stuffing and gravy.

NOTE: I prefer dried herbs in my turkey gravy and stuffing. To me, they give it more of a Thanksgiving flavor. It's hard to explain exactly what that means— but you'll understand when you taste them! 🌿

HARVEST CORN BREAD STUFFING

MAKES ENOUGH FOR AN 18-POUND TURKEY, WITH PLENTY LEFT OVER TO BAKE SEPARATELY

Spicy sausage, available in all supermarkets, gives a super bite to this stuffing. The dried fruit acts as a foil for the sausage, adding sweetness and contributing to a luscious flavor. I love plenty of thyme and sage at Thanksgiving, but adjust the seasonings to your taste.

12 cups cubed corn bread or sourdough bread
(1-inch cubes)

2 pounds well-spiced pork or turkey sausage,
casings removed, meat broken into clumps

2 tablespoons olive oil

4 cups chopped red onions (¼-inch pieces)

4 cups chopped celery (¼-inch pieces)

2 tablespoons finely minced garlic

2 teaspoons dried thyme leaves (see Note above)

2 teaspoons crumbled dried sage leaves
(see Note above)

2 Granny Smith apples, unpeeled, cored and
cut into ½-inch pieces

1 cup dried cherries

1 cup dried apricots, quartered

Salt and freshly ground black pepper, to taste

1½ cups chicken broth, preferably homemade
(see page 434)

1. Preheat the oven to 350°F.

2. Spread the corn bread on two baking sheets and bake it for 15 minutes. Remove the baking sheets from the oven and let the bread rest for 30 minutes to dry out. Place the bread cubes in a large bowl.

3. Cook the sausage in a heavy pot over medium heat, breaking up the clumps, until it is browned, 10 to 12 minutes. Using a slotted spoon, remove the sausage and add it to the bread cubes. Discard the fat in the pot.

4. Heat the oil in the same pot over low heat. Add the onions, celery, and garlic, and cook, stirring occasionally, until tender, about 15 minutes. While the vegetables are cooking, sprinkle the thyme and sage over them.

5. Add the vegetable mixture to the bread and sausage, and toss in the apples, cherries, and apricots. Season well with salt and pepper.

6. Drizzle the broth over the stuffing, ½ cup at a time, tossing, until it is well moistened. Let the stuffing cool to room temperature; then transfer it to a container, cover, and refrigerate it until you are ready to stuff the turkey. 🌿

"AN ULTIMATE DINING EXPERIENCE."

SIZZLING STEAK,

perfectly marbled and well aged, cut nice and thick and then grilled to an exactly right doneness, is unbeatably satisfying but also as elusive as a baseball no-hitter. Is it the grade, the thickness, the cut, the aging, and the marbling that create that elusive steak experience? And how about the preparations used—do they make the steaks better or does a good cut need nothing more than salt and pepper? Rib eye has great texture and flavor. A porterhouse combines two top-notch cuts: tenderloin and sirloin. I love a T-bone; it's smaller than a porterhouse but a similar type of steak, with a portion of the sirloin and less of the tenderloin. The New York strip is well marbled, a perfect shape and size, infinitely versatile, and sublime. An elegant tenderloin is ideal for roasting—with no bones, it's easy to carve and perfect to serve to guests.

I used to buy 2-inch-thick steaks but eventually decided that was too thick. Now I prefer 1¼ to 1½ inches. But timing is important. A perfectly cooked steak will thrill when cooked the way you like it. I prefer mine rare, juicy, and full-flavored, with plenty left over for a sliced steak sandwich the next day. Here are nine terrific cooked steaks and one amazing tartare. 🎋

THE PERFECT PORTERHOUSE
WITH HERB BUTTER

SERVES 2 TO 3

there are few steaks that command as much respect as the porterhouse. For example, it's the only steak served at the renowned Peter Luger Steak House in Brooklyn, New York. What earns the praise is that it is the best of both steak worlds: part tenderloin and part sirloin, divided by a T-shaped bone. It's sheer luxury in my house and bound to be in yours. Pour a rich Cabernet Sauvignon when you serve this porterhouse.

1 porterhouse steak, cut 1¼ inches thick
    (about 1¾ pounds), at room temperature
1 to 2 tablespoons chopped fresh
    thyme leaves
Freshly ground black pepper, to taste
Sea salt, to taste
4 thyme sprigs, for garnish
2 or 3 disks Herb Butter (recipe follows),
    sliced ¼ inch thick, for serving

1. Preheat a barbecue grill to high, or preheat the broiler. If using the broiler, position the rack 6 to 7 inches from the heat source.

2. Pat the steak dry with paper towels. Sprinkle the thyme and a generous amount of pepper over both sides, patting to make sure the seasonings adhere to the meat.

3. Oil the grill grate or the rack in a broiling pan, place the steak on it, and broil or grill for 5 minutes.

4. Turn the steak over, sprinkle it with salt, and cook for 3 minutes for medium-rare meat (135° to 140°F on an instant-read thermometer). Add 1 minute for medium-cooked meat.

5. Transfer the steak to a cutting board and let it rest for 5 minutes for the juices to settle. Then carefully carve the bone out of the steak. Slice the sirloin and the tenderloin into ½-inch-thick slices, arrange them on a warmed platter, and garnish with the thyme sprigs. Serve with the disks of Herb Butter to top each serving.

HERB BUTTER

MAKES ½ CUP

there are several reasons to make an herb butter and keep it close at hand in your freezer: It's delicious with simple fish, poultry, and vegetable dishes. You'll forget garlic bread once you taste herb butter spread on a hot loaf. And it is a perfect topping for a grand porterhouse steak. No need to bother with a sauce—all you'll need to do is slice off a generous disk, center it on the steak, and serve.

> 8 tablespoons (1 stick) unsalted butter,
>   at room temperature
> 1½ tablespoons chopped fresh flat-leaf
>   parsley leaves
> 2 teaspoons chopped fresh tarragon leaves,
>   or ½ teaspoon dried
> 1½ teaspoons chopped fresh thyme leaves,
>   or ½ teaspoon dried
> 1½ teaspoons chopped fresh oregano leaves,
>   or ½ teaspoon dried
> ¼ teaspoon freshly ground black pepper

1. Combine all the ingredients in a bowl and stir until well blended.

2. Mound the butter in the center of a large piece of wax paper. Cover the top of the butter with the paper and roll the butter to form a log about 1½ inches in diameter and 5 inches long. Twist the ends of the paper to seal the roll closed, and wrap it well in plastic wrap. Store in the freezer for up to 2 months.

3. To serve, slice off ⅛- to ¼-inch-thick disks as needed. ❧

A FEW STEAK TIPS

Nowadays, top chefs are creating spice rubs for their steaks, but I prefer them simply salted and peppered. For a great crust on your meat, brush your steaks with olive oil before grilling or broiling and then sprinkle them with coarse (kosher) salt and freshly ground pepper. Lay them on the hottest part of a well-oiled grill grate, and if there's a flare-up, move the meat to the side until the flame subsides.

Knowing when a steak is cooked to your liking is not an exact science, even to a professional chef (I have sent steaks back). Cutting into the meat allows those important juices to escape—something you don't want to have happen. An instant-read thermometer is a great help—poke it into the side of the steak to find out if your steak is ready.

T-BONE FIORENTINA-STYLE

SERVES 4

While we're known for our great steaks in America, marvelous beef, pungent olive oil, and wood-burning fires put this Tuscan classic on the culinary map. A Fiorentina is a good thick T-bone steak, coated with coarsely ground or crushed peppercorns, grilled quite rare, salted on one side, and served with lemon halves. Very simple—and that is why the quality of the meat is so important. The Frisée and Apple Salad (page 258) is heavenly alongside.

Coarsely ground black pepper or crushed
　　black peppercorns, to taste
4 T-bone steaks, cut 1½ inches thick
　　(each about 1½ pounds), at room temperature
Coarse (kosher) salt or Maldon (flaky)
　　sea salt (see Notes), to taste
¼ cup extra-virgin olive oil
2 lemons, halved, for garnish
4 bunches fresh watercress, for garnish

1. Preheat a grill (preferably a charcoal grill) to high.

2. Press the pepper into both sides of the meat.

3. When you're ready to grill the steaks, oil the grate well. Grill the steaks for 3 minutes. Then turn them over and sprinkle the salt over the grilled side. Grill the second side for 5 minutes for medium-rare meat (135° to 140°F on an instant-read thermometer), or to the desired doneness.

4. Before removing the steaks from the grill, drizzle the olive oil over them. Transfer the steaks to a cutting board and let them rest for 5 to 10 minutes.

5. Remove the meat from the bone and slice it ½-inch thick. Serve garnished with the lemon halves and watercress.

NOTES:

✦ Flaky Maldon sea salt can be found at Whole Foods, Williams-Sonoma, and other fine food and cookware stores.

✦ These steaks can also be cooked under the broiler. Set the oven rack 3 inches from the heat source, and oil the rack in the broiler pan.

STRIP STEAKS
WITH A TOUCH OF LATIN AMERICA

SERVES 2

Each of these steaks is perfect to serve one. While the Kansas City or New York strip hardly needs any embellishing, the robust flavor of Chimichurri Sauce, with its garlic and fresh herbs, complements the juicy texture of the meat. The steak is great cooked on an outdoor grill, and it's equally delicious when broiled.

FOR THE RUB:

½ teaspoon ground cumin

½ teaspoon sweet paprika

½ teaspoon chipotle chile powder

½ teaspoon coarse (kosher) salt

FOR THE STEAKS:

2 strip steaks (12 ounces each), cut 1¼ inches thick,
    at room temperature

FOR SERVING:

Chimichurri Sauce (page 366)

1. Preheat a barbecue grill to high.

2. Prepare the rub: Combine all of the rub ingredients in a small bowl, and stir well.

3. Prepare the steaks: Pat the steaks dry with a paper towel. Rub the spice mixture all over them.

4. When you are ready to grill, set the grate 3 inches from the heat source and oil the grate well. Grill the steaks for 3 minutes. Then turn them over and grill the second side for 3 minutes for rare meat (125°F on an instant-read thermometer), 4 minutes for medium-rare (135° to 140°F), or 5 minutes for medium (140° to 145°F).

5. Transfer the steaks to a cutting board, and let them rest for 5 minutes for the juices to settle.

6. Cut the steaks on the diagonal into ½-inch-thick slices, and serve them on a warmed platter with Chimichurri Sauce alongside.

NOTE: This recipe can be doubled.

A CUT ABOVE

A thick and perfectly cooked steak intoxicates. Here are some favorite cuts.

PORTERHOUSE: What a steak—and most would say, the King of Steaks. Two for one in this fabulous piece of meat: Separated by a T-shaped bone, half is tender and luscious tenderloin, and half New York strip, juicy and pleasantly chewy in comparison. Some of each is a delectable experience.

T-BONE: Smaller than a porterhouse, but not dissimilar, this terrific steak has it all as well. Identified by its T-bone, it has a section of fillet along one side, although smaller than the porterhouse, and a top loin along the other side. I've prepared mine in the Fiorentina style—simple, with a splash of fresh lemon before taking a bite.

SIRLOIN: This is the one to order when you want a large, juicy steak. There are round bone, pin bone, and double-bone steaks. The one with the medium-size pin bone is considered the tenderest of all. Any which way, I love marinating mine and serving it with a Chopped Steak-House Salad for a true steakhouse experience.

TENDERLOIN: The fillet—always elegant, tender, and delicious. The popular name for an individual steak, cut from the whole tenderloin, is filet mignon. To punch up the flavor, I prepare mine with an orange glaze.

NEW YORK STRIP: Also known as the Kansas City strip. This is a well-marbled piece of top loin. I grill mine with a south-of-the-border-inspired rub and serve it with a Chimichurri Sauce.

LONDON BROIL AND FLANK STEAK: Flank steak is a lean, boneless piece of beef from the underside of the cow—the lower section of the short loin. This cut is used mainly for London broil. It takes very well to marinades. It has wonderful flavor and tender texture when thinly sliced on the diagonal. It must be cooked quickly or it will toughen. I've marinated it in Chinese flavoring with delicious results.

HANGER STEAK: Known as the hanging tender, butcher's steak, or *onglet,* it hangs between the last rib and the loin. Its intense flavor is hard to resist, and if I see one on a menu, I pounce. My Asian seasonings combine well with the steak's natural taste.

RIB EYE: The rib eye, cut from the rib of the cow, deserves high-class treatment with its ideal texture and big flavor. It can absorb zesty sauces or shine under uptown toppings such as my Wild Mushroom Ragoût. I like my rib eyes cut thick. You can buy them boneless and on the bone.

SKIRT STEAK: Long, thin, moist, and full-flavored, skirt steak is a true downtown cut of meat. Cut from the plate of the beef, it's chewier than other steaks and benefits from time spent in a marinade. This piece of meat gained in status when fajitas became popular countrywide. I've piled mine high with a riot of sweet sautéed peppers.

RIB EYE
WITH WILD MUSHROOM RAGOUT

SERVES 4

When you are cooking for company, what could be more luxurious than well-seasoned steaks topped with a pile of Wild Mushroom Ragoût? For the greatest flavor, choose rib eyes that are marbled with just the right amount of fat. (The best marbling appears to be woven throughout the meat like a fine tapestry thread. It guarantees a high degree of tenderness.) For the more delicate table, and of course to avoid who-gets-the-bone fights, buy them boneless. But when cooking for one, savor that bone!

For the quick mushroom sauté, I've combined fresh shiitake, cremini, and porcini mushrooms with shallots, garlic, and parsley. It's ready in less than 15 minutes and makes a rib-eye steak even more spectacular than it already is.

FOR THE MUSHROOM RAGOUT:

8 ounces fresh shiitake mushrooms

8 ounces fresh cremini mushrooms

4 ounces fresh porcini mushrooms (cèpes)

2 to 2½ tablespoons salted butter

2 tablespoons extra-virgin olive oil

1 shallot, finely minced

1 tablespoon finely minced garlic

Salt and freshly ground black pepper,
    to taste

2 tablespoons finely chopped fresh flat-leaf
    parsley leaves

FOR THE STEAKS:

4 rib-eye steaks, cut 1½ inches thick
    (each about 8 ounces), at room temperature

Coarsely ground black pepper, to taste

Sea salt, to taste

1. Prepare the Mushroom Ragoût: Wipe the mushroom caps clean with a damp paper towel, or clean them with a mushroom brush. Cut off the stems and reserve them for another use. Quarter the mushroom caps and set them aside.

2. Melt the butter in the oil in a large nonstick skillet over medium-low heat. Add the mushrooms,

AGING

In many of the best steak houses, you may see prime meat hanging to be aged in cool meat lockers. The aging allows the meat's natural enzymes to break down the hard connective tissues and for water to evaporate, concentrating the flavor. For aging to substantially improve the quality of the meat, the meat should be well marbled. The ideal time can be anywhere from 10 days to 3 weeks.

raise the heat to medium, and cook, stirring, until they are lightly colored and cooked through, 5 to 7 minutes. (You raise the heat so the mushrooms will cook through without releasing too much liquid.) Then add the shallot and garlic and cook, tossing, for 2 minutes. Season the mixture with salt and pepper, and toss with the parsley. Set it aside, covered loosely with aluminum foil.

3. Preheat a barbecue grill or the broiler to high. Lightly oil the grill grate or the rack in a broiler pan.

4. Prepare the steaks: Sprinkle the steaks well with pepper, and place them on the grate or in the pan.

Grill or broil until the steaks are well crusted on the first side, about 3 minutes for rare meat, 4 minutes for medium-rare. Turn the steaks over, sprinkle the grilled side with salt, and grill for 3 to 4 minutes for rare meat (125°F on an instant-read thermometer), 5 to 6 for medium-rare (135° to 140°F).

5. Transfer the steaks to a cutting board and sprinkle the second side with salt. Let them rest for 5 minutes for the juices to settle.

6. Carve the steaks into ½-inch-thick slices, and divide them among four dinner plates. Top with the Mushroom Ragoût, and serve immediately. 🍀

SEARING SIRLOIN

SERVES 4

Whenever my family sits down for a steak, sirloin is usually my choice. It is large, flavorful, and goes a long way. It's great grilled or broiled, and especially served with baked potatoes heaped with butter, sour cream, and chives. The Chopped Steak-House Salad is a perfect accompaniment, next to or on top of the steak.

FOR THE STEAK AND MARINADE:
1 sirloin steak (boneless top sirloin, also called
  a butt sirloin), cut 1¼ inches thick
  (1½ pounds), at room temperature
¼ cup red wine vinegar
Salt and freshly ground black pepper,
  to taste
1 large clove garlic, grated

2 tablespoons Dijon mustard
⅓ cup extra-virgin olive oil

Chopped Steak-House Salad (recipe follows),
  for serving

1. Pat the steak dry with a paper towel, and place it in a shallow bowl.

2. Prepare the marinade: Combine the vinegar, salt and pepper, garlic, and mustard in a small bowl. Whisk in the olive oil until slightly thickened. Pour the marinade over the steak, coating it completely. Cover, and refrigerate for 4 hours or overnight. Turn the steak about halfway through the marinating time.

3. Remove the steak from the bowl and bring it to room temperature. Scrape off the garlic.

4. Preheat a barbecue grill or the broiler to high. Lightly oil the grill grate or the rack in a broiler pan.

5. Grill or broil until the steak is well-crusted on the first side, about 3 minutes. Turn it over and grill or broil on the second side for 3 minutes more for rare meat (125°F on an instant-read thermometer), 4 minutes for medium-rare (135° to 140°F), or 5 minutes for medium (145° to 150°F).

6. Transfer the steak to a cutting board and let it rest for 5 minutes for the juices to settle. Then carve it into generous ½-inch-thick slices and divide them among four dinner plates. Serve the Chopped Steak-House Salad alongside or atop the sirloin. ❧

CHOPPED STEAK-HOUSE SALAD

MAKES 4 CUPS

The first chopped salad appeared at Hollywood's Brown Derby restaurant in the 1920s when Bob Cobb needed to whip up something on short notice for his friends (hence the Cobb Salad). When chopped salads became popular once again in steak houses, they included iceberg lettuce, chickpeas, and feta cheese. I came up with this version, which I thought would be great served over sirloin steak. I've left out the lettuce, and in fact this small salad is more like a Greek salad. It freshens a steak and gives it a lighter twist—and it's great on its own with crusty bread.

> 1 cup diced hothouse (seedless) cucumber (¼-inch dice)
> 1 cup diced seeded ripe tomatoes (¼-inch dice)
> 1 cup diced feta cheese (½-inch dice)
> ½ cup diced red onion (¼-inch dice)
> ½ cup coarsely chopped pitted black olives
> ¼ cup chopped fresh flat-leaf parsley leaves
> Salt and freshly ground black pepper, to taste
> ¼ cup extra-virgin olive oil
> ¼ cup red wine vinegar

Combine the cucumber, tomatoes, feta, onion, olives, and parsley in a large bowl. Season with salt and pepper. Drizzle the olive oil and vinegar over the salad, and lightly toss it together. Serve immediately. ❧

ORANGE-GLAZED FILLETS

SERVES 8

beef fillets are extremely mild in flavor. In fact, they can be disappointing because although they're dressy and very tender, they need a real flavor boost. This does the trick: a gooey orange glaze that reduces and intensifies to a rich orange flavor without overwhelming the beef.

FOR THE GLAZE:

2 tablespoons olive oil

½ cup diced onion (¼-inch dice)

1 tablespoon finely minced garlic

2½ cups fresh orange juice

½ cup unsulfured molasses

¼ cup dark rum

Salt and freshly ground black pepper,
   to taste

FOR THE BEEF:

2 fillets of beef (each 2 pounds)

2 tablespoons olive oil

Salt and freshly ground black pepper, to taste

2 scallions (white bulb and 3 inches green),
   for garnish

1. Prepare the glaze: Heat the oil in a heavy saucepan over low heat. Add the onions and cook until softened, about 5 minutes. Add the garlic and cook for 3 minutes longer.

2. Stir in the orange juice, molasses, and rum. Season with salt and pepper, and bring to a boil. Then reduce the heat to medium and simmer until the mixture has reduced to 1½ cups, about 15 minutes. Let the glaze cool to room temperature.

3. Meanwhile, preheat a barbecue grill or the broiler to high. Generously oil the grill grate or the rack in a broiler pan.

4. Brush the fillets with the olive oil, and season them with salt and pepper. Arrange them on the grate or in the pan, and grill or broil until the fillets are well-crusted on the first side, about 5 minutes.

5. Using tongs, turn the fillets over. Brush some of the glaze over the top and sides. Grill or broil for 5 minutes for medium-rare meat (135° to 140°F on an instant-read thermometer).

6. Transfer the fillets to a cutting board and let them rest for 5 to 10 minutes. Then cut them into ½-inch-thick slices and arrange them on a warmed serving dish. Drizzle the remaining glaze over the slices, and sprinkle with the scallions. Serve immediately. 🕸

PAN-SIZZLED HANGER STEAK

SERVES 4

the hanger steak—known as the hanging tender, butcher's steak, or *onglet*—hangs between the last rib and the loin. It is well known in France, where butchers often keep it for themselves—and once you taste one, you'll see why! I have always found its intense flavor hard to resist if I see it on a menu—especially if there are some crisp fries, a good salad, and some Côtes du Rhône to enjoy along with it. Asian seasonings, mellowed with a little honey, work well to temper the pungent flavor of the meat and bring it up to today's taste preferences. It's a delicious piece of beef.

FOR THE MARINADE:

¼ cup light soy sauce

2 tablespoons toasted sesame oil

1 tablespoon honey

2 tablespoons slivered soft inner
    stalk of lemongrass

2 tablespoons chopped fresh cilantro leaves

1 tablespoon finely minced garlic

FOR THE STEAKS:

2 hanger steaks (each about 8 ounces),
    at room temperature

2 tablespoons olive oil

1. Combine all the marinade ingredients in a medium-size bowl, and stir well. Add the hanger steaks and coat them well with the mixture. Let the steaks marinate for 2 hours at room temperature, turning them once or twice. (If the kitchen is very hot, marinate the meat in the refrigerator.)

2. Remove the steaks from the marinade, scraping off any bits of lemongrass, cilantro, or garlic.

3. Heat the olive oil in a large nonstick skillet over medium heat. Add the steaks, in batches if necessary (cut the steaks in half crosswise if necessary to fit in the skillet), and sear for 5 minutes on each side for medium-rare meat (135° to 140°F on an instant-read thermometer).

4. Transfer the steaks to a cutting board and let them rest for 5 minutes. Then thinly slice them on the diagonal, and serve immediately.

LONDON BROIL
WITH ASIAN ACCENTS

SERVES 4

Flank steak and Chinese seasonings: two delicious flavors that are irresistible when combined. Ginger, garlic, sherry, and soy sauce set the tone for the marinade, and a little honey smooths out the flavors. The final results will become a favorite in your grilling repertoire, indoors or out!

FOR THE MARINADE:

¼ cup soy sauce
¼ cup dry sherry
1 tablespoon finely minced fresh ginger
1 tablespoon finely minced garlic
1 tablespoon toasted sesame oil
1 tablespoon peanut oil or corn oil
1 tablespoon honey
1 tablespoon rice vinegar
2 teaspoons chile oil
Salt and freshly ground black pepper, to taste

FOR THE STEAK:

1 flank steak (about 2 pounds), at room temperature
2 tablespoons chopped fresh flat-leaf parsley leaves, for garnish

1. Combine all the marinade ingredients in a shallow bowl, and stir well. Add the flank steak and coat it well with the mixture. Cover the bowl, and let the steak marinate for 8 hours at room temperature, or overnight in the refrigerator, turning it once or twice.

2. If refrigerated, remove the bowl from the refrigerator thirty minutes before grilling. Remove the steak from the marinade, scraping off any bits of ginger and garlic.

3. Preheat the barbecue grill or broiler to high. Generously oil the grill grate or the rack in a broiler pan.

4. Grill or broil the steak for 4 minutes per side for medium-rare meat (135° to 140°F on an instant-read thermometer).

5. Transfer the steak to a cutting board and let it rest for 10 minutes. Then thinly slice it on the diagonal and arrange the slices on a warmed platter. Sprinkle with the chopped parsley, and serve immediately.

MARINATED SKIRT STEAK
WITH A KALEIDOSCOPE OF PEPPERS

SERVES 4

◯

Ifirst fell for skirt steak at Sammy's Romanian Restaurant on New York's Lower East Side. It was served on a chop plate with some horseradish grated over the top—nothing fancy, but the flavor was marvelous. Shortly thereafter skirt steak became the "hot" steak—great for a fajita or to marinate, sauté, and slice up. This long, thin steak loves an intense marinade, cooks up quickly, and bursts with flavor—which is often the case with less expensive cuts of meat. Melting-soft peppers served atop the meat marry beautifully with it. Serve some of My Roasted Beet and Fig Fantasy (page 270) alongside.

FOR THE MARINADE AND STEAK:

¼ cup extra-virgin olive oil

3 tablespoons red wine vinegar

2 teaspoons Dijon mustard

1 large clove garlic, finely minced

Salt and freshly ground black pepper, to taste

1 skirt steak (1½ pounds)

FOR THE PEPPERS:

2 tablespoons unsalted butter

¼ cup extra-virgin olive oil

1 large onion, halved and slivered

2 yellow bell peppers, stemmed, seeded,
  and cut lengthwise into thin strips

2 red bell peppers, stemmed, seeded,
  and cut lengthwise into thin strips

1 tablespoon finely chopped fresh thyme leaves,
  or ½ teaspoon dried

Salt and freshly ground black pepper, to taste

¼ cup chopped fresh flat-leaf parsley leaves plus
  2 tablespoons, for garnish

2 teaspoons finely minced garlic

1. Prepare the marinade: Combine the olive oil, vinegar, mustard, garlic, and salt and pepper in a large shallow bowl. Add the skirt steak and coat it well with the marinade. Let it rest, loosely covered, at room temperature for 1½ hours, turning the meat occasionally.

2. While the meat is marinating, prepare the peppers: Melt the butter in the oil in a large heavy pot over medium-low heat. Add the onion, bell peppers, thyme, and salt and pepper. Cook, uncovered, stirring frequently, until the vegetables are completely tender, 30 to 45 minutes.

3. Add the ¼ cup parsley and the garlic, and cook for another 5 minutes. Adjust the seasonings as needed. Set aside, loosely covered, until serving time.

4. Shortly before serving, preheat the broiler. Position the rack 3 inches from the heat source.

5. Remove the steak from the marinade and scrape off the garlic. Oil the rack in a broiler pan, arrange the steak on it, and broil for 3 minutes. Turn it over and broil for 4 minutes for medium-rare meat (135° to 140°F on an instant-read thermometer).

6. Meanwhile, if necessary, rewarm the reserved peppers.

7. Slice the steak crosswise into four portions, arrange them on individual plates, and top them with the peppers. (Alternatively, cut the steak into ½-inch-thick slices and divide them among the plates.) Sprinkle with the 2 tablespoons chopped parsley, and serve immediately. ✿

BALTHAZAR'S STEAK TARTARE

SERVES 6 TO 8 AS AN APPETIZER

There is no restaurant in New York City that I frequent more than I do Keith McNally's Balthazar. Its warmth, luscious food, and magic take me right back to the years when I lived in Paris. There's a quality at Balthazar that makes everyone dining there feel like a movie star—but if the food weren't as good as it is, people wouldn't keep coming back night after night. Lee Hanson and Riad Nasr make the best steak tartare I've ever had, and their special mayonnaise pulls it all together. Serve the steak garnished with fresh greens and lightly toasted slices of baguette. This is an instance where you'll want to use the very best quality beef—filet mignon.

1¼ pounds best-quality filet mignon, very cold

½ onion, minced

2 tablespoons drained tiny capers

8 cornichons, finely diced

2 tablespoons chopped fresh flat-leaf parsley leaves

1 anchovy fillet, minced

2 tablespoons extra-virgin olive oil

1 clove garlic, minced

½ teaspoon salt

Freshly ground white pepper, to taste

6 tablespoons Balthazar's Tartare Mayonnaise
   (recipe follows)

Assorted fresh salad greens, such as mâche and
   watercress, for garnish

1 baguette, sliced and lightly toasted,
   for serving

1. Fill a large bowl with crushed ice, and set it aside.

2. Remove the filet mignon from the refrigerator; it should be very cold. Using a very sharp knife, cut the steak into ¼-inch-thick slices. Stack 2 slices and cut them into ¼-inch-wide lengthwise slices. Turn the stack 90 degrees and slice it again, forming ¼-inch dice. Place the chopped steak in a bowl, and set the bowl in the larger bowl of crushed ice. Repeat with the remaining steak.

3. When all the beef has been chopped, add the onion, capers, cornichons, parsley, anchovy, oil, garlic, salt, and white pepper. Mix gently with a fork until just combined. Add the Tartare Mayonnaise, and mix until just combined.

4. Serve on individual plates, garnished with the salad greens and slices of toasted baguette. ☘

BALTHAZAR'S TARTARE MAYONNAISE

MAKES 1 CUP

This mayonnaise is the real thing, with raw eggs, so use the freshest eggs and keep them in the refrigerator. Leftover mayo is delicious spread on a roast beef or sliced steak sandwich.

FOR THE MAYONNAISE:

2 large egg yolks

2 tablespoons Dijon mustard

2 teaspoons fresh lemon juice

1 teaspoon sherry vinegar

½ teaspoon Worcestershire sauce

½ teaspoon Tabasco sauce

½ teaspoon salt

½ cup grapeseed oil

½ cup olive oil

FOR THE FLAVORINGS:

½ cup ketchup

3 tablespoons Dijon mustard

1 tablespoon Tabasco sauce

1 teaspoon Worcestershire sauce

½ teaspoon salt

1. Place all of the mayonnaise ingredients except the oils in the bowl of a food processor, and process for 30 seconds. With the motor running, slowly drizzle the oils in through the feed tube. Process until the mayonnaise is thick, with a creamy body.

2. Whisk the flavorings into the mayonnaise. Refrigerate, covered, for up to 1 week.

NOTE: If you don't have all the ingredients for Balthazar's mayonnaise, substitute ⅓ cup good-quality prepared mayonnaise and whisk in the additional flavorings. ☘

"ON A COLD WINTER SUNDAY, THERE IS NOTHING MORE IRRESISTIBLE."

SUNDAY SUPPERS

There's a nostalgic quality to meats cooked for Sunday suppers that goes back to an earlier generation and big family get-togethers at Grandma and Grandpa's house. They were never light meals, but they were always wonderful meals and the dishes were memorable. For me, there are few things more comforting than a richly tender brisket that has cooked all day, its wonderful scent flowing from the kitchen and perfuming the rest of the house. Now, *that* is my heaven.

Meats used for Sunday meals should be the less expensive cuts. Extremely flavorful, yes, but not the tenderloins and prime ribs. Those are special-occasion choices, and there's another chapter for them (see page 47). These are the cuts that the whole family will enjoy, and that leave scrumptious leftovers for later in the week.

When I'm cooking a hearty Sunday supper and looking for a change from brisket, I might choose beef short ribs or pork shoulder. But I'll always add something to freshen up the flavor—preserved kumquats with the pork, star anise with the ribs. These suppers are both cozy *and* new.

SUNDAY BRISKET

SERVES 6

brisket is a sumptuous cut of meat that comforts and satisfies. While a large brisket dazzles my family on holidays, a smaller brisket provides a cozy family dinner on Sunday. In the past I've embellished brisket with everything from carrots to olives. Now I keep it simple and delicious with red wine and tomatoes, and I prefer the results.

1 first-cut beef brisket (3¼ pounds; see Note)

Salt and freshly ground black pepper,
    to taste

2 tablespoons olive oil

1 large onion, halved lengthwise and slivered

6 cloves garlic, bruised (see box, page 82)

1 cup dry red wine

1 can (28 ounces) peeled Italian plum tomatoes
    (do not drain)

½ cup chicken broth, preferably homemade
    (see page 434)

2 tablespoons tomato paste

1 tablespoon dark brown sugar

2 tablespoons chopped fresh flat-leaf parsley leaves,
    for garnish

Cooked egg noodles, for serving

1. Preheat the oven to 300°F.

2. Sprinkle the brisket generously with salt and pepper. Heat the oil in a flameproof casserole over medium heat. Add the brisket and cook until it is well browned on both sides, 6 to 8 minutes per side. Sprinkle the brisket with extra salt and pepper if desired, and transfer it to a plate.

3. Reduce the heat to low and add the onion and garlic to the casserole. Cook, stirring, until softened, 5 minutes. Pour in the wine and simmer, stirring, for 2 minutes.

4. Puree the tomatoes, with their juices, in a food processor and pour the puree into the casserole. Add the broth, tomato paste, and brown sugar, and stir. Return the meat to the casserole and spoon the sauce over it. Cover the casserole, place it in the oven, and bake until the brisket is very tender, about 3 hours.

5. Transfer the meat to a cutting board and let it cool slightly. Taste the sauce, and season it if desired. Then cut the cooled brisket into ½-inch-thick slices, against the grain. Re-form the brisket, pressing the slices close together, and place it back in the casserole. Spoon the sauce over the brisket and bake, covered, for 30 minutes.

6. Sprinkle the parsley over the brisket, and serve over hot egg noodles.

NOTE: The brisket lies between the plate and the foreleg of the beef. Brisket is sold in two cuts: the first cut being the leaner and the second containing quite a bit more fat (the fat can always be skimmed off before serving). Both cuts have superb flavor.

POT ROAST PAPRIKASH

SERVES 6

One of Hungary's most famous dishes is its chicken paprikash, and with good reason: The rich sour cream sauce, flavored with sweet paprika and caraway seeds, creates a lush coating for the meat. While I have made many a luscious chicken paprikash, I've discovered that this delectable sauce complements the deep flavors of a chuck roast, making a nice change from another familiar Hungarian dish—goulash. Red bell peppers and onions add texture. Serve this with a bowl of buttered egg noodles tossed with chopped fresh dill leaves.

1 boneless beef chuck roast (about 5½ pounds)

Salt and freshly ground black pepper, to taste

3 tablespoons extra-virgin olive oil

4 red bell peppers, stemmed, seeded, and cut
    lengthwise into ½-inch-wide strips

2 onions, halved lengthwise and slivered

2 tablespoons chopped garlic

3 tablespoons good-quality sweet Hungarian
    paprika

1 tablespoon caraway seeds

2 cups beef broth, preferably homemade
    (see page 435)

1 can (28 ounces) peeled Italian plum tomatoes,
    chopped, with their juices

1 cup dry red wine

2 tablespoons all-purpose flour

¾ cup sour cream

2 tablespoons chopped fresh flat-leaf
    parsley leaves, for garnish

1. Preheat the oven to 325°F.

2. Season the pot roast all over with salt and pepper.

3. Heat the olive oil in a large, heavy, flameproof casserole over medium-high heat. Add the pot roast and brown it on all sides, about 6 minutes per side. Remove the roast to a plate.

4. Reduce the heat to medium. Add the bell peppers and the onions to the casserole, and cook, stirring occasionally, until softened, about 10 minutes. Add the garlic and cook for 2 minutes longer.

5. Reduce the heat to medium-low, sprinkle the paprika and caraway seeds over the onion mixture, and cook, stirring, for 1 minute. Add the beef broth, 2 cups of the chopped tomatoes with their juices (reserve the rest for another use), and the wine. Return the meat to the casserole and spoon the sauce over the meat. Bring to a boil, and then reduce the heat and simmer for 5 minutes.

6. Cover the casserole, transfer it to the oven, and bake, basting once or twice, until the meat is very tender, 3 hours.

7. Transfer the roast to a cutting board and cover it loosely with aluminum foil to keep it warm.

8. Strain the cooking liquid into a bowl, reserving the onions and peppers. Pour the strained cooking liquid through a gravy separator to remove the fat. Pour 2 cups of the defatted cooking liquid into a saucepan, and bring it to a boil over high heat. Reduce the heat to medium and simmer for 5 minutes. While the sauce is simmering, whisk the flour and sour cream together in a small bowl.

9. Whisk ½ cup of the hot cooking liquid into the sour cream mixture (this tempers the sour cream so that it doesn't curdle). Then, off the heat, slowly whisk the sour cream mixture into the liquid in the pan. Continue whisking until smooth. Return the vegetables to the pan.

10. Cut the pot roast into ½ inch-thick slices, and arrange them, overlapping, in a shallow serving dish.

Spoon the sauce over the meat, and sprinkle with the parsley. Serve immediately. ❧

BRUISE, CRUSH, OR PRESS?

BRUISED GARLIC: Place the garlic clove on a flat surface and hit it with the flat side of a large chef's knife so it is bruised. Remove and discard the peel.

PRESSED GARLIC: Put a peeled clove through a garlic press.

CRUSHED GARLIC: Place the garlic clove on a flat surface and hit it with the flat side of a large chef's knife. Remove and discard the peel. Sprinkle a bit of coarse salt over the garlic, and very finely mince and mash the two together.

EMMA'S SHORT RIBS

SERVES 6

On a cold winter Sunday, there is nothing more irresistible than a large pot of short ribs hot from the oven, ready to be served with mashed potatoes. Emma Feigenbaum, a chef who has cooked alongside me and Laurie for this book, braised these unforgettable ribs. The star anise and orange add exotic richness and layers of flavor to the sauce. Let's eat!

6 pounds short ribs of beef, cut crosswise
    between the bones

1½ teaspoons freshly ground black pepper, or
    to taste

2 tablespoons olive oil, or more if needed

4 large carrots, halved lengthwise and cut into
    1-inch pieces

4 ribs celery, halved lengthwise and cut into
    1-inch pieces

6 cloves garlic, sliced

3 whole star anise

1 tablespoon finely chopped fresh
    rosemary leaves

Finely grated zest and juice of 1 lemon

Finely grated zest of 1 orange

1 bottle (750 ml) dry red wine,
    preferably Beaujolais

4 cups beef broth, preferably homemade
    (see page 435)

2 cans (each 28 ounces) peeled Italian plum
    tomatoes, chopped, juices reserved

1 tablespoon dark brown sugar

1 tablespoon Dijon mustard

1 teaspoon dry mustard

Silky Mashed Potatoes (page 328), for serving

2 tablespoons chopped fresh flat-leaf parsley leaves,
    for garnish

1. Preheat the oven to 350°F.

2. Season the ribs with the pepper.

3. Heat the 2 tablespoons olive oil in a large flameproof casserole over medium heat. In batches, add the ribs and brown them well, 6 minutes per side. Transfer the ribs to a bowl.

4. Reduce the heat to medium-low, and add the carrots and celery to the casserole with a little more olive oil if needed. Cook, stirring, until wilted, about 15 minutes, adding the garlic during the last 3 minutes. Stir in the star anise, rosemary, lemon zest and juice, and orange zest.

5. Place the ribs on top of the vegetables. Pour the wine, broth, chopped tomatoes, and 2 cups of the reserved tomato juices over the ribs. Sprinkle the brown sugar over the ribs and bring to a gentle boil. Then cover the casserole, transfer it to the oven, and bake for 2 hours.

6. Remove the casserole from the oven, turn the ribs over, and adjust the seasonings as needed. Return the casserole to the oven and cook until the ribs are tender and the meat is falling off the bone, about 1 hour.

7. Using a large slotted spoon, carefully transfer the ribs and vegetables to a bowl. Set the bowl aside. Defat the sauce with a metal spoon or by pouring it through a gravy separator. Return the defatted sauce to the casserole, discarding the star anise.

8. Place the Dijon mustard and the dry mustard in a small bowl, and stir together. Whisking constantly, drizzle in some of the sauce; whisk until combined.

Then whisk this mixture back into the sauce and place the casserole over medium-low heat. Simmer until it has thickened slightly, about 20 minutes.

9. Taste the sauce, and adjust the seasonings as needed. Return the ribs and vegetables to the casserole. Simmer over medium-low heat for 5 to 7 minutes to reheat. Serve over the mashed potatoes, garnished with the chopped parsley. ❧

BRAISED OSSO BUCO
WITH GREMOLATA

SERVES 6

this osso buco is fairly traditional, but it is such an extremely delicious preparation that in this case, I let the meat and tradition speak for themselves. Serving the osso buco over Saffron Orzo enhances all the flavors and makes for a stunning presentation.

Marrow is one of those rare treats, and osso buco is a great excuse to indulge. Be sure to provide little spoons for scooping the marrow out of the bones. Enjoy it spread on toasted peasant bread.

6 center-cut veal shanks, cut 2 inches thick
(each about 12 ounces)
Salt and freshly ground black pepper,
to taste
¼ cup olive oil
2 ribs celery, cut into ¼-inch dice
2 carrots, cut into ¼-inch dice
1 large onion, cut into ¼-inch dice
1 tablespoon finely minced garlic

2 cups prepared marinara sauce or
Basic Tomato Sauce (page 437)
2 cups chicken broth, preferably homemade
(see page 434)
2 cups dry white wine
2 teaspoons chopped fresh thyme leaves, or
½ teaspoon dried
Saffron Orzo (page 347), for serving
Gremolata (recipe follows), for garnish

Why wait to make osso buco—gremolata is an easy to prepare condiment that adds spark to many a dish. Sprinkle it over grilled fish and chicken, especially an otherwise lackluster chicken breast. Stir it into steamed spinach, a bowlful of noodles, and even mashed potatoes. When you're looking to perk up a bland entrée or side dish, think gremolata.

1. Preheat the oven to 375°F.

2. Sprinkle the veal shanks generously with salt and pepper.

3. Heat the oil in a heavy flameproof casserole over medium heat. Add the veal shanks and cook until browned all over, 6 to 8 minutes per side. Transfer them to a plate and set it aside.

4. Reduce the heat to medium-low and add the celery, carrots, and onion to the casserole. Cook, stirring occasionally, for 10 minutes, adding the garlic during the last 5 minutes.

5. Add the marinara sauce, broth, wine, and thyme to the casserole, and bring to a boil. Reduce the heat and simmer for 5 minutes.

6. Return the veal shanks to the casserole. (The sauce should reach about halfway up the meat.) Cover, transfer to the oven, and bake until the meat is very tender, 2 to 2½ hours. (Do not overcook the meat.)

7. Remove the casserole from the oven and carefully skim the fat from the surface, using a metal spoon. Serve the osso buco over Saffron Orzo in shallow bowls, and sprinkle a tablespoon of gremolata over each portion. Don't forget the small spoons for scooping out the lush marrow. ❧

GREMOLATA

MAKES ABOUT ⅔ CUP

Gremolata is a fresh condiment traditionally served with osso buco. The combination of parsley, lemon zest, and garlic is a refreshing, unexpected contrast when sprinkled over the meat. It adds to the dramatic and complex flavors of the dish.

½ cup chopped fresh flat-leaf parsley leaves
Finely grated zest of 2 large lemons
2 tablespoons finely minced garlic

Combine all the ingredients in a small bowl, and toss with a fork. For the freshest taste, use within 2 to 3 hours. ❧

CHINESE-STYLE BRAISED PORK SHOULDER WITH PRESERVED KUMQUATS

SERVES 8

Whether a dish like this would ever be served in China is questionable, but my notion was ingredient-driven: kumquats, soy sauce, Chinese five spice powder, and star anise. All in all, when combined with pork, rosé wine, and carrots, the result is a splendid fusion creation.

1 boneless pork shoulder (about 5 pounds)

1 teaspoon coarse (kosher) salt

½ teaspoon freshly ground black or white pepper

½ teaspoon Chinese five spice powder

3 tablespoons peanut oil or olive oil

1 large onion, halved lengthwise and slivered

2 cups apple cider

1 cup Provençal rosé or sauvignon blanc wine

4 carrots, peeled and cut into ½-inch pieces

3 whole star anise

1 cup drained preserved kumquats, homemade (recipe follows) or store-bought

1 tablespoon cornstarch

1 tablespoon light soy sauce

1 bunch fresh watercress, for garnish

Cooked white rice, for serving

1. Preheat the oven to 325°F. Wipe the pork clean with damp paper towels.

2. Combine the salt, pepper, and five spice powder in a small bowl, and rub the mixture all over the pork.

3. Heat the oil in a large flameproof pot over medium-high heat. Add the pork and brown it well on all sides, about 8 minutes per side. Then transfer it to a plate.

4. Reduce the heat to medium-low, add the onion to the pot, and cook, stirring occasionally, until softened, about 10 minutes.

5. Add the cider, wine, carrots, and star anise, and bring to a boil. Reduce the heat and simmer for 10 minutes to blend the flavors. Then add the kumquats. Place the pork and any accumulated juices on top of the vegetables and fruit, cover the pot, and transfer it to the oven. Bake, turning the meat twice and basting it occasionally, until it is very tender, 2½ hours.

6. Remove the pot from the oven and let the meat rest in the covered pot for 10 to 12 minutes. Then transfer the pork to a cutting board. Using a slotted spoon, transfer the vegetables to a bowl, discarding the star anise. Set the bowl aside. Carve the meat into ½-inch-thick slices, and cover them with aluminum foil to keep them warm.

7. Pour the sauce through a gravy separator to remove any fat, and return the defatted sauce to the pot.

8. In a small bowl, whisk ½ cup of the sauce with the cornstarch until smooth. Place the pot over medium heat, and whisking constantly, slowly add the cornstarch mixture to the sauce. Continue whisking until the sauce has thickened slightly, 5 to 7 minutes. Add the soy sauce and the reserved vegetables to the sauce.

9. Arrange the sliced meat on a platter, and garnish it with the watercress. Serve the vegetables and sauce in a bowl alongside, along with a bowl of white rice. 🍀

PRESERVED KUMQUATS

MAKES 1 CUP

With all the interest in Asian food, there has also been a surge of interest in fresh kumquats, both for putting by and for use as a fresh garnish. With their tiny orange fruits and green leaves, kumquats look stunning arranged around roast pork dishes and on the tray holding your Thanksgiving turkey. Once preserved, the sour little fruit contrasts well with its sugary syrup. Discard the small pits (although they can be swallowed). As it softens, the whole fruit is edible.

8 ounces fresh kumquats, washed,
    halved crosswise, and pitted
¾ cup plus 2 tablespoons sugar
1 piece (1 inch) peeled fresh ginger
1 tablespoon fresh lemon juice
Salt, to taste

1. Place all the ingredients in a heavy saucepan. Add ¾ cup water and bring to a boil over medium-high heat. Reduce the heat to medium-low and simmer until the kumquats are just tender, 10 to 12 minutes.

2. Remove the pan from the heat and let the kumquats cool to room temperature in the liquid. Using a slotted spoon, remove the kumquats needed for the pork. Transfer any remaining kumquats, with their syrup, to a container; cover, and store in the refrigerator for up to 1 month. 🍀

FRESH KUMQUATS

You don't have to preserve a kumquat in order to enjoy it. Pop one in your mouth whole—no nibbling—and start chewing. You may be surprised to discover that the rind is sweet, but the juice is tart. Keep chewing and the delicious sweet rind will counter the tart juice. As for the seeds, they're small enough to be swallowed or you can just spit them out.

FILIPINO PORK ADOBO

SERVES 4

adobo is a seasoning containing vinegar, soy sauce, chiles, and garlic. It's also the name of the Filipino national dish, cooked with these flavorings. The addition of Thai fish sauce adds pungent sweet and slightly salty layers. Pork always adds great flavor to any dish, but chicken simmers up beautifully in this sauce as well. I came across this recipe in Bruce Aidells's *Complete Book of Pork,* went right to the stove, and tossed it up. It's ideal for a Sunday supper because it's so easy to put together. The flavors are intense, just the way I like them, and the pork is delicious served with Pineapple Ginger Rice (page 324).

2 pounds boneless Boston butt, cut into
    1½- to 2-inch pieces

2 onions, thinly sliced

¼ cup minced garlic

2 cups chicken broth, preferably homemade
    (see page 434)

¾ cup soy sauce

½ cup rice vinegar, or more to taste

¼ cup Asian fish sauce

2 teaspoons dark brown sugar

1 teaspoon Asian hot chile oil, or more
    to taste

½ teaspoon freshly ground black pepper

Pineapple Ginger Rice, for serving

2 tablespoons chopped fresh cilantro leaves,
    for garnish

1. Place the pork, onions, and garlic in a flameproof casserole or a large Dutch oven. Mix the chicken broth, soy sauce, rice vinegar, fish sauce, brown sugar, hot chile oil, and pepper together in a medium-size bowl and add it to the casserole. Bring to a boil. Then reduce the heat to medium and simmer, uncovered, stirring occasionally, until the pork is tender, about 1 hour and 20 minutes. (Do not let it boil—if necessary, reduce the heat.)

2. Taste the sauce and adjust the vinegar, brown sugar, and chile oil to your taste. Then partially cover the casserole and continue cooking over medium-low heat for 15 minutes.

3. Serve over Pineapple Ginger Rice, sprinkled with the cilantro.

CHOUCROUTE GARNIE

SERVES 4

After two years of enjoying the delicious choucroute at Les Halles restaurant in New York City, I finally asked Anthony Bourdain for his recipe, which can also be found in his *Les Halles Cookbook*. After all, I am a tremendous fan of choucroute and enjoy making my own. Tony also makes an elegant seafood choucroute with scallops and salmon—quite a revelation.

I suggest that you follow Tony's recipe the first time you make it. The next time you do it, think about improvising. Tony says, "You can, and should, improvise on the recipe. We do at the restaurant. Just handle the sauerkraut (including the pork belly) the same way."

2 pounds high-quality sauerkraut, fresh or
    packaged in plastic bags or refrigerated jars
    (do not use canned)

8 new potatoes (about 2 pounds), peeled

2 tablespoons rendered duck fat
    (or pork or bacon fat)

1 onion, finely chopped

10 dried juniper berries

1 small clove garlic, crushed (see box, page 82)

3 cups dry white wine, preferably Riesling

1 dried bay leaf

1 teaspoon coriander seeds

Salt and freshly ground black pepper, to taste

4 ounces slab bacon, cut into ¼-inch dice

4 slices smoked pork loin, each cut ½ inch thick

4 good-quality frankfurters, bratwurst, or
    knockwurst (see Note)

4 good-quality boudins blancs or German
    white veal sausage (see Note)

3 tablespoons chopped fresh flat-leaf parsley leaves,
    for garnish

Grainy German mustard, for serving

1. Rinse the sauerkraut in cold water and let it drain in the colander.

2. Bring a medium-size pot of salted water to a boil. Add the potatoes and cook until tender but not mushy, 10 to 15 minutes. Drain and set aside.

3. Heat the duck fat in a large pot over medium heat. Add the onion and cook, stirring occasionally, until translucent, about 5 minutes. Add the sauerkraut, juniper berries, garlic, white wine, bay leaf, coriander seeds, and salt and pepper. Cover, and bring to a simmer. Add the bacon and smoked pork loin. Cover the pot and simmer for 1 hour.

4. In a separate pot, bring 8 cups of water to a boil, and then reduce the heat to a simmer. Add the frankfurters (or wursts), boudins blancs, and potatoes, and simmer until hot, about 5 minutes.

5. Drain the sauerkraut, discarding the bay leaf, and place it in the center of a large serving platter. Arrange the bacon, pork, and sausages and the boiled potatoes around it. Sprinkle with the parsley just before serving. Pass the mustard at the table.

NOTE: If possible, buy your sausages from a German butcher, who will advise you on the best sausages to use. They'll probably also sell fresh sauerkraut. 🍀

LENNY SCHWARTZ'S MARKET STREET MEAT LOAF

SERVES 8

I have never had a better meat loaf than this one, which Lenny Schwartz created for the late, lamented 72 Market Street, a restaurant in Los Angeles known for high-style yet down-home American food. It's large and moist and packs a huge flavor wallop. It's the carrots, celery, and bell peppers that get the flavors going; the half-and-half and ketchup tie the sausage, beef, and vegetables together. Hope for leftovers, because this is definitely one for sandwiches for the week ahead. Serve it with mashed potatoes and a great mixed salad or a Caesar salad.

3 tablespoons unsalted butter

¾ cup finely chopped onion

¾ cup finely chopped scallions
(white bulbs and 3 inches green)

½ cup finely chopped carrots

¼ cup finely chopped celery

¼ cup chopped red bell pepper

¼ cup chopped green bell pepper

2 teaspoons minced garlic

3 large eggs, well beaten

½ cup ketchup

½ cup half-and-half

1 teaspoon ground cumin

½ teaspoon ground nutmeg

¼ teaspoon cayenne pepper

Salt and freshly ground black pepper,
to taste

2 pounds lean ground beef chuck

12 ounces ground sweet Italian sausage
meat

¾ cup fine fresh toasted bread crumbs
(see box, facing page)

1. Melt the butter in a heavy skillet over medium-low heat, and add the onions, scallions, carrots, celery, bell peppers, and garlic. Cook, stirring often, until the moisture from the vegetables has evaporated, about 10 minutes. Set the mixture aside to cool; then refrigerate it, covered, until chilled, 1 to 2 hours.

2. Beat the eggs, ketchup, half-and-half, cumin, nutmeg, cayenne, and salt and black pepper together in a mixing bowl. Add the ground beef, sausage, and bread crumbs. Then add the chilled vegetables and knead with your hands until well mixed, 5 minutes.

3. Preheat the oven to 350°F.

4. Form the mixture into a loaf shape, approximately 12 inches long, 5 inches wide, and 2½ inches high, on a rimmed baking sheet. Bake until the loaf is cooked through (160°F on an instant-read thermometer), about 1 hour. Let the meat loaf rest for 20 minutes before slicing it. ❧

HOW TO MAKE FRESH BREAD CRUMBS

Tear lightly toasted bread into coarse pieces and place them in a food processor. Pulse the machine on and off for coarse crumbs. Store in an airtight container for up to 2 days.

BLUE RIBBON CHILI

SERVES 6 TO 8

I have always been a great fan of chili, and so have my family and friends. I've whipped up many a bowl of red, and eaten quite a few outside of my own as well. The Blue Ribbon pot is a fusion of many of the best, including a few ideas from the original *Silver Palate Cookbook*'s Chili for a Crowd. I've started it off with bite-size cubes of beef, pork, and chorizo instead of chopped meat. Ancho and regular chili powder, cumin, and chopped veggies simmer together with beer and wine, resulting in a new pot of red to be proud of.

4 tablespoons olive oil, plus more if needed

1½ pounds boneless pork shoulder, cut into
  ½-inch cubes

1½ pounds boneless beef chuck, cut into
  ½-inch cubes

3½ ounces dried chorizo, cut into ¼-inch
  dice

2 cups diced onions (¼-inch dice)

1 cup diced red bell peppers (¼-inch dice)

2 tablespoons finely minced garlic

1 to 2 teaspoons very finely minced green
  jalapeño pepper

3 tablespoons chili powder

1 tablespoon ground cumin

2 teaspoons ancho chile powder

2 teaspoons dried oregano

Salt and freshly ground black pepper,
  to taste

1 bottle (12 ounces) flat beer (see Note)

2 cans (each 28 ounces) peeled Italian plum
  tomatoes, drained and chopped

1 cup dry red wine

1 cinnamon stick (3 inches long)

1 can (15¼ ounces) dark red kidney beans,
  drained and rinsed

Cooked white rice, for serving

Sour cream, for serving

Grated Cheddar cheese, for serving

1. Pour 2 tablespoons of the olive oil into a large heavy pot over medium-high heat. Add the pork, beef, and chorizo, in batches, and cook until browned, about 6 minutes per batch. As each batch is done, use a slotted spoon to transfer it to a bowl. If needed, add the remaining olive oil to the pot while you are browning the meat.

2. Reduce the heat to medium-low and add the onions, bell peppers, garlic, and jalapeño to the pot. Cook, stirring occasionally, until soft, about 10 minutes. Sprinkle with the chili powder, cumin, ancho chile powder, oregano, and salt and pepper, and cook over low heat, stirring, to mellow the spices, 2 minutes. Return the meat to the pot.

3. Stir in the beer, tomatoes, wine, and cinnamon stick. Bring to a boil over medium-high heat. Then reduce the heat to low, cover the pot, and simmer, stirring occasionally, for 1 hour. Test the meat for doneness—it should be tender—and adjust the seasonings as desired.

4. Uncover the pot and cook the chili over low heat for 45 minutes.

5. Remove the cinnamon stick, stir in the beans, and cook for another 15 minutes. Serve the chili over rice, and pass bowls of sour cream and grated cheese to use as toppings.

NOTE: No flat beer around the house? Before you start the recipe, just open the bottle, pour the beer into a bowl, and let it stand until you need it. 🌿

SUNDAY SUGO DI CARNE

SERVES 4 TO 6

What is the famous sublime "gravy" that Italians make to serve with their Sunday pasta? My friend Donaldo Soviero—an Italian chef who for years ran a cooking school in Umbria—showed me how he made his *sugo* with lamb shanks: unusual but yummy. As he puts it, "Its sweet simplicity is what appeals most." I like it with a wide noodle, such as fettuccine or pappardelle.

FOR THE SAUCE:

2 tablespoons extra-virgin olive oil

4 cloves garlic, bruised (see box, page 82)

2 lamb foreshanks (each about 12 ounces)

¼ teaspoon crushed red pepper flakes

¼ teaspoon crushed dried basil

⅛ teaspoon ground nutmeg

Coarse salt and freshly ground black pepper,
     to taste

½ cup dry vermouth

6 cups pureed Italian plum tomatoes
     (from two 28-ounce cans)

1 tablespoon sugar

1 onion, peeled and halved

1 teaspoon finely minced garlic

FOR THE PASTA:

1 tablespoon salt

1 tablespoon olive oil

1 pound dried fettuccine

Freshly grated Parmesan cheese, for serving

1. Heat the oil in a large heavy pot over medium heat. Add the bruised garlic and sauté until it is lightly browned, 5 to 7 minutes. Remove the garlic from the pot with a slotted spoon, and set it aside.

2. Add the lamb shanks to the same pot and cook them over medium-high heat until browned, about 6 minutes per side. Sprinkle the red pepper flakes, basil, nutmeg, and salt and pepper over the lamb. Return the garlic to the pot. Add the vermouth and deglaze the pot over high heat, loosening any brown bits with a wooden spoon. Cook until the vermouth has caramelized the lamb, 3 to 5 minutes. Then stir in the tomatoes, sugar, and onion. Simmer for 5 minutes.

3. Add the minced garlic, reduce the heat, and simmer, partially covered, stirring occasionally, until the sauce is thick and the lamb shanks are tender, 1 hour.

4. Remove the lamb from the sauce and discard the onion halves. Taste the sauce, and adjust the seasonings as needed. Cut the lamb from the bones, return the meat to the sauce, and keep it warm.

5. Bring a large pot of water to a boil over high heat. Add the salt and olive oil. Then add the fettuccine and cook until just tender, about 12 minutes. Drain the pasta, reserving 1 cup of the cooking water, and place it in a warm serving bowl. Toss the pasta with the sauce, adding some of the reserved cooking water if it is too thick. Serve immediately, with the Parmesan cheese alongside.

"CHOPS MAKE FOR A SHOW-STOPPING MEAL."

CHOPS

Whether you cook them in a rack or individually, these tempting cuts of veal and venison, pork and lamb are memorably elegant, yet too good not to pick up in your fingers to get that last remaining luscious bit of meat off the bone.

Here are ten recipes that make chops stand out. Grilled frenched veal chops, accompanied by a fresh-tasting Tangerine and Tomato Salsa, resemble lollipops. A rack of veal, somewhat new on the scene, yields sumptuous large chops that look even more inviting when dressed with watercress and kumquats.

Also working their way up the popularity poll are racks of venison. In my version, they are coated with an unusual crust made from pulverized dried orange peel. Meat enhanced by orange flavors intrigues and inspires me, and I think you'll enjoy how well the combination works in an easy orange-flavored béarnaise sauce I've created to accompany lamb chops that have rested in an orange-flavored marinade.

And don't forget pork chops. Grilled with Thai flavors and accompanied by a vegetable salad that's both spicy and cooling, they make any dinner memorable.

Yes, it's easy to just grill or broil a plain chop, but until you begin to experiment with them you'll never know how exciting they can be. ✿

LOLLIPOP VEAL CHOPS
WITH TANGERINE AND TOMATO SALSA

SERVES 2

Veal chops have a delicate flavor, and when they are cut thick with the bones frenched, the rib chops resemble lollipops. A simple marinade of olive oil and fresh lemon juice is all that's necessary to punch up the flavor of these luxurious chops before setting them on the grill. I serve them crowned with a bright-tasting Tangerine and Tomato Salsa. This recipe serves two, but it is easily doubled.

2 veal rib chops (each 8 ounces), 1½ inches thick,
  bones frenched (see box, page 56)
2 tablespoons extra-virgin olive oil
2 tablespoons fresh lemon juice
Salt and freshly ground black pepper, to taste
Tangerine and Tomato Salsa (recipe follows),
  for serving

1. Place the chops in a bowl. Add the olive oil, lemon juice, and salt and pepper, and toss to coat the chops. Cover, and refrigerate for 2 hours.

2. Twenty minutes before grilling time, remove the chops from the refrigerator so they can come to room temperature.

3. Preheat a barbecue grill to high.

4. Oil the grill rack well, and arrange the chops on it. Grill until they are cooked through, being careful not to overcook them: 6 to 7 minutes per side for medium-rare to medium meat.

5. Let the chops rest for 5 minutes. Center each on a dinner plate, top with the salsa, and serve.

TANGERINE AND TOMATO SALSA

MAKES 2 CUPS

There is nothing quite like the surprisingly fresh flavor of tangerines when oranges seem tired. Combined with tomatoes and mint, they really shine.

3 tangerines
2 ripe plum tomatoes, cut into ¼-inch pieces
2 tablespoons finely diced red onion
1 teaspoon finely minced green jalapeño pepper
2½ tablespoons coarsely chopped fresh
  mint leaves

1. Peel 2 of the tangerines and separate them into segments. Remove as much of the stringy pith as possible. Cut each segment crosswise into 3 pieces.

2. Combine the tangerine pieces, tomatoes, onion, and jalapeño in a bowl, and toss to combine.

3. Finely grate the zest of the remaining tangerine, then juice it. Add the zest and 2 tablespoons of the juice to the salsa. Before serving, toss with the mint. 🌿

RACK OF VEAL

SERVES 4

For a fine and elegant dinner centerpiece, you can't beat a rack of veal—the chops are succulent and delicious. My butcher sells rack of veal as five chops, but you can order four chops, or six, depending on the appetites at the table. A garnish of fresh kumquats (see box, page 87) perks up the color.

1 rack of veal (about 5½ pounds; 5 rib chops),
    bones frenched (see box, page 56)
2 to 3 cloves garlic, slivered
3 tablespoons extra-virgin olive oil
Salt and freshly ground black pepper, to taste
Finely grated zest and juice of 2 lemons
2 teaspoons dried oregano
1½ cups dry white wine
2 to 3 large bunches watercress, for garnish
5 to 6 large bunches fresh kumquats, for garnish

1. With the tip of a small sharp knife, make slits into the rack of veal. Insert the garlic slivers in the slits.

2. Brush the rack of veal all over with the olive oil. Season it generously with salt and pepper. Then gently rub in the lemon zest and drizzle the lemon juice over the meat. Sprinkle with the oregano. Cover loosely with aluminum foil and refrigerate for 3 to 4 hours.

3. Thirty minutes before cooking time, remove the meat from the refrigerator.

4. Preheat the oven to 425°F.

5. Place the veal rack in a shallow baking pan, curved (meaty) side up. Pour the wine into the pan.

6. Roast the veal for 1½ hours, basting it once or twice, until it is cooked through and an instant-read thermometer registers 135° to 140°F when inserted in the center of the end chop.

7. Let the meat rest for 5 to 10 minutes before carving it into individual chops. Serve them on a platter garnished with watercress and kumquats. 🌿

GRILLED VEAL CHOPS CAPRI

SERVES 4

While the germ of this idea was borrowed from veal chops à la Milanese, the resemblance to that dish is distant. In a Milanese, the famous chop is pounded, flattened, breaded, and fried until browned and crispy, much like schnitzel. A squeeze of lemon juice is the final touch. Here I've marinated the chop in a lemon juice mixture and grilled it—a bit of fresher, more modern thought.

FOR THE MARINADE AND CHOPS:

¼ cup fresh lemon juice

¼ cup extra-virgin olive oil

1 teaspoon Dijon mustard

Salt and freshly ground black pepper,
    to taste

4 veal chops, cut 1 inch thick
    (each about 12 ounces), bones frenched
    (see box, page 56)

FOR THE SALAD:

4 cups baby arugula leaves, rinsed,
    patted dry, and coarsely chopped

2 cups ripe pear or cherry tomatoes,
    halved

¼ cup diced red onion (¼-inch dice)

1 tablespoon extra-virgin olive oil

1 tablespoon red wine vinegar

Salt and freshly ground black pepper,
    to taste

2 tablespoons chopped fresh flat-leaf parsley
    leaves, for garnish

1. Combine the lemon juice, olive oil, mustard, and salt and pepper in a container with a tight-fitting lid, and shake well. Place the veal chops in a shallow bowl and coat them well with the marinade. Cover, and refrigerate for 4 to 6 hours or overnight.

2. Shortly before serving, place the arugula, tomatoes, and onion in a bowl. Sprinkle the olive oil over the salad, followed by the vinegar and salt and pepper. Toss to blend the flavors.

3. Preheat a barbecue grill to high.

4. Oil the grill grate well, and arrange the chops on the grate. Grill until they are cooked through, about 8 minutes per side. Do not overcook them. Let them rest for 5 minutes before serving.

5. Place a chop on each of four dinner plates. Divide the salad equally among the chops, piling it on top. Sprinkle with the chopped parsley, and serve immediately. 🌸

ORANGE-DUSTED VENISON CHOPS

SERVES 8

When you're cooking, it's fun to experiment. Laurie thought of making this orange dust after grinding up some dried mushrooms to coat venison chops and finding that the results were too bland to use. This was an inspired idea and ever so delicious.

FOR THE ORANGE DUST (makes ¼ cup):

4 large oranges

FOR THE VENISON:

4 venison racks (each 4 chops, 1 to
1½ pounds)
¼ cup olive oil
Salt and freshly ground black pepper, to taste

1. Preheat the oven to 250°F.

2. Prepare the orange dust: Cut a thin slice off the bottom of each orange so the orange sits flat on a cutting board. With a sharp knife, working from top to bottom, cut off the peel of the orange, leaving as much white pith behind as possible. If necessary, scrape off any excess pith from the peel with the knife.

3. Lay the peels on a baking sheet and bake until they are completely dried out, about 45 minutes. Set aside to cool.

4. Pulverize the cooled dried peels to a powder in a mini food processor or a spice grinder. (The dust will keep for 3 or 4 days in an airtight glass jar.)

5. When you are ready to cook the venison chops, preheat the oven to 475°F.

6. Pat the chops dry with paper towels. Brush the racks with the olive oil, and season them well with salt and pepper.

7. Sprinkle the orange dust all over the meaty side of each of the racks. Arrange the racks, curved (meaty) side up, on a rimmed baking sheet and roast until medium-rare, 20 minutes. (If you prefer them cooked to medium, add an extra 3 to 4 minutes cooking time.) Transfer the racks to a cutting board and let them rest for 10 minutes.

8. Carve each rack into 4 chops, and arrange 2 on each dinner plate. Serve immediately.

SMOKED PORK CHOPS
WITH SOUR CHERRY BRANDY
SAUCE & CARAMELIZED FENNEL

SERVES 4

bruce Aidells—a cookbook author and founder of Aidells Sausage Co.—has an uncanny way with pork, and his marriage of sour cherries and smoked chops creates the most delicious dish. Bruce suggests that regular pork chops will do as well but must cook about 8 minutes longer than the smoked chops when added to the sauce. For a perfect combination, serve Caramelized Fennel with these chops.

⅔ cup dried cherries

½ cup brandy or kirsch

1 tablespoon olive oil

4 smoked pork chops, cut 1 inch thick

½ cup finely diced shallots

1 tablespoon minced garlic

2 dried juniper berries, crushed

1 teaspoon chopped fresh thyme leaves,
    or ¼ teaspoon dried

½ teaspoon freshly ground black pepper

½ cup ruby port

2 cups chicken broth, preferably homemade
    (see page 434)

1 tablespoon sour cherry or red currant jelly

Coarse (kosher) salt and freshly ground black
    pepper, to taste

Caramelized Fennel (recipe follows), for serving

1. Soak the cherries in the brandy in a small bowl for 1 hour, stirring occasionally.

2. Heat the olive oil in a very large deep skillet over medium heat. Add the pork chops and brown them well, about 3 minutes per side. Transfer the chops to a plate, and set them aside.

3. Reduce the heat to low and add the shallots, garlic, juniper berries, thyme, and pepper to the skillet. Cook, stirring occasionally, until the shallots have wilted, about 5 minutes. Add the port and cook for 3 minutes longer. Add the broth, bring to a boil over high heat, and then reduce the heat and simmer gently to blend the flavors, 15 minutes.

4. Add the jelly and the soaked cherries with their brandy. Raise the heat to medium-high and cook until the sauce is syrupy, about 3 minutes.

5. Return the chops to the skillet and spoon the sauce over them. Cover, and cook over low heat for 5 minutes (if using regular pork chops, cook them over low heat for 13 to 15 minutes). Season with salt and pepper. Serve immediately, with the sauce spooned over the chops and the fennel alongside. ⚜

CARAMELIZED FENNEL

SERVES 4 TO 6

Roasted fennel takes on a golden hue and a subtle sweet flavor, and partners beautifully with both pork and roast chicken.

    4 fennel bulbs
    ¼ cup extra-virgin olive oil
    Coarse (kosher) salt and freshly ground black
        pepper, to taste
    2 tablespoons chopped fresh flat-leaf parsley leaves,
        for garnish

1. Preheat the oven to 375°F.

2. Trim the tops off the fennel bulbs. Remove any badly bruised outer layers. Quarter the fennel bulbs lengthwise, leaving the cores intact, and place them in a bowl.

3. Drizzle the olive oil over the fennel, and sprinkle with salt and pepper. Toss well to coat the fennel with the oil.

4. Spread the fennel quarters out on a baking sheet. Bake until they are browned and caramelized, 1½ hours, turning them after 45 minutes. When they are fully cooked, turn the fennel quarters again so that they get coated in any remaining oil on the baking sheet.

5. Transfer the fennel to a platter, sprinkle with the chopped parsley, and serve immediately.

MIAMI PORK CHOPS

SERVES 6

This was inspired by a magazine article by Miami entertaining guru Jennifer Rubell—the flavors sounded so sexy together. I combined some of my favorites—Mojo Sauce, pork, and a lush tropical salsa—and the results were as lively as their muse.

    ½ cup fresh lime juice
    ¼ cup extra-virgin olive oil
    1 tablespoon very finely minced garlic
    2 teaspoons ground cumin
    Coarse salt and freshly ground black pepper, to taste
    6 center-cut pork chops, bones frenched (see page 56)
    1 cup Mojo Sauce (page 53), for serving
    1 cup Tropical Salsa (page 372) or Fresh Mango Salsa
        (page 369), for serving

1. Combine the lime juice, olive oil, garlic, cumin, and salt and pepper in a large bowl; stir well. Add the pork chops and turn to coat them well with the marinade. Refrigerate, covered, for 3 to 4 hours.

2. Preheat a barbecue grill or the broiler to high. If using the broiler, set the oven rack 3 inches from the heat source.

3. Oil the grill grate or rack in a broiler pan. Arrange the chops on the grill grate or in the broiler pan, and grill or broil until they are cooked through, about 6 minutes per side. Do not overcook or they will become dry.

4. Serve the chops topped with a spoonful of the Mojo Sauce, and pass the salsa alongside. ❧

THAI PORK CHOPS
WITH A SPICY VEGETABLE SALAD

SERVES 4

familiar pork chops come alive with new tastes when they are presented on a decorative platter topped with this exciting Thai-dressed salad. Asian fish sauce, with its pungent, slightly sweet, salty taste, is an essential ingredient in Thai cooking. When combined with other ingredients, its flavor is quite subtle.

FOR THE PORK CHOPS:

4 center-cut pork chops, cut about 1¼ inches thick
  (each about 12 ounces)
Salt and freshly ground black pepper, to taste
¼ cup fresh lime juice
¼ cup olive oil
2 tablespoons Asian fish sauce

FOR THE SPICY VEGETABLE SALAD:

Juice of 2 limes
2 tablespoons Asian fish sauce
1 teaspoon sugar
1 medium-size ripe tomato, halved lengthwise and
  cut into thin wedges
½ hothouse (seedless) cucumber, peeled and
  thinly sliced
4 scallions (white bulbs and 3 inches green),
  thinly sliced

½ cup pale green celery heart leaves,
  coarsely chopped
3 shallots, thinly sliced
1 to 2 teaspoons finely minced green jalapeño
  pepper, to taste

1. Place the pork chops in a bowl. Sprinkle them generously with salt and pepper. Combine the lime juice, olive oil, and fish sauce in a spouted measuring cup, and pour the marinade over the chops. Toss to coat them well. Marinate, loosely covered, at room temperature for 2 to 4 hours; or cover and refrigerate for 6 hours, turning the chops occasionally.

2. Shortly before serving time, prepare the Spicy Vegetable Salad: Whisk the lime juice, fish sauce, and sugar together in a small bowl. Set it aside.

3. In a large bowl, toss together the tomato, cucumber, scallions, celery leaves, shallots, and jalapeño. Set this aside.

4. Preheat a barbecue grill to high.

5. Remove the chops from the marinade. Oil the grill rack well, and arrange the chops on it. Grill, basting often with the marinade, for 7 minutes per side.

6. Arrange the chops on an oval serving platter. Toss the reserved dressing and the salad together, and spoon over the pork chops. Serve immediately. ❧

ORANGE-SCENTED RACK OF LAMB

SERVES 4

the Asian flavors in the marinade bring out the best in lamb, and the orange juice and zest add a welcome freshness to the meat. This dish allows for two chops a person. While that may not sound like much, lamb is a rich meat, therefore the amount is just right.

FOR THE MARINADE:

2 tablespoons grated orange zest

½ cup fresh orange juice

3 tablespoons honey

3 tablespoons soy sauce

2 tablespoons toasted sesame oil

1 tablespoon finely minced garlic

1 tablespoon finely minced fresh ginger

FOR THE LAMB:

1 rack of lamb (8 chops, about 2½ pounds),
    bones frenched (see box, page 56)

Salt and freshly ground black pepper,
    to taste

4 scallions (white bulbs and 3 inches green),
    thinly sliced, for garnish

4 mint sprigs, for garnish

1. Combine all the marinade ingredients in a large shallow bowl, and stir together well.

2. Cut the lamb rack in half so that you have two 4-chop racks. Place the lamb in the marinade meat side and coat it well. Cover, and refrigerate overnight, basting the lamb once or twice.

3. Thirty minutes before cooking time, remove the lamb from the refrigerator so it can come to room temperature.

4. Preheat the oven to 400°F.

5. Place the lamb in a shallow roasting pan, curved (meaty) side up. Season it generously with salt and pepper. Pour half of the marinade over the lamb.

Roast the lamb, basting it after 10 minutes, until it is medium-rare (an instant-read thermometer should register 130°F when inserted into the end chop), about 25 minutes total.

6. Transfer the rack to a carving board and let it rest for 10 minutes. Then cut it into individual chops and serve 2 per person, each serving garnished with the scallions and a mint sprig. ❧

LOIN LAMB CHOPS WITH ORANGE BEARNAISE MAYONNAISE

SERVES 4

While Americans love their lamb with mint jelly, and the English with mint sauce, I prefer a dollop of orange-flavored béarnaise mayonnaise for the finesse that these sumptuous loin chops deserve. A hint of orange and tarragon balances their pungent flavor.

Finely grated zest and juice of 1 orange

2 teaspoons crumbled dried tarragon

2 tablespoons extra-virgin olive oil

2 cloves garlic, smashed (see box, page 82)

Salt and freshly ground black pepper, to taste

8 loin lamb chops, cut 1½ inches thick

½ cup Orange Béarnaise Mayonnaise, for serving
(recipe follows)

1. Combine the orange zest and juice, tarragon, olive oil, garlic, and salt and pepper in a large bowl or container, and stir well. Add the lamb chops and coat them well with the marinade. Cover, and refrigerate for 8 hours or overnight, turning the chops once or twice. Thirty minutes before cooking time, remove the chops from the refrigerator.

2. Preheat a barbecue grill or the broiler to high. If using the broiler, set the rack 3 inches from the heat source.

3. Remove the chops from the marinade, scraping off any excess.

4. Lightly oil the grill grate or the rack in a broiler pan, and arrange the chops on it. Grill or broil for 4 to 5 minutes per side for medium-rare meat. Serve, with the Béarnaise Mayonnaise alongside. ❧

ORANGE BEARNAISE MAYONNAISE

MAKES ½ CUP

While a classic béarnaise sauce is a delicious emulsion of egg yolks, butter, vinegar, tarragon, and shallots, in today's faster-moving times I came up with this easier and luscious version. The addition of olive oil smoothes out prepared mayonnaise, resulting in a silky-textured béarnaise mayonnaise.

    ½ cup prepared mayonnaise, such as Hellmann's

    2 teaspoons finely grated orange zest

    1 tablespoon fresh orange juice

    2 teaspoons crumbled dried tarragon

    1 tablespoon olive oil

    Salt and freshly ground black pepper, to taste

Whisk the mayonnaise, orange zest, orange juice, and tarragon together in a small bowl. Whisking constantly, add the oil; season with salt and pepper. Store in a covered container in the refrigerator for up to 3 days. ♣

GINGER LAMB CHOPS

SERVES 4

h ere's another lamb dish with a hint of Asian influence. Lamb's succulent taste marries well with the intensity of soy sauce, ginger, and garlic. Green Apple Salsa (page 370) would be a bright and enjoyable accompaniment here.

    6 tablespoons dry red wine

    6 tablespoons soy sauce

    1½ tablespoons finely minced fresh ginger

    1½ tablespoons finely minced garlic

    3 tablespoons chopped fresh flat-leaf parsley leaves

    Freshly ground black pepper, to taste

    8 loin lamb chops, cut ¾ inch thick

1. Combine all the ingredients except the lamb chops in a large bowl or other container. Add the lamb chops and turn to coat them well with the marinade.

2. Loosely cover the bowl and let the chops marinate in the refrigerator for 2 hours, turning them occasionally; or let them marinate for 6 hours or overnight, turning the chops once or twice.

3. Preheat a barbecue grill or the broiler to high. If using the broiler, set the oven rack 3 inches from the heat source.

4. Remove the chops from the marinade and carefully scrape the excess marinade off them.

5. Lightly oil the grill rack or the rack in a broiler pan. Arrange the chops on the rack, and grill or broil for 4 to 5 minutes per side for medium-rare. Serve immediately. ♣

"FOR BURGERS LIKE THESE, YOU NEED THE TASTIEST BUNS."

BURGERS

Just watch someone eat a hamburger in a restaurant and I'll bet you crave that burger. There is something absolutely inherent in a sumptuous burger that makes us want to take a big bite out of it, even if we're eating a 1½-pound lobster! Is it because it's rare and juicy, or because it smells so good, or because the condiments look so great? For some, it's the works: ripe tomato, sliced red onion, ketchup, relish, even mayo and mustard. And how about melted cheese, sautéed mushrooms, and bacon too?

Burgers aren't just any-night affairs. For a big celebration, when you're ready to open your very best red wine, prepare Jeremiah Tower's Black Truffled Hamburgers. They're so good, they deserve a superlative bottle alongside.

And what about the range of new burgers? They run the gamut from tuna burgers (here with a slather of sesame sauce) to a well-spiced curried turkey burger embellished with a lively carrot salad. A giant portobello burger is a new classic vegetarian-style between-the-bun meal.

And what about the buns? Set aside the packaged variety for ones with a little more pizzazz: whole-grain or Kaiser rolls or soft sesame-seede buns. And when ketchup seems just too ordinary, add a little salsa or Chimichurri Mayonnaise for a bang-up finish! ✿

THE ALL-AMERICAN
JUICY HAMBURGER

SERVES 4

there are few people in the food world whose opinions about burgers I trust more than Coleman Andrews, a restaurant critic for *Gourmet* magazine and a true burger aficionado. With inspiration from his favorites and the addition of my own preferred condiments, I offer you this take on an American classic.

1 pound ground beef chuck (see Note)

Coarse (kosher) salt and freshly ground

    black pepper, to taste

Vegetable oil, for grilling

4 soft white hamburger buns, for serving

½ cup Russian Dressing (page 357)

4 slices ripe tomato (¼ inch thick)

4 slices red onion (¼ inch thick)

Pickle spears, for serving

Potato chips, for serving

1. If you are using a barbecue grill, preheat it to medium-high.

2. Place the meat in a large bowl and season it generously with salt and pepper. Toss lightly with a fork to combine. Do not overmix.

3. Shape the meat into 4 patties, each about 3 inches in diameter and 1 inch thick. Set them aside.

4. Lightly oil the grill grate or a nonstick skillet, and cook the burgers over medium-high heat for 3 minutes per side for rare, 4 to 4½ minutes for medium-rare, or more or less to your desired doneness.

5. While the burgers are cooking, lightly toast the buns—either on the grill or under the broiler.

6. Spread 1 tablespoon of the Russian Dressing over the cut side of each bun. Set a burger on each bottom half, top it with a slice of tomato and onion, and cover with the top half of the bun. Serve with pickle spears and potato chips.

NOTE: These are 4-ounce burgers. If you prefer 6-ounce burgers, you'll need 1½ pounds of meat.

HOLD THE KETCHUP

Nowadays we've got many options for topping a burger. Have a look at some of the great condiments in the Salsa chapter (page 365) before hauling out the ketchup and pickle relish. How about a Sparkling Pineapple or Green Apple Salsa? Or Corn and Mango Salsa? A great burger deserves an inspired go-with.

BACON SWISS BURGERS
WITH TOMATO AND AVOCADO

SERVES 4

a bacon Swiss burger embellished with ripe tomato and avocado: delectable! In this burger, I've spiced up the meat with thyme and Worcestershire sauce, which hint at the Mediterranean and at the steak house. In this case, a soft white bun is the best choice—any other type of bun and the burger might become too huge to eat. But of course, that's what helps to make it delectable. Serve your favorite condiments alongside.

8 slices bacon

1 pound ground beef chuck or sirloin

1 teaspoon Worcestershire sauce

1 or 2 dashes Tabasco sauce

¼ teaspoon dried thyme leaves

Salt and freshly ground black pepper,
    to taste

Vegetable oil, for grilling

4 slices Swiss cheese

4 hamburger buns, toasted, for serving

Thinly sliced ripe tomato, for garnish

Thinly sliced red onion, for garnish

Sliced ripe avocado, for garnish

Boston lettuce leaves, for garnish

1. If you will be grilling the burgers, preheat a barbecue grill to medium-high.

2. While the grill is heating up, cook the bacon on the stovetop in a large skillet over medium-low heat until it is just crisp, 6 to 7 minutes. Transfer the bacon to a plate lined with paper towels and set it aside to drain. (If you prefer to panfry the burgers, reserve 2 tablespoons of the bacon fat in the skillet.)

3. Place the beef, Worcestershire, Tabasco, thyme, and salt and pepper in a bowl, and toss lightly with a fork to combine. Form the mixture into 4 patties, each about 3 inches in diameter and 1 inch thick.

4. When you are ready to grill the burgers, oil the grill grate well. Add the burgers and grill for about 3 minutes for rare, 4 minutes for medium-rare meat. Turn them over and grill for another 3 or 4 minutes, topping the burgers with the cheese in the last minute of cooking. (Or panfry the burgers in the hot bacon fat over medium heat for 3 minutes per side for rare meat, adding the cheese as described.)

5. Place the burgers on the toasted buns, and top them with the bacon, tomato, onion, avocado, and lettuce. Cover with the tops of the buns and serve immediately. 🌿

JEREMIAH TOWER'S BLACK TRUFFLED HAMBURGERS

SERVES 4

Jeremiah Tower, a pioneering California chef, is the master of lush excess, and combining truffles and burgers is exactly his style—and thoroughly delicious. If fresh truffles are not available, bottled black truffles are an excellent alternative. With these large, luxurious burgers, Jeremiah recommends an old-fashioned, deep red, rich, powerful Burgundy in a large balloon glass. Oh, how I wish he was still at the helm of Stars, an iconic San Francisco restaurant of the 1980s.

2 pounds ground beef chuck

Coarse (kosher) salt and freshly ground black
    pepper, to taste

2 ounces fresh black truffle (or bottled, drained),
    finely chopped

¼ cup prepared mayonnaise, preferably
    Hellmann's

4 English muffins (preferably Thomas'), split

3 tablespoons unsalted butter

1 tablespoon olive oil

1. Place the beef in a bowl, and season it with salt and pepper. Add three quarters of the chopped truffles, and mix lightly with your hands until just combined. Cover the bowl loosely with aluminum foil and let it rest in the refrigerator for 4 hours (this lets the flavor of the truffles permeate the meat).

2. Meanwhile, combine the remaining chopped truffles with the mayonnaise in a small bowl and refrigerate it, covered, for 4 hours.

3. Form the beef into 4 patties, each 3 inches in diameter and 1½ inches thick. Do not compact the meat.

4. Just before cooking the hamburgers, toast the English muffins and spread the butter over each half. Set them aside.

5. Line a plate with paper towels and set it aside.

6. Heat the olive oil in a nonstick skillet over medium heat. Add the burgers and sauté for 5 minutes per side for medium-rare meat. While they are cooking, lightly season the burgers on both sides with salt and pepper.

7. Transfer the burgers to the paper-towel-lined plate and let them drain for a few seconds. Then place them on the muffin bottoms, spoon a tablespoon of the mayonnaise onto each burger, and cover with the muffin tops. Serve immediately.

ASIAN BEEF BURGERS
WITH SESAME SAUCE

SERVES 4

a little soy and a sprinkling of scallions add tremendous flavor to the beef in these burgers, giving it just the right hint of Asian seasonings. The lemon juice and zest are unusual and spark up the other flavors. Note that the Sesame Sauce is best when made a day ahead.

1 pound ground beef chuck

4 scallions (white bulbs and 3 inches green),
   thinly sliced

2 tablespoons chopped fresh flat-leaf parsley leaves

4 teaspoons fresh lemon juice

1 teaspoon finely grated lemon zest

4 teaspoons soy sauce, plus extra for brushing

Salt and freshly ground black pepper, to taste

2 tablespoons olive oil

Sesame Sauce (recipe follows), for serving

4 sesame-seed buns, toasted, for serving

Sliced ripe tomatoes, for serving (optional)

1. Place the ground beef, scallions, parsley, lemon juice and zest, and the 4 teaspoons soy sauce in a bowl, and combine gently. Season with salt and pepper. Form the mixture into 4 patties, each about 3 inches in diameter and 1 inch thick.

2. Heat the olive oil in a nonstick skillet over medium heat. Add the burgers and cook for 4 minutes. Then turn them over, brush the tops with some soy sauce, and cook for 4 minutes on the second side for medium-rare meat.

3. Spread about 1 tablespoon of the Sesame Sauce on each side of the toasted buns. Add the burgers, top them with the tomato slices if desired, and serve.

CHOOSING MEAT FOR BURGERS

The "prime" meat for burgers is beef. Go for the most flavorful cuts: Chuck, with its high fat content, or round usually give you the best results. Just the right amount of fat—about 20 percent—is what to look for. I often add just salt and pepper to the ground meat, and many purists feel that no more than that is needed for the ideal burger. Other times, I can't resist gussying up the meat with a variety of spices.

For a rich south-of-the-equator flavor, I like to mix ground beef with ground pork. And a ground lamb burger can transport us to the Mediterranean. Any way you look at it, the key is to handle the meat as little as possible when mixing it, to keep the burgers nice and juicy. And if you're grilling, don't forget to oil the grill grate well!

SESAME SAUCE

MAKES 1¼ CUPS

a sauce thick enough to slather on a bun or toss over noodles must have a rich and creamy consistency to do its job: lend whatever food it is blanketing that "wow" factor. This sauce tastes like the peanut dipping sauce for satés. Once it's made, refrigerate the Sesame Sauce overnight for the perfect consistency. Toss any leftovers with hot noodles—perfect!

> ¼ cup soy sauce
>
> ¼ cup rice vinegar
>
> 2 teaspoons cold water
>
> 1 tablespoon light brown sugar
>
> Salt, to taste

> 2 teaspoons minced fresh ginger
>
> 1 teaspoon minced garlic
>
> 6 tablespoons smooth peanut butter, at room temperature
>
> 3 tablespoons toasted sesame oil
>
> 3 tablespoons peanut or corn oil
>
> ½ teaspoon chile oil

1. Place the soy sauce, rice vinegar, cold water, brown sugar, salt, ginger, garlic, and peanut butter in a blender and process on high speed until smooth, 1 to 2 minutes.

2. Combine the three oils in a spouted measuring cup, and with the blender running on low speed, drizzle the mixture into the sauce.

3. Refrigerate overnight, or up to 2 days, in an airtight container to thicken up.

TANGO BURGERS
WITH CHIMICHURRI MAYONNAISE

SERVES 4

W ith a nod to South America, these burgers are made from a mixture of beef and pork, both for flavor and for added moisture. They are spiced up with a little cumin and oregano, favorite complements to pork. Ripe avocado smooths the effect of the spices to ready the palate for a lively Chimichurri Mayonnaise.

8 ounces ground beef chuck

8 ounces ground pork

2 tablespoons red wine vinegar

1 tablespoon finely minced garlic

2 teaspoons dried oregano

2 teaspoons ground cumin

Salt and freshly ground black pepper, to taste

Vegetable cooking spray, for oiling the broiler pan

4 English muffins, split

3 tablespoons unsalted butter

1 ripe avocado, peeled, pitted, and cut into
     large slices

¼ cup Chimichurri Mayonnaise (recipe follows)

1. Preheat the broiler, and if possible, set an oven rack 7 inches from the heat source.

2. Place the beef, pork, vinegar, garlic, oregano, cumin, and salt and pepper in a bowl, and mix lightly with your hands until just combined. Form the mixture into 4 patties, each 3 inches in diameter and 1 inch thick. Do not compact the meat. Lightly oil a ridged broiler pan or a slotted broiler rack, and place the patties on the pan.

3. Just before broiling the hamburgers, toast the English muffins and spread the butter over each half. Set them aside.

4. Broil the burgers for 4 minutes per side for medium-well-done meat, or 5 minutes per side for more well-done.

5. Place the burgers on the muffin bottoms. Top each one with some avocado slices and a dollop of Chimichurri Mayonnaise. Cover with the muffin tops, and serve immediately. 🌿

CHIMICHURRI MAYONNAISE

MAKES 1 CUP

Put very simply, chimichurri is an Argentinian-style steak sauce, resembling a salsa verde. I've combined the traditional chimichurri ingredients—parsley, olive oil, vinegar, and salt (no garlic)—with mayonnaise to create a dynamite Nuevo Latino burger sauce. Serve any extra sauce with cold meats—it will keep in the refrigerator for 2 days.

1 cup prepared mayonnaise,
     preferably Hellmann's

2 tablespoons chopped fresh flat-leaf
     parsley leaves

2 tablespoons chopped fresh mint leaves

1 teaspoon dried oregano

Salt and freshly ground black pepper,
     to taste

1 teaspoon finely minced green
     jalapeño pepper

1 tablespoon extra-virgin olive oil

2 teaspoons sherry vinegar

Combine all the ingredients in a bowl. Let rest, covered, in the refrigerator for a few hours before serving. 🌿

GREEK-STYLE LAMB
CHEESEBURGERS

SERVES 4

t he flavors of Greece are rich and distinctive. Even a burger can reflect the beauty of that food culture if you use traditional Greek ingredients: lamb, oregano, mint, feta, and a little ripe tomato and you're there. Some good olives on the side, a little bouzouki music, and you have it all.

1 pound ground lamb

1 tablespoon grated onion

1 large clove garlic, very finely minced

2 teaspoons dried oregano

Salt and freshly ground black pepper, to taste

⅓ cup chopped fresh mint leaves

3 ounces Greek cheese, such as feta or
    manouri, cut into 4 chunks

2 tablespoons vegetable oil

4 whole-grain hamburger buns, toasted, for serving

Sliced ripe tomato, for serving

Sliced red onion, for serving

½ cup Kalamata olives, for serving

1. Place the lamb, onion, garlic, oregano, salt and pepper, and mint in a bowl. Mix together lightly with your hands.

2. Form the meat mixture into 4 thick patties, each about 3 inches in diameter and 1½ inches thick. Remove some of the meat from the top center of each patty, insert a chunk of the cheese, and re-cover with the meat.

3. Heat the oil in a nonstick skillet over medium heat. Add the burgers, two at a time, and sauté for 5 minutes on the first side. Then turn them over and cook for 3 minutes on the second side for medium-rare meat, or longer if you prefer. (The burgers can be broiled, 8 inches from the heat source, for 5 minutes on the first side and 3 minutes on the second side.)

4. Serve the burgers on the toasted buns, topped with the sliced tomatoes and red onions, and with the olives on the side. 🍀

CURRIED TURKEY BURGERS
WITH CARROT SALAD

SERVES 4

*G*round turkey and chicken have become popular burger ingredients, originally as a change from beef. When making a turkey or chicken burger or meat loaf, it's essential to add strong seasonings— I chose curry powder here—to compensate for the mild flavor of the meat. And because the meat can be dry, I've added mango chutney and apple—both familiar partners of curry—and egg to contribute some moisture as well as wonderful flavor.

2 tablespoons olive oil

½ cup diced red onion (¼-inch dice)

2 teaspoons curry powder

1 pound ground turkey or chicken

1 small egg, lightly beaten

½ cup fresh bread crumbs (see box, page 91)

¼ cup grated peeled Granny Smith apple

¼ cup chopped store-bought mango chutney

2 scallions (white bulbs and 3 inches green),
      thinly sliced on the diagonal

Salt and freshly ground black pepper, to taste

Vegetable oil, for oiling the grill grate

Mayonnaise, preferably Hellmann's, for spreading

4 hamburger buns, toasted, for serving

Carrot Salad (recipe follows), for garnish

1. Place the oil and onions in a nonstick skillet and cook over medium-low heat, stirring, until the onions are wilted, 10 minutes. Reduce the heat to low, add the curry power, and cook, stirring, for 1 minute to mellow the flavors. Transfer the onions to a bowl and let them cool to room temperature.

2. Meanwhile, preheat a barbecue grill to medium.

3. Add the turkey, egg, bread crumbs, apple, chutney, scallions, and salt and pepper to the onions, and combine lightly. Form the mixture into 4 patties, each about 3 inches in diameter and 1 inch thick.

4. Brush the grill grate with vegetable oil. Add the burgers and grill until they are cooked through, 5 minutes per side.

5. Spread the mayonnaise over the cut sides of the hamburger buns. Place the burgers on the bottom halves, spoon 2 tablespoons of the Carrot Salad over each one, and cover with the tops of the buns. Serve immediately. ❧

CARROT SALAD

MAKES ABOUT 3 CUPS; SERVES 6

there's something refreshing about grated carrots. A light lemon dressing hits the spot, complementing the carrots' sweet flavor and bringing out the brightness. Fresh chives finish it off and add a mild bite to play against the sweetness. This salad is the perfect condiment to serve atop Curried Turkey Burgers. Use any leftovers as part of a crudités plate—delicious! It will keep in the refrigerator for up to 2 days.

FOR THE DRESSING:

3 tablespoons olive oil

1½ tablespoons fresh lemon juice

1 teaspoon Dijon mustard

½ teaspoon sugar

Salt and freshly ground black pepper,
    to taste

FOR THE SALAD:

6 carrots, peeled and grated

1 tablespoon snipped fresh chives

Combine all the dressing ingredients in a large bowl, and stir thoroughly with a whisk. Add the grated carrots and chives, and toss with the dressing.

RAISE A GLASS

Wine with burgers? Absolutely. Here are some suggestions for the burgers in this chapter:

THE ALL-AMERICAN JUICY BURGER
ZINFANDEL

BACON SWISS BURGERS
CHATEAUNEUF-DU-PAPE

JEREMIAH TOWER'S
BLACK TRUFFLED HAMBURGERS
CABERNET SAUVIGNON

ASIAN BEEF BURGERS
COTES-DU-RHONE

TANGO BURGERS
MALBEC

CURRIED TURKEY BURGERS
PINOT GRIGIO

GREEK-STYLE LAMB CHEESEBURGERS
MERLOT

TUNA BURGER EXTRAVAGANZA
GEWURZTRAMINER

FRESH SALMON BURGERS
CHARDONNAY

PORTOBELLO MUSHROOM BURGERS
PINOT NOIR

TUNA BURGER EXTRAVAGANZA

SERVES 4

Yellowfin tuna is the best choice for this burger. When selecting your fish, look for dark red flesh. My choice is to prepare the fish by hand with a sharp knife so that it won't be too mushy (you can ask your fishmonger to do this). Panko, the rough and flaky Japanese bread crumbs, are an excellent choice to bind the burgers because they are light and slightly coarse. The Asian seasonings work very well with the tuna. It's essential to refrigerate the burgers before cooking so that they hold their shape while grilling. The Sesame Sauce echoes their flavor on the bun, while the Green Apple Salsa refreshes. Altogether, this burger is an extravaganza.

1½ pounds skinless best-quality tuna steak,
　　coarsely chopped with a very sharp knife

½ cup panko (available in most supermarkets,
　　or see Sources, page 439)

1 large egg, lightly beaten

3 tablespoons honey mustard

1 tablespoon finely minced fresh ginger

1 tablespoon finely minced garlic

1 tablespoon toasted sesame oil

1 or 2 dashes Tabasco sauce

Coarse (kosher) salt and freshly ground black
　　pepper, to taste

Vegetable oil, for oiling the grill grate

4 soft sesame-seed buns, for serving

5 tablespoons Sesame Sauce (page 112),
　　for serving

Green Apple Salsa (page 370), for serving

1. Preheat a barbecue grill to medium-high.

2. Combine the tuna, panko, egg, mustard, ginger, garlic, sesame oil, Tabasco, and salt and pepper in a bowl and toss together lightly. Form the mixture into 4 patties, each 3½ inches in diameter and 1 inch thick. Place them on a plate and refrigerate, loosely covered, for 1 hour to firm up.

3. When you are ready to grill the burgers, oil the grill grate well. Add the burgers and grill them for 4 minutes on each side for medium-rare, 1 minute longer for medium.

4. Meanwhile, lightly toast the buns on the grill.

5. Spread the Sesame Sauce over both sides of each bun. Place the tuna burgers on the bottom halves and top them with some Green Apple Salsa. Cover with the top halves of the buns, and serve.

FRESH SALMON BURGERS
WITH SPARKLING PINEAPPLE SALSA

SERVES 6

fresh salmon burgers with the subtle flavors of lemon and scallion are a revelation! The texture is light, yet the burger is substantial—and unusual. I like the addition of a sesame-seed topping on the bun. When the bun is toasted, it adds a nice crunch. The pineapple salsa tops it all off to perfection.

FOR THE BURGERS:

2 pounds skinless and boneless center-cut
    salmon fillets

½ cup fresh bread crumbs (see box, page 91)

1 large egg, lightly beaten

2 scallions (white bulbs and 3 inches green),
    thinly sliced on the diagonal

Finely grated zest of 1 lemon

2 tablespoons finely snipped fresh chives

1 tablespoon minced garlic

1 tablespoon extra-virgin olive oil

1 teaspoon red wine vinegar

1 or 2 dashes Tabasco sauce

Salt and freshly ground black pepper, to taste

FOR COOKING AND SERVING:

Vegetable oil, for oiling the grill grate

6 sesame-seed buns, for serving

6 tablespoons Sparkling Pineapple Salsa
    (page 371), for garnish

1. Preheat a barbecue grill to high.

2. Using a knife, coarsely chop the salmon. Place it in a food processor, and pulse to achieve a coarse texture. Do not overprocess.

3. Transfer the salmon to a large bowl and add all the remaining burger ingredients. Combine lightly, and form into 6 patties, each about 3 inches in diameter and 1 inch thick.

4. Brush the grill grate with vegetable oil, and add the burgers. Grill until they are just cooked through, turning them over carefully, 3 to 4 minutes per side. While the burgers are cooking, lightly toast the buns.

5. Serve the burgers on the toasted buns, each burger topped with 1 tablespoon of the pineapple salsa. ❖

PORTOBELLO MUSHROOM BURGERS

SERVES 4

Of all the veggie burgers I have eaten, this is the most satisfying because biting into a portobello mushroom is very close to eating a good piece of meat. Spicing it up with Boursin cheese serves two purposes: it keeps the bun from getting soggy, and it's a great combination with the mushroom and the bell peppers. Peppery greens not only add color; they spark up all the other flavors. Best of all, this burger is *soooo* juicy!

8 tablespoons olive oil

4 large portobello mushrooms, stems removed,
    caps wiped clean with a damp paper towel

8 cloves Roasted Garlic (page 433)

4 hamburger buns, preferably whole-grain,
    lightly toasted

4 tablespoons Boursin cheese

2 red or orange bell peppers, roasted (see
    page 438)

1 large bunch arugula or watercress,
    tough stems removed, rinsed and
    patted dry; or 2 cups mixed salad
    greens

1. Heat 2 tablespoons of the oil in a nonstick skillet over medium heat. Add one of the mushroom caps, rounded side down, and sauté, pressing down on it with a spatula, until it is golden brown, about 2 minutes. Turn the mushroom over and sauté the underside until the mushroom is cooked through,

1 minute (see Note). Transfer the mushroom to a plate and pat it dry with paper towels. Repeat with the remaining mushroom caps, adding 2 tablespoons oil to the skillet for each one.

2. Squeeze 1 clove of the roasted garlic over the cut side of each bun, and spread the garlic over the surface.

3. Spread 1 tablespoon of the Boursin over the bottom half of each bun. Top it with a portobello mushroom and half a roasted pepper. Divide the greens evenly among the mushrooms, and cover them with the top halves of the buns. Cut in half, and serve immediately.

NOTE: I usually sauté one mushroom at a time because they're so large; two might give off too much liquid and prevent the mushrooms from browning nicely. 🌿

"SHINY AND GOOEY, THE WAY WE LOVE THEM."

BARBECUED RIBS AND SAUCES

While I was growing up, my rib exposure was limited to the spareribs from a local Chinese restaurant. They were awfully good and on a Sunday night my family could put away plenty. My awakening came when I did a guest-chef stint in Dallas. Chef Stephen Pyles led me to Sonny Bryan's on Inwood, and introduced me to some Texas ribs. I never looked back. Those ribs—those sauces, that smoke, that flavor! I not only went crazy for the ribs, but the brisket was blue ribbon too. But that's another story.

That visit got me doing some creating of my own. The ribs and sauces in this chapter run the flavor gamut from Texas to Shanghai, and they're fun, gooey, dress-up, and just right for the Fourth of July.

There is a choice of ribs to slather with good sauces: large, succulent, pork spareribs; delicate, leaner baby backs; meaty country ribs—more like pork chops with very little bone; and luscious beef short ribs.

Here are two truths: "Life is short" and "You can never have too many ribs." Stoke up the fire and get going. 🌿

BARBECUED BABY BACKS
WITH SHEILA'S RAUCOUS BBQ SAUCE

SERVES 4

For a great summertime meal right off the grill, nothing's yummier than baby backs slathered with a rich and tangy brick-colored Texas-style sauce. Great potato salad, crunchy slaw, and cold beer finish off the menu. Could I make you any hungrier? Stock up on brightly colored paper napkins and have fun!

2 racks baby back ribs (each about 2 pounds)
Vegetable oil, for oiling the grill grate
Sheila's Raucous BBQ Sauce (recipe follows)

1. Preheat the oven to 350°F.

2. Place the ribs, meaty side up, in a shallow roasting pan. Pour 1½ cups of the barbecue sauce over the ribs, and pour ½ cup water into the bottom of the pan. Bake, basting occasionally, for 1 hour.

3. Meanwhile, preheat a barbecue grill to high and then reduce the heat to medium. Oil the grill grate well.

4. Remove the ribs from the oven and arrange them, meaty side down, on the grill. Grill, brushing them occasionally with the extra barbecue sauce, until they are caramelized and have some nice grill marks, about 5 minutes.

5. Put the ribs on a large cutting board and cut them apart, slicing between the bones. Arrange them on a large platter and serve, with extra sauce on the side for dipping.

SHEILA'S RAUCOUS BBQ SAUCE

MAKES 3 CUPS

I find barbecue sauces irresistible and I have a fondness for that sweet Texas tang, so I've cooked up a batch here that should blow away some baby back ribs. It has a similar effect on barbecued chicken. This recipe is easily doubled, but I prefer to make two separate batches for better control.

1 onion, finely chopped

4 cloves garlic, finely minced

2 cups ketchup

½ cup cider vinegar

¼ cup canola oil

¼ cup Worcestershire sauce

¼ cup fresh lemon juice

⅓ cup (packed) dark brown sugar

1 tablespoon honey

1 tablespoon chili powder

1 tablespoon ground cumin

2 dashes Tabasco sauce

1. Combine all the ingredients in a heavy saucepan. Add 1 cup water, stir well, and bring to a boil. Reduce the heat to medium-low and simmer until the sauce has thickened slightly and the flavors have blended, 10 to 15 minutes.

2. Pour the sauce through a fine-mesh strainer into a bowl, discarding the onion and garlic. Taste, and adjust the seasonings as needed. Use immediately, or let the sauce cool to room temperature, transfer it to a covered container, and refrigerate it for up to 1 week.

RIB LEXICON

So many types of ribs and only 10 ways to serve them up! Still, they are 10 great ways. Here's a brief lexicon of the type of ribs included in this chapter.

BABY BACK RIBS (PORK): The most delicate ribs, baby backs are not from small or baby pigs—but they are small. Each slab weighs about 2 pounds, includes about 13 ribs, and is perfect for 2 good-size servings. I think of baby backs as the Porsche of ribs—sleek. They are succulent, and while small, they satisfy that real rib craving.

COUNTRY RIBS (PORK): Also known as blade end ribs, country ribs are cut from the butterflied blade chops from the shoulder end of the pork loin. They are nice meaty pieces (about 8 ounces in weight), looking more like chops than ribs. Unlike spareribs, 1 per person is plenty.

SPARERIBS (PORK): These ribs are cut from the pork belly, and a slab may include 11 ribs. They are great for barbecuing and are often used in Chinese-style recipes. They are easy to eat with your fingers.

SHORT RIBS OF BEEF: Short ribs of beef are cut from different sections of the cow that begin at the chuck shoulder and end at the loin. An inexpensive cut, the meat is highly flavorful and cooks up wonderfully tender.

SPICED-UP BABY BACKS

SERVES 4

a briskly spiced barbecue sauce lends just the right piquancy as it cooks along with the ribs. It's the combination of hot, sweet, and sour in these Texas-style sauces that does the job. Bake the ribs, basting them with the sauce, before you grill them—it may be cheating a little, but this will create a beautiful glaze for perfect grill marks.

FOR THE BARBECUE SAUCE
(makes 2½ cups):

2 cups ketchup

½ cup cider vinegar

2 tablespoons Dijon mustard

2 teaspoons Tabasco sauce

2 tablespoons unsulfured molasses

2 tablespoons Worcestershire sauce

Grated zest and juice of 1 lemon

1 tablespoon dark brown sugar

2 teaspoons very finely minced garlic

FOR THE RIBS:

2 racks baby back ribs (each about 2 pounds)

Salt and freshly ground black pepper, to taste

Vegetable oil, for oiling the grill grate

1. Prepare the barbecue sauce: Combine all the sauce ingredients in a heavy nonreactive saucepan, and stir in ¼ cup water. Cook, stirring, over medium-low heat until the flavors have blended and the sauce is heated through, about 5 minutes. Do not let it boil. Let the sauce cool to room temperature. Then strain the sauce into a container, discarding the garlic.

2. When you are ready to cook the ribs, preheat the oven to 350°F.

3. Prepare the ribs: Season the ribs all over with salt and pepper. Place the ribs, meaty side down, in a shallow baking pan. Brush each rack of ribs with ¼ cup of the barbecue sauce, and bake for 15 minutes. Then turn the ribs over, brush each rack with 1 cup of the sauce, and bake, basting them every 15 minutes, until they are cooked through, about 45 minutes.

4. Meanwhile, preheat a barbecue grill to high and then reduce the heat to medium. Oil the grill grate well.

5. Transfer the ribs to the grill grate, and grill, basting them with any remaining barbecue sauce from the pan, until they are caramelized and have some nice grill marks, about 5 minutes per side. (Do not let the sauce burn.)

6. Cut the ribs apart and serve them on a platter.

NOTE: You can use the sauce immediately or you can refrigerate it in a covered container for up to 2 weeks. 🌸

HULA RIBS

SERVES 4

Seasoned with some favorite Asian flavors and finished off with orange zest and juice, this sauce, rich with mango chutney and curry powder, lends a fruity flair to spareribs or baby back ribs. They'll be all shiny and gooey, the way we love them. (If you miss the grill marks, you can grill the ribs for 5 minutes on each side over medium heat when they have finished baking.)

FOR THE SAUCE (makes 2 cups):

½ cup ketchup

6 tablespoons store-bought mango chutney, pureed

¼ cup honey

¼ cup cider vinegar

3 tablespoons soy sauce

3 tablespoons dry sherry

2 tablespoons toasted sesame oil

3 tablespoons curry powder

Finely grated zest and juice of 1 orange

2 teaspoons Asian chile paste (see Note)

Salt and freshly ground black pepper, to taste

FOR THE RIBS:

2 racks baby back ribs (each about 2 pounds)

Salt and freshly ground black pepper, to taste

1. Preheat the oven to 350°F.

2. Combine all the sauce ingredients in a bowl, and stir together well.

3. Place the ribs, meaty side up, in an ovenproof dish, and season them well with salt and pepper. Cover the ribs with 1 cup of the sauce, brushing it all over them. Bake until the ribs are cooked through and glistening, 1 hour, basting with ½ cup of the sauce after 30 minutes.

4. Cut the ribs apart, arrange them on a platter, and serve immediately, with the remaining sauce on the side.

NOTE: Asian chile paste is a blend of hot chile peppers, garlic, oil, and salt. It is a common ingredient in Asian dishes and can be found in Asian markets and in well-stocked supermarkets.

OLD-FASHIONED CHINESE BARBECUED RIBS

SERVES 4

both familiar and delicious, the easy sauce doubles as a marinade for the ribs. Fresh ginger and dry sherry contribute to the Asian flair, while honey and hoisin add just the right sweetness to lacquer the ribs. While they are reminiscent of old-fashioned Chinese restaurant ribs, the flavors here are layered and complex.

FOR THE SAUCE:

½ cup soy sauce

¼ cup cider vinegar

¼ cup hoisin sauce

¼ cup honey

2 tablespoons rice vinegar

2 tablespoons dry sherry

2 teaspoons dark brown sugar

2 teaspoons finely minced fresh ginger

2 teaspoons finely minced garlic

FOR THE RIBS:

2 racks baby back ribs (each about 2 pounds)

2 scallions (white bulbs and 3 inches green),
thinly sliced, for garnish

2 tablespoons chopped fresh cilantro, for garnish

1. Prepare the sauce: Combine all the sauce ingredients in a heavy saucepan and heat it over medium heat until the flavors have blended, 3 to 4 minutes (do not let it boil). Let the sauce cool slightly.

2. Prepare the ribs: Place the ribs, meaty side up, in a 13-x-9-x-2-inch baking dish and pour the sauce over them. Set the dish aside at room temperature, covered loosely with aluminum foil for 1 hour.

3. Preheat the oven to 350°F.

4. Bake the ribs, uncovered, for 30 minutes, basting them once or twice. Then cover them loosely with aluminum foil and bake for another 30 minutes. Uncover the ribs, baste them well with the sauce, and bake until cooked through and glistening, 15 minutes more.

5. Cut the ribs apart and serve them on a platter, garnished with the scallions and cilantro.

SHANGHAI BABY BACKS

SERVES 6

Malaysian spice mixtures combine Chinese and Indian influences and often include cinnamon. It occurred to me to try cinnamon on these Chinese-style ribs—it marries beautifully with the hoisin sauce. Just a light touch on the grill caramelizes these deliciously tender ribs.

FOR THE SHANGHAI RIB SAUCE
  (makes 5 cups):

1½ cups rice vinegar

1 cup ketchup

⅔ cup light soy sauce

⅔ cup fresh lime juice (from about 6 limes)

½ cup hoisin sauce

¼ cup toasted sesame oil

2 tablespoons finely minced garlic

2 tablespoons finely minced fresh ginger

1 to 2 teaspoons crushed red pepper flakes

FOR THE RIBS:

3 racks baby back ribs
  (each about 2 pounds)

1 teaspoon ground cinnamon

Salt and freshly ground black pepper,
  to taste

Vegetable oil, for oiling the grill

2 scallions (white bulbs and 3 inches green),
  thinly sliced, for garnish

1. Prepare the Shanghai Rib Sauce: Combine all the sauce ingredients in a heavy saucepan and bring to a boil. Then reduce the heat to medium-low and simmer until the flavors have blended, 5 minutes. Set the sauce aside.

2. Prepare the ribs: Place the ribs, meaty side up, in two shallow baking pans and season them on both sides with the cinnamon and generous amounts of salt and pepper. Cover the pans loosely with aluminum foil and set aside, at room temperature, for 1 hour.

3. Meanwhile, preheat the oven to 350°F.

4. Pour 1½ cups of the sauce over each rack of ribs. Bake, uncovered, basting often, for 45 minutes. (If the sauce dries up, add ½ cup water to each pan and swirl it in. Continue baking until the ribs are cooked through.)

5. While the ribs are baking, preheat a barbecue grill to high and then reduce the heat to medium. Oil the grill grate well.

6. Transfer the ribs to the grill and cook, brushing them with the sauce, until they are caramelized and have nice grill marks, 5 minutes per side.

7. Remove the ribs from the grill and let them rest on a cutting board for 10 minutes. Then cut the ribs apart, slicing between the bones, and arrange them on a platter. Garnish with the scallions, and serve.

ORANGE MAPLE SPARERIBS

SERVES 4

Sauces and glazes on ribs serve two purposes: First, they deliver powerful flavor, and second, they deliver a beautiful sheen and extra succulence to one of our favorite foods. While this sauce contains a number of sweet ingredients, the bite of ginger and garlic provide an excellent foil.

FOR THE ORANGE MAPLE BARBECUE SAUCE
(makes about 2½ cups):

¼ cup canola oil

¼ cup diced onion (¼-inch dice)

2 tablespoons finely minced fresh ginger

1 teaspoon finely minced garlic

2 tablespoons finely grated orange zest

1 cup fresh orange juice

½ cup unsulfured molasses

¼ cup pure maple syrup

3 tablespoons ketchup

2 tablespoons honey

Salt and freshly ground black pepper, to taste

FOR THE RIBS:

2 racks pork spareribs (each 3 to 4 pounds),
   or 2 racks baby back ribs (each about 2 pounds)

Salt and freshly ground black pepper, to taste

1 tablespoon snipped fresh chives, for garnish

1. Prepare the sauce: Heat the canola oil in a small, heavy saucepan over low heat. Add the onion, ginger, and garlic, and cook, stirring occasionally, until wilted, 5 to 8 minutes.

2. Add all the remaining sauce ingredients, bring to a boil over medium-high heat, and cook for 3 minutes. Then reduce the heat to medium-low and simmer, stirring occasionally, until the sauce has thickened, about 10 minutes.

3. Strain the sauce through a fine-mesh sieve, reserving the solids. When the solids have cooled, finely mince them to a pastelike consistency. Return them to the sauce to thicken it slightly. Let the sauce cool.

4. When you are ready to cook the ribs, preheat the oven to 350°F.

5. Prepare the ribs: Place the ribs, meaty side up, in a large shallow baking pan and season them well with salt and pepper. Coat the ribs generously with the sauce. Bake until the ribs are cooked through, tender, and nicely glazed, about 1 hour.

6. Cut the ribs apart and serve them on a large platter, garnished with the chives. ❧

MICHAEL'S CHERRY COLA–GLAZED SPARERIBS

SERVES 6

Michael McLaughlin was a great friend and a very talented cook and cookbook writer—he worked at The Silver Palate for years and helped Julee Rosso and me write the original *Silver Palate Cookbook*. When he was living in Santa Fe, Michael created these wildly delicious spareribs. On his recommendation, I ran to the supermarket and bought a six-pack of cherry cola. Surprisingly, the ribs aren't too sweet. In fact, they are every pleasure a rib should be: succulent, meaty, pork-flavored, sweet, gooey, and utterly delicious, with just the right caramelized cherry flavor. *Bon Appétit* magazine called this recipe an "All-American Great," and it is!

FOR THE GLAZE:

4 cans (each 12 ounces) flat cherry cola (see Notes)

2 cups cherry jam or preserves

⅔ cup Dijon mustard with horseradish

3 tablespoons soy sauce

2 tablespoons cider vinegar

1 tablespoon Tabasco or other hot pepper sauce

FOR THE RIBS:

3 racks (each 3 to 4 pounds) pork spareribs,
   well trimmed

Salt and freshly ground black pepper, to taste

FOR SERVING:

State Fair Potato Salad (page 271)

1. Prepare the glaze: Bring the flat cherry cola to a slow boil in a large heavy saucepan over medium heat, and cook until it is reduced to 1½ cups, about 45 minutes. Then stir in all the remaining glaze ingredients, reduce the heat to medium-low, and simmer, stirring occasionally, until the mixture is reduced to 2½ cups, about 35 minutes. Transfer the glaze to a large bowl.

2. Preheat the oven to 350°F.

3. Prepare the ribs: Lay the racks of ribs, meaty side up, in two shallow baking pans and sprinkle them generously with salt and pepper. Coat the ribs generously with the glaze and bake, basting every 15 minutes, until cooked through and glistening, 1 hour. (Reserve the remaining glaze.)

4. Meanwhile, preheat a barbecue grill to high, then reduce the heat to medium. Oil the grill grate well.

5. Transfer the ribs to the grill, arranging them meaty side down, and grill, brushing them with the remaining glaze, until they are caramelized, about 5 minutes per side.

6. Place the ribs on a cutting board and cut them apart, slicing between the bones. Arrange the ribs on a platter and serve the potato salad along with them. Pass any extra glaze in a small pitcher.

NOTES:

◆ Pour the cherry cola into a pitcher and let it rest at room temperature until it is flat, about 4 hours.

◆ The glaze can be made up to 1 week ahead and refrigerated, covered.

◆ Be careful not to let the ribs burn in the oven or on the grill—there's a lot of sugar in the cola. 🦋

HONEY SPARERIBS

SERVES 4

this is a simple but wonderful preparation for regular pork spareribs, which are meatier than baby backs—but both are delicious. I had similar ribs in China, and I loved them. The combination of honey and salt is irresistible.

2 racks pork spareribs (each 3 to 4 pounds),
 partially split by the butcher; or 2 racks
 baby back ribs (each about 2 pounds)
Coarse (kosher) salt and freshly ground black
 pepper, to taste
2 cups honey
3 scallions (white bulbs and 3 inches green),
 thinly sliced, for garnish
Maldon (flaky) sea salt (see Note, page 66) or coarse
 (kosher) salt, for serving

1. Preheat the oven to 350°F.

2. Lay the rack of ribs, meaty side up, in a large baking pan, and sprinkle them generously with salt and pepper. Bake for 30 minutes.

3. Remove the pan from the oven and brush ½ cup of the honey over the ribs. Bake for 30 minutes longer.

4. Drain off any cooking liquid from the pan. Brush the ribs with another ½ cup of the honey and bake until the ribs are cooked through and browned and glistening, 15 minutes. Then remove the pan from the oven and let the ribs cool slightly.

5. Place the ribs on a cutting board and cut them apart, slicing between the bones. Arrange them on a platter, and sprinkle the scallions over them. Pour the remaining 1 cup honey into a bowl and serve it with the ribs, along with a bowl of the sea salt, for sprinkling. 🦋

MAPLE BOURBON COUNTRY RIBS

SERVES 6

There's something about bourbon and pork—they just seem to have an affinity for each other. And with the addition of ginger and maple syrup, the magic starts to happen. Country ribs are more chops than ribs—they come from the shoulder end of the pork loin and are often called end chops. The bourbon gives them a distinctive Southern flavor. I like to make these ribs for those big summer holidays. Serve them with the Fluffy Grits Soufflé on page 325.

FOR THE SAUCE:

⅔ cup ketchup

⅔ cup pure maple syrup

½ cup bourbon

⅓ cup soy sauce

2 tablespoons (packed) dark brown sugar

2 tablespoons finely minced fresh ginger

FOR THE RIBS:

6 country-style bone-in pork ribs
    (each about 8 ounces)

Vegetable oil, for oiling the grill

1. Whisk all the sauce ingredients together in a bowl.

2. Place the ribs in a bowl or other container, and coat them well with the sauce. Cover and refrigerate, turning them occasionally, for 8 hours or overnight.

3. Bring the ribs to room temperature before baking (this will take about 45 minutes).

4. Preheat the oven to 350°F.

BAKING RIBS

I think baking is the way to prepare the most succulent ribs if they're not being smoked on the grill. Basting with a sauce keeps them moist and luscious, and the fat inherent in both pork ribs and beef short ribs completes the job. The cooking is easy to control and the results are usually perfect.

If you're not grilling, you may want to create a little crust on the ribs for textural interest. After baking the ribs for 1 hour, very carefully run them under the broiler, 3 inches from the heat source, for 3 to 5 minutes per side. Watch them very closely—you don't want them to burn.

5. Remove the ribs from the marinade and place them in a 13-x-9-inch baking dish. Brush them well with the marinade, reserving the remaining marinade. Bake the ribs, basting them once or twice, until they are cooked through and an instant-read meat thermometer registers 160°F when inserted in the thickest part of the meat, 40 minutes.

6. Meanwhile, preheat a barbecue grill to high. Oil the grill grate well.

7. Transfer the ribs to the grill, and grill them, brushing them occasionally with the remaining marinade, until they are browned, glazed, and tender, about 4 minutes per side. Serve immediately. ⚜

KOREAN-STYLE
BEEF SHORT RIBS

SERVES 4 TO 6

Anyone who eats fairly frequently in Korean restaurants is probably familiar with their version of barbecue. The types of beef used for barbecuing—specially cut short ribs (or flanken), and top round, rib eye, or sirloin presliced into thin, wide pieces—can be found in Korean grocery stores. All are ready to be quickly grilled over hot coals or cooked in a heavy skillet and served with a tempting dipping sauce made with a mix of soy sauce, chili paste, sesame oil, and a variety of flavorings. I've made my version of Korean barbecue using beef short ribs cut into small pieces. Ask your butcher to cut the ribs for you. There is plenty here to serve four hearty appetites or six delicate ones. These ribs are also a perfect finger food at cocktail parties (as long as there are plenty of napkins).

FOR THE SAUCE (makes 3 cups):

1½ cups soy sauce

6 tablespoons rice vinegar

2 tablespoons toasted sesame oil

6 cloves garlic, finely minced with a pinch
    of coarse (kosher) salt

6 tablespoons sugar

3 tablespoons Asian (Thai) chile paste

6 tablespoons finely minced scallions,
    including 3 inches green

2 tablespoons finely minced fresh ginger

1 tablespoon toasted sesame seeds, crushed (see Note)

6 pounds short ribs of beef, cut crosswise into
    2-inch pieces

Salt and freshly ground black pepper, to taste

2 tablespoons olive oil

4 scallions (white bulbs and 3 inches green),
    thinly sliced, for garnish

1. Prepare the sauce: Whisk all the sauce ingredients together in a bowl. Set it aside. (The sauce can be made 6 to 8 hours ahead; store it, covered, in the refrigerator.)

2. Preheat the oven to 350°F.

3. Prepare the ribs: Season the short ribs well with salt and pepper. Heat the oil in a large heavy ovenproof pot over medium-high heat. Add the ribs, in small batches, and cook until browned all over, about 6 minutes per batch. When all the ribs are browned, return them to the pot and toss with 1½ cups of the sauce.

4. Bring the ribs and sauce to a boil on top of the stove. Then cover the pot, transfer it to the oven, and bake, stirring them occasionally, until the ribs are tender and falling off the bones, 2½ to 3 hours.

5. Serve the ribs in a large bowl or on a platter, sprinkled with the scallions. At each place setting, place a small ramekin containing about ¼ cup of the remaining sauce.

NOTE: To toast sesame seeds, place a small skillet over medium-low heat. Add the sesame seeds and cook, shaking the skillet constantly, until they are light gold, about 3 minutes. To crush them, place the cooled seeds in a self-seal plastic bag, press out all the air and seal it, and then run a rolling pin over the bag to crush the seeds. 🌿

"THERE'S NOTHING MORE SATISFYING THAN A WELL-ROASTED CHICKEN."

CHICKEN—
ROASTED AND BAKED

I'm not the first to say it and I won't be the last, but it's something I believe: A well-roasted chicken is the sign of an excellent cook. It takes talent to get the skin a deep golden brown and crispy in the same amount of time that it takes for the white meat to cook without drying out and the dark meat to have its juices run clear.

Everyone has a favorite way to roast a chicken, everyone cherishes their grandmother's recipe, and everyone has their own rules. Unless you are a master carver worthy of an audience, present a whole bird on a serving platter, well garnished, and then carve it in the kitchen. I always garnish my roasted birds with bundles of fresh herbs because it adds an elegant and fresh look.

Not every roasted chicken needs to go into the oven whole. This chapter also includes wonderful recipes for all manner of cut-up chicken—quartered pieces with Asian accents or glazed with a tomato marmalade. Cut into smaller pieces, chicken is given Tandoori-style flavoring, slowly pot-roasted South American style, and prepared the French way with plenty of onions and garlic. Accompany your chickens with something to absorb the marvelous juices—like potatoes, noodles, or a grain. 🌿

AN HERB-ROASTED CHICKEN

SERVES 4

there is no dish handier to have in your repertoire than a perfect roast chicken. Cooks in the know will respect the crisp skin and juicy meat—and your friends and family, whether they are cooks or not, will too. Subtle flavoring is also a telltale sign of a cook who knows what he or she is doing. Begin with a hot oven to brown the skin and seal in the juices, and then shift to a slower finish to guarantee a moist bird. Now let's roast . . .

1 roasting chicken (3½ pounds)

Salt and freshly ground black pepper,
    to taste

4 sprigs fresh tarragon or rosemary

4 tablespoons (½ stick) salted butter,
    at room temperature

¼ teaspoon sweet paprika

2½ cups chicken broth, preferably homemade
    (see page 434)

2 tablespoons olive oil

1 large shallot, finely minced

1 tablespoon cider vinegar

1. Preheat the oven to 425°F.

2. Rinse the chicken well, removing any excess fat, and pat it dry. Sprinkle the chicken cavity with salt and pepper. Place 2 tarragon sprigs in the cavity and truss the chicken.

3. Using your fingers carefully loosen the skin on the breast and insert a sprig of tarragon under the skin on each side.

4. Spread 3 tablespoons of the butter over the outside of the chicken. Sprinkle it with salt and pepper, and dust the breast with the paprika.

5. Place the chicken on a rack in a shallow roasting pan and roast it for 15 minutes, basting it occasionally with a mixture of 1½ cups of the chicken broth, the olive oil, and any drippings in the pan. Then reduce the oven temperature to 350°F and roast until the juices run clear when the thigh is pricked with the point of a small knife, about 1 hour and 10 minutes. (An instant-read thermometer inserted in the thigh should read 170°F.)

6. Transfer the chicken to a platter and let it rest for 5 to 10 minutes, so the juices can settle before carving.

7. While the chicken rests, prepare the pan gravy: Defat the pan juices, either by skimming the fat off the surface with a metal spoon or by pouring the juices through a gravy separator. Return the defatted juices to the roasting pan and add the shallot. Bring to a boil. Add the remaining 1 cup chicken broth and the vinegar to the pan, and boil the mixture, scraping

up the brown bits on the bottom of the pan, for 10 minutes. Season with salt and pepper. Remove the pan from the heat and whisk in the remaining 1 tablespoon butter.

8. Present the chicken on a platter, if desired; then take it into the kitchen to carve it. Spoon a bit of the sauce over the carved chicken, and pass the rest in a small pitcher. 🌿

ROASTED BRINED CHICKEN

SERVES 4

Any food lover will agree that there's nothing more satisfying than a well-roasted chicken. You don't have to be a classically trained chef to come up with a great bird. I find that an overnight brine results in especially juicy, flavorful meat; it also gives the finished chicken a glistening sheen—crisp on the outside and moist on the inside. Perfect! Just remember that 12 hours is the limit for the brine; any longer and the meat becomes mushy.

Small chickens roast quickly and evenly at a high heat, resulting in succulent meat and crisp skin. Don't go above 3½ pounds when buying a bird.

FOR THE BRINE:

1 cup sugar

1 cup coarse (kosher) salt

8 cloves garlic, bruised (see box, page 82)

8 whole black peppercorns, crushed

8 whole allspice berries, crushed

2 small dried red chile peppers

2 star anise pods

FOR THE CHICKEN:

1 roasting chicken (3½ pounds; see headnote)

Freshly ground black pepper, to taste

1 onion, halved

3 sprigs fresh thyme

2 tablespoons unsalted butter, melted

1. Prepare the brine: Combine all of the brine ingredients with 8 cups water in a large pot and bring to a boil. Then reduce the heat, partially cover the pot, and simmer for 15 minutes. Remove the pot from the heat and let the brine cool to room temperature.

2. Snip off the wing tips and remove any excess fat from the chicken. Rinse it well, and pat it dry with paper towels. Place the chicken, breast side down, in a nonreactive pot (not too big, because you want

the brine to cover it as much as possible). Cover with the brine and refrigerate, covered, for up to 12 hours.

3. Thirty minutes before roasting time, preheat the oven to 425°F.

4. Remove the chicken from the brine and pat it dry. Season the inside of the chicken with pepper, and place the onion halves and thyme sprigs in the cavity. Tie the ends of the chicken legs together with kitchen string, and tuck in the wings. Place the chicken in a shallow roasting pan, brush it all over with the melted butter, and sprinkle with pepper.

5. Roast the chicken until the juices run clear when the thickest part of the thigh is pierced with the tip of a small knife, 1¼ hours. (Check the bird after 1 hour. If it is browning too quickly, tent it loosely with aluminum foil.) Let the chicken rest for 10 minutes before carving. 🌿

JUST BETWEEN US CHICKENS

When shopping for chicken, I want to make sure I buy the variety that's right for my recipe, whether I'm frying, roasting, baking, or turning it into a luscious soup. And I want to be sure I choose the right bird. And frankly, at first glance the various chickens in the market look alike. So here's a primer, going from small to large.

POUSSIN, OR BABY CHICKEN: 4 to 6 weeks old. Weight: ¾ to 1 pound. Fancy little party bird, good for a single serving. Serve as you would a Cornish game hen.

CORNISH GAME HEN: a hybrid of the Cornish and White Rock breeds. Weight: 1 to 2 pounds. Meaty; good for stuffing, roasting, broiling, and grilling.

BROILER OR FRYER: 2 to 3 months old. Weight: 1½ to 3½ pounds. Good all-purpose chicken. Tender meat; use for broiling or frying, or for roasting, grilling, sautéing, or poaching.

ROASTER, OR ROASTING CHICKEN: 3 to 5 months old. Weight: 4 to 6 pounds. Flavorful bird with more fat to keep it moist. Large cavity for stuffing; great roasted but fine also for grilling, broiling, or poaching.

STEWING CHICKEN, FOWL, HEN, OR BOILING HEN: 10 to 18 months old. Weight: 4 to 6 pounds. Great flavor but tough meat. Use for stocks, long-simmered stews, and braises.

CAPON: a young castrated rooster, under 10 months old. Weight: 4 to 10 pounds. Tender meat; large cavity for stuffing; full-breasted; excellent alternative to a small turkey.

ASIAN-SCENTED
ORANGE CHICKEN

SERVES 6 TO 8

h ere soy sauce, sesame oil, and ginger blend beautifully with the juice and zest of fresh oranges to give the chicken a delightfully bright Asian flavor. Honey lacquers the skin to a rich golden brown. The Watercress and Mushroom Salad is just the right counterpoint to the sweet chicken.

2 chickens (each 2½ to 3 pounds), each
    cut into 8 pieces
Finely grated zest of 4 oranges
⅔ cup fresh orange juice
¼ cup honey
3 tablespoons soy sauce
2 tablespoons toasted sesame oil
1 tablespoon minced fresh ginger
2 teaspoons finely minced garlic
¼ teaspoon crushed red pepper flakes
Salt and freshly ground black pepper,
    to taste
4 scallions (white bulbs and 3 inches green),
    thinly sliced on the diagonal, for
    garnish
Watercress and Mushroom Salad (page 254),
    for serving

1. The day before serving, rinse the chicken pieces well, removing all excess fat, and pat them dry. Place the chicken in a large bowl.

2. Combine the orange zest and juice with the honey, soy sauce, sesame oil, ginger, garlic, and red pepper flakes in a small bowl. Stir well, and coat the chicken pieces thoroughly with this mixture. Refrigerate, covered, overnight.

3. Thirty minutes before cooking time, preheat the oven to 375°F and remove the chicken from the refrigerator. Arrange the pieces in a large shallow roasting pan, and sprinkle with salt and pepper. Pour ⅔ cup of the marinade into the pan.

4. Bake the chicken, basting it frequently, until it is golden brown and shiny, 1 hour.

5. Transfer the chicken pieces to a large serving platter. Strain the pan juices into a small saucepan and boil until thickened, about 10 minutes. Drizzle the sauce over the chicken, and sprinkle with the scallions. Serve immediately, with the Watercress and Mushroom Salad alongside.

ORANGE-GINGER-TOMATO GLAZED CHICKEN

SERVES 8

there is something about a glistening orange chicken that has universal appeal. The salty olives balance the sweetness, and the oven-roasted tomatoes inject a little sophistication into this easy-to-prepare party dish. Serve it with Dress-Up Rice (page 322).

FOR THE OVEN-ROASTED TOMATOES:

8 ripe plum tomatoes, halved lengthwise

3 tablespoons extra-virgin olive oil

2 tablespoons sugar

Freshly ground black pepper, to taste

FOR THE CHICKEN:

2 chickens (each 3½ pounds), each quartered

Salt and freshly ground black pepper, to taste

1 cup bitter orange marmalade

¼ cup finely minced fresh ginger

Finely grated zest and juice of 2 oranges

½ cup pitted green Spanish olives

½ cup chicken broth, preferably homemade
    (see page 434)

2 tablespoons chopped fresh mint leaves, for garnish

1. One day ahead, prepare the Oven-Roasted Tomatoes: Preheat the oven to 375°F.

2. Place the tomatoes, cut side up, on a baking sheet. Drizzle them with the olive oil and sprinkle with the sugar and pepper. Bake for 1½ hours. Cool to room temperature. Refrigerate, covered, until ready to use. They will keep up to 2 days.

3. When you are ready to prepare the chicken, preheat the oven to 350°F.

4. Rinse the chicken well, removing any excess fat, and pat it dry. Place the chicken, skin side up, in a large roasting pan. Do not crowd it—use two pans if necessary. Season well with salt and pepper. Tuck the Oven-Roasted Tomatoes among the chicken pieces.

5. Spread the marmalade over the chicken. Sprinkle with the ginger and the orange zest. Scatter the olives over the chicken, and pour the orange juice and chicken broth into the pan. Bake until the chicken is golden brown and the juices run clear when the thickest part of the chicken is pricked with the tip of a small knife, about 1¼ hours.

6. Using a slotted spoon, transfer the chicken, tomatoes, and olives to a platter. Moisten the chicken with some of the pan juices, and sprinkle the chopped mint over it. Pass the remaining pan juices in a warmed sauceboat. ❧

KOOPER FAMILY FAVORITE
VIETNAMESE-STYLE CHICKEN

SERVES 6 TO 8

My friend Mike Kooper and his children Sophie, Luke, and Jake cook this chicken to perfection and were kind enough to share the recipe with me. It's great served over rice noodles in a shallow bowl to catch all the sauce. It's also excellent accompanied by Pineapple Ginger Rice (page 324). Extra limes served alongside are always delicious for squeezing.

2 chickens (each about 3½ pounds),
    each cut into 8 pieces

¼ cup minced fresh ginger

¼ cup minced garlic

2 teaspoons crushed red pepper flakes

½ cup soy sauce

2 tablespoons Asian fish sauce

2 tablespoons fresh lime juice

½ cup (packed) dark brown sugar

2 tablespoons chopped fresh cilantro leaves, for garnish

2 scallions (white bulbs and 3 inches green),
    thinly sliced on the diagonal, for garnish

4 limes, halved crosswise, for serving

1. Rinse the chicken pieces well, removing any excess fat, and pat them dry.

2. Combine the ginger, garlic, red pepper flakes, soy sauce, fish sauce, lime juice, and ½ cup water in a large bowl. Stir well. Add the chicken pieces and stir to coat them with the marinade. Cover the bowl and refrigerate for 8 hours or overnight.

3. Preheat the oven to 350°F.

4. Arrange the chicken in a single layer in one or two shallow baking pans. Spoon the marinade evenly over the chicken, and sprinkle with the brown sugar. Bake, basting occasionally with the pan juices, until the chicken is browned and glistening, 50 to 60 minutes.

5. Transfer the chicken to a decorative platter. Pour the pan juices into a small saucepan and boil to thicken them slightly and create a sauce, about 5 minutes. Drizzle the sauce over the chicken, and sprinkle with the cilantro and scallions. Serve immediately, with the limes alongside. ❧

TANDOORI-STYLE ROAST CHICKEN

SERVES 6 TO 8

While we all can't be fortunate enough to have a tandoori oven in our kitchen, we can emulate the flavors of tandoori chicken by seasoning the bird with spices from the richly aromatic Indian palate. Vegetables lend flavor and color to the sauce, which combines with the chicken to make this an ideal party dish. For a refreshing condiment, serve Pineapple Apple Raita alongside.

2 chickens (each about 3½ pounds),
    each cut into 8 pieces
8 tablespoons (1 stick) unsalted butter
1 tablespoon vegetable oil
1½ tablespoons curry powder
1½ teaspoons ground turmeric
½ teaspoon ground cinnamon
½ teaspoon coarse (kosher) salt
½ teaspoon freshly ground black pepper
2 onions, cut into ¼-inch dice
1 red bell pepper, stemmed, seeded,
    and cut into ¼-inch dice
2 ripe tomatoes, seeded and cut into
    ¼-inch dice
1 cup chicken broth, preferably homemade
    (see page 434)
¼ cup chopped fresh cilantro leaves,
    for garnish
Pineapple Apple Raita (page 370), for serving
Mango chutney (store-bought), for serving

1. Preheat the oven to 375°F.

2. Rinse the chicken pieces well, removing any excess fat, and pat them dry. Clip off the wing tips. Divide the pieces evenly between two shallow baking dishes, arranging them skin side up.

3. Melt the butter in the oil in a small saucepan over low heat. Add the curry powder, turmeric, cinnamon, salt, and pepper, and cook to mellow the spices, 2 to 3 minutes. Let cool slightly. Then drizzle the spiced butter over the chicken. Use a brush to make sure the chicken is well coated.

4. Sprinkle the chopped onions, bell pepper, and tomatoes over the chicken. Pour ½ cup of the broth into the bottom of each baking dish. Bake, basting often, until the chicken is reddish-brown and is cooked through, about 1 hour.

5. Arrange the chicken pieces in a large shallow bowl, and spoon the vegetables and sauce over them. Sprinkle with the chopped cilantro. Serve the Pineapple Apple Raita and mango chutney alongside.

DANIEL BOULUD'S CHICKEN GRAND-MERE FRANCINE

SERVES 4

Grandmas know a thing or two about preparing top-notch chicken dishes and Daniel Boulud, a great French chef with several extraordinary restaurants in New York and other locations, shares his grandmother's recipe with us (the recipe here is adapted from *Daniel Boulud's Café Boulud Cookbook*). This fricassee, a classic family recipe, is a classic in French cuisine as well. Daniel's grandmother, Francine, prepared this chicken at the original Café Boulud, outside of Lyon. It was especially wonderful during the mushroom harvest.

Daniel suggests that diners spread the soft, caramel-y garlic, easily squeezed out of the skins, over pieces of crusty baguette—marvelous for sopping up the tasty sauce. Serve a rustic Bandol rouge with Grand-mère Francine's chicken.

1 chicken (3 pounds), cut into 8 pieces

Salt and freshly ground black pepper, to taste

2 tablespoons extra-virgin olive oil

2 tablespoons unsalted butter

12 cipollini onions, peeled and trimmed

4 shallots, peeled and trimmed

2 heads garlic, cloves separated but not peeled

3 thyme sprigs

4 small Yukon Gold potatoes, peeled and
    cut into 1½-inch chunks

2 small bulbs celery root (celeriac), peeled and
    cut into 1½-inch chunks

2 ounces slab bacon, cut into short, thin strips

12 small cremini or oyster mushrooms, wiped clean
    with a damp paper towel and trimmed

2 cups unsalted chicken broth, preferably
    homemade (see page 434) or canned

1. Position a rack in the center of the oven and preheat the oven to 375°F.

2. Rinse the chicken pieces well, removing any excess fat, and pat them dry. Season the chicken all over with salt and pepper. Heat the olive oil in a 12-inch ovenproof sauté pan or skillet (choose one with high sides and a cover) over medium-high heat. Add the chicken pieces and cook until they are well browned on all sides, 10 to 15 minutes altogether. Take your time: you want a nice deep color and you also want to cook the chicken three-quarters through at this point. When the chicken is a deep gold, transfer it to a platter and keep it in a warm place.

3. Pour off all but 2 tablespoons of the fat from the pan. Reduce the heat to medium, and add the butter, onions, shallots, garlic cloves, and thyme sprigs. Cook, stirring, until the vegetables just start to take on a little color, about 3 minutes. Then add the potatoes, celery root, and bacon, and cook just to start rendering the bacon fat, 1 to 2 minutes. Cover the pan and cook, stirring every 2 minutes, for 10 minutes.

4. Add the mushrooms, season with salt and pepper, and return the chicken pieces to the pan. Add the broth and bring to a boil. Transfer the pan to the oven and bake, uncovered, until the chicken is cooked through, 20 to 25 minutes.

5. Spoon the chicken and vegetables onto a warm serving platter or into an attractive casserole, and serve immediately. 🌺

ZUNI ROAST CHICKEN
WITH SAVORY BREAD SALAD

SERVES 2 TO 4

this sumptuous recipe comes to us from Judy Rodgers, chef-owner of Zuni Café in San Francisco. Judy believes in salting her birds well in advance. She says it improves the flavor, keeps in moisture, and makes the meat tender. I love her food, so I'm a believer. The recipe looks long, but it is not difficult. Just follow the directions carefully for a great roast chicken that is worth taking the time to prepare.

FOR THE CHICKEN:

1 chicken (3 to 3½ pounds)

4 tender sprigs fresh thyme, marjoram, rosemary,
    or sage, each about 2 inches long

Salt

About ¼ teaspoon freshly cracked black pepper

FOR THE SALAD:

1 round loaf slightly stale, open-crumbed, chewy
    peasant-style bread (a generous 8 ounces)

6 to 8 tablespoons mild olive oil

1½ tablespoons champagne vinegar or
    white wine vinegar

Salt and freshly cracked black pepper, to taste

1 teaspoon red wine vinegar, or more
    as needed

1 tablespoon warm water

1 tablespoon dried currants

2 tablespoons pine nuts

3 cloves garlic, slivered

4 scallions (white bulbs and 3 inches green),
    thinly sliced

2 tablespoons lightly salted chicken broth,
    preferably homemade (see page 434)

A few handfuls of arugula, frisée, or red
    mustard greens, rinsed and patted dry

1. Prepare the chicken 2 to 3 days before serving: Rinse the chicken well, removing any excess fat, and pat it very dry inside and out. Slide a finger under the skin on each side of the breast, making two little pockets. Use the tip of your finger to gently loosen a pocket of skin on the thickest section of each thigh. Using your finger, shove an herb sprig into each of the four pockets. Season the chicken liberally all over with salt (using about 2¼ teaspoons salt), sprinkling the thick sections a little more heavily than the thinner parts. Sprinkle on the cracked pepper then sprinkle a little salt just inside the cavity, on the backbone. Tuck the wing tips behind the shoulders. Cover the chicken loosely with aluminum foil, and refrigerate.

2. Up to several hours in advance of cooking the chicken, prepare the bread salad: Preheat the broiler.

3. Cut the bread into a couple of large chunks. Slice off all of the bottom crust and most of the top and side crust. Brush the bread all over with 2 to 3 tablespoons of the olive oil. Broil very briefly, to crisp and lightly color the surface. Turn the bread chunks over and crisp the other side. Trim off any badly charred tips; then tear the chunks into a combination of irregular 2- to 3-inch pieces, bite-size bits, and fat crumbs. You should have about 4 cups. Put the bread in a wide salad bowl.

4. In a small bowl, combine about 4 tablespoons of the olive oil with the champagne vinegar, and salt and pepper to taste. Toss about ¼ cup of this vinaigrette with the torn bread in the salad bowl; the bread will be unevenly dressed. Taste one of the more saturated pieces. If it is bland, add a little salt and pepper and toss again.

5. Combine the 1 teaspoon red wine vinegar and the warm water in a small bowl. Add the currants and stir to moisten them. Set aside.

6. When you are ready to roast the chicken, preheat the oven to 475°F (see box below).

7. Choose a shallow flameproof roasting pan that is barely larger than the chicken, or use an ovenproof 10-inch skillet. Preheat the pan over medium heat. Wipe the chicken dry and set it, breast side up, in the pan. It should sizzle. Place the pan in the center of the oven, and listen and watch for the chicken to start sizzling and browning within 20 minutes. If it doesn't, raise the temperature progressively until it does. The skin should blister, but if the chicken begins to char

PERFECT ROASTING

———

+ Be thorough when you dry a chicken after rinsing it. A wet chicken will spend too much time steaming before it begins to turn golden brown.

+ Depending on the size, efficiency, and accuracy of your oven, and the size of your bird, you may need to adjust the heat to as high as 500°F or as low as 450°F during the course of roasting the chicken to get it to brown properly. If that proves to be the case, begin at that temperature the next time you roast a chicken. If you have a convection function on your oven, use it for the first 30 minutes; it will enhance the browning and may reduce the overall cooking time by 5 to 10 minutes.

or the fat is smoking, reduce the temperature by 25°F. After about 30 minutes, turn the bird over (by drying the bird and preheating the pan before adding the chicken, the skin should not stick). Roast until it starts to blister and brown, another 10 to 20 minutes, depending on size.

8. While the chicken is roasting, place the pine nuts in a small baking dish and set it in the hot oven for a minute or two, just to warm them through. Add them to the bowl of bread.

9. Heat 1 tablespoon of the olive oil in a small skillet over medium-low heat, add the garlic and scallions, and cook, stirring constantly, until softened, 5 minutes. Don't let them color. Add this to the bread and fold to combine. Drain the plumped currants and fold them in. Drizzle the chicken broth over the salad, and fold again. Taste a few pieces of bread—a fairly saturated one and a dryish one. If they are bland, add salt, pepper, and/or a few drops of red wine vinegar, then toss well. Since the basic character of a bread salad depends on the bread you use, these adjustments can be essential.

10. Pile the bread salad in a 1-quart baking dish and tent it with aluminum foil; set the salad aside.

11. Check the chicken: When it is done, the juices will run clear when the thickest part of the thigh is pricked with the tip of a knife. (The total cooking time will be 45 minutes to 1 hour.)

12. Turn the chicken back over to recrisp the breast skin, 5 to 10 minutes. At the same time, place the salad in the oven.

13. Remove the chicken from the oven and turn off the heat. Leave the bread salad to continue warming for another 5 minutes or so.

14. Place the chicken on a plate. Carefully pour the clear fat from the roasting pan, leaving the lean drippings behind. Add about 1 tablespoon water to the hot pan and swirl it around. Slash the stretched skin between the thighs and breast of the chicken, and then tilt the plate over the roasting pan to drain the juices into the drippings. Set the chicken in a warm spot (like your stovetop), and let it rest while you finish the bread salad. The meat will become more tender and uniformly succulent as it cools.

15. Set a platter in the oven to warm for a few minutes.

16. Tilt the roasting pan and skim off the last of the fat. Place the pan over medium-low heat, add any juice that has collected under the chicken, and bring to a simmer. Stir and scrape to soften any hard golden drippings. Taste—the juices will be extremely flavorful.

17. Return the bread salad to the salad bowl. Drizzle a spoonful of the pan juices over the salad, and toss. Add the greens and a drizzle of the remaining vinaigrette, and fold well. Taste again.

SAN FRANCISCO DREAMING

For a very special evening—an anniversary, a visit from good friends whom you haven't seen in a while, a new job—celebrate with style. Prepare San Francisco chef Judy Rodgers's chicken dish, and open a bottle of Viognier to go along with it. Here's to happiness!

SPICED GOAT CHEESE SLATHER
with Ficelle Toasts
PAGE 18

KUMAMOTO OYSTERS

ZUNI ROAST CHICKEN
with Savory Bread Salad
PAGE 144

ROASTED BEETS
with Tangerine Vinaigrette
PAGE 22

BITTERSWEET CHOCOLATE CAKE
PAGE 376

---

18. Cut the chicken into pieces. Spread the bread salad on the warm platter, and nestle the chicken in the salad. Serve immediately.

POT-ROASTED CHICKEN SANTIAGO

SERVES 2 TO 4

the colorful and simple ingredients of the South American larder add delicious flavor to this comfy pot-roasted chicken. Whole corn kernels, added shortly before the cooking is finished, lend a vibrant crunch and fresh contrast to the slowly roasted chicken.

1 chicken (3 pounds), cut into 8 pieces

½ cup all-purpose flour

Salt and freshly ground black pepper, to taste

¼ teaspoon sweet paprika

2 tablespoons unsalted butter

4 tablespoons olive oil, plus more if needed

1 onion, cut into ¼-inch dice

1 tablespoon finely minced garlic

½ cup diced red bell pepper (¼-inch dice)

½ cup diced carrots (¼-inch dice)

½ cup diced celery (¼-inch dice)

2 cups chopped canned peeled Italian plum
    tomatoes, with their juices

2 teaspoons ground cumin

⅔ cup chopped pimento-stuffed green olives

⅔ cup fresh corn kernels (from 1 ear of corn) or
    thawed frozen corn

2 tablespoons chopped fresh cilantro leaves,
    for serving

Saffron Orzo (page 347) or cooked rice, for serving

1. Preheat the oven to 325°F.

2. Rinse the chicken pieces well, removing any excess fat, and pat them dry.

3. Combine the flour, salt, pepper, and paprika in a large bowl. Mix well. Add the chicken pieces and dredge them in the seasoned flour, shaking off any excess.

4. Melt the butter in 2 tablespoons of the olive oil in a large skillet over medium-high heat. Add the chicken and cook, turning, until it is golden brown on all sides, about 20 minutes total (add extra oil if necessary). Transfer the chicken to a plate.

5. Pour the remaining 2 tablespoons olive oil into a large Dutch oven set over low heat. Add the onion, garlic, bell pepper, carrots, and celery, and cook, stirring occasionally, until softened, 10 minutes. Then stir in the tomatoes with their juices, the cumin, and salt and pepper to taste. Add the chicken to the pot.

6. Bring the mixture to a low boil on top of the stove. Then cover the pot, transfer it to the oven, and bake for 50 minutes.

7. Stir the olives and corn into the chicken mixture, distributing them evenly. Bake, covered, until the chicken is cooked through, 10 to 15 minutes. Sprinkle with the cilantro, and serve over Saffron Orzo.

LEMON HERB-ROASTED CHICKEN DRUMSTICKS

SERVES 6

Planning a picnic? There is nothing better to pack in your basket than flavorful chicken drumsticks, so easy to pick up and enjoy while sitting on your quilt, basking in a summer day. These easy drumsticks are tossed with the complementary flavors of lemon and thyme. If lemon thyme is available, even better.

12 chicken drumsticks (3 pounds total)

Finely grated zest and juice of 2 lemons

2 tablespoons chopped fresh thyme leaves

2 tablespoons extra-virgin olive oil

Coarse salt and freshly ground black pepper, to taste

1. Rinse the drumsticks well, removing any excess fat, and pat them dry.

2. Combine the lemon zest and juice, thyme, olive oil, and salt and pepper in a large bowl. Add the drumsticks and toss to coat. Cover and set aside to marinate at room temperature for 1 to 2 hours.

3. Preheat the oven to 375°F.

4. Arrange the drumsticks in a large shallow roasting pan (use two if necessary to avoid crowding). Pour the marinade over the chicken and bake, basting occasionally, until the drumsticks are cooked through and golden brown, about 1¼ hours.

5. If the chicken has not browned enough, place it under the broiler, 4 inches from the heat source, and broil until browned on both sides, 2 to 3 minutes, watching carefully.

6. Transfer the drumsticks to a serving dish, or let them cool and then transfer them to a picnic container. Pour the pan juices into a small saucepan and boil until slightly thickened, about 10 minutes. Pour the juices over the chicken and let rest for 10 to 15 minutes for the flavors to develop. Serve immediately, or remove from the pan juices and pack them into your picnic basket (don't forget the napkins). ❧

"THERE IS NO BOTTOM TO MY STEW POT."

STEWS

Stews are an ideal way to slow-cook flavor into a dish using less expensive cuts of meat. Many of the stews that we savor may be family recipes handed down through generations, but most of us have had the good fortune—through travel, restaurants, TV shows, and cookbooks—to become familiar with intensely flavored stews from cultures outside our own. Morocco inspired my Lamb and Vegetable Tagine enhanced with cumin, coriander, and thyme and Seven-Vegetable Couscous. Time spent in France inspired a rich Pork Marengo and a succulent Beef Daube.

The stews in this chapter are as exciting and appealing to serve for family dinners as they are to serve for your fancy dinner parties. For cozy winter eves, there's Rabbit Stewed in Holiday Spices or Tom Valenti's Braised Duck in Red Wine and Tomatoes. And when summer arrives and you want something light, Shellfish Stew is absolutely the right choice. I serve it in shallow bowls with a twirl of pasta on the bottom, accompanied by a crisp Sauvignon Blanc or a fruity red wine, crusty bread, and a lavish Greek salad.

Another word of advice: Add extra fresh herbs shortly before your stews finish cooking—they enliven the flavors. Egg noodles, couscous, and rice are a perfect base for most any stew. They soak up all of the luscious sauce.

BEEF DAUBE

SERVES 8

daube is the well-known beef stew of Provence, where each household has its own version. It is the most popular beef dish in the South of France, especially beloved in the Camargue, the cowboy terrain west of Marseille. A long, slow simmer brings out the best in our beef chuck, a perfect cut for stew. Flavoring vegetables, chorizo, thyme, bay leaves, and red wine all add their flavors. A strip of orange peel perfumes the stewing liquid, lending its special character to the daube.

½ cup all-purpose flour

¼ teaspoon sweet paprika

Salt and freshly ground black pepper

4 pounds boneless beef chuck, cut into 2-inch pieces

6 tablespoons olive oil, or more as needed

1 cup diced onion (¼-inch dice)

1 cup diced carrots (¼-inch dice)

1 cup diced celery (¼-inch dice)

2 tablespoons finely minced garlic

4 ounces hard chorizo, cut into ¼-inch dice

2 bay leaves

1 tablespoon fresh thyme leaves, chopped,
    or 1 teaspoon dried thyme

2 cups diced seeded tomatoes (¼-inch dice)

2 tablespoons tomato paste

2½ cups chicken broth, preferably homemade
    (see page 434)

1½ cups dry red wine

2 tablespoons dark brown sugar

Zest of 1 orange, removed in 1 long strip
    with a sharp paring knife if possible
    (see Note, page 155)

½ cup pitted Niçoise olives

⅓ cup chopped fresh flat-leaf parsley leaves

Lightly buttered egg noodles, for serving

1. Combine the flour, paprika, 1 teaspoon salt, and black pepper to taste in a plastic bag. Seal the bag and shake it to mix well. Then add the beef, in batches, and shake it in the flour to dredge it. Shake off any excess flour.

2. Heat 4 tablespoons of the oil in a large heavy pot over medium-high heat. Add the beef in batches and brown it well on all sides, about 6 minutes per batch. As each batch is browned, transfer it to a bowl. Add more oil to the pot between batches if necessary.

3. Wipe the pot clean and heat the remaining 2 tablespoons oil in it over low heat. Add the onion, carrots, and celery, and cook, stirring, until almost softened, 7 minutes. Add the garlic and cook for 3 minutes. Then add the chorizo, bay leaves, and thyme; cook, stirring, until the flavors are blended, 3 minutes.

4. Stir in the tomatoes, tomato paste, broth, wine, brown sugar, and orange zest. Return the meat and any accumulated juices to the pot.

5. Bring the liquid to a boil over medium-high heat. Reduce the heat to medium or medium-low, partially cover the pot, and simmer, stirring occasionally, until the meat is very tender, 2 hours.

6. Remove and discard the bay leaves. Season the stew with salt and pepper to taste. Stir in the olives and parsley and cook, partially covered, for 15 minutes.

7. Remove and discard the orange zest. Serve the daube over buttered noodles. ❧

LAMB AND VEGETABLE TAGINE

SERVES 6 TO 8

tagine refers to two wonderful things: a delectable, slowly simmered Moroccan stew made with lamb, beef, or chicken; vegetables; dried fruits; and aromatic spices; and the shallow earthenware pot with a high conical lid in which the stew is cooked and served. This tagine is typical in its ingredients—lamb, vegetables, prunes, and spices—and it delivers the pure flavors of an old-style Moroccan dish. It is a true favorite of mine.

3 tablespoons olive oil

1 tablespoon sweet paprika

1 teaspoon ground turmeric

1 teaspoon ground coriander

½ teaspoon ground cumin

½ teaspoon ground ginger

3 pounds boneless lamb shoulder, cut into
 1½-inch pieces

1 cup finely minced onion

2 teaspoons finely minced garlic

1¾ cups chicken broth, preferably homemade
 (see page 434)

¾ cup dry red wine

Zest of 1 lemon, removed in 1 long strip with a sharp
 paring knife if possible (see Note, page 155)

2 cinnamon sticks (each 3 inches long)

1½ cups pitted prunes, halved

1 cup canned chickpeas (garbanzo beans),
 rinsed and drained

4 carrots

Salt and freshly ground black pepper,
 to taste

Juice of ½ lemon

¼ cup coarsely chopped fresh mint leaves

Couscous, for serving

1. Heat the olive oil in a large heavy pot over low heat. Sprinkle in the paprika, turmeric, coriander, cumin, and ginger. Cook, stirring, to mellow the spices, 1 to 2 minutes.

2. Add the lamb to the spice mixture and toss well to coat. Stir in half of the onions and all of the garlic. Add the broth, wine, lemon zest, and cinnamon sticks. Bring to a boil over high heat. Then reduce the heat, partially cover the pot, and simmer for 45 minutes.

3. Add the remaining onions, the prunes, and the chickpeas to the stew and simmer for 15 minutes.

4. While the stew is simmering, peel and halve the carrots lengthwise and cut them into 1-inch lengths. Bring a small pot of salted water to a boil, add the carrots, and cook for 3 minutes. Drain, and set aside.

5. Add the carrots to the stew and cook until the meat is tender, about 15 minutes. Season with salt and pepper.

6. Remove the lemon zest and cinnamon sticks. Just before serving, stir in the lemon juice and chopped mint. Serve in shallow bowls, spooned over couscous.

TAGINE SALOUI

The *tagine saloui* is a shallow earthenware pot in which a tagine is cooked and also served. It has a high conical top, which allows the condensation from the cooking stew to slide easily back into the pot. But it is easy to understand where confusion lies because that luscious, slowly simmered Moroccan stew is also called a *tagine*. There are hundreds of recipes for outstanding tagines using lamb, poultry, vegetables, and dried fruits.

Most Moroccan tagines are made out of glazed terra-cotta. While they are suitable for the oven, they can also be used on the stovetop. Nowadays, with the popularity of ethnic foods, various cookware companies have caught on and are designing their own models—but I do love the old earthenware ones and the romance of the old souks that comes along with them.

PORK MARENGO

SERVES 4 TO 6

the basic flavorings of the classic veal or chicken marengo—tomatoes, white wine, garlic, and orange—blend beautifully with pork, turning the French classic into a luscious new kind of stew. I've added my own touches with brown sugar, which sweetens the tomatoes and makes them less acidic, and mint, not usually found in marengo. It's delicious served over buttered noodles.

2½ pounds boneless pork shoulder,
    cut into 2-inch cubes

Salt and freshly ground black pepper, to taste

2 tablespoons olive oil, or more if needed

2 cups diced onions (¼-inch dice)

1 tablespoon finely minced garlic

1 can (28 ounces) peeled Italian plum tomatoes,
    drained and chopped (about 2 cups)

1 tablespoon dark brown sugar

Zest of 1 orange, removed in 1 long strip with a
    sharp paring knife if possible (see Note)

3 cups chicken broth, preferably homemade
    (see page 434)

1 cup dry white wine

4 carrots

4 tablespoons chopped fresh mint leaves

1. Season the pork generously with salt and pepper.

2. Heat the olive oil in a large heavy pot over medium-high heat. Add the pork in batches and brown it on all sides, about 6 minutes per batch. As the batches are browned, transfer them to a bowl.

3. Reduce the heat under the pot to low, add more oil if needed, and cook the onions and garlic, stirring occasionally, until wilted, about 10 minutes.

4. Add the tomatoes, brown sugar, orange zest, broth, and wine. Return the pork to the pot, and bring to a boil over high heat. Then reduce the heat to medium-low, partially cover the pot, and simmer for 1 hour.

5. While the stew is simmering, peel and halve the carrots lengthwise and cut them into 1-inch lengths. Bring a small pot of salted water to a boil, add the carrots, and cook until they are slightly softened, 3 minutes. Drain, and set aside.

6. After the stew has cooked for 1 hour, stir the carrots and 2 tablespoons of the mint into it. Season it with salt and pepper. Cook, partially covered, until the pork is tender, about 15 minutes more.

7. Remove and discard the orange zest. Sprinkle the remaining 2 tablespoons mint over the stew, and serve.

NOTE: One long strip of orange zest is elegant and easy to remove, but if it ends up breaking into two or more pieces, that is perfectly acceptable.

CHICKEN IN A TOMATO-HONEY JAM

SERVES 6 TO 8

When Laurie and I were at the Maison Arabe in Marrakech, we were served a chicken tagine smothered in a honeyed tomato jam. Rarely do I have a totally new food experience, but this was one. Cooking ripe tomatoes with honey helps to bring out all their sweetness. Of course, this dish must be made with fresh tomatoes. The aromatic spiced gravy from the chicken makes the sauce even yummier as it all comes together.

Note that you will want to prepare the Tomato-Honey Jam at least 2 hours before starting the chicken. It can be prepared up to 2 days in advance and stored in a covered container in the refrigerator. Leftover jam is wonderful spread on toasted peasant bread, and served with Taleggio cheese, ripe figs, and prosciutto.

FOR THE TOMATO-HONEY JAM:

6 pounds ripe plum tomatoes, seeded and
    coarsely chopped

½ cup sugar

¼ cup honey

FOR THE CHICKEN:

2 chickens (each about 3 pounds), quartered,
    wing tips removed, rinsed and patted dry

2 onions, halved lengthwise and slivered

¼ cup olive oil

1 tablespoon finely minced garlic

1 teaspoon ground cumin

1 teaspoon ground cinnamon

¼ teaspoon ground coriander

¼ teaspoon ground ginger

¼ teaspoon crumbled saffron threads
    diluted in ¼ cup hot water

1 cup chicken broth, preferably homemade
    (see page 434)

Salt and freshly ground black pepper, to taste

¼ cup slivered almonds, toasted, or 2 tablespoons
    sesame seeds, toasted, for garnish

1. At least 2 hours before preparing the chicken, make the Tomato-Honey Jam: Combine the tomatoes, sugar, and honey in a heavy saucepan and bring to a boil. Then reduce the heat to medium-low and cook, uncovered, stirring occasionally, until thickened, about 1 hour. Set aside to cool.

2. Preheat the oven to 375°F.

3. Prepare the chicken: Combine the chicken quarters, onions, oil, and garlic in a large bowl. Toss to mix thoroughly.

4. Stir the cumin, cinnamon, coriander, and ginger together in a small bowl. Sprinkle this over the chicken pieces, and toss. Add the diluted saffron mixture, and salt and pepper to taste, and toss again.

5. Arrange the chicken and onions in a single layer in a shallow oven-to-table roasting pan. Do not crowd the chicken; if necessary, use two pans. Pour the chicken broth into the pan. Bake, basting once or twice, until the chicken is golden and cooked through, 1 hour.

6. Top the chicken pieces evenly with the tomato jam, spooning some of the cooking juices over the jam to loosen it up slightly. Sprinkle the toasted almonds over the chicken, and serve. ✿

CHICKEN TAGINE
WITH EGGPLANT, TOMATOES, AND ONIONS

SERVES 6 TO 8

ruce Aidells, founder of Aidells Sausage Company and the author of many books, has created one of the most delicious Moroccan tagines I have ever enjoyed. He uses moist dark chicken meat and a souk's worth of aromatic spices—just the right amount of sweet flavor with a little lemon juice to balance it out. Under a tent or around a table, surrounded by apricot-colored roses and turquoise glass candlesticks, you'll be in heaven with Bruce's fragrant tagine.

6 tablespoons olive oil

3 cups slivered onions

6 large cloves garlic, finely minced

1 tablespoon sweet paprika

1 teaspoon ground turmeric

1 teaspoon ground coriander

1 teaspoon fennel seeds

½ teaspoon ground cumin

½ teaspoon ground ginger

Coarse (kosher) salt and freshly ground black pepper

1 can (28 ounces) whole tomatoes, drained and diced (about 2 cups)

3 tablespoons fresh lemon juice

8 chicken legs, drumsticks and thighs separated, skinned

1 large eggplant, cut into 1-inch cubes (see Note)

2 tablespoons coarsely chopped fresh flat-leaf parsley leaves

⅓ cup slivered blanched almonds, for garnish

1. Heat 2 tablespoons of the olive oil in a large heavy, wide pot over low heat. Add the onions and garlic, cover the pot, and cook, stirring occasionally, until they are softened, 10 to 15 minutes. Sprinkle in the paprika, turmeric, coriander, fennel seeds, cumin, ginger, 1 teaspoon salt, and black pepper to taste. Stir over low heat to mellow the spices, 1 minute.

2. Add the tomatoes, lemon juice, and 1 cup water. Bring to a boil and boil for 2 minutes. Then arrange the chicken pieces in a single layer in the pot, spooning some of the sauce over them. Bring to a boil. Reduce the heat to medium-low, cover, and simmer for 15 minutes.

3. Meanwhile, preheat the oven to 400°F.

4. Carefully turn the chicken pieces over and simmer until the meat is tender, about 20 minutes more.

5. While the chicken is cooking, toss the eggplant with the remaining 4 tablespoons olive oil. Spread it out on in a single layer on a baking sheet, and bake in the oven, tossing it once with a spatula, until it is soft and golden, about 25 minutes.

6. Stir the eggplant and 1 tablespoon of the parsley into the tagine. Season with salt and pepper to taste. Transfer the mixture to a large shallow serving bowl. Sprinkle with the almonds and the remaining 1 tablespoon chopped parsley, and serve.

NOTE: I like that the eggplant in this dish is tossed with oil then baked. The cubes soften nicely and hold their shape better in the final dish. When I'm preparing eggplant for a traditional ratatouille, I like to oven-bake it, too. (And, for a different take on ratatouille—the vegetables are grilled—see page 177.)

RABBIT STEWED IN HOLIDAY SPICES

SERVES 6

My friend Donaldo Soviero, a great Italian chef at restaurants in both Massachusetts and Umbria some years ago, prepared a stunning rabbit stewed in Barbaresco. I have added my touches, very slightly, and I suggest that the stew be served over creamy polenta to appreciate every drop of the luscious sauce.

2 domestic rabbits (each about 2½ pounds),
    each cut into 6 pieces, rinsed and patted dry

1 lemon, halved

2 carrots, cut into ¼-inch dice

2 ribs celery, cut into ½-inch dice

1 onion, cut into ¼-inch dice

2 bay leaves

6 dried juniper berries

2 cups dry red wine (Barbaresco if you're splurging!)

2 tablespoons extra-virgin olive oil, or more if necessary

4 cloves garlic, bruised (see box, page 82)

Salt and freshly ground black pepper, to taste

½ teaspoon ground nutmeg

½ teaspoon ground cloves

½ teaspoon ground cinnamon

1 tablespoon red currant jelly

2 tablespoons chopped fresh flat-leaf parsley leaves,
    for garnish

1. Place the rabbit pieces in a bowl. Squeeze the lemon halves over the rabbit and toss well to coat all the pieces. Add the carrots, celery, onion, bay leaves, juniper berries, and 1 cup of the wine. Cover, and marinate in the refrigerator for 3 hours or overnight.

2. Preheat the oven to 325°F.

3. Heat the olive oil in a large heavy ovenproof pot over low heat. Add the garlic and cook, stirring occasionally, until the cloves are golden brown and the oil has been flavored, about 5 minutes. Remove and reserve the garlic. Raise the heat to medium. Remove the rabbit pieces from the marinade, reserving the vegetables and marinade. Season the rabbit with salt and pepper and add it, in batches, to the pot. Cook until golden, about 6 minutes per side. As they turn golden, transfer the pieces to a bowl.

4. Using a slotted spoon, remove the vegetables from the marinade and add them to the pot, along with the reserved garlic. Reduce the heat to low and cook the vegetables, stirring, until the onion is translucent, about 10 minutes.

5. Sprinkle the nutmeg, cloves, and cinnamon over the vegetables and cook, stirring, for 1 minute. Add the reserved marinade, the remaining 1 cup wine, and the red currant jelly. Bring to a boil. Then reduce the heat to medium, cover the pot, and simmer for 3 minutes.

6. Return the rabbit pieces to the pot and spoon the sauce over them. Cover the pot, transfer it to the oven, and bake, basting occasionally, until the meat is tender, 1 hour and 20 minutes.

7. Remove the pot from the oven and spoon the sauce over the rabbit. Remove the bay leaves and sprinkle with the chopped parsley. Serve immediately. 🌿

TOM VALENTI'S
BRAISED DUCK
IN RED WINE AND TOMATOES

SERVES 6

om is one of my favorite chefs in New York, and this delicious dish is served in his restaurant Ouest, happily just around the corner from my apartment. I use Moulard duck legs in my recipe—they are a perfect match with the red wine, tomatoes, carrots, and touch of vinegar. When you feel the first chill of autumn coming, try this over wide egg noodles or over a rich Lemon-Dill Parsnip Mash (page 336). Or have friends over and cook up the menu suggested on the facing page.

4 plum tomatoes, seeded and cut into
    ¼-inch dice
Coarse (kosher) salt and freshly ground black
    pepper, to taste
6 Moulard duck legs (see Sources, page 439),
    trimmed of as much fat as possible
2 tablespoons olive oil
4 ounces slab bacon, cut into ¼-inch dice
1 onion, cut into ¼-inch dice
2 carrots, cut into ¼-inch dice
2 cups dry red wine
¼ cup cider vinegar
⅓ cup tomato paste
3 tablespoons chopped fresh flat-leaf parsley
    leaves, for garnish

1. Place the tomatoes in a bowl and season them with salt and pepper (do this no more than 30 minutes before cooking).

2. Preheat the oven to 350°F.

3. Season the duck legs with salt and pepper.

4. Heat the olive oil in a large heavy ovenproof pot over medium-low heat. Add the duck legs, in batches, skin side down, and cook until golden, 8 to 10 minutes per side. As they are browned, transfer the duck legs to a plate. Between batches, remove the excess fat from the pot. When done browning, discard all the fat in the pot.

AN AUTUMN GET-TOGETHER

When the air is crisp and summer is definitely only a memory, celebrate the great indoors with this menu of remarkable dishes. If time is a crunch, no need to prepare them all yourself—why not have your friends join in? You braise the duck and assign the other dishes to willing participants. That way, everyone can relax come dinnertime.

ROASTED CARROT GINGER SOUP
PAGE 43

FRISEE AND APPLE SALAD
PAGE 258

TOM VALENTI'S BRAISED DUCK IN RED WINE AND TOMATOES
FACING PAGE

BUTTERNUT BARLEY RISOTTO
PAGE 318

LAURA'S STICKY TOFFEE DATE CAKE
with Crème Fraîche
PAGE 400

5. Add the bacon to the pot and cook over medium-low heat, stirring, to render its fat, about 7 minutes.

Then add the tomatoes, onion, carrots, red wine, and vinegar. Cook, stirring, for 1 minute. Stir in the tomato paste.

6. Return the duck legs to the pot and bring the liquid to a boil. Then cover the pot, transfer it to the oven, and bake until the duck is thoroughly tender, about 1¼ hours.

7. Remove the duck legs from the pot and set them aside on a plate to cool. When they are cool enough to handle, remove the meat from the bones, discarding all skin and fat. Shred the meat into large pieces and place it in a bowl.

8. Use a slotted spoon to remove all the vegetables and bacon from the sauce. Add them to the duck meat.

9. Pour the sauce through a gravy separator to remove all the fat. Mix the defatted sauce with the duck and vegetables, and gently reheat. Season with salt and pepper. Serve garnished with the chopped parsley.

NOTE: You can cook the duck a day ahead. In that case, in Step 9, pour the sauce through a gravy separator as described. Refrigerate the sauce and the duck mixture separately overnight. The next day, remove and discard the layer of fat that has formed on the surface of the sauce. Reheat the duck and vegetables in the sauce, and serve. 🌿

SHELLFISH STEW

SERVES 6

there's nothing more dazzling than a shellfish stew, and this one, a festive combination of clams, mussels, shrimp, and scallops, leads the way. I add fennel and fresh tarragon to flavor the tomato sauce, and a small amount of Pernod to enhance the flavor further. Serve the stew in bowls with garlic-rubbed peasant bread toasts, a rich red Côtes de Provence, and a marvelous cheese selection to follow.

12 littleneck clams, scrubbed

12 mussels, scrubbed (and debearded if necessary)

1 tablespoon cornmeal

¼ cup extra-virgin olive oil

3 onions, halved lengthwise and slivered

1 fennel bulb, trimmed, halved lengthwise, and
    slivered

1 tablespoon finely minced garlic

¼ teaspoon crushed red pepper flakes

1 can (28 ounces) peeled Italian plum tomatoes,
    undrained

2 cups canned tomato sauce

1 cup dry white wine

1 bottle (8 ounces) clam juice

¼ cup Pernod

Salt and freshly ground black pepper, to taste

18 large shrimp, peeled and deveined

12 sea scallops

3 tablespoons chopped fresh tarragon leaves, or
    2 teaspoons crushed dried tarragon

½ cup chopped fresh flat-leaf parsley leaves

6 large slices peasant bread, toasted, brushed with
    oil and rubbed with garlic, for serving

1. Place the clams and mussels in a large bowl of water. Stir in the cornmeal and soak for 1 hour to remove any sand. Drain the shellfish, rinse well, and set aside.

2. Meanwhile, heat the oil in a large heavy pot over medium-low heat. Add the onions, fennel, garlic, and red pepper flakes, cover the pot, and cook, stirring occasionally, until the onions are translucent, about 15 minutes.

3. Pour the tomatoes and their juices into a food processor or blender, and process until pureed.

4. Add the pureed tomatoes, tomato sauce, wine, clam juice, and Pernod to the pot, and bring to a boil. Reduce the heat to medium, season with salt and pepper, and simmer, uncovered, until slightly thickened, about 15 minutes.

5. Add the reserved clams and mussels, cover the pot, and cook until they begin to open, 5 to 6 minutes.

6. Add the shrimp and scallops, and cook, uncovered, until they are cooked through, about 3 minutes. Stir in the tarragon and ¼ cup of the parsley. Adjust the seasonings, adding salt and pepper to taste.

7. Transfer the stew to a serving bowl, discarding any clams or mussels that have not opened, and sprinkle with the remaining ¼ cup of the parsley. Serve with the toasted peasant bread.

RICH VEGETABLE CURRY

SERVES 8

a blend of curry, honey, cinnamon, and mango chutney cooked up with fresh vegetables makes for a richly flavored stew. Slow simmering brings the vegetables to just the right tenderness. I serve this curry over rice in shallow bowls in order to enjoy the sauce to the fullest.

3 tablespoons olive oil

1 onion, cut into ¼-inch dice

1 green bell pepper, stemmed, seeded, and
    cut into ¼-inch dice

1 tablespoon finely minced garlic

2 tablespoons curry powder

1 can (28 ounces) Italian plum tomatoes,
    drained and chopped (about 2 cups)

2 cups vegetable or chicken broth, preferably
    homemade (see pages 434 and 436)

3 tablespoons chopped mango chutney

2 tablespoons honey

1 cinnamon stick (3 inches long)

4 carrots, halved lengthwise and cut into 1-inch pieces

2 Idaho potatoes (each 8 ounces), peeled and
    cut into ½-inch dice

1 head cauliflower, trimmed and cut into small florets

1 can (15 ounces) chickpeas (garbanzo beans),
    rinsed and drained

3 tablespoons dried currants

Salt and freshly ground black pepper, to taste

¼ cup chopped fresh flat-leaf parsley leaves

Cooked white rice, for serving

1. Heat the olive oil in a large heavy pot over low heat. Add the onion, bell pepper, and garlic, and cook, stirring occasionally, until the onion is soft and translucent, about 10 minutes.

2. Sprinkle with the curry powder and cook, stirring, for the flavor to mellow, 1 minute.

3. Add the chopped tomatoes, broth, chutney, honey, cinnamon stick, carrots, potatoes, and cauliflower. Bring to a boil. Then reduce the heat to a simmer and cook, uncovered, until the vegetables are tender, about 20 minutes.

4. Stir in the chickpeas, currants, and salt and pepper, and cook for 5 minutes longer.

5. Just before serving, remove the cinnamon stick and stir in the parsley. Serve over rice in shallow bowls. 🌺

SEVEN-VEGETABLE COUSCOUS

SERVES 6 TO 8

When I traveled to Marrakech, I enjoyed a splendid modern seven-vegetable couscous in the cooking style of the city of Fez, which I wrote about in my *All Around the World Cookbook*. I have since made some changes, yet the seven vegetables remain the same: onions, leeks, zucchini, turnips, carrots, tomatoes, and potatoes.

I add 2 tablespoons of small whole fresh mint leaves just before serving.

6 medium-size leeks (white bulb and 3 inches green)

2 tablespoons distilled white vinegar

3 quarts chicken or vegetable broth, preferably homemade (see pages 434 and 436)

¼ cup olive oil

6 cilantro sprigs, roots and stems crushed

8 cloves garlic, bruised (see box, page 82)

2 cinnamon sticks (each 3 inches long)

2 teaspoons ground cumin

2 teaspoons curry powder

¼ teaspoon crumbled saffron threads

Salt and freshly ground black pepper, to taste

2 medium-size zucchini, ends trimmed

2 medium-size carrots, peeled, halved lengthwise, and cut into 2-inch lengths

3 Idaho potatoes, peeled and cut into quarters

8 ounces small white turnips, peeled and quartered

3 small yellow onions, peeled and halved lengthwise

3 large ripe tomatoes, cored and quartered

1 can (16 ounces) chickpeas (garbanzo beans), drained and rinsed

1 cup pitted prunes, halved

½ cup golden raisins

4 tablespoons chopped fresh cilantro leaves

2 tablespoons small fresh mint leaves, for garnish

8 cups cooked couscous (2⅔ cups dried), for serving

1. Trim the roots from the leeks and cut a 2-inch-long slit through the green leaves. Place the leeks in a bowl and cover with water. Add the vinegar and let soak for 30 minutes to remove any sand.

2. While the leeks are soaking, prepare the seasoned broth: In a large pot, combine the broth, olive oil, cilantro sprigs, garlic, cinnamon sticks, cumin, curry powder, saffron, and salt and pepper to taste. Bring just to a boil. Then reduce the heat and simmer, uncovered, for 30 minutes. Do not let the mixture return to a boil.

3. Meanwhile, using a potato peeler, peel the zucchini lengthwise at intervals to make three or four stripes in the skin. Cut the zucchini into 1½-inch lengths. Set aside.

4. Drain the leeks, rinse them under cold running water, and pat dry. Tie each leek at the top and bottom with thick kitchen string to keep the leaves from separating during cooking.

5. Place the leeks, carrots, potatoes, turnips, and onions in the broth and bring to a boil. Reduce the heat and simmer, uncovered, until the vegetables are tender, 20 minutes.

6. Add the zucchini, tomatoes, chickpeas, prunes, and raisins to the pot. Stir gently so that the vegetables don't break up. Simmer until the vegetables soften and the flavors are blended, 20 minutes.

7. Just before serving, remove and discard the cinnamon sticks and the string around the leeks. Stir in 3 tablespoons of the chopped cilantro. Serve in a large decorative bowl, sprinkled with the remaining 1 tablespoon cilantro and the whole mint leaves. Serve the couscous in a separate serving bowl alongside. ✿

"KEBABS ARE JUST PLAIN FUN."

PICKUP STICKS

I love kebabs. You simply thread skewers—they can be wood or metal—with cubes of meat and vegetables or fruit, set them on a grill, and within minutes you have the perfect main dish (and, occasionally, dessert). What I enjoy most about kebabs is that they're almost a whole meal on a stick with great savory flavor.

And as easy as they are to prepare, they look stylishly tempting on a platter, and are perfect for warm weather. Wait till you try sumptuous minty lamb grilled with a festive array of bell peppers or sweet and sour pork combined with chunks of fresh pineapple. Or how about a hearty helping of Steak and Potatoes on a Stick? Serve it with a Grilled (on a stick) Tomato Bread Salad. Dad just may want to forgo those hamburgers and hot dogs forever!

I haven't forgotten seafood and how good it tastes grilled. Shrimp sprinkled with a powerful spice mixture become easier to grill when loaded onto skewers, and so do the lemony scallops that I serve with a citrus and watercress salad, and the cubes of halibut that work beautifully on a Niçoise salad. End your dinner-on-a-stick with fresh juicy peaches quartered and grilled to serve over creamy vanilla ice cream. Summer meals don't get any better than this.

STEAK AND POTATOES
ON A STICK

SERVES 6

What could be more appealing than steak and potatoes on the grill? Here is a simply delicious way to do the job. Begin your meal with a Stack of Heirloom Tomatoes (page 356) or Tomato Bonanza (page 356) and serve a mountain of corn on the cob on the side—summer produce at its best. If it's winter and you're cooking on an indoor grill, begin your meal with the Caesar Salad on page 257. Roasted Beets with Tangerine Vinaigrette (page 22) makes a wonderful accompaniment, and to pour, choose a robust Châteauneuf-du-Pape. These kebabs call for six 12-inch-long metal skewers.

FOR THE MARINADE:

¼ cup extra-virgin olive oil

⅓ cup balsamic vinegar

2 tablespoons light soy sauce

1 tablespoon Worcestershire sauce

1 tablespoon Dijon mustard

1 tablespoon chopped flat-leaf parsley leaves

Coarsely ground black pepper, to taste

FOR THE KEBABS:

2 pounds sirloin steak, cut into 1½-inch cubes

12 small red-skinned new potatoes
    (about 1 pound)

Vegetable oil, for the grill

2 small red or white onions, peeled and
    quartered, leaving the root ends intact

2 tablespoons chopped fresh flat-leaf parsley leaves,
    for garnish

1. Combine all the marinade ingredients in a measuring cup or a bowl, and set it aside.

2. Place the steak cubes in a separate bowl, add half of the marinade, and toss to coat them well. Let the meat sit at room temperature for 2 hours, or cover and refrigerate for 8 hours, tossing the meat once or twice.

3. Place the potatoes in a saucepan, add cold water to cover, and bring to a boil. Then reduce the heat slightly and cook at a slow boil until tender, about 15 minutes.

4. Drain the potatoes well, place them in a bowl, and add the remaining marinade. Toss, and set the potatoes aside until the steak is ready.

5. Preheat a barbecue grill to high.

6. Thread the meat and vegetables on each of six metal skewers in this order: a beef cube, a potato, a beef cube, an onion quarter, a beef cube, a potato, a beef cube.

7. Oil the grill grate well and arrange the skewers on the grate. Grill, basting with any remaining marinade, for 5 minutes. Turn them over and grill, basting, for another 5 minutes for medium-rare meat.

8. Arrange the skewers on a platter, garnish with the chopped parsley, and serve. ❧

PORK AND PINEAPPLE PICKUP STICKS
WITH SAVORY MINT MAYONNAISE

SERVES 4 TO 6

Pork and pineapple have a natural affinity for each other, and both are served well by some time on the grill. Marinating the pork in a combination of sweet and sour—a dash of wine vinegar, a dab of honey, and cumin for a touch of the exotic—seals the deal on a well-flavored dish.

You'll need ten thin 12-inch metal skewers for these kebabs. If you prefer to use wooden skewers, soak them in water for 2 hours first, to prevent burning.

FOR THE MARINADE:

½ cup dry red wine

⅓ cup red wine vinegar

⅓ cup extra-virgin olive oil

¼ cup dry white wine

2 tablespoons chopped fresh mint leaves

1 tablespoon honey

1 shallot, finely minced

1 teaspoon ground cumin

Salt and freshly ground black pepper,
    to taste

FOR THE KEBABS:

2 pork tenderloins (1¾ pounds total),
    cut into 1-inch cubes

1 ripe pineapple, peeled, cored, and cut into
    1½-inch cubes

Vegetable oil, for the grill

Savory Mint Mayonnaise (recipe follows), for serving

1. Combine all the marinade ingredients in a medium-size bowl. Add the pork cubes and toss to coat them well with the marinade. Cover, and refrigerate for 4 to 6 hours or overnight.

2. Preheat a barbecue grill to high.

3. Thread each skewer, alternating 3 pork cubes with 3 pineapple cubes, beginning with a pork cube and ending with a pineapple cube. (Reserve the marinade.)

4. Oil the grill grate well and arrange the skewers on it. Grill the skewers, brushing them with the marinade, until the meat is cooked through and the pineapple is glazed, 10 minutes in all. (Do not brush with marinade during the last 3 minutes of cooking.)

5. Serve immediately, with the Savory Mint Mayonnaise alongside. 🌿

SAVORY MINT MAYONNAISE

MAKES 1¾ CUPS

Here's a condiment with enough character to hold up to dashing pork on a stick. I'd choose it for a roast pork sandwich any day, and most any lamb dish wouldn't be far behind.

> 1½ cups prepared mayonnaise, such as Hellmann's
> 1 tablespoon extra-virgin olive oil
> ½ teaspoon honey
> ¼ cup minced shallots
> 1 tablespoon drained tiny capers
> Salt and freshly ground black pepper, to taste
> ¼ cup chopped fresh mint leaves

Combine the mayonnaise, olive oil, honey, shallots, capers, and salt and pepper in a small bowl. Stir well, and then gently fold in the mint. Let the mayonnaise rest in the refrigerator, covered, for 1 hour for the flavors to blend. (The Savory Mint Mayonnaise will keep for up to 2 days in the refrigerator.) 🌿

MINTY LAMB KEBABS

SERVES 8

When I was growing up, come Memorial Day, we'd fire up the grill and out would come the kebabs—lamb marinated in bottled Italian salad dressing sharing a skewer with tomatoes, mushrooms, and onions. Not bad, but it's time for something more contemporary. Mint and lamb are natural partners. A fresh mint sauce serves as the base for this marinade, and the grilled kebabs are garnished with a lavish bunch of the herb. If you just can't get enough, pass the mint jelly. These kebabs call for eight 8-inch metal skewers.

FOR THE MINT SAUCE (makes 1 cup):

1 cup finely chopped fresh mint leaves

⅔ cup red wine vinegar

2 tablespoons dark brown sugar

Pinch of salt

¼ cup boiling water

Pinch of freshly ground black pepper

FOR THE KEBABS:

4 pounds boneless leg of lamb, cut into
    1½-inch cubes

2 red bell peppers, stemmed, seeded, and
    cut into 1½-inch pieces

2 orange bell peppers, stemmed, seeded,
    and cut into 1½-inch pieces

2 tablespoons dark brown sugar

3 tablespoons extra-virgin olive oil

Salt and freshly ground black pepper, to taste

Vegetable oil, for the grill

FOR GARNISH AND SERVING:

1 large bunch fresh mint

Bright Green Tabouleh (page 319)

1. Prepare the mint sauce: Place the chopped mint in a small bowl, and pour the vinegar over it. In

---

JULY BIRTHDAY LUNCH

Birthdays are better in the summer. No one feels guilty lingering over a delicious lunch, because the days are longer and there is always lots more time left to get things done—that is, if you really need to. A Merlot or Pinot Noir rounds out the menu.

MINTY LAMB KEBABS
THIS PAGE

GREEK-STYLE LUNCH SALAD
PAGE 259

BRIGHT GREEN TABOULEH
PAGE 319

FRESH APRICOT-ALMOND TART
PAGE 412

---

another small bowl, dissolve the brown sugar and the salt in the boiling water; add this to the mint mixture. Stir in the black pepper. Set the bowl aside for 30 minutes for the flavors to blend.

2. Place the lamb and the bell peppers in a large bowl. Sprinkle the brown sugar over them, and toss lightly. Add the oil, sprinkle with the salt and pepper, and toss to coat the meat well. Pour the mint sauce over the meat and peppers, and stir. Cover the bowl and set it aside for 2 hours at room temperature.

3. Preheat a barbecue grill to high.

4. Thread eight metal skewers with the lamb and peppers, alternating the two and leaving a small space between them.

5. Oil the grill grate well, and arrange the skewers on it. Grill for 4 minutes per side for rare to medium-rare meat. Let the skewers rest off the heat for 5 minutes before serving.

6. Arrange the skewers on a platter, garnish it with the mint, and serve. Pass the Bright Green Tabouleh. ✿

PICKUP THAI-STYLE WINGS

SERVES 4 AS AN APPETIZER

Chicken wings are high up in the popularity poll, and when they're marinated in honey, soy sauce, lime juice, and ginger, they become absolutely irresistible. Because of the amount of honey in this marinade, I bake the skewers instead of grilling them, to prevent burning. If you have any extra baking sauce left, cook it down to thicken it a bit and serve alongside for dipping. Use eight 12-inch metal skewers for these wings.

FOR THE MARINADE:

½ cup light soy sauce

½ cup honey

2 tablespoons finely minced garlic

2 tablespoons finely minced fresh ginger

Juice of 1 lime

FOR THE KEBABS:

16 chicken wings, rinsed and patted dry

1. Combine all the marinade ingredients in a large bowl. Add the chicken wings and toss to coat them well with the marinade. Refrigerate, covered, for 6 hours or overnight, tossing the wings once or twice.

2. Preheat the oven to 375°F.

3. Remove the chicken wings from the marinade, reserving the marinade. Carefully thread 2 chicken

wings on each of eight skewers, pushing the skewer through the drumstick, the middle section, and out the tip of each wing. Arrange the skewers in two 13-x-9-x-2-inch glass or ceramic baking dishes.

4. Pour ½ cup of the reserved marinade over the wings and bake, basting them with more marinade every 10 to 15 minutes, until the wings are cooked through and lacquered a deep golden brown, about 45 minutes. (The frequent basting is well worth it—you'll see.)

5. Arrange the skewers on a platter and serve immediately. 🍂

A LITTLE HELP FROM MY FORK

How best to get a chicken wing off a skewer and into your mouth? Well, you could use your hands for the whole job, but you might have an easier time if you slip the skewer between the tines of a fork and use it to push the wing off. That way if the skewer is still really hot, there's less of a chance of burning your fingers.

BARBECUED SPICED SHRIMP ON A STICK

SERVES 6

If you're looking for that great barbecue taste, look no further. The spices that coat these succulent shrimp are as right on as they come: smoked paprika, cumin, and ancho chile powder all contribute the kick. Thread up twelve 12-inch metal skewers and you're set to go.

FOR THE SPICE MIXTURE:

¼ cup (packed) light brown sugar

1 tablespoon smoked paprika

2 teaspoons ancho chile powder

2 teaspoons chili powder

1½ teaspoons ground cumin

1 teaspoon (kosher) salt

FOR THE KEBABS:

2 pounds large shrimp, peeled and deveined but tails left on, rinsed and patted dry

2 tablespoons olive or canola oil

Vegetable oil, for the grill

4 to 6 scallions (white bulbs and 4 inches green), cut into 1-inch lengths on the diagonal, for garnish

3 limes, halved, for serving

1. Combine all the ingredients for the spice mixture in a small bowl, and stir together well. Set it aside.

2. Preheat a barbecue grill to high.

3. Toss the shrimp with the olive oil in a large bowl. Then thread each shrimp, through the head end, then through the tail end so it forms a "C" shape, on twelve metal skewers, 4 shrimp per skewer.

4. Line two baking sheets with wax or parchment paper. Lay six skewers crosswise on each of the prepared baking sheets. Sprinkle the spice mixture evenly over both sides of the shrimp, patting it in slightly. Let the shrimp rest for 15 minutes to absorb the flavors.

5. Oil the grill grate well and arrange the skewers, in batches if necessary, on the grate. Grill, turning them carefully, until the shrimp are cooked through, 2 to 3 minutes per side.

6. Arrange the skewers on a serving platter, sprinkle the scallions over them, and surround them with the lime halves. Serve hot or at room temperature. ❧

LEMON SCALLOPS
WITH GRAPEFRUIT, ORANGE, AND WATERCRESS SALAD

SERVES 4 AS AN APPETIZER

to retain their pure fresh flavor, it's best to cook sea scallops for about 2 minutes per side—they will be just cooked through, never overdone. A citrus salad offset with peppery watercress makes this dish come alive. It's a delightful beginning for a winter meal, now that we grill indoors and outdoors all year round. You'll need four thin 12-inch metal skewers.

12 large sea scallops

3 tablespoons fresh lemon juice

4 tablespoons extra-virgin olive oil

Coarse (kosher) salt and freshly ground black pepper, to taste

1 ruby grapefruit

2 blood oranges, or 1 small navel orange

Vegetable oil, for the grill

1 or 2 large bunches watercress, rinsed and patted dry, tough stems removed

2 tablespoons chopped fresh flat-leaf parsley leaves, for garnish

1. Preheat a barbecue grill to high.

2. While the grill is heating, place the scallops in a

bowl and add the lemon juice, 2 tablespoons of the olive oil, and the salt and pepper. Toss, and let rest for 20 minutes at room temperature.

3. While the scallops are marinating, cut the skin and the white pith off the grapefruit and oranges. Using a small sharp knife, cut out the segments, holding the fruit over a bowl to catch the juices. Place the segments in a second bowl. Squeeze the membranes over the juice bowl to extract any extra juice. Season the juice with salt and pepper to taste, and then whisk in the remaining 2 tablespoons olive oil. Set both bowls aside.

4. Thread 3 scallops on each of four skewers, leaving a little space between them for even cooking.

5. Oil the grill grate well and arrange the skewers on the grate. Grill until the scallops are just cooked through, 2 minutes per side.

6. Divide the watercress among four large salad plates. Drizzle it lightly with the citrus dressing, and

then arrange the grapefruit and orange segments on top. Place 3 grilled scallops in the center of each plate. Garnish with the parsley, and serve.

SUMMER SUNDAY LUNCH

Stretch the weekend out with one more delicious meal before the car is packed up and everyone heads back to the work week ahead. A glass of Sauvignon Blanc from New Zealand toasts the good times past and ahead.

WHITE GAZPACHO
PAGE 34

LEMON SCALLOPS
FACING PAGE

WHEAT BERRY SALAD WITH FRUITS
PAGE 317

SINFUL CHOCOLATE TART
PAGE 386

HALIBUT NIÇOISE
ON A STICK

SERVES 6

I adore Niçoise salads and was recently served a totally original version in Nice: tossed on a bed of frisée and radicchio, it included green bell peppers, radishes, scallions, olives, and canned tuna. There were no potatoes, no string beans, no tomatoes—yet it was absolutely delicious. I'm taking it a step further here and grilling marinated halibut kebabs, in place of the tuna, to accompany the salad. The result: stunning. You'll need six metal skewers, 12 to 18 inches long, for the halibut.

FOR THE KEBABS:

⅓ cup extra-virgin olive oil

¼ cup fresh lemon juice

1 tablespoon red wine vinegar

2 tablespoons pressed garlic

Coarse (kosher) salt and freshly ground
     black pepper, to taste

4 halibut steaks (about 1½ pounds total),
     cut 1 inch thick, skin removed, each cut
     into 6 pieces

30 fresh bay leaves (available in the produce
     department of well-stocked supermarkets) or
     thin lemon wedges

FOR THE SALAD:

1 head frisée lettuce, tough outer leaves
     discarded

2 heads Bibb lettuce, tough outer leaves discarded

1 head radicchio, outer leaves discarded

Salt and freshly ground black pepper, to taste

¼ cup Red Wine Vinaigrette (page 23)

3 radishes, thinly sliced

2 inner ribs celery, thinly sliced

⅓ cup Niçoise olives

1 green bell pepper, stemmed, seeded, and
     cut into thin rings (you'll need about
     6 rings)

6 scallions (white bulbs and 3 inches green),
     halved crosswise on the diagonal

8 anchovies, rinsed and patted dry

4 hard-cooked eggs, halved lengthwise,
     for garnish

2 tablespoons chopped fresh flat-leaf parsley
     leaves, for garnish

Vegetable oil, for the grill

1. Prepare the kebabs: Combine the oil, lemon juice, vinegar, garlic, and salt and pepper in a large bowl. Stir together well. Add the halibut pieces and toss well to coat them with the marinade. Cover the bowl and refrigerate for 30 minutes.

2. Preheat a barbecue grill to medium-high, or preheat the broiler.

3. While the grill is heating, prepare the skewers and the salad: Thread each of six skewers with 4 pieces of the halibut, alternating with 5 bay leaves (start with a bay leaf and end with a bay leaf). Leave a little bit of space around each piece of fish. Set the skewers aside, reserving any remaining marinade.

4. Separate the frisée, Bibb, and radicchio leaves and rinse them under cold water. Drain, and thoroughly pat them dry. Just before grilling the fish, tear the salad greens into large pieces and place them in a large bowl and season them with salt and pepper. Add the vinaigrette and toss very lightly. Arrange the greens on a large platter. Sprinkle the radishes, celery, and olives over the greens. Lay the bell pepper rings, scallions, and anchovies over the top. Arrange the hard-cooked eggs decoratively around the salad, and sprinkle with the parsley.

5. Oil the grill grate well and arrange the skewers on it, or on an oiled rack in a broiler pan. Grill, brushing with any extra marinade, until the fish is cooked through, 6 to 8 minutes per side.

6. Arrange the skewers on a platter and serve immediately, with the salad.

RATATOUILLE ON THE GRILL

SERVES 8

While ratatouille is native to the South of France, its popularity has certainly spread. In this recipe, the vegetables are grilled, giving them an even greater depth of flavor that is complemented by a rich marinade of extra-virgin olive oil and vibrant rosemary. You will need six to eight 12-inch metal or wooden skewers for the ratatouille. If you choose wooden skewers, soak them in water for 2 hours before using them or see the box on page 170.

FOR THE MARINADE:

¼ cup red wine vinegar

¼ cup extra-virgin olive oil

2 teaspoons Dijon mustard

1 tablespoon finely minced garlic

1 tablespoon finely chopped fresh
    rosemary leaves

Salt and freshly ground black pepper, to taste

FOR THE RATATOUILLE:

1 Japanese (long, thin) eggplant, halved lengthwise
    and cut crosswise into 1-inch pieces

2 red bell peppers, stemmed, seeded, and cut into
    1½-inch pieces

1 zucchini, halved lengthwise and cut crosswise into
    ½-inch pieces

1 yellow summer squash, halved lengthwise and cut
    crosswise into ½-inch pieces

4 ripe plum tomatoes, halved crosswise

2 small red onions, quartered

Vegetable oil, for the grill

Salt and freshly ground black pepper, to taste

¼ cup chopped fresh flat-leaf parsley leaves

1. Combine all the marinade ingredients in a large bowl, and stir well. Add the eggplant, bell peppers, zucchini, yellow squash, tomatoes, and onions. Season with salt and pepper, and toss well. Let the mixture rest at room temperature, tossing it occasionally, for 3 hours.

2. Preheat a barbecue grill to high.

3. Thread the vegetables, one type per skewer, onto the skewers, leaving ½ inch between the pieces. Reserve the marinade in the bowl.

4. Oil the grill grate well and arrange the skewers on the grate. Grill, turning them carefully, for 3 to 5 minutes on each side. Watch them carefully: the vegetables cook at slightly different times, with the tomatoes cooking the fastest.

5. Slide the hot vegetables off the skewers into the bowl containing the reserved marinade. Let them cool slightly. Then adjust the salt and pepper, toss with the parsley, and serve.

GRILLED TOMATO BREAD SALAD

SERVES 6

Lately some terrific tomato bread salads—*panzanella* in Italian—have appeared in restaurants all around the country. Whether it's the availability of stunning heirlooms that has brought the tomato front and center or simply the irresistible taste of those summer-fresh orbs, I can't say. Any way you slice them, tomato bread salads are inventive and fun. This one is grilled on a stick. Once the tomatoes and bread cubes are grilled, toss them up with fresh cucumbers, oil, vinegar, and basil. It has the best of both summer worlds: the grill and the garden. You'll need eight 12-inch metal skewers.

4 cups cubed French or peasant bread
    (1-inch cubes)
6 tablespoons extra-virgin olive oil, or
    more if desired
1 teaspoon dried thyme leaves
Salt and freshly ground black pepper, to taste
3 red onions, cut into ½-inch-thick slices
8 ripe plum tomatoes
2 cucumbers, peeled, halved lengthwise, seeded,
    and cut into 1-inch pieces (about 2 cups)
½ cup fresh basil leaves, slivered
2 tablespoons red wine vinegar

1. Preheat a barbecue grill to high.

2. Place the bread cubes in a bowl and drizzle 2 tablespoons of the olive oil over them. Sprinkle with the thyme, add salt and pepper to taste, and toss well. Thread the bread on six skewers, leaving some space between the cubes. Set the skewers aside.

3. Brush 1 tablespoon of the remaining olive oil over both sides of the onion slices, and grill the onions directly on the grill grate until they have some light grill marks and are softened, about 5 minutes per side. Set the onion slices aside.

4. Place 4 plum tomatoes on each of two metal skewers and brush them lightly with 1 tablespoon of the oil. Grill, turning the skewers, until the tomatoes have softened and have light grill marks, about 5 minutes total. Slide the tomatoes off the skewers onto a plate and set it aside.

5. Grill the skewered bread cubes until they are nicely toasted, about 1½ minutes per side (grill on all four sides). Slide the bread cubes into a separate bowl.

6. Cut the reserved grilled onion slices into quarters and add them to the bread.

7. Using a serrated knife, cut the grilled tomatoes into quarters and add them to the bread. Add the cucumbers and the basil. Drizzle the remaining 2 tablespoons olive oil over the vegetables, adding more if desired, and then drizzle the vinegar over them. Toss well. Taste, and adjust the seasonings if needed. Serve immediately. ❧

GRILLED VANILLA PEACHES ON A STICK

SERVES 4

When ripe peaches are cooking on the grill, their natural sugars caramelize, making them especially luscious. Coax even more goodness out of them with a dab of butter and a sprinkling of sugar. These are sublime when served over vanilla ice cream. Just serving the peaches, minus the ice cream? Then halve them instead of quartering them. Either way, use four 12-inch metal skewers.

4 tablespoons (½ stick) unsalted butter

½ teaspoon pure vanilla extract

Vegetable oil, for the grill

4 ripe peaches, halved, pitted, and quartered
    (do not peel them)

1 tablespoon sugar

1 bunch fresh mint, for garnish

Vanilla ice cream, for serving

1. Preheat a barbecue grill to medium-high.

2. Melt the butter in a small saucepan over low heat. Remove the pan from the heat and stir in the vanilla.

3. Oil the grill grate well. Thread 4 peach quarters on each of four skewers. Place the skewers on a baking sheet, and brush the cut sides of the peaches with the vanilla butter. Sprinkle them with the sugar.

4. Arrange the skewers so the fruit is cut side down on the grill grate. Grill, turning the skewers, for 4 to 5 minutes total.

5. Slide the peaches off the skewers onto a small serving platter, and garnish it with the mint. Fill individual bowls with vanilla ice cream, and top each serving with some of the hot grilled peaches. ❧

"WHEN COOKING FISH, KEEP IT SIMPLE."

BIG FISH

Fish has finally won over the American palate and we're eating it more than ever. We've progressed from that thin, paprika-ed, and over-broiled piece of fish of years ago to some of the best fish cooking in the world. Many varieties of fish are available in our markets—and we are serving them in aromatic broths, on a bed of Provençal vegetables, and over a hash of fresh heirloom tomatoes.

If you're still afraid to cook fish—don't be. If you choose your fish well (make sure it's fresh or just flash frozen) and don't overdo the preparation, it's easy. I use high temperature methods to cook fish quickly and retain the moisture, and frequently flavor them with easy marinades of citrus juice, olive oil, and seasonings—all modern and delicious.

Not all the fish in these recipes are big fish, but they all deliver big flavor. There's Wild Striped Bass with Tomatoes & Roasted Corn, the epitome of summer flavors; broiled Red Snapper with Citrus Salsa, simple, classic, and fast; and Glazed Salmon Teriyaki, the reinvention of a tired standard.

Again: Remember when selecting, always go for the freshest. With this in mind, you'll find a new excitement in preparing and eating fish.

ANDREW ENGLE'S MONTAUK
WILD STRIPED BASS
WITH TOMATOES & ROASTED CORN

SERVES 4

this dish was created by my friend Andrew Engle, chef of The Laundry in East Hampton, on New York's Long Island. With all of the spectacular heirloom tomatoes available in the summer, and with Andrew's way with fish, this is the choice for a dinner party. Your friends will go wild!

FOR THE TOMATO SALAD:

2 pounds assorted ripe tomatoes (heirloom if
    available, or a combination of plum, cherry,
    and medium-size tomatoes)

3 ears corn, grilled or broiled (see Note), kernels
    stripped off the cobs

1 small red onion, halved lengthwise and slivered

3 tablespoons coarsely chopped fresh flat-leaf
    parsley leaves

3 tablespoons coarsely chopped fresh basil leaves

Grated zest of 1 lemon

¼ cup extra-virgin olive oil

2½ tablespoons fresh lemon juice

Freshly ground black pepper, to taste

FOR THE FISH:

3 tablespoons butter, at room temperature

4 striped bass fillets (each 6 ounces)

Salt and freshly ground black pepper, to taste

2 tablespoons olive oil

½ lemon, for squeezing

2 tablespoons chopped fresh flat-leaf parsley leaves,
    for garnish

1. Prepare the tomato salad: Cut the tomatoes into different shapes—thin wedges, halves, and dice—and place them in a large bowl. Add the corn kernels, onion, parsley, basil, lemon zest, olive oil, and lemon juice. Season with black pepper, and set aside.

2. Rub the butter over the skin side of the fish. Season both sides with salt and pepper. Heat the olive oil in a nonstick skillet over medium heat. Add the fish, skin side down, and sauté until golden brown, about 6 minutes. Carefully turn the fillets over, and cook the other side, 3 to 4 minutes.

3. Divide the tomato salad evenly among four dinner plates, and place a fish fillet on top of each serving. Drizzle with a little lemon juice, garnish with the chopped parsley, and serve immediately.

NOTE: To grill or broil corn, first heat a barbecue grill or the broiler to high heat. If using the broiler, set a rack 3 inches from the heat source. While the grill or broiler is heating, bring a large pot of salted water to a boil. Add the ears of corn and cook for

2 minutes. Remove the corn and dry the ears with a towel. Then oil the grill grate well, or oil the rack in a broiler pan, and brush some olive oil over the ears of corn. Arrange the corn on the grate or rack and grill or broil, turning the ears, until they have nice grill marks, about 3 minutes. 🌿

GINGER-LIME COD
IN A BOWL

SERVES 6

Comfort food comes in many guises. Inspired by the inventive chicken noodle soups of Indonesia, here succulent codfish is served alongside thin noodles and vegetables in a hot broth. Arrange the ingredients decoratively in the serving bowls to show off your creativity.

FOR THE FISH:

2 cups chicken broth, preferably homemade
    (see page 434)
4 sprigs cilantro, lightly crushed
4 large sprigs flat-leaf parsley
4 cloves garlic, crushed
1 piece (1 inch) fresh ginger, sliced and
    crushed
½ teaspoon salt
1½ pounds cod fillet, cut crosswise into six 4-ounce
    pieces (try to keep the pieces similarly sized by
    trimming off the thin area on the bottom of
    each piece)

FOR THE SERVING BROTH:

2 tablespoons olive oil
2 medium-size shallots, minced
2 tablespoons minced garlic

2 tablespoons minced fresh ginger
6 cups chicken broth, preferably homemade
    (see page 434)
2 cinnamon sticks (each 3 inches long)
Salt and freshly ground black pepper,
    to taste

FOR FINISHING THE DISH:

12 ounces angel-hair pasta
1 head broccoli (about 1½ pounds), cut into
    small florets
2 ripe tomatoes, each seeded and cut into
    8 pieces
4 scallions (white bulbs and 3 inches green),
    thinly sliced on the diagonal, for garnish
6 lime slices, for garnish
4 tablespoons thinly sliced fresh basil or
    flat-leaf parsley leaves, for garnish

COOL SUMMER EVE DINNER

When the heat of August has cooled off to a light September chill, comfort your friends with a slightly Asian-themed dinner. Accompany the meal with a dry Riesling or a Gewurztraminer.

1. Prepare the fish: Combine the chicken broth, cilantro, parsley, garlic, ginger, salt, and 2 cups water in a large skillet. Bring to a boil. Then reduce the heat to a simmer, add the fish, and simmer until the fish is cooked through, about 7 minutes.

Using a slotted spatula, gently transfer the fish to a plate; set it aside. Discard the cooking broth and seasonings.

2. Prepare the serving broth: Heat the olive oil in a heavy saucepan over medium-low heat. Add the shallots, garlic, and ginger and cook, stirring, until softened, 3 to 4 minutes. Add the broth and the cinnamon sticks, partially cover the pan, and cook for 10 minutes. Remove the pan from the heat. Season the broth with salt and pepper. Let it steep, covered, for 15 minutes. Then strain the broth into another saucepan and set it aside until serving time.

3. About 15 minutes before serving time, bring a large pot of salted water to a boil, add the pasta, and cook according to the package directions. Drain, and set it aside.

4. While the pasta is cooking, bring a saucepan of water to a boil, add the broccoli florets, and blanch them lightly, 2 to 3 minutes. Drain the broccoli and set it aside.

5. To serve, reheat the serving broth. Arrange the cod, pasta, tomatoes, and broccoli in a pinwheel fashion in each of six shallow soup or pasta bowls. Top each serving with a cup of the hot broth, and sprinkle the scallions on top. Place a lime slice in the center of each bowl, garnish each with the basil, and serve immediately. ❧

HALIBUT
ON A BED OF PROVENÇAL VEGETABLES

SERVES 4

The tastes and colors of Provence come through in this sublime fish dish. The robust flavors can support a wine with some body—I would serve an excellent Provençal Bandol. Afterward, offer a selection of regional cheeses along with some ripe figs, melon, and cherries.

4 tablespoons extra-virgin olive oil

1 cup coarsely chopped onion

1 tablespoon finely minced garlic

1½ pounds zucchini (about 4 medium), halved
    lengthwise and cut into ½-inch pieces

1½ pounds ripe tomatoes (about 4 medium),
    cut into ½-inch pieces

4 boneless halibut steaks (each 6 to 8 ounces),
    cut 1½ inches thick

Juice of ½ lemon

Salt and freshly ground black pepper, to taste

1 tablespoon chopped fresh thyme leaves

½ cup torn fresh basil leaves

2 tablespoons chopped fresh flat-leaf
    parsley leaves, for garnish

1. Heat 3 tablespoons of the oil in a heavy pot over low heat. Add the onion and cook, stirring, until almost softened, 7 minutes. Add the garlic and cook for another 3 minutes.

2. Add the zucchini and tomatoes, raise the heat to medium, and cook, partially covered, for 10 minutes.

Remove the cover and cook for another 15 minutes to reduce the liquid.

3. Meanwhile, position a rack in the center of the oven, and preheat the oven to 400°F.

4. While the vegetables are cooking, place the fish steaks in a shallow bowl, add the remaining 1 tablespoon olive oil and the lemon juice, and turn to coat the fish. Season with salt and pepper. Let the fish rest in the dressing while the vegetables finish cooking.

5. Add the thyme and basil to the vegetables. Season them with salt and pepper. Transfer the vegetables to a 13-x-9-x-2-inch oven-to-table baking dish. Arrange the fish on top of the vegetables, and spoon some of the vegetables over the fish. Bake in the oven until the fish is cooked through and flakes easily with a fork, about 10 minutes.

6. Remove the baking dish from the oven, sprinkle with the parsley, and serve immediately. 🐟

SKILLET-SEARED SALMON
ON FRESH TOMATO HASH

SERVES 4

Seared salmon on a bed of uncooked ripe tomatoes is a smashing combination, blending the sweet flavors of both foods. The hot and cold enhance each other while the scallions, herbs, and lime juice pull it all together.

FOR THE TOMATO HASH:

2 pounds assorted ripe tomatoes,
    a combination of cherry, grape,
    pear, plum, and vine
5 scallions, (white bulbs and 3 inches green),
    thinly sliced on the diagonal
¼ cup whole flat-leaf parsley leaves
3 tablespoons extra-virgin olive oil
3 tablespoons torn fresh basil leaves
Freshly ground black pepper, to taste

FOR THE MARINADE AND SALMON:

2 tablespoons fresh lime juice
2 tablespoons extra-virgin olive oil
1 teaspoon finely chopped garlic
Salt and freshly ground black pepper, to taste
4 center-cut salmon fillets (each about 6 ounces),
    skin on

FOR FINISHING THE DISH:

2 tablespoons extra-virgin olive oil
2 scallions (white bulbs and 3 inches green),
    sliced on the diagonal, for garnish
2 tablespoons chopped fresh flat-leaf parsley leaves,
    for garnish
1 lime, quartered, for garnish

1. Prepare the tomato hash: Cut the tomatoes up in different shapes—thin wedges, halves, and dice—so that they resemble a hash. Combine them in a bowl and add all the remaining hash ingredients. Set it aside.

2. Prepare the marinade: Combine the lime juice, olive oil, garlic, and salt and pepper in a shallow bowl. Add the salmon, coat them well, and let sit for 15 minutes.

3. Heat the 2 tablespoons olive oil in a large, heavy nonstick skillet over medium heat. Scrape the marinade off the salmon and place the fillets in the hot skillet, skin side down (do this in batches if necessary). Raise the heat to medium-high and cook for 2 to 3 minutes, shaking the pan and lifting the salmon with a spatula to loosen it.

4. Reduce the heat to medium, cover the pan, and cook, shaking the pan occasionally, until the salmon is cooked through, 3 to 4 minutes. The salmon skin should be crisp and browned; the flesh should be medium-rare.

5. Divide the tomato hash among four dinner plates. Arrange a salmon fillet on each serving of hash, and sprinkle with the scallions and the chopped parsley. Place a lime quarter on each plate, and serve.

GLAZED
SALMON TERIYAKI

SERVES 4

For many, teriyaki steak, salmon, or chicken once defined Japanese cooking. Now our repertoire of Japanese dishes has expanded so greatly that teriyaki feels dated and less exciting. It shouldn't. This glazed salmon, prepared with a homemade teriyaki sauce, will remind you just how good that old friend is. And those memories will brighten even further when the salmon teriyaki is matched with fluffy Wasabi Mashed Potatoes. Either hot or cold sake suits this meal.

4 center-cut salmon fillets (each about 8 ounces)
¾ cup light soy sauce
6 tablespoons (packed) dark brown sugar
6 tablespoons dry sherry or Madeira
3 tablespoons olive oil
1½ tablespoons finely minced garlic
1½ tablespoons finely minced fresh ginger
3 scallions (white bulbs and 3 inches green),
    thinly sliced on the diagonal, for garnish
Wasabi Mashed Potatoes (page 330), for serving

1. Place the salmon fillets in a shallow bowl.

2. Combine the soy sauce, brown sugar, sherry, olive oil, garlic, and ginger in a blender or a food processor, and process until well blended. Pour the marinade over the salmon, coating it well, and marinate, loosely covered, at room temperature for 1 hour.

3. Preheat the oven to 450°F. Lightly oil a baking dish.

4. Remove the salmon fillets from the marinade and arrange them, skin side down, in the baking dish.

5. Pour the marinade into a small saucepan and bring it to a boil. Reduce the heat to medium and simmer until the marinade is slightly thickened, 5 to 8 minutes. Spoon about 1 generous tablespoon over each fillet, transfer the baking dish to the oven, and bake for 8 to 10 minutes for medium-rare fish.

6. Garnish the fish with the sliced scallions. Serve with the Wasabi Mashed Potatoes, passing any extra warmed marinade to spoon on top.

ROASTED
SEA BREAM

SERVES 2

O

I first tasted sea bream at Moro, a trendy Moorish-inspired restaurant in London, and never forgot how much I loved it. This fish, with its firm white flesh, is moist and made for roasting. The results are succulent and would be marvelous served along with the Frisée and Apple Salad (page 258). If you can't find sea bream, substitute red snapper.

2 whole sea breams (each about 1 pound),
    cleaned and skinned (see Notes)

2 bay leaves

2 tablespoons extra-virgin olive oil

2 tablespoons fresh lemon juice

Maldon (flaky) sea salt (see Note, page 66),
    to taste

Freshly ground black pepper, to taste

¼ teaspoon sweet smoked paprika
    (see Notes)

2 tablespoons chopped fresh flat-leaf parsley leaves,
    for garnish

2 scallions (white bulbs and 3 inches green),
    thinly sliced, for garnish

1. Arrange the fish in a 13-x-9-x-2-inch baking dish. Place a bay leaf in the cavity of each fish. Drizzle the olive oil and lemon juice over the fish, and then turn the fish to coat it well. Sprinkle each side with sea salt and black pepper. Dust the tops with the paprika. Let rest for 30 minutes at room temperature.

2. Meanwhile, position a rack in the center of the oven and preheat the oven to 425°F.

3. Place the baking dish in the oven and roast the fish until it is cooked through and the flesh flakes easily with a fork, 13 to 15 minutes.

4. Serve each person a whole fish, garnished with the parsley and scallions.

NOTES:

✦ Have the fishmonger remove the skin from the fish, from just behind the head just to the tail, on both sides.

✦ Smoked paprika is a popular ingredient in Spanish dishes. The sweet variety is readily available in specialty food markets and some larger supermarkets. Look for Pimentón "El Angel," a popular brand. If you can't find it, use a good regular sweet paprika.

GREY SOLE
WITH GREMOLATA BUTTER

SERVES 4

there is something inherently old-world, yet so classy, about a perfectly cooked fillet of grey sole. I've tweaked the butter with gremolata flavors—lemon zest, parsley, garlic—adding a little punch. Whether it's the butter or the broiling that brings out the sweet flavors of this delicate flatfish is anyone's guess—probably a little of each. But I wouldn't pass this up for anything—it's marvelous.

FOR THE GREMOLATA BUTTER:

6 tablespoons (¾ stick) unsalted butter,
    at room temperature
Finely grated zest of 1 large lemon
2 tablespoons chopped fresh flat-leaf parsley leaves
1 tablespoon finely minced garlic
Salt and freshly ground black pepper, to taste

FOR THE SOLE:

4 fillets grey sole (each 6 ounces)

FOR SERVING:

Fresh clover sprouts or radish sprouts
    (see Note, page 242)
1 lemon, quartered

1. Prepare the Gremolata Butter: Combine all the ingredients in a small bowl, and stir together well. Set the bowl aside.

2. Position a rack 4 inches from the heat source, and preheat the broiler.

3. Prepare the fish: Line two baking sheets with aluminum foil, and oil them lightly. Arrange 2 sole fillets on each baking sheet. Pat the tops dry with paper towels. Using a kitchen knife, carefully spread 1 tablespoon of the Gremolata Butter over each fillet.

4. Broil until the fish is lightly browned on top and flakes easily when tested with a fork, about 4 minutes. Be careful not to overcook the fish.

5. Using a large metal spatula, transfer the fillets to four dinner plates. Sprinkle some sprouts over each serving, place a lemon wedge alongside, and serve immediately.

RED SNAPPER
WITH CITRUS SALSA

SERVES 6

Citrus is refreshing and delightful when combined with basil atop a delicate broiled red snapper. The honey and jalapeño are ideal foils for the pucker of the citrus. What a way to eat—fast and fresh!

FOR THE SALSA:

1 ruby red grapefruit

2 navel oranges

1 tablespoon extra-virgin olive oil

1 tablespoon honey

1 teaspoon finely minced green
    jalapeño pepper

Salt and freshly ground black pepper, to taste

6 fresh basil leaves, slivered

FOR THE FISH:

Vegetable oil, for the broiler pan

6 red snapper fillets (each about 6 ounces)

2 tablespoons olive oil

2 tablespoons fresh lime juice

Salt and freshly ground black pepper,
    to taste

6 basil sprigs, for garnish

1. Prepare the salsa: Cut a thin slice off the top and bottom of the grapefruit and the oranges. With the fruit standing on a flat end, carefully slice off the remaining peel, from top to bottom, taking as much of the white pith as possible. Carefully slice between the membranes to section the fruit. Place the sections and any juice in a bowl, and then squeeze the grapefruit and orange halves over the bowl to extract any remaining juice. Fold in the remaining salsa ingredients. Set it aside.

2. Position a rack 4 inches from the heat source and preheat the broiler. Lightly oil a broiler pan with vegetable oil.

3. Place the fish, flesh side up, in the broiler pan, and brush the fillets with the olive oil. Drizzle the lime juice over them, and season with salt and pepper. Broil until the fish is cooked through and flakes easily when tested with a fork, 7 to 8 minutes.

4. Place a snapper fillet in the center of each dinner plate, and spoon the salsa over them. Garnish each portion with a basil sprig, and serve immediately. ❧

SWORDFISH CLUB SANDWICH

SERVES 6

When I was in Hawaii I was served a swordfish club for lunch—and I never forgot it. Here is my version, not far from the one I enjoyed so much. Now that chips are so varied in types and flavors, choose your favorite and serve them in a napkin-lined basket alongside. It's a delightful summer lunch!

18 slices bacon

6 thin swordfish fillets (each 6 ounces), skin removed

¼ cup chicken broth, preferably homemade
(see page 434)

¼ cup dry white wine

6 tablespoons extra-virgin olive oil, plus more
if needed

1 large clove garlic, bruised (see box, page 82)

Salt and freshly ground black pepper, to taste

12 slices whole-grain or peasant bread,
lightly toasted

About ½ cup prepared mayonnaise, such as
Hellmann's

6 slices large ripe tomato, cut ¼ inch thick

2 bunches arugula (about 12 ounces total),
tough stems removed, washed and patted dry

1. Place as many slices of bacon as will fit in a large skillet over medium heat, and cook until crisp. Transfer the bacon to a paper-towel-lined baking sheet to drain. Pour off the fat, and repeat with the remaining bacon slices. Set the baking sheet aside.

2. Place the swordfish fillets between two pieces of wax paper, and use the back of a metal spatula to flatten them until they are ½ inch thick.

3. Combine the broth, wine, 4 tablespoons of the olive oil, garlic, and salt and pepper in a large bowl. Add the swordfish fillets and coat them well with the marinade. Let rest for 15 minutes.

4. Heat the remaining 2 tablespoons olive oil in a large nonstick skillet over medium-low heat. Add the fish, in batches if necessary, and cook until seared, 1½ minutes per side. If necessary, add an extra tablespoon of oil between batches. Transfer the swordfish to a plate.

5. To assemble the sandwiches, spread one side of each piece of toast with the mayonnaise. Lay a swordfish fillet on 6 of the toasts. Top each fillet with 3 bacon slices. Cover with a tomato slice and a few arugula leaves. Cover each sandwich with the top slice of toast and press down slightly. Cut them in half, and serve immediately. ♣

SEARED TUNA STEAKS
WITH A PEPPERCORN CRUST

SERVES 6

fresh tuna, like all fish, can be a little tricky to cook. I watch it like a hawk while I am searing it. When ready, the medium-rare meat should have an airbrushed look—for me, that's not deep red but more of a pinkish color. If you prefer more well-done fish, cook it a minute more per side. A dollop of the orange mayonnaise adds a robust flavor. (Fresh salsa is also an excellent topper.)

6 tuna steaks (each 6 to 8 ounces),
    cut 1 inch thick
2 tablespoons extra-virgin olive oil
2 tablespoons fresh lemon juice
Salt and freshly ground black pepper,
    to taste
3 to 4 tablespoons whole black peppercorns
Roasted Garlic-Orange Mayonnaise
    (recipe follows), for serving

1. Place the tuna in a shallow bowl. Add the oil, lemon juice, and salt and ground pepper. Turn the tuna to coat it well. Let it rest for 15 minutes, turning it once more.

2. Place the peppercorns in a double thickness of plastic bags. Using the handle of a heavy chef's knife or the blade of a cleaver, pound the peppercorns to crush them coarsely. Place the crushed peppercorns in a shallow bowl.

3. When you are ready to cook the tuna, heat a nonstick skillet over medium heat. Dip the edges (not the flat top and bottom) of the tuna steaks into the crushed peppercorns.

4. Sear the tuna steaks in the skillet, in batches if necessary, for 4 minutes per side for medium-rare fish. (If necessary to prevent sticking, add 2 to 3 tablespoons of the marinade to the skillet.)

5. Serve with the Roasted Garlic-Orange Mayonnaise alongside. ❧

ROASTED GARLIC-ORANGE MAYONNAISE

MAKES ABOUT 1 CUP

this seemingly simple mayonnaise gets its rich flavors from two cooking methods that take a little extra time and care: reducing some fresh orange juice to a thick syrup, and roasting garlic to add a sweet flavor. The mayonnaise is delightful served with pork, game, steak, as well as a variety of grilled fish.

1 cup fresh orange juice

1 large head garlic, outer papery layers removed

1 cup prepared mayonnaise, such as Hellmann's

Salt and freshly ground black pepper,
    to taste

1. Place the orange juice in a small, heavy saucepan and bring it to a boil. Reduce the heat to medium and simmer until the juice is thick and syrupy, watching it carefully so it does not burn, 20 to 25 minutes. Cool to room temperature and refrigerate until ready to use (it will keep for 1 day).

2. Preheat the oven to 350°F.

3. Cut the top ¼ inch off the top of the head of garlic, and wrap the head in aluminum foil. Bake until the cloves are very soft, about 1¼ hours.

4. Remove the garlic from the oven and let it cool slightly. Then squeeze the soft garlic pulp out of the cloves into a bowl. Add 2 to 3 tablespoons of the reduced orange juice, and stir well. Fold in the mayonnaise. Season with salt and pepper. Taste, and adjust the flavorings as needed.

5. Transfer the mayonnaise to a container, cover, and refrigerate for at least 6 hours for the flavors to blend (it will hold for as long as 2 days).

"THERE'S NOTHING MORE SPECTACULAR THAN LOTS OF LOBSTERS."

LOBSTER ANYTIME

Lobster, whether steamed, broiled, or on a roll, makes anytime feel like the very best special occasion. Its sweet, succulent flavor exudes both comfort and luxury.

Perhaps the brakes screech to halt when you think of lobster and your wallet, but cooking lobster at home is not half as expensive as ordering it in a restaurant. The trick for the most sumptuous lobster meat at the best price is to curb your desires until the summer season arrives and then GO WILD! I've cooked up a Creamy Lobster Stew, a rich Lobster Tomato Risotto, and for the hottest months, an elegant Lobster Cobb Salad.

The Great Lobster Bake is brilliant in any season: lobsters baked with clams, mussels, and shrimp, perfumed to the hilt with fresh herbs. This feast is grand enough to be your Christmas dinner, served with big pieces of toasted peasant bread and an Apple Vichyssoise to begin.

Since lobster is such a favorite, I figured while we're being excessive, why not add another recipe and make it an even 11 in this chapter. You can never have enough top "10s". ❧

SUCCULENT BOILED LOBSTERS

SERVES 6

a sunny day. The perfect seaside café. Bib in place in anticipation of a bright red boiled lobster about to arrive at your table. It's a wonderful memory for some, a daydream for others. But lobster can make any setting special. For those who need help cooking lobsters at home, here's my favorite method. Though steaming lobsters is more than acceptable (and often confused with boiling), boiling in well-salted water produces the best results. The lobsters flavor the water, which flavors the lobsters. One-and-a-half-pound lobsters give you just the right amount of meat.

6 live lobsters (about 1½ pounds each)

Drawn butter, for serving (see Note)

Lemon wedges, for serving

1. Bring a large pot of salted water to a boil over high heat.

2. Holding a lobster by the tail, plunge it into the boiling water. Repeat with a second lobster. Cover the pot, return the water to a boil, and cook until they are bright red and cooked through, 8 to 10 minutes. Using tongs, transfer the lobsters to a colander to drain. Repeat with the remaining lobsters.

3. Crack the lobster claws a bit and let any water drain off. Serve each lobster with drawn butter and lemon wedges, a lobster cracker, and a pick. Don't forget the napkins!

NOTE: Drawn butter is melted butter with the milk solids removed—also known as clarified butter. Melt the butter in a saucepan and then let it rest off the heat for a few minutes. When the solids have settled to the bottom of the pan, carefully pour off the clarified butter, leaving the solids behind.

THE GREAT LOBSTER BAKE

SERVES 8

there is nothing more spectacular than lots of lobsters and a great bake to go along with them—jumbo shrimp, clams, and mussels. What fun! Invite your friends over and pop the cork on a steely cold Sauvignon Blanc.

1 pound littleneck or cherrystone clams

1 tablespoon cornmeal

1 pound large mussels

4 live lobsters (each 1½ pounds)

8 tablespoons (1 stick) unsalted butter,
    at room temperature

6 tablespoons chopped fresh flat-leaf parsley leaves

2 tablespoons minced garlic

Salt and freshly ground black pepper, to taste

1½ pounds jumbo shrimp, peeled and deveined
    but tails left on

8 lemons, halved crosswise, for garnish

1. Rinse the clams under cold water and place them in a bowl. Sprinkle the cornmeal over the clams, add cold water to cover, and let soak for 1 hour. Drain, rinse again under cold water, and drain again.

2. Scrub the mussels well and rinse them in several changes of cold water to remove any sand. Drain. If they have beards, don't pull them off until right before you cook the mussels.

3. Place a lobster on a cutting board and plunge the tip of a sharp knife about 1½ inches down from the eyes into the center of the head; cut straight through the body and head. Then cut lengthwise completely through the whole tail. Remove and discard the sac in the top of the head, the tomalley (green liver), and the intestine. Carefully crack the claws with the back of the knife. Repeat with the remaining lobsters.

4. Preheat the oven to 475°F.

5. Combine the butter, 4 tablespoons of the parsley, the garlic, and salt and pepper in a small bowl.

6. Divide the lobster halves, cut side up, and the clams, mussels, and shrimp between two large rimmed baking sheets. Season the seafood well with salt and pepper. Spread the butter mixture over the lobsters and shrimp and on the clams and mussels.

7. Bake until the lobsters and shrimp are cooked through (the meat should be opaque) and the clams and mussels have opened, about 20 minutes. Discard any clams or mussels that do not open.

8. Arrange the shellfish on one or two large platters. Sprinkle with the remaining 2 tablespoons parsley and garnish with the lemon halves. Serve immediately.

LOBSTER FRA DIAVOLO

SERVES 4

While reminiscent of a marinara sauce, red bell pepper, cognac, and jalapeño add hints of newness to this luscious, traditional favorite lobster dish.

5 cups canned Italian plum tomatoes,
    with their juices

4 tablespoons extra-virgin olive oil, or
    more if needed

3 fresh lobsters (each 1½ pounds),
    each cut into 8 pieces (see Note)

Salt and freshly ground black pepper,
    to taste

2 large shallots, finely minced

2 tablespoons finely minced garlic

¾ cup dry white wine

¼ cup cognac

1 small red bell pepper, stemmed, seeded,
    and cut into ¼-inch dice

2 teaspoons finely minced fresh red jalapeño or
    serrano chile, with seeds and ribs;
    or ½ teaspoon crushed red pepper flakes

3 tablespoons tomato paste

½ teaspoon sugar

8 tablespoons chopped fresh flat-leaf
    parsley leaves

2 tablespoons torn fresh basil leaves

2 teaspoons dried oregano

12 ounces spaghettini

1. Pour the tomatoes, with all their juices, into a food processor and pulse until well blended. Set aside.

2. Heat the olive oil in a large heavy pot over medium heat. Add the lobster pieces, and season with salt and pepper. Cook, stirring frequently (and adding more oil if needed), until the lobster turns bright red, 10 to 12 minutes.

3. Add the shallots and garlic to the lobster, and toss with tongs. Add the wine and cognac, and cook over medium heat, turning the lobster carefully with tongs, until most of the liquid has evaporated, about 5 minutes. Then add the bell pepper, jalapeño, processed tomatoes, tomato paste, sugar, 6 tablespoons of the parsley, and the basil and oregano. Simmer (do not boil), stirring occasionally, over medium to medium-low heat until the flavors blend together, 20 minutes.

4. While the mixture is cooking, bring a large pot of salted water to a boil. Add the spaghettini and cook until al dente, according to the package directions. Drain, and set aside.

5. To serve, make delicate swirls of spaghettini in the center of four shallow pasta bowls. Arrange the lobster tails and claws, with the sauce, on top of the pasta. Sprinkle with the remaining 2 tablespoons parsley. Serve the lobster bodies and legs in a separate bowl and let the guests help themselves. Serve immediately, with plenty of napkins.

NOTE: If you're not boiling lobsters, either have your fishmonger cut them up and crack the claws for you, or prepare them in a humane way: Plunge the tip of a sharp knife about 1½ inches down from the eyes into the center of the head. That quickly kills it. To section it for Fra Diavolo, separate the head and body (top) portion from the tail. Cut the tail in half lengthwise and remove the intestine. Split each half in half crosswise so that you have 4 tail pieces. Now remove the knuckles and claws from the top portion. Cut the knuckles from the claws for 4 more lobster pieces. Since the head of the lobster isn't used in this recipe, either discard the pieces or clean them out, removing the head sac, the tomalley, and roe, if any. Rinse the shells, dry them, wrap them well, and freeze them for fish stock. They will keep for up to 1 month in the freezer. ❧

CREAMY LOBSTER STEW

SERVES 4

*a*ny lobster dish feels celebratory simply because it's lobster, but add cream and sherry and it becomes comforting as well. Serve generous bowlsful of this dish to your best friends on a Saturday night. Be sure to accompany it with plenty of crusty peasant bread on the side. Sautéing the lobster shells adds a subtle flavor to the sauce.

4 live lobsters (each 1½ pounds)

3 tablespoons olive oil

Salt and freshly ground black pepper, to taste

1 cup amontillado sherry

3 tablespoons unsalted butter

3 carrots, peeled and cut into ¼-inch dice

1 russet potato, peeled and cut into ¼-inch dice

1 cup chicken broth, preferably homemade
   (see page 434)

1½ cups green peas, thawed if frozen

2 cups heavy (whipping) cream

3 tablespoons chopped fresh flat-leaf parsley leaves

1. Bring a large pot of well-salted water to a boil. Drop 2 lobsters into the boiling water, cover the pot, and boil for 5 minutes. The shells won't be that fully-cooked bright red color. Remove the lobsters from the water with tongs, and transfer them to a colander to drain. Repeat with the remaining 2 lobsters, making sure to let the water return to a rolling boil before adding them.

2. Allow the lobsters to cool slightly. While they are still warm, remove the meat from the lobsters: Place the lobsters, belly up, on a flat surface and split them from head to tail, separating the thin membrane that covers the tail meat. Remove and discard the head sac, the tomalley (green liver), and the intestinal vein. Reserve the coral (red roe), if any. Crack the claw shells lightly on one side with the back of the knife. Carefully remove the meat from the tails, claws, and knuckles and cut it into ½-inch pieces; you should have about 4 cups of lobster meat. Place the lobster shells in a bowl. Reserve the meat in another bowl, covered, in the refrigerator.

3. Heat the olive oil in a large heavy pot over medium heat. Add the reserved lobster shells, sprinkle with salt and pepper, and cook, shaking the pot and turning them with tongs, until the shells turn bright red, 4 to 5 minutes. Transfer the shells to a bowl.

4. Add the sherry to the pot and deglaze it, scraping up any brown bits on the bottom. Let the sherry simmer for 2 minutes. Then pour the sherry through a strainer over the reserved lobster shells. Set aside.

5. In the same pot, melt the butter over low heat. Add the carrots and potato, and cook until slightly softened, about 5 minutes. Add the broth and the peas, and simmer until all the vegetables are tender, about 5 minutes.

6. Add the cream and 2 tablespoons of the parsley. Partially cover the pot, and simmer over medium heat for 5 minutes.

7. Pour the reserved sherry through a strainer into the pot. Add the reserved lobster meat, along with the reserved roe, if any. Heat until just cooked through, 2 to 3 minutes. Garnish with the remaining 1 tablespoon chopped parsley, and serve immediately. ✿

BROILED
LOBSTER SALAD

SERVES 2

When I lived near Long Island Sound, a special-occasion meal meant perfect broiled lobsters stuffed with rich bread crumbs laced with the faint taste of the tomalley and roe. I haven't seen such a presentation in years, yet I often yearn for a broiled lobster—but with a fresh presentation. A basting sauce of lemon juice, olive oil, and tarragon produces just the right result. A fresh tomato salad tops the lobster off perfectly, with a hint of scallion and garlic offsetting the sweet shellfish.

FOR THE LOBSTERS AND THE BASTING SAUCE:

2 live lobsters (each 1½ pounds; see Note)

¼ cup olive oil

1 tablespoon fresh lemon juice

1 tablespoon chopped fresh tarragon leaves

2 teaspoons finely grated lemon zest

Freshly ground black pepper, to taste

FOR THE TOMATO SALAD (makes 1¼ cups):

2 cups diced ripe tomatoes (¼-inch dice)

3 scallions (white bulbs and 3 inches green),
    thinly sliced on the diagonal

2 teaspoons minced garlic

½ teaspoon finely minced green jalapeño
    pepper

1 tablespoon extra-virgin olive oil

1 tablespoon fresh lemon juice

¼ cup coarsely torn fresh basil leaves

1. Prepare the lobsters: Place the lobsters, belly up, on a flat surface and split them from head to tail, separating the thin membrane that covers the tail meat. Do not cut through the back outer shell. Remove and discard the intestine that runs down the length of the tail, and remove the sac from the head. Hold open the cavity and remove the tomalley (green liver) and coral (red roe), if any; discard. With the side of the knife, crack the center of each claw on one side only.

2. Prepare the basting sauce: Combine the olive oil, lemon juice, tarragon, lemon zest, and pepper in a small bowl. Stir well, and set it aside.

3. Prepare the tomato salad: Combine all of the ingredients in a medium-size bowl. Toss, and set it aside.

4. Position a rack 6 to 8 inches from the heat source, and preheat the broiler.

5. Arrange the lobsters, belly up, in a broiler pan or on a rimmed baking sheet. Insert a thin metal skewer diagonally through the tail of each lobster to help keep it flat. The lobster tail meat must be completely exposed. Brush the meat and the claws (in the cracks) with the basting sauce. Broil for 5 minutes.

6. Brush the lobsters well again with the basting sauce, and broil until the meat is still moist but opaque and cooked through, 5 minutes.

7. Transfer the lobsters to individual dinner plates and remove skewers. Fill the cavities with the tomato salad. Brush the tails with any remaining basting sauce, and serve.

NOTE: Have your fishmonger prepare the lobsters for you as described in Step 1, or see the Note on page 199 for the best way to dispatch a lobster. Then split the lobsters lengthwise as described.

LOBSTER TOMATO RISOTTO

SERVES 4 (OR 6 AS AN APPETIZER)

he perfect risotto is a work of love that requires a little skill, a little patience, and top-quality ingredients. I make my risotto with arborio rice, a short, round, pearl-centered grain that is able to absorb a great amount of liquid and to release its surface starch, adding creaminess to the dish. I like risotto to be particularly creamy and moist—the way the Venetians cook it. The addition of ripe tomatoes and lobster enhances the luxury of this risotto.

2 tablespoons extra-virgin olive oil

1 cup diced onion (¼-inch dice)

2 tablespoons finely minced garlic

1 pound ripe tomatoes, peeled (see page 266),
    seeded, and chopped

6 cups chicken broth, preferably homemade
    (see page 434)

1¼ cups arborio rice

8 ounces cooked fresh lobster meat (from one
    2-pound lobster), cut into ½-inch pieces

Salt and freshly ground black pepper, to taste

¼ cup chopped fresh tarragon leaves

1. Heat the oil in a heavy pot over low heat. Add the onion and cook, stirring, until softened, 5 minutes. Add the garlic and cook for 4 minutes longer (do not let the garlic brown).

2. Add the tomatoes, raise the heat to medium, and cook, stirring, until most of the moisture has evaporated, about 10 minutes.

3. While the tomatoes are cooking, bring the broth to a boil in a medium-size saucepan. Reduce the heat to a simmer, and keep it at that heat.

4. Add the rice to the tomato mixture and cook, stirring, to coat the grains, 2 minutes.

5. Add ½ cup of the hot broth to the rice mixture and cook, stirring frequently, until all the liquid has been absorbed into the rice, 3 to 4 minutes. Continue to add the broth, ½ cup at a time, cooking and stirring until each addition has been absorbed, and all the broth has been added. This will take about 45 minutes total.

6. Meanwhile, if the lobster meat is in the refrigerator, set it out on the counter to come to room temperature, about 20 minutes.

7. Season the risotto with salt and pepper, and remove it from the heat. Fold in the lobster and the tarragon. Serve immediately.

LOBSTER COBB SALAD

SERVES 6

○

Ilove arranging large dramatic salads for company. While most everyone knows what's in a traditional Cobb Salad, the *aahs* can be heard around the table when this exquisite version is presented. Once all the ingredients are prepared, there's nothing to putting the salad together in nice straight rows—making it look gorgeous.

8 strips bacon

4 hard-cooked eggs

2 ripe avocados, preferably Hass

Juice of 2 limes

4 cups cut-up tender inner romaine lettuce leaves
    (1-inch pieces)

4 ripe plum tomatoes, seeded and cut into
    ½-inch pieces

1 pound cooked fresh lobster meat, cut into
    ½-inch dice (see Note)

8 ounces Danish blue or Maytag blue cheese,
    chilled, cut into ½-inch cubes

Coarse (kosher) salt and freshly ground black
    pepper, to taste

2 tablespoons chopped fresh flat-leaf parsley
    leaves, for garnish

8 ounces fresh salmon caviar, for garnish

½ cup Light Lemon Vinaigrette (page 205), for serving

1. Cut the bacon crosswise into 1-inch pieces, and cook them in a skillet over medium heat until just crisp, 7 minutes. Set aside on paper towels to drain.

2. Cut the eggs in half lengthwise. Then cut each half into quarters, so you have a total of 16 pieces.

3. Cut the avocados in half and remove the pits. Peel the avocados and cut them into ½-inch pieces. Put the pieces in a small bowl, add the lime juice, and toss.

4. Arrange the following ingredients in straight crosswise rows on a large oval or rectangular platter (approximately 15 x 19 inches) in this order: romaine lettuce, tomatoes, lobster, bacon, avocados, blue cheese, and eggs.

5. Season lightly with salt and pepper. Sprinkle with the chopped parsley. Dollop the caviar in ½ teaspoon dollops, equally spaced, alongside the lobster and the eggs. Serve the Light Lemon Vinaigrette alongside.

NOTE: This will amount to about 2½ cups of diced lobster meat, from two 2-pound lobsters.

GORGEOUS LOBSTER SALAD
WITH GREEN GODDESS AVOCADO DRESSING

SERVES 8

there are occasions where a truly elegant salad is called for: Mother's Day, a bridal shower, a black-tie dinner. This is the time to pull out all the stops—and of course the lobster. Lobster is sweet enough to combine with the sweetest fruits, which is why I've offered up a couple of delicious combinations in this chapter. The creamy avocado dressing is the perfect foil for the tart lemon vinaigrette.

1 ripe avocado, preferably Hass

2 tablespoons fresh lemon juice

1½ pounds cooked fresh lobster meat,
    cut into ¾-inch pieces (see Note)

1 ripe papaya, peeled, seeded, and cut into
    ½-inch pieces

3 ripe plum tomatoes, seeded and cut
    into ¼-inch

3 scallions (white bulbs and 2 to 3 inches green),
    thinly sliced on the diagonal

Salt and freshly ground black pepper,
    to taste

⅔ cup Light Lemon Vinaigrette
    (recipe follows)

2 heads Boston lettuce, tough outer leaves
    discarded, leaves separated, rinsed,
    and patted dry

2 tablespoons snipped fresh chives,
    for garnish

Green Goddess Avocado Dressing
    (recipe follows), for serving

1. Cut the avocado in half and remove the pit. Peel the avocado and cut it into ½-inch pieces. Put the pieces in a small bowl, add the lemon juice, and toss. Set it aside.

2. Combine the lobster, papaya, tomatoes, and scallions in a large bowl. Drain the avocado, and add it to the salad. Toss together very gently.

3. Shortly before serving, season the salad with salt and pepper and toss it with about ¼ cup of the Light Lemon Vinaigrette. Arrange the lettuce leaves on a decorative platter and top them with the lobster salad. Sprinkle with the chives. Serve the Green Goddess Avocado Dressing in a bowl alongside, to dollop atop each portion.

NOTE: Three 2-pound (6 pounds total) lobsters will yield 1½ pounds of cooked lobster meat. Alternatively, you can order cooked lobster meat from your fishmonger. ✿

GREEN GODDESS AVOCADO DRESSING

MAKES 2 CUPS

Normally this dressing would be made with 2 cups of mayonnaise, but an avocado can take the place of a cup of mayonnaise for me any day. It has all the rich, creamy properties of mayonnaise plus its own luscious flavor. Combined with the fresh herbs that add the distinctive flavor to the dressing, avocado creates an ideal Green Goddess. It's perfect with seafood, and great with chicken.

> 1 ripe avocado, preferably Hass, halved, pitted,
>   and peeled
> 2 tablespoons fresh lemon juice
> 1 cup prepared mayonnaise, such as
>   Hellmann's
> 6 canned anchovy fillets, rinsed and squeezed
>   dry in a paper towel
> ¼ cup snipped fresh chives
> ¼ cup chopped fresh flat-leaf parsley leaves
> 1½ teaspoons dried tarragon, crumbled
> 2 tablespoons tarragon vinegar

1. Combine the avocado pulp and the lemon juice in a small bowl, and mash together thoroughly. Fold in the mayonnaise.

2. Chop the anchovies fine, and stir them into the mixture. Add the chives and parsley.

3. Combine the tarragon and the vinegar in a small bowl. Set it aside for 5 minutes for the tarragon to moisten. Then stir this into the dressing. Let the dressing rest, loosely covered in the refrigerator, for 1 hour for the flavors to blend. 🦞

LIGHT LEMON VINAIGRETTE

MAKES ⅔ CUP

This delicate vinaigrette is delicious tossed over a fruit-and-vegetable combination. The addition of honey takes the bite out of the lemon juice and mellows the flavors.

> ¼ cup fresh lemon juice
> 1 tablespoon honey
> 1 tablespoon Dijon mustard
> Salt and freshly ground black pepper, to taste
> ¼ cup olive oil

Combine the lemon juice, honey, mustard, and salt and pepper in a small bowl. Whisking constantly, slowly drizzle in the olive oil. Continue whisking until thickened. (The dressing will keep, covered, in the refrigerator for up to 2 days.) 🦞

SUNSHINE LOBSTER SALAD

SERVES 4

You usually can't pull me away from a lobster salad slathered with mayonnaise, but this refreshing, light variation will delight even the traditionalist. Fresh fruits enhance the sweetness of the lobster, and mint works a wonderful magic as a garnish. The dazzling colors suit summer entertaining to a tee. A crisp Sauvignon Blanc would be just the ticket to pour alongside.

Cooked tail meat from four 1½-pound lobsters
    (see Note)
2 cups diced ripe pineapple (¼-inch dice)
2 cups diced ripe cantaloupe (¼-inch dice)
2 cups diced seeded ripe tomatoes
    (¼-inch dice)
Orange Vinaigrette (recipe follows)
Salt and freshly ground black pepper, to taste
2 tablespoons chopped fresh mint leaves,
    for garnish

1. Place each lobster tail on a cutting board, rounded side up (they naturally curl this way), and press down on it while you slice it crosswise into ¼-inch-thick medallions.

2. Arrange the medallions in a tight spiral in the center four dinner plates.

3. Surround the lobster with a neat ring, about 1¼ inches wide, of diced pineapple. Follow with a 1-inch-wide ring of cantaloupe, and end with a ½-inch-wide ring of tomatoes.

4. Drizzle 2 tablespoons of the Orange Vinaigrette over each salad. Season them with salt and pepper, and sprinkle with the fresh mint. Garnish with the lobster claws. Serve immediately.

NOTE: This salad uses only the tail meat from the lobsters. Use the delicious claw and knuckle meat chopped and mixed with a little chopped celery and mayonnaise as an easy lobster roll filling or as a filling for a tomato shell. It makes a great bonus lunch.

ORANGE VINAIGRETTE

MAKES ½ CUP

fresh and fruity—ideal for seafood and light vegetable salads. A drop of honey always brings out the fruit flavor even more, while cider vinegar is a delightful soft acid.

¼ cup fresh orange juice

1 teaspoon cider vinegar

2 teaspoons Dijon mustard

½ teaspoon honey

Salt and freshly ground black pepper, to taste

¼ cup extra-virgin olive oil

Combine the orange juice, vinegar, mustard, honey, and salt and pepper in a small bowl. Whisking constantly, slowly drizzle in the olive oil. Continue whisking until the dressing has thickened slightly. (This will keep for up to 2 days, covered, in the refrigerator.) 🏵

LUSCIOUS LOBSTER ROLLS
WITH CREAMY COLESLAW

SERVES 6

there is nothing like a lobster roll. The most winning presentation is not necessarily the most elaborate. Look for red oval woven plastic baskets (sold in housewares stores) and line them with cute paper napkins. Tuck in a lobster roll and some potato chips. Pass a bowl of coleslaw. Make up a pitcher of sweet lemonade or pop the cork on a bottle of Veuve Clicquot!

FOR THE DRESSING:

½ cup prepared mayonnaise, such as
    Hellmann's

½ cup sour cream

1 tablespoon drained tiny capers

1 tablespoon coarsely chopped sweet pickles

1 to 2 tablespoons chopped fresh tarragon
    leaves, or 1 to 2 teaspoons crumbled
    dried tarragon

Dash of Tabasco sauce

Freshly ground black pepper, to taste

FOR THE LOBSTER ROLLS:

1 pound cooked fresh lobster meat (from two
    2-pound lobsters), cut into ½-inch pieces

1 cup diced celery (¼-inch dice)

2 scallions (white bulbs and 3 inches green),
    thinly sliced on the diagonal

6 top-split hot dog rolls

2 tablespoons unsalted butter (optional)

FOR SERVING:

Creamy Coleslaw (recipe follows)

1. Prepare the dressing: Combine all the dressing ingredients in a bowl. Stir together well and set it aside.

2. Prepare the lobster rolls: In another bowl, combine the lobster, celery, and scallions. Using a rubber spatula, fold the dressing into the lobster mixture, making sure the ingredients are well coated.

3. Lightly toast the hot dog rolls. Spread them with butter if desired. Fill each roll with about ⅓ cup of the lobster salad. Top them off with a little extra lobster salad for the *wow*! effect. Be careful not to break the rolls. Serve immediately, with the Creamy Coleslaw alongside. ❧

CREAMY COLESLAW

SERVES 6 TO 8

simple and yummy slaw is easy to make, delicious, and perfect to serve with lobster rolls. I just go crazy for homemade slaw. One word of caution, however: If you're flavoring your slaw with celery salt, as I do here, season it only with pepper—no more salt! It's always a good idea to taste as you go. Leftovers are great with hot dogs, sausage or ham sandwiches, burgers—just about anything.

> 1 head cabbage, tough outer leaves removed
> 1 large carrot, coarsely grated
> 1 small onion, coarsely grated
> 1 cup prepared mayonnaise, such as Hellmann's
> 1 cup sour cream
> 2 tablespoons heavy (whipping) cream
> 2 tablespoons cider vinegar
> 2 teaspoons Dijon mustard
> ½ to 1 teaspoon celery salt, to taste
> Freshly ground black pepper, to taste
> 2 tablespoons chopped fresh flat-leaf
>   parsley leaves

1. Halve, core, and thinly slice the cabbage. Place it in a large bowl, and add the carrot and onion.

2. In a separate bowl, combine the mayonnaise, sour cream, heavy cream, vinegar, mustard, celery salt, and pepper. Fold the mayonnaise mixture into the cabbage, mixing very well.

3. When the cabbage is well coated with the dressing, fold in the parsley. Cover the bowl with plastic wrap, and chill the coleslaw for at least 4 hours before serving. ❧

LOBSTER MELT

SERVES 4

When we think of melts, it's most often the tuna melt that comes to mind as a sensible, easy midweek meal. But when lobster is the main event and avocado joins the melt, we're dealing with something way beyond sensible.

FOR THE DRESSING:

¼ cup prepared mayonnaise, such as Hellmann's

2 tablespoons sour cream

1 tablespoon Heinz chili sauce

½ teaspoon crushed dried tarragon

FOR THE LOBSTER MELT:

8 ounces cooked fresh lobster meat (from one 2-pound lobster), cut into ½-inch pieces

½ cup finely diced celery

2 scallions (white bulbs and 3 inches green), thinly sliced on the diagonal

½ cup finely diced unpeeled Granny Smith apple, tossed in a bowl with 1 tablespoon fresh lemon juice to prevent discoloration

2 English muffins, split and toasted

1 ripe avocado, preferably Hass, peeled, pitted, and sliced

½ cup alfalfa sprouts

4 ounces Vermont Cheddar cheese, coarsely grated

1. Prepare the dressing: Combine all the ingredients in a medium-size bowl. Stir together well, and set aside.

2. In another bowl, combine the lobster, celery, scallions, and the apple, including the lemon juice. Fold the dressing into the lobster mixture, coating the ingredients well.

3. Position an oven rack about 7 inches from the broiler heat source, and preheat the broiler.

4. Place the toasted English muffin halves on a baking sheet. Top each one with some of the lobster salad, followed by a couple of avocado slices and some alfalfa sprouts. Sprinkle the grated cheese evenly over the top.

5. Place the baking sheet under the broiler, and broil until the cheese melts, 5 to 10 minutes. Serve immediately. ❧

"SHRIMP ARE JUST PLAIN CLASSY, AND WE LOVE THEM."

SHRIMP, BIG AND SMALL

Despite our access to a wealth of cuisines and a variety of dishes, America's favorite restaurant meal is still a snazzy shrimp cocktail followed by a thick, well-cooked steak. Shrimp are just plain classy, and we love them. Of the hundreds of species, the one we enjoy most often is the familiar Gulf White, with its firm texture and great flavor. But we are now farming shrimp, and whether they come from Asia or the Gulf area, we have a much larger selection in our markets. Look for Black Tiger Shrimp, dark gray with black stripes and red feelers—beautiful, firm, and tasty. Our Gulf Pink can be farm-raised or wild; the shell is often redder than the Whites. Rock Shrimp are in a class of their own—much smaller, caught off the mid-Atlantic and southern states. Your fishmonger can help you choose.

To begin a great evening, I often serve delicate Coconut Shrimp with an Apricot Dipping Sauce. I assure you that there won't be one left. Serve Shrimp Tacos when friends come by for casual noshing. They'll adore all the fixings and the fun of it. But for a sit-down dinner, wow them with Shrimp Curry or a pot of Shrimp Creole, with some Allen Toussaint music playing for a perfect evening.

SPIRITED SHRIMP COCKTAIL

SERVES 4 AS AN APPETIZER

Shrimp cocktail says "special occasion," so it should be all gussied up, and I think this one fits the bill. Cocktail sauce—that pungent and classic dip for the shrimp—is set aside for a more modern sweet-hot fruit salsa that complements the shellfish perfectly. If you can find some martini glasses with colorful stems to serve them in, go for it! And just in case you crave that cocktail sauce, I've included a recipe here as well. Serve it alongside for anyone who wants a dollop.

FOR THE SHRIMP:

½ cup dry white wine

2 ribs celery with leaves, chopped

4 sprigs fresh flat-leaf parsley

4 whole black peppercorns

32 large shrimp (1½ to 2 pounds), peeled and
    deveined, half with tails left on

FOR THE SALSA:

1 ripe papaya, seeded, peeled, and cut into
    ½-inch pieces

1 cup diced ripe tomato (½-inch dice)

½ cup diced peeled hothouse (seedless) cucumber
    (½-inch dice)

¼ cup diced red onion (¼-inch dice)

2 tablespoons fresh lime juice

1 teaspoon finely minced green jalapeño pepper

1 tablespoon olive oil

Salt and freshly ground black pepper, to taste

6 tablespoons coarsely chopped fresh mint leaves

FOR GARNISH:

8 large mint sprigs

1. Prepare the shrimp: Fill a medium-size saucepan halfway with water. Add the wine, celery, parsley sprigs, and peppercorns. Bring to a boil over high heat. Reduce the heat to medium-low, add the shrimp, and simmer until they are opaque and pink, 2 minutes. Drain the shrimp, discarding the celery, parsley, and peppercorns. Rinse the shrimp under cold running water, and drain them well. Transfer them to a bowl and refrigerate, loosely covered, for 2 hours.

2. Prepare the salsa: Using a rubber spatula, combine the papaya, tomato, cucumber, red onion, lime juice, jalapeño, and olive oil in a large bowl. Season with salt and pepper. Fold in the chopped mint.

3. To serve, place 4 shrimp (ones with tails removed), in the bottom of each of four martini glasses. Top with ½ cup of the salsa. Arrange 4 shrimp (ones with tails left on) on the rim of each glass, grouped together. Garnish with mint sprigs, and serve.

COCKTAIL SAUCE

MAKES ABOUT ½ CUP

While I was trying to make up a new, more delicious sauce for my shrimp cocktail, I kept thinking that I couldn't *not* include this classic. So simple yet so delicious.

¼ cup ketchup

¼ cup Heinz chili sauce

1 tablespoon drained white horseradish

1. Combine all the ingredients in a small bowl.

2. Refrigerate, covered, until ready to use. This sauce will keep for up to 1 day. 🥢

BUFFALO SHRIMP
WITH BLUE CHEESE SAUCE

SERVES 6 AS AN APPETIZER

taking some liberty with the classic buffalo chicken wing, I've substituted shrimp and served it along with crisp veggies and a super blue cheese sauce for a hot new appetizer. It's as good as it gets! Don't miss this one for the Super Bowl!

8 tablespoons (1 stick) unsalted butter

1 to 1½ tablespoons Tabasco sauce, to taste

1 pound (about 24) large shrimp, cleaned and
    deveined but tails left on, rinsed and patted dry

Coarse (kosher) salt, to taste

4 large ribs celery, trimmed and cut into sticks,
    for serving

4 large carrots, peeled and cut into sticks, for serving

6 scallions, trimmed, for serving

Blue Cheese Sauce (recipe follows), for serving

1. Combine the butter and the Tabasco sauce in a small saucepan over medium-low heat, and cook until the butter has melted. Stir, and let cool slightly.

Then divide the butter mixture between two large mixing bowls.

2. Place the shrimp in one of the bowls and coat them well with the butter mixture. Cover the bowl loosely and let the shrimp marinate at room temperature for 20 minutes.

3. Heat a nonstick skillet over medium heat. Using tongs, lift the shrimp from the marinade and cook them, in batches, in the skillet until they are pink and opaque, 2 minutes per side. As they are cooked, transfer the shrimp to the second bowl and toss them well in that batch of butter-Tabasco mixture.

4. Again using tongs, transfer the cooked shrimp to a serving bowl. Sprinkle them with coarse salt. Serve immediately, along with the celery, carrots, and scallions, and a bowl of Blue Cheese Sauce for dipping. If you have extra Blue Cheese Sauce, drizzle it over a wedge of iceberg lettuce: another classic! ❧

BLUE CHEESE SAUCE

MAKES 2 CUPS

buffalo Shrimp will be the hit of any party when dipped into this delicious sauce. While a blue cheese sauce made with Roquefort can be delicious, I prefer mine mellow, made with a milder-flavored Danish blue. It's mild enough to take the bite off the Tabasco on the shrimp, and ideal for the vegetables too!

¾ cup prepared mayonnaise, such as Hellmann's

¾ cup sour cream

1 tablespoon fresh lemon juice

1 to 2 teaspoons Worcestershire sauce,
    to taste

1 dash Tabasco sauce

2 tablespoons finely minced shallots

2 tablespoons chopped fresh flat-leaf
    parsley leaves

Coarsely ground black pepper, to taste

¾ cup crumbled Danish blue cheese or other
    mild blue cheese

EXTRA SAUCE

Whenever I prepare a dish that comes with a dip or sauce, I like to make sure I have plenty on hand. Some are so good, they get dolloped on or scooped up by the table-spoonful, and running out of a sauce (like running out of gravy on Thanksgiving) can be pretty disappointing. Of course, this means that I usually have some left over and that holds true with the Blue Cheese Sauce I serve with Buffalo Shrimp. If you're lucky enough to have some extra, here are a few serving ideas:

+ Drizzle it over a wedge of iceberg lettuce.

+ Serve it alongside slices of cold chicken breast, garnished with a sprig or two of fresh parsley.

+ Arrange thin slices of ripe tomatoes and cucumbers on a plate and serve a little bowl of Blue Cheese Sauce alongside.

+ And—does this go without saying?—it makes a great dip for celery and carrot sticks, crisp radishes, and raw broccoli florets.

Combine all of the ingredients except the cheese in a bowl. Gently fold in the blue cheese, being careful not to break it up too much (or it will turn the sauce an unappetizing gray). Adjust the seasonings to taste. Refrigerate, covered, for as long as overnight. ❧

COCONUT SHRIMP
WITH APRICOT DIPPING SAUCE

SERVES 6 AS AN APPETIZER

lthough I can't place the origin of coconut shrimp—Is it the Caribbean? Is it Thailand?—the combination of flavors results in a delicious dish. I've taken the liberty of blending the coconut with panko (slightly coarse and fluffy Japanese bread crumbs), resulting in a crust with just the right texture. The coconut marries well with the shrimp and is excellent served with the slightly tart Apricot Dipping Sauce, which you'll want to prepare a day ahead.

½ cup all-purpose flour

¼ teaspoon sweet paprika

Salt and freshly ground black pepper, to taste

2 large eggs

½ cup shredded sweetened coconut

½ cup panko (available in most supermarkets, or see Sources, page 439)

Peanut, vegetable, or canola oil, for frying

1 pound large shrimp, peeled and deveined but tails left on, rinsed and patted dry

Apricot Dipping Sauce (recipe follows)

1. Combine the flour, paprika, and salt and pepper in a shallow bowl.

2. In another shallow bowl, lightly beat the eggs.

3. In a third shallow bowl, combine the coconut and the panko.

4. Pour peanut oil into a skillet to a depth of ¼ inch. Place the skillet over medium-high heat.

5. Dredge the shrimp in the seasoned flour, shaking off any excess. Then dip them into the eggs, followed by the coconut-panko mixture, covering them completely.

6. Using long-handled tongs, carefully sauté the shrimp in the hot oil until they are just golden brown, about 2 minutes per side, being careful not to burn them. Transfer them to paper towels to drain.

7. Serve warm, with the Apricot Dipping Sauce alongside.

APRICOT DIPPING SAUCE

MAKES 1¼ CUPS

angy with a slight aftertaste of sweetness, apricot sauce complements the delicacy of the Coconut Shrimp. Just a dip will do you.

½ cup apricot preserves

¾ cup rice vinegar, plus extra if needed

1 tablespoon finely minced garlic

1 tablespoon dark brown sugar

2 teaspoons soy sauce

1 to 2 dashes Tabasco sauce, to taste

Coarse (kosher) salt, to taste

1. Combine the apricot preserves, ¾ cup vinegar, garlic, brown sugar, soy sauce, and Tabasco in a small saucepan over medium-low heat. Stir in ¾ cup water and the salt. Simmer, uncovered, stirring occasionally, until the sauce has thickened slightly, about 20 minutes. Remove from the heat and let cool to room temperature.

2. Transfer the mixture to a food processor, and process until smooth. Refrigerate, covered, overnight.

3. If the sauce is too thick (it thickens as it rests), stir in an additional 1 to 2 tablespoons rice vinegar. ❖

GRILLED JUMBO SHRIMP
WITH SAUCE CHIEN

SERVES 6

andrew Engle, chef at The Laundry in East Hampton, threads four jumbo shrimp on a small bamboo skewer, grills them, and then serves them with a small bowl of Sauce Chien, a sauce served in Martinique. Andrew calls for half of a Scotch bonnet chile in his Sauce Chien—Scotch bonnets are wickedly hot, so be careful! A serrano, or even a jalapeño (the coolest of the lot), would be a fine substitute. The flavor of Sauce Chien falls somewhere between a Thai dipping sauce and an exotic vinaigrette.

FOR THE SAUCE CHIEN:

5 cloves garlic

½ Scotch bonnet chile (see Note)

3 scallions (white bulbs and 2 inches green), thinly sliced

¼ cup finely chopped fresh flat-leaf parsley leaves

1 tablespoon fresh thyme leaves

Coarse (kosher) salt and freshly ground black pepper, to taste

1½ cups extra-virgin olive oil

FOR THE SHRIMP:

30 jumbo shrimp, head and tail left on, carefully peeled and deveined between the head and tail, rinsed and patted dry

Coarse (kosher) salt and freshly ground black pepper, to taste

3 to 4 tablespoons extra-virgin olive oil

FOR FINISHING THE DISH:

½ cup fresh lemon juice (from 2 or 3 lemons)

4 tablespoons boiling water (optional)

6 large thyme sprigs, for garnish

1. If you are using bamboo skewers, soak six skewers in water to cover for 1 hour.

2. Prepare the Sauce Chien: Finely mince the garlic and the chile together, and place in a small bowl. Add the scallions, parsley, thyme, and coarse salt and pepper. Whisk in the olive oil. Set aside for now.

3. Preheat a barbecue grill to medium-high.

4. Prepare the shrimp: Place the shrimp in a bowl and season them with coarse salt and black pepper. Drizzle the olive oil over the shrimp, and toss to lightly coat them. (Too much oil will cause the grill to flare up.) Thread 5 shrimp crosswise, through the middle of the body, onto each skewer.

5. Grill the shrimp, turning them carefully, until they are just cooked through (pink and opaque), about 3 minutes per side—be careful not to let them char too much.

6. Just before serving, whisk the lemon juice into the Sauce Chien. Taste, and correct the seasonings as needed. If you prefer a mellower sauce, whisk in some or all of the boiling water. Pour the sauce into six individual ramekins.

7. Place a skewer of shrimp on each plate, accompanied by a ramekin of sauce for dipping and a thyme sprig for garnish.

NOTE: When handling any chile, remember not to touch your eyes, lips, or anywhere the oils might cause a burn. Wash your hands well when you're finished.

SHRIMP TOASTS

MAKES 20 PIECES

It's difficult to decide which were my favorite foods on a trip I made to China. Almost everything I ate became an instant favorite, since I'm a great fan of the cuisine to begin with! One delicious appetizer, a bit nostalgic but every bit a contender, was a delicate golden shrimp toast, deep-fried and perfectly crisp. I enjoyed mine with a chilled Tsingtao beer. When I returned, Laurie and I quickly made up some shrimp toasts of our own. It is easy to make the shrimp paste to coat the bread; it's the frying that takes some practice—you want the toasts to be the color of honey.

8 ounces medium shrimp, peeled and
    deveined
4 canned water chestnuts, drained and
    coarsely chopped
1 tablespoon Madeira or dry sherry
1 teaspoon sugar
¼ teaspoon salt
1 tablespoon cornstarch
1 large egg, lightly beaten
2 scallions (white bulbs and 2 inches green),
    thinly sliced
2 teaspoons snipped fresh chives
10 slices firm white bread, crusts removed,
    cut in half diagonally (I used Pepperidge
    Farm sandwich bread, approximately
    3½ x 3½ inches)
Vegetable or peanut oil, for frying

1. Place the shrimp, water chestnuts, Madeira, sugar, salt, cornstarch, egg, and scallions in a food processor, and puree until the mixture forms a spreadable paste. Transfer the paste to a bowl and stir in the chives.

2. Neatly spread 1 tablespoon of the shrimp paste on each piece of bread, making sure to cover it evenly and completely to the edges.

3. Pour the oil to a depth of 1 inch in a heavy pot. Heat it over medium heat until a small square of bread dropped into it immediately bubbles and browns.

Gently lower the coated bread pieces, shrimp side down, into the hot oil. (Do this in batches so you do not overcrowd the pot.) Cook, using tongs to turn them, until they are golden brown, 1 minute per side. Drain the shrimp toasts on paper towels.

4. While they are still hot, arrange the shrimp toasts on a serving dish, and serve. ✤

SUMMER IN THE BACKYARD

It's midsummer, the corn is piled high in the market, the grill is waiting to be fired up for the next great meal, and everyone's hungry for something tasty but easy to prepare. Here's the perfect meal. A pitcher of fresh lemonade and some cold beer rounds it out.

GRILLED SHRIMP ROLLS
FACING PAGE

BARBECUED BABY BACKS
with Sheila's Raucous BBQ Sauce
PAGE 122

FARMERS' MARKET CORN SALAD
PAGE 307

SUMMER BERRY CRISP
PAGE 418

GRILLED SHRIMP ROLLS

SERVES 8

Here's an updated take on a beloved summer classic—the lobster roll. The flavors of just-off-the-grill shrimp add special fun to these summer rolls and lend a neat idea for your campfire overnights. While scallions and celery are basic fare, the results go to town with the kick of lemon and cornichons. You'll need eight to ten 12-inch metal skewers for the shrimp.

1½ pounds large shrimp, peeled, deveined,
   well rinsed, and patted dry
2 tablespoons extra-virgin olive oil
Finely grated zest of 1 lemon
2 tablespoons fresh lemon juice
Salt and freshly ground black pepper, to taste
Vegetable oil, for the grill
¾ cup diced celery (¼-inch dice)
4 scallions (white bulbs and 3 inches green),
   thinly sliced
3 tablespoons chopped cornichons
½ cup prepared mayonnaise, such as Hellmann's
1 tablespoon chopped fresh tarragon leaves
8 top-split hot dog rolls, toasted and lightly buttered
Radish sprouts, cress, or other baby sprouts, for garnish

1. Preheat a barbecue grill to high.

2. Place the shrimp in a large bowl. Add the olive oil, lemon zest and juice, and salt and pepper, and toss. Let rest at room temperature for 15 minutes.

3. Thread the shrimp crosswise on metal skewers, leaving space between them.

4. Oil the grill grate well and arrange the shrimp on the grate. Grill until they are pink and opaque, about 2 minutes per side.

5. Let the shrimp cool slightly, and then remove them from the skewers. Place them in a medium-size bowl, and add the celery, scallions, and cornichons.

6. Combine the mayonnaise and tarragon together in a small bowl. Add this to the shrimp mixture, and stir to combine. Adjust the seasonings if necessary.

7. Using a soupspoon, fill the rolls with the shrimp mixture (about ½ cup per roll). Garnish the top of each roll with a few sprouts, and serve. 🌸

SHRIMP TACOS

SERVES 4

there is something about eating tacos that's just plain fun—both kids and adults love them. They're great filled with chili, but they morph into a *wow!* when shrimp are the centerpiece. These are worthy of a fresh corn salsa, minty yogurt topping, and the whole nine yards (make that ten yards). Since football starts at the beginning of September and corn is still available at the farm stands, I'd serve these for Monday Night Football for as long as possible! They are real TD food.

FOR THE MINTED LIME YOGURT:

1 cup plain yogurt

Finely grated zest of 1 lime

1 tablespoon extra-virgin olive oil

2 tablespoons chopped fresh mint leaves

Freshly ground black pepper, to taste

FOR THE SHRIMP:

1 pound large shrimp, peeled, deveined, rinsed,
    and patted dry

2 tablespoons extra-virgin olive oil

1 tablespoon fresh lime juice

½ teaspoon ancho chile powder (see Notes)

Salt and freshly ground black pepper, to taste

FOR ASSEMBLING:

8 hard corn taco shells or soft flour tortillas
    (see Notes)

1 heart of romaine lettuce, thinly shredded
    crosswise

1 cup Farm Stand Corn Salsa (page 367)

1. Prepare the Minted Lime Yogurt: Combine all of the ingredients in a bowl, and stir well. Cover and refrigerate for 4 hours.

2. Prepare the shrimp: Place the shrimp in a bowl, and add the olive oil, lime juice, chile powder, and salt and pepper. Toss, and let marinate for 15 minutes at room temperature.

3. Heat a nonstick skillet over medium heat. Add the shrimp and sauté until they are pink and opaque, 2 minutes per side. Transfer the shrimp to a bowl and let them cool to room temperature. Then cut the shrimp in half crosswise (there will be 2 cups of shrimp).

4. To assemble the tacos, place ¼ cup of the cooked shrimp in each taco shell. Top with a small handful of the shredded lettuce, followed by 2 tablespoons of the Farm Stand Corn Salsa. Dollop with a tablespoon of the Minted Lime Yogurt. Serve immediately, passing the extra Minted Lime Yogurt in a small bowl.

NOTES:

+ Ancho chile powder is available in large supermarkets and in specialty food stores.

+ If serving tortillas, wrap them in aluminum foil and heat them for 3 minutes in a 350°F oven.

GRILLED SAIGON SHRIMP

SERVES 4 AS AN APPETIZER

With Vietnamese restaurants proliferating around the country, lemongrass and fish sauce have comfortably taken their places in our kitchen pantry. While these delicious shrimp grill, the sugar in the marinade caramelizes slightly, adding a distinctive Southeast Asian flavor. Serve them over Frisée and Apple Salad for an irresistible first course. You'll need four 12-inch skewers for the shrimp. If you use wooden ones, see the box on page 170.

8 jumbo shrimp, peeled and deveined but
    tails left on
1 stalk lemongrass
2 tablespoons Asian fish sauce
1 tablespoon sugar
1 tablespoon olive oil
Frisée and Apple Salad (page 258),
    for serving

1. Rinse the shrimp under cold running water; drain and pat dry.

2. Trim the ends from the stalk of lemongrass and remove the tough outer layer. Thinly slice and then finely mince the first 6 inches of the stalk (at the bulb end). Combine the lemongrass, fish sauce, sugar, and olive oil in a bowl, and mash the mixture with the back of a spoon. (Alternatively, the mixture can be chopped in a mini-chopper and then transferred to a bowl.) Add the shrimp and coat them well with the mixture. Cover, and refrigerate for 2 hours.

3. Preheat a barbecue grill to high.

4. Remove the shrimp from the refrigerator. Thread 2 shrimp on each of four 12-inch skewers, spacing them ½ inch apart.

5. Oil the grill grate well and arrange the shrimp on the grate. Grill until they are opaque and pink, 2½ to 3 minutes per side.

6. Remove the shrimp from the skewers. Divide the Frisée and Apple Salad among four shallow bowls, top each serving with 2 shrimp, and serve immediately. ❧

A POT OF
CREOLE SHRIMP

SERVES 8

While Shrimp Creole is a mainstay of American home cooking, I have caramelized the onions to sweeten the pot and enriched the sauce further with extra butter—all while retaining its basic Louisiana flair.

2 pounds large shrimp, peeled and deveined

3 tablespoons unsalted butter

2 tablespoons olive oil

1½ cups diced onion (¼-inch dice)

1½ cups diced celery (¼-inch dice)

1½ cups diced green bell pepper (¼-inch dice)

1 tablespoon finely minced garlic

1 bay leaf

Salt and freshly ground black pepper, to taste

1 to 2 teaspoons Tabasco sauce, to taste

2 teaspoons dried oregano

1 teaspoon dried thyme leaves

3 cups chopped canned peeled Italian plum
    tomatoes, drained

1 cup Basic Tomato Sauce (see page 437) or
    marinara sauce

2 teaspoons sugar

1 cup chicken broth, preferably homemade
    (see page 434), plus up to ½ cup extra
    if needed

¼ cup chopped fresh flat-leaf parsley leaves

Cooked white rice, for serving

1. Rinse the shrimp under cold water; drain and pat dry. Set them aside.

2. Melt the butter in the oil in a heavy pot over low heat. Raise the heat to medium, add the onions, and cook, stirring, for 3 minutes. Then reduce the heat to medium-low and cook until the onions begin to caramelize, 5 minutes. Add the celery and bell peppers, and cook, stirring occasionally, until they soften, about 15 minutes. Add the garlic and cook until softened, 5 minutes.

3. Add the bay leaf, salt and pepper, Tabasco, oregano, and thyme. Stir in the tomatoes and simmer, stirring occasionally, over low heat to blend the flavors, 5 minutes.

4. Add the tomato sauce, sugar, and the 1 cup broth. Bring to a boil. Then reduce the heat to medium-low and simmer the sauce for 15 minutes, tasting and adjusting the seasonings as needed. Add the additional broth if you prefer a thinner sauce.

5. Stir in the shrimp, cover the pot, and let rest off the heat until the shrimp are pink and opaque, about 10 minutes. Stir in the parsley and serve immediately over rice. 🌿

SHRIMP CURRY

SERVES 6

Nowadays there's nothing more desirable for entertaining than a sumptuous bowl of curry. An exotic and elegant menu is easily built around this luscious shrimp curry, thickened with a flavorful apple and sweetened with coconut milk. It's delicious spooned over plain white rice, but Pineapple Ginger Rice gilds the lily in the most wonderful way.

2 tablespoons olive oil

1 onion, cut into ¼-inch dice

2 carrots, peeled and cut into ¼-inch dice

1 Granny Smith apple, peeled, cored, and cut
    into ¼-inch dice

1 tablespoon finely minced garlic

1 tablespoon finely minced fresh ginger

2 teaspoons finely minced seeded green
    jalapeño pepper

1 large ripe tomato, peeled, seeded, and cut
    into ½-inch dice

2 tablespoons curry powder

2 bay leaves

1 cinnamon stick (3 inches long)

2 cups chicken broth, preferably homemade
    (see page 434)

1 can (15 ounces) unsweetened coconut milk

2 pounds large shrimp, peeled and deveined

Salt, to taste

¼ cup chopped fresh cilantro

Pineapple Ginger Rice (page 324), for serving

1. Heat the oil in a heavy pot over medium-low heat. Add the onion, carrots, and apple, and cook, stirring occasionally, until softened, about 7 minutes. Add the garlic, ginger, and jalapeño, and cook to incorporate the flavors, 7 minutes longer.

2. Add the tomato, curry powder, bay leaves, and cinnamon stick. Cook, stirring, for 2 minutes.

3. Add the broth and bring it to a boil. Then reduce the heat and simmer, uncovered, until the vegetables and apple are very soft, about 10 minutes.

4. Using the back of a spoon, mash some of the vegetables a little so they "melt" into the sauce a bit. Whisk in the coconut milk, and simmer the sauce gently, stirring occasionally, until it thickens slightly, about 10 minutes.

5. Stir the shrimp into the sauce and cook until they are pink and opaque, about 5 minutes. Season with salt. Stir in the cilantro. Discard the bay leaves and cinnamon stick, and serve immediately over Pineapple Ginger Rice. ♣

"I THINK YOU'LL HAVE A GREAT DEAL OF FUN WITH THESE CLAMS!"

A BUCKET OF CLAMS

From the first time I watched my mother eat littlenecks on the half shell, I couldn't wait to be old enough to try one. However, my first clam experience wasn't quite so daring. It was a fried clam roll, slathered with tartar sauce. Not bad. Next came spaghetti with white clam sauce. Definitely delicious but not unusual. I've come a long way since then. Yes, that includes enjoying raw clams, but I put mine in little sake cups atop a dab of some great cocktail sauce, and spear the clams with bamboo picks—perfect for serving with drinks at a party.

Jason Epstein, my brilliant food mentor, suggested mascarpone to freshen up an old favorite, clam dip, and it did the trick in spades. Lemongrass and White Wine Steamers are a classy update of a classic shore appetizer.

The Creamy Clam Chowder is intoxicating (I may live in New York, but I like my chowder New England–style) and the Clams Casino just may be the best you've ever tasted. And don't overlook the fresh clam sauce created for a twirl of thin spaghetti. In fact, try them all!

CLAM COCKTAIL IN A SAKE CUP WITH "HOT" COCKTAIL SAUCE

MAKES 24

to me, clams on the half shell say "summer," and they're one of my favorite hors d'oeuvres to serve as soon as the days get long and the trees are in full bloom. But they can be a little tricky because they can get pretty messy. So I've dreamed up a way to enjoy them and still come away as pretty as a picture: Serve the clams, speared with top-knotted bamboo picks, in individual sake cups or shot glasses or even Chinese-restaurant soupspoons.

¼ cup Heinz chili sauce

¼ cup ketchup

2 tablespoons prepared white horseradish, drained

1 tablespoon fresh lemon juice

½ teaspoon Worcestershire sauce

1 to 2 dashes Tabasco sauce, to taste

24 littleneck clams, scrubbed, soaked, rinsed, and shucked, (see box, page 231) in their liquor

1. Combine all the ingredients except the clams in a bowl. Taste, and adjust the seasonings as needed. Refrigerate, covered (the sauce will keep for up to 1 day).

2. To serve, drain the clams. Place 1 teaspoon of the cocktail sauce in the bottom of each of 24 small sake cups or shot glasses. Spear a clam with a top-knotted bamboo pick and stand it upright in the sauce in the cup. Place the little cups on an attractive tray, and pass as an hors d'oeuvre. ❧

JASON EPSTEIN'S
CLAM DIP DELUXE

MAKES 1½ CUPS

don't underestimate the power of the dip! Dips were popular in the '50s and are still going strong today. Set out a bowl of guacamole, a spicy salsa, and this extraordinary clam dip, and I assure you, no one will be disappointed. I've always loved clam dip, so I prodded my ever-creative friend Jason Epstein, former editorial director of Random House, cofounder of *The New York Review of Books,* and renowned cook with the best culinary imagination I know, to develop a slightly different version for this book. And he graciously complied.

18 to 20 littleneck clams, scrubbed, soaked,
    and rinsed (see box, page 231)

¼ cup dry white wine

3 flat-leaf parsley sprigs

1 shallot, halved

¾ cup mascarpone cheese

¼ cup full-fat plain yogurt

¼ cup bottled clam juice

1 large clove garlic, pressed

2 teaspoons fresh lemon juice

1 teaspoon Worcestershire sauce

1 dash Tabasco sauce

2 tablespoons chopped fresh flat-leaf parsley
    leaves, plus ½ teaspoon for garnish

Salt and freshly ground black pepper,
    to taste

Potato chips or Belgian endive leaves,
    for serving

1. Place the clams in a large pot and add the wine, parsley sprigs, shallot, and ½ cup water. Cover the pot and cook over high heat, shaking the pot occasionally, until the clams open, 5 to 10 minutes. Let rest for 5 minutes, covered, off the heat. Discard any clams that have not opened.

2. Remove the clams from the shells and blot them dry on paper towels. Coarsely chop them; you should have about ½ cup. Cover, and set aside.

3. Combine the mascarpone, yogurt, clam juice, garlic, lemon juice, Worcestershire sauce, Tabasco sauce, the chopped clams, and the 2 tablespoons chopped parsley in a bowl. Season with salt and pepper, and toss well. Transfer the mixture to a pretty serving bowl, and garnish it with the remaining ½ teaspoon chopped parsley. Serve with potato chips or endive leaves for scooping.

LEMONGRASS AND WHITE WINE STEAMERS

SERVES 4

○

I am a big fan of steamed clams. The touch of lemongrass here, along with the fresh ginger, freshens the broth. Enjoy the steamers with a dip of melted lemon butter. (Avoid buying the very large steamers—the smaller clams are sweeter.)

8 tablespoons (1 stick) unsalted butter

Juice of 1 lemon

1 bottle (750 ml) dry white wine

2 stalks fresh lemongrass, trimmed, peeled,
    and thinly sliced (see box, at right)

1 piece (1 inch) peeled fresh ginger, sliced
    and smashed

4 pounds steamer clams, scrubbed, soaked,
    and rinsed (see box, page 231)

¼ cup chopped fresh flat-leaf parsley leaves,
    for garnish

1. Melt the butter in a small saucepan over low heat. Stir in the lemon juice and remove from the heat. Cover to keep warm.

2. Combine the wine, lemongrass, and ginger in a heavy saucepan and bring to a boil. Reduce the heat to a simmer, cover the pan, and cook for 5 minutes.

3. Add the clams, return the liquid to a boil over high heat, and then reduce the heat slightly. Cover the pan and cook, shaking the pan once or twice, until the clams have opened, 5 to 10 minutes. Discard any clams that haven't opened.

HOW TO PREPARE LEMONGRASS

Prized for its subtle citrus fragrance, lemongrass is most often used in Thai and Vietnamese cooking. All the flavor is located in the bottom 6 inches of the long, pale, woody stalk. To prepare lemongrass, cut off and discard all but the lower 6 inches of the stalk, and then remove the tough outer layer. Slice the tender interior of the stalk as called for in the recipe. Discard the lemongrass after it has flavored the dish.

Look for fresh lemongrass. Most dried or frozen lemongrass has very little flavor.

4. Serve the clams immediately in shallow bowls, sprinkled with the parsley. (Discard the lemongrass and ginger.) Line a strainer with a paper towel, and strain the cooking broth through it into small bowls. Place a bowl of broth and a small ramekin of the melted lemon butter at each setting.

5. To eat the clams, first dip them in the broth to remove any sand that might cling to them, and then dip them into the lemon butter. Afterward, you might enjoy the clam broth on its own, but avoid the last few drops, as any sand will have settled at the bottom. ♣

JASON EPSTEIN'S
CLAMS CASINO

SERVES 6 AS AN APPETIZER

any recipe that my friend Jason Epstein shares with me is irresistible, and half of the dish is usually long gone before I finish my notes. These clams are no exception. Notice that there are no bread crumbs, thereby updating this recipe from the status of dry old-fashioned restaurant cliché. These clams are both creative and luxurious.

4 tablespoons (½ stick) unsalted butter,
    at room temperature

¼ cup finely chopped green bell pepper

¼ cup finely chopped sweet white onion

1 medium-size bottled pimento, finely
    chopped

2 teaspoons finely minced seeded green
    jalapeño pepper

2 teaspoons Worcestershire sauce

1 to 2 dashes Tabasco sauce, to taste

1 teaspoon fresh lemon juice

6 slices lean bacon, cut crosswise into
    1-inch-wide pieces

24 littleneck or small cherrystone clams,
    scrubbed, soaked, rinsed, and shucked
    (see box, page 231), on the half shell

1. Combine the butter, bell pepper, onion, pimento, and jalapeño in a bowl. Using a fork, stir in the Worcestershire, Tabasco, and lemon juice. Set aside.

2. Fry the bacon in a nonstick skillet over medium-low heat until it is translucent but not cooked through, about 4 minutes.

3. Meanwhile, position an oven rack 7 inches from the heat source and preheat the broiler.

4. Set the clams on a baking sheet, and top each clam with about 1 teaspoon of the butter mixture. Place a piece of bacon on top of that.

5. Broil the clams until the bacon has just begun to crisp (do not let it burn), 2 to 3 minutes. Serve immediately. ♣

CREAMY CLAM CHOWDER

SERVES 8

◯

Ilove this chowder—not too heavy, not too rich, thickened with potatoes only. Littlenecks are the ideal choice here because they have good flavor and chop beautifully. Scallions add a bright touch just before serving.

FOR STEAMING THE CLAMS:

8 pounds littleneck clams, scrubbed, soaked
    (use 2 tablespoons cornmeal for this amount),
    and rinsed (see box, facing page)

2 onions, halved

2 ribs celery, with leaves, halved

1 bay leaf

FOR THE CHOWDER:

4 ounces slab bacon, rind removed, cut into
    ¼-inch dice

1 tablespoon vegetable oil, if needed

1 onion, cut into ¼-inch dice

1½ ribs celery, with leaves, cut into ¼-inch dice

1 bay leaf

½ teaspoon dried tarragon, crumbled

2 medium-size russet potatoes, peeled and
    cut into ¼-inch dice

2 tablespoons unsalted butter

1⅔ cups half-and-half

Salt and freshly ground black pepper, to taste

2 tablespoons chopped fresh flat-leaf
    parsley leaves

3 scallions (white bulbs and 3 inches green),
    thinly sliced on the diagonal

1. Place the cleaned clams in a very large pot, and add the onion halves, celery ribs, and bay leaf. Add water to cover (but at least 10 cups) and bring just to a boil. Then reduce the heat, cover the pot, and simmer until the clams open, 5 to 10 minutes.

2. Using a slotted spoon, transfer the clams to a bowl. Discard any that have not opened. Let the clams cool slightly, and then remove them from the shells and set them aside (discard the shells).

3. Line a strainer with a paper towel, and strain the cooking broth through it into a bowl, to catch the sand. You should have about 10 cups of broth. Set it aside.

4. Prepare the chowder: Place the bacon in a large heavy pot over medium-low heat and cook to render the fat, 6 to 7 minutes. (If the bacon is lean, it may be necessary to add the tablespoon of vegetable oil.) Add the onion, celery, bay leaf, and tarragon, and cook, stirring occasionally, until the vegetables are wilted, about 10 minutes.

5. Add the potatoes and the butter, and cook, stirring, to melt the butter, 2 to 3 minutes.

6. Add 5 cups of the reserved strained broth. Simmer until the potatoes are tender and the soup is beginning to thicken, about 15 minutes. (Freeze the remaining broth for the next time you make fish chowder. Frozen, it keeps for 1 month.)

7. Chop the reserved clams and add them, along with the half-and-half, to the chowder. Simmer gently over medium-low heat to warm through, about 5 minutes.

8. Season the chowder with salt and pepper. Remove the bay leaf, and stir in the parsley and the scallions. Serve immediately. 🌿

CLEANING AND OPENING CLAMS

Buy clams on the day you intend to eat them, and make sure your clams are alive when you buy them. The shells should be shut tight. Any open clams should be discarded.

HOW TO CLEAN CLAMS: First, scrub them under cold running water. Then put them in a large bowl, add cold water to cover, and stir in 1 tablespoon cornmeal. Set them aside to soak for about 30 minutes. Then rinse them very well.

If you're not preparing the clams immediately, store them in a ceramic or stainless steel bowl in the fridge (no plastic—the clams will die in plastic).

HOW TO SHUCK CLAMS: Shucking clams is not easy, so it's best to have your fishmonger open them for you if you're not cooking them in the shell. Ask for the clams and liquid in one container and the shells in another. However, if that's not possible (you went clamming with friends, none of whom are expert shuckers), here's a brief how-to.

To shuck the clams yourself, you'll need a shucking knife—a wide, short, stiff knife, available at kitchenware stores. Place a clam on a towel in the palm of your hand, with the hinge facing away from you. Insert the tip of the shucking knife between the two halves of the shell, near the hinge. Holding the clam level, so as not to lose the liquor, carefully work the knife back and forth to pry the shell apart. Then work the knife along the edge of the upper shell and carefully cut the hinge. Discard the top shell. Cut the clam from underneath to free it from the bottom shell.

A LITTLE CLAM
AND POTATO SALAD

SERVES 4

this may seem like an unusual presentation, but the liquid from the clams is delicious over the potatoes and it makes a robust little meal. Serve it with a chilled Pinot Grigio.

FOR THE POTATO SALAD:

1 pound small red and white (mixed) boiling
    potatoes, quartered

2 tablespoons dry white wine

2 tablespoons chicken broth, canned or made from
    a bouillon cube

Salt and freshly ground black pepper, to taste

3 scallions (white bulbs and 3 inches green),
    thinly sliced

3 tablespoons red wine vinegar

2 teaspoons Dijon mustard

¼ cup extra-virgin olive oil

2 tablespoons chopped fresh flat-leaf parsley leaves

FOR THE CLAMS:

2 tablespoons extra-virgin olive oil

1 tablespoon finely sliced garlic

½ cup dry white wine

1½ pounds littleneck or Manila clams, scrubbed,
    soaked, and rinsed (see box, page 231)

Salt and freshly ground black pepper, to taste

2 tablespoons chopped fresh flat-leaf parsley leaves,
    for garnish

Crusty bread, warmed or at room temperature,
    for serving

1. Prepare the potato salad: Bring a pot of salted water to a boil. Add the potatoes, reduce the heat to medium, partially cover the pot, and simmer until the potatoes are tender, 15 minutes. Drain, and place them in a large bowl.

2. While the potatoes are still warm, toss them with the wine and broth. Season with salt and pepper, and toss with the scallions.

3. Whisk the vinegar and mustard together in a small bowl. Slowly drizzle in the olive oil, whisking constantly, until the dressing has thickened slightly. Combine this with the potatoes. Taste and adjust the seasonings if needed, and then stir in the parsley. Set the salad aside.

4. Prepare the clams: Heat the olive oil in a large heavy pot over low heat. Add the garlic and cook, stirring, until golden, 2 minutes. Add the wine and the clams, and season with salt and pepper. Raise the heat to medium so that the wine is simmering, cover the pot, and steam the clams, shaking the pan occasionally, until they open, 5 to 10 minutes (raise the heat if necessary). Discard any clams that do not open.

5. To serve, spoon the potato salad into four shallow pasta bowls. Divide the clams, still in their shells, among the servings of salad. Line a strainer with a paper towel, and strain the cooking liquid through it into a spouted measuring cup; then spoon 2 or 3 tablespoons of the strained liquid over each serving. Sprinkle with the chopped parsley, and serve with wedges of crusty bread. 🍂

CLAMS, CHORIZO, AND RICE

SERVES 4

Whether the origins of this dish belong to Portugal or South America barely matters, the allure is so intense and the flavors and texture so comforting. Serve some crusty peasant bread alongside. A crisp chilled white is the wine of choice.

2 tablespoons extra-virgin olive oil

1 small onion, cut into ¼-inch dice

4 ounces chorizo sausage, cut into ¼-inch pieces

1½ cups long-grain white rice

1 tablespoon ground cumin

Salt and freshly ground black pepper, to taste

3½ cups chicken broth, preferably homemade
    (see page 434)

36 littleneck clams, scrubbed, soaked, rinsed, and
    shucked (see box, page 231) in their liquor

4 tablespoons chopped fresh flat-leaf parsley leaves

3 scallions (white bulbs and 3 inches green),
    thinly sliced, for garnish

1. Heat the oil in a large heavy pot over medium heat. Add the onion and chorizo and cook, stirring occasionally, until the onion is translucent, about 10 minutes. Add the rice and stir to coat it well with the oil. Sprinkle with the cumin, salt, and pepper. Cook, stirring, for 1 minute to mellow the spices.

2. Add the broth, bring it to a boil, stir, and reduce the heat to medium-low. Cover the pot and simmer until most of the liquid has been absorbed, about 15 minutes.

3. Meanwhile, drain the clams in a fine-mesh strainer set over a bowl. Gently rinse the clams to remove any sand; or soak them in cold water and rinse again.

4. Stir 2 tablespoons of the parsley and the cleaned clams into the rice mixture. Cover, and cook for 2 minutes. Taste, and adjust the seasonings if needed. Transfer the mixture to a serving bowl, and sprinkle the remaining 2 tablespoons parsley and the scallions on top. Serve immediately. 🍂

HONG KONG CLAMS

SERVES 4

These Asian-flavored clams served over Thai rice sticks remind me a little of an excellent linguine with white clam sauce, and they're just as much fun to eat. Make the sauce as hot or as moderate as you choose. Serve the clams with plenty of sauce in shallow bowls, with a flourish of scallions and parsley. Some cold Tsingtao beer is the drink for these.

3 ounces Thai rice noodles

2 tablespoons olive oil

1 tablespoon finely minced garlic

1 tablespoon finely minced fresh ginger

3 pounds littleneck clams (36 clams), scrubbed,
    soaked, and rinsed (see box, page 231)

½ cup chicken broth, preferably homemade
    (see page 434)

2 tablespoons dry sherry

1 tablespoon light soy sauce

2 dashes Tabasco sauce

Freshly ground black pepper, to taste

3 scallions (white bulbs and 3 inches green),
    thinly sliced, for garnish

2 tablespoons chopped fresh flat-leaf
    parsley leaves, for garnish

1. Prepare the rice noodles: Bring 4 cups water to a boil in a saucepan. Remove the pan from the heat and add the noodles to the hot water. Soak until soft (but not mushy), about 5 minutes. Drain, rinse under cold water, and drain again. Set aside.

2. Heat the olive oil in a wok or a large wide pot over medium heat. Add the garlic and ginger and cook, stirring, until the garlic is lightly golden, 1 minute. Add the clams and stir. Raise the heat to medium-high, cover the wok, and cook, shaking the pan, until the clams begin to open, 4 to 5 minutes. Add the broth, sherry, soy sauce, Tabasco, and pepper. Lower the heat to medium and continue to cook until all of the clams have opened, 5 to 10 minutes. Discard any that do not open.

3. To serve, divide the rice noodles among four shallow bowls. Arrange the clams over the noodles, and pour the liquid over them. Sprinkle with the scallions and parsley, and serve immediately. ✿

BEER BATTER–FRIED CLAM ROLL
WITH TARTAR DELIGHT

SERVES 12

There is just something compelling about fried clam rolls. They are a real side-of-the-road, shack-at-the-end-of-a-pier, State-of-Maine treat. I believe they use steamers in their rolls. This version calls for littlenecks, which are quite meaty. The beer batter is a good deal lighter than most—almost fluffy. When all is said and done, this is one great—and light—clam roll. Enjoy!

FOR THE BEER BATTER:

1 cup all-purpose flour

1 teaspoon coarse (kosher) salt

2 tablespoons unsalted butter,
    melted

2 large eggs, beaten

1 cup flat beer (see Note)

2 large egg whites

FOR THE CLAM ROLLS:

Vegetable oil, for deep-frying

1 quart (60 to 65) littleneck clams,
    scrubbed, soaked, rinsed, and shucked
    (see box, page 231), drained, and
    patted dry

12 split-top hot dog rolls, for serving

Tartar Delight (recipe follows), for serving

1. One hour ahead of time, prepare the beer batter: Sift the flour and salt into a bowl. Stir in the melted butter and the beaten eggs. Gradually add the beer, stirring until the batter is smooth. Let the batter stand, loosely covered, in a warm place for 1 hour.

2. Beat the egg whites in a bowl until they form stiff peaks. Carefully fold them into the beer batter.

3. Fill a deep heavy pot halfway with vegetable oil, and heat the oil to 350°F.

4. In small batches, dip the clams into the beer batter and then drop them carefully into the hot oil. Cook until they are golden brown, about 4 minutes. Use a slotted spoon to carefully transfer them to paper towels to drain.

5. Meanwhile, preheat the broiler.

6. Gently spread open the hot dog rolls (be careful not to break them apart), and toast them lightly under the broiler. Spread 2 tablespoons of Tartar Delight over the interior of each roll, and then fill it with the fried clams. 5 clams per roll. Serve immediately, passing any extra tartar sauce in a small bowl.

NOTE: To flatten beer, pour it into a glass and let it sit for 30 minutes to 1 hour. If it still seems too fizzy, stir it until it loses its bubbles. 🌺

TARTAR DELIGHT

MAKES 2 CUPS

homemade tartar sauce—what could be better for hot batter-fried clams? I've added a touch of yogurt for an ever-so-slight tang—it works beautifully with all sweet summer shellfish.

> ½ cup prepared mayonnaise, such as Hellmann's
> ¼ cup sour cream
> ¼ cup nonfat plain yogurt
> 2 tablespoons coarsely chopped sweet pickles
> 1 tablespoon drained tiny capers
> 1 to 2 tablespoons chopped fresh tarragon leaves,
>   or 1 to 2 teaspoons dried
> Dash of Tabasco sauce
> Freshly ground black pepper, to taste

Combine all the ingredients in a bowl. Refrigerate, covered, until ready to use (it will keep for up to 2 days). 🌺

SPAGHETTINI
WITH CLAMS AND TOMATO HERB SAUCE

SERVES 4

Spaghetti with clam sauce has always been a favorite of mine. I prefer using tiny New Zealand cockles in this version, because they add a sweet finesse to spaghettini tossed with fresh tomatoes, garden-fresh basil, and tarragon. But, if you can't find them, littlenecks work very well. This pasta dish is easy to prepare and elegant enough to serve up for any significant dinner. Accompany it with a delicate green salad and a chilled Pinot Grigio. And don't forget to set a little bowl by each place setting to hold the empty clam shells.

12 ounces spaghettini

¼ cup extra-virgin olive oil

2 tablespoons finely minced garlic

½ cup bottled clam juice

½ cup dry white wine

4 pounds cockles or littleneck clams, scrubbed,
    soaked, and rinsed (see box, page 231)

4 cups diced ripe tomatoes

4 scallions (white bulbs and 3 inches green),
    thinly sliced

⅓ cup slivered fresh basil leaves

2 tablespoons coarsely chopped fresh tarragon
    leaves

Salt and freshly ground black pepper, to taste

1. Bring a large pot of salted water to a boil. Add the spaghettini and cook according to the package directions until al dente. Drain, toss with a little of the olive oil to prevent sticking, and set aside, covered, to keep warm.

2. Heat the olive oil in a large heavy pot over low heat. Add the garlic and cook, stirring, until it is wilted, 2 minutes.

3. Add the clam juice and wine, cover the pot, raise the heat to medium-low, and simmer for 3 minutes to blend the flavors.

4. Add the clams, cover, and simmer, shaking the pan, until they open, about 5 minutes (raise the heat if necessary). Discard any clams that do not open.

5. Transfer the clams, along with the juices, to a large shallow serving bowl. Add the tomatoes and scallions, and toss. Sprinkle with the basil and tarragon, and season with salt and pepper. Toss lightly to combine.

6. Divide the cooked spaghettini among four shallow pasta bowls, and top it with the clams and the tomato sauce. Serve immediately. 🍃

SATURDAY NIGHT WITH FRIENDS

A little pasta, a little wine, a few friends, a hot game of Scrabble, and a wedge of cheesecake to celebrate the winner—an easy, fun, late-summer Saturday night. Pour a Chianti Classico or a Montepulciano.

TUNA BREAD SALAD
PAGE 248

SPAGHETTINI
with Clams and Tomato Herb Sauce
FACING PAGE

A REFINED LITTLE SALAD
PAGE 252

FRESH RICOTTA LEMON CHEESECAKE
PAGE 403

"EASY, LIGHT, AND DELICIOUS—YOU CAN'T ASK MORE OF A SALAD."

SEAFOOD SALADS

are refreshing and delightful for luncheons, light suppers, and as delicate first plates. They're easy to create, make colorful presentations, and are varied enough to suit every palate and pocketbook. I enjoy tuna both canned and fresh, and offer up a Tuna Bread Salad, resplendent with Italian tuna, ripe tomatoes, robust croutons, and fresh basil. On the other hand, my Tuna Niçoise Chopped Salad is prepared with skillet-seared lightly marinated fresh tuna, giving it a special-occasion feel.

I enjoyed my first *insalate di mare* sitting at a seaside restaurant in Italy—shrimp, perfectly poached calamari, crabmeat, and tiny dice of celery and carrots dressed with olive oil and a splash of vinegar. It appears in my book as a Seaside Seafood Salad. I just couldn't resist substituting lobster for the calamari.

Poached halibut, combined with red onions, capers, celery, and mayonnaise, becomes a delectable salad spread over multigrain toast with a slab of ripe tomato for Sunday brunch. For a variation, substitute smoked whitefish for the halibut and serve the salad with bagels.

HERRING AND CREAM
AND MORE

SERVES 6

Pickled herring is a favorite of some and a joke to others, but I grew up with it on tables laden with deli spreads, and for me it's a deliciously nostalgic dish. The addition of thinly sliced cucumber adds freshness to this Scandinavian staple. Radicchio lends its beautiful magenta color, and dill gives it finesse. Serve it with Roasted Beets with Tangerine Vinaigrette (page 22). Or enjoy your herring the traditional way: with fresh pumpernickel and unsalted butter.

1 pound pickled herring and onions in sour cream
(from the deli counter or bottled)

½ hothouse (seedless) cucumber, unpeeled, halved
lengthwise and cut into thin half-rounds

⅓ cup thinly sliced tender inner radicchio leaves
(about ½- x ¼-inch strips)

3 scallions (white bulbs and 3 inches green),
thinly sliced

½ cup sour cream

2 tablespoons chopped fresh dill leaves

Salt and freshly ground black pepper, to taste

1. Remove the herring from the cream sauce and onions (reserving the sauce and onions), and cut it into 1-inch pieces. Place the pieces in a bowl. Add the cucumber, radicchio, scallions, sour cream, dill, and the reserved cream sauce and onions. Season with salt and pepper. Using a rubber spatula, gently fold all the ingredients together.

2. Transfer the salad to a serving bowl, cover, and refrigerate until well chilled, up to 4 hours. Serve cold. ❧

BRUNCH HALIBUT SALAD

MAKES 2 CUPS; SERVES 6

On a lazy summer morning, invite a few friends over for brunch and serve them this fish salad. It's one of my favorites, delicious with a slice of ripe tomato on a toasted bagel or multigrain bread. Try the same salad using smoked whitefish or bluefish.

½ cup dry white wine

2 flat-leaf parsley sprigs

1 bay leaf

4 whole black peppercorns

1½ pounds halibut fillet, halved crosswise

½ cup diced celery (¼-inch dice)

¼ cup diced red onion (¼-inch dice)

1 tablespoon drained tiny capers

⅓ cup prepared mayonnaise, such as Hellmann's

Toasted multigrain bread or bagels,
    for serving

Sliced ripe tomatoes, for serving

1. Combine the wine, parsley sprigs, bay leaf, peppercorns, and 2 cups water in a heavy saucepan and bring to a boil over high heat. Reduce the heat to medium-low and add the halibut. Gently simmer the fish, uncovered, until it is opaque and cooked through, about 10 minutes. Using a large spatula, transfer the halibut to a colander and allow it to drain and cool completely.

2. Pat the halibut dry. Remove the skin and gently scrape off the dark layer of fat. Flake the fish into a large bowl.

3. Add the celery, red onion, and capers to the fish, and toss to mix. Stir in the mayonnaise. Cover the bowl and refrigerate for at least 4 hours.

4. Serve the salad in a bowl, with the toast and sliced tomatoes alongside. ❧

GRAVLAX SALMON SALAD

SERVES 6

○

I chose to make this salad with gravlax rather than uncured salmon because the unique curing process, using both sugar and salt, adds spectacular flavor to the fish. Combined with the contrasting flavors of cool cucumbers and licorice-y fennel, the result is sublime. A splash of cider vinegar brightens the palate, and a dollop of crème fraîche is the icing on the cake. Serve this with fresh raisin-pumpernickel bread.

1 center-cut piece salmon gravlax
    (2 pounds; see box, page 242)

1 fennel bulb

1 hothouse (seedless) cucumber, unpeeled,
    cut into thin rounds

1 cup chopped tender radicchio leaves
    (½-inch pieces)

¼ cup cider vinegar

1 cup crème fraîche, for serving

1 cup fresh radish sprouts, for garnish (see Note)

1. Preheat the oven to 450°F.

2. Lightly oil a baking sheet. Place the gravlax, skin side down, on the baking sheet and bake until the fish is cooked to medium-rare and flakes easily when tested with a fork, 15 to 20 minutes.

3. While the gravlax is cooking, prepare the fennel: Trim off the fronds, chop them, and set them aside. Cut the bulb in half lengthwise, cut out and discard the core, and cut the bulb into thin slivers. Set the slivers aside.

4. When the gravlax is cooked, flake off large pieces of salmon from the skin (the skin will probably be sticking to the baking sheet) and remove any fat. Place the pieces of salmon in a large bowl, and add the slivered fennel, chopped fennel fronds, cucumber, and radicchio. Using a large rubber spatula, gently fold the ingredients together until just combined.

5. Drizzle the vinegar over the salad and toss lightly. Divide the salad among six plates. Top each serving with a dollop of crème fraîche and a sprinkling of radish sprouts.

NOTE: Fresh radish sprouts are found in plastic containers in the produce department of specialty markets and well-stocked supermarkets.

GRAVLAX

Gravlax is one of my favorite ways to enjoy salmon and one of the many delights of Scandinavian cuisine. The classic Nordic process uses both sugar and salt to cure the raw salmon. Plenty of fresh dill is also part of the curing process. To prepare gravlax, a mixture of the sugar, salt, and dill is sandwiched between two salmon fillets. The fillets are tightly wrapped in plastic wrap and refrigerated for between 24 and 36 hours. Once cured, the cure mixture is scraped off and the salmon is ready to serve. Most often, it is thinly sliced for serving—it's very delicious this way—however, I think it reaches it's full potential in this salad. Specialty markets should have gravlax on hand for you to purchase.

CRABMEAT-APPLE SALAD

SERVES 4

Snowy white lump crabmeat is always an elegant choice to serve, and this salad is delicious as a starter or as a light luncheon dish. The crisp apples add delicous crunch, and the chives and lemon give the salad just the right flavor accents.

1 Granny Smith apple

3 tablespoons fresh lemon juice

1 pound cooked fresh lump crabmeat, picked over to remove any cartilage

2 scallions (white bulbs and 3 inches green), thinly sliced

Salt and freshly ground black pepper, to taste

2 tablespoons olive oil

1 tablespoon snipped fresh chives

4 large tender inner radicchio leaves, rinsed and patted dry, to use as cups

¼ cup radish sprouts (see Note, facing page)

1 cup Sparkling Pineapple Salsa (page 371) or Tropical Salsa (page 372)

1. Halve and core the apple, and then cut it into ¼-inch dice. Place the diced apple in a large bowl, add 1 tablespoon of the lemon juice, and toss (this will keep the apple from discoloring).

2. Add the crabmeat and scallions to the apple, and season with salt and pepper. Drizzle the remaining 2 tablespoons lemon juice and the olive oil over the mixture, and toss together gently. Add the chives and toss gently again.

3. To serve, place a radicchio leaf on each of four salad plates. Spoon the crab salad evenly into the lettuce cups, and sprinkle the sprouts on top. (Alternatively, the salad can be served in a decorative bowl, sprinkled with the sprouts.) Serve with a large spoonful of salsa alongside.

PARTY SHRIMP SALAD

SERVES 8

almost everyone I know has a favorite shrimp salad. Most are slathered with mayonnaise. This light and colorful version combines the shrimp with tomatoes, olives, and small chunks of uncooked summer squash and bathes the mix in a vinaigrette instead. Serve it on a warm day, along with a potato or corn salad. For a buffet table, grilled flank steak or butterflied leg of lamb would be a delicious companion.

FOR THE SHRIMP:

½ cup dry white wine

2 ribs celery with leaves, chopped

4 sprigs flat-leaf parsley

4 whole black peppercorns

2¼ pounds large shrimp, peeled and
    deveined

FOR THE SALAD:

1½ pounds green beans, trimmed and cut into
    1-inch lengths

6 cups coarsely torn tender lettuce leaves
    (Boston, romaine hearts, or leaf lettuce),
    rinsed and patted dry

3 cups diced seeded ripe tomatoes
    (½-inch dice)

3 small yellow squash or zucchini, quartered
    lengthwise, seeded, and cut into ½-inch
    pieces

¾ cup pitted Niçoise or ripe California
    black olives, coarsely chopped

¼ cup chopped fresh flat-leaf parsley leaves

Salt and freshly ground black pepper,
    to taste

¾ cup Red Wine Vinaigrette (page 23)

4 hard-cooked eggs, halved, for garnish

1. Prepare the shrimp: Fill a medium-size saucepan halfway with water. Add the wine, celery, parsley sprigs, and peppercorns. Bring to a boil over high heat. Reduce the heat to medium-low, add the shrimp, and simmer until they are opaque and pink, 2 minutes. Drain the shrimp, discarding the celery, parsley, and peppercorns. Rinse the shrimp under cold running water, and drain them well. Set aside.

2. Fill a large bowl with ice water.

3. Bring a large saucepan of lightly salted water to a boil. Add the green beans and cook until tender, 3 to 4 minutes. Drain them in a colander, plunge the colander in the ice water, and leave it until the beans are thoroughly cooled. Drain again.

4. Pat the green beans dry, and place them in a large bowl along with the lettuce, shrimp, tomatoes, squash, olives, and chopped parsley.

5. Just before serving, season the salad with salt and pepper and toss it lightly with the vinaigrette.

6. Serve in a large shallow bowl or on a decorative platter, garnished with the hard-cooked eggs.

ROASTED BLACK COD SALAD

SERVES 6

black cod, also known as sablefish, is found in northern Atlantic waters and is as sumptuous as it is delicious. The texture lends itself beautifully to high-temperature roasting. Once the fish is flaked, it combines well with a fresh vegetable salad. A brisk vinaigrette is an ideal foil for the buttery flavor of the fish. Enjoy this as a luncheon or a light supper.

4 black cod fillets (each 8 ounces)

5 tablespoons olive oil

Salt and freshly ground black pepper

1 yellow bell pepper, stemmed, seeded,
    and thinly sliced lengthwise

1 red bell pepper, stemmed, seeded,
    and thinly sliced lengthwise

½ hothouse (seedless) cucumber, unpeeled, thinly sliced

2 ribs celery, thinly sliced

1 small red onion, halved lengthwise and
    cut into thin lengthwise slivers

2 cups tiny pear tomatoes, halved lengthwise

4 scallions (white bulbs and 3 inches green), thinly sliced

¼ cup chopped fresh flat-leaf parsley leaves

¼ cup red wine vinegar

1. Preheat the oven to 450°F.

2. Lightly oil a large baking dish, and arrange the cod fillets in it. Brush them with 1 tablespoon of the olive oil and season them generously with salt and pepper. Roast until the fish is cooked through and flakes easily, 15 to 18 minutes. Set it aside to cool.

3. Remove any bones and carefully flake the fish into large pieces. Set it aside.

4. Combine the bell peppers, cucumbers, celery, onion, tomatoes, scallions, and 2 tablespoons of the chopped parsley in a large bowl.

5. In another bowl, whisk the remaining 4 tablespoons olive oil with the vinegar. Season with salt and pepper.

6. Shortly before serving, toss the vegetables with the dressing. Using a large rubber spatula, carefully fold in the reserved flaked fish. Transfer the salad to a serving bowl, and sprinkle the remaining 2 tablespoons chopped parsley over it.

SAFFRON MUSSEL SALAD

SERVES 6

farmed mussels, readily available these days, are, for the most part, wonderfully clean and easy to prepare. When robed in a delicate saffron mayonnaise, which seems to me the perfect silky fit, the mussels acquire a Spanish overtone. The frisée salad with apples and red pepper provides a crisp freshness that beautifully balances the fish.

FOR THE SAFFRON MAYONNAISE:

4 cloves garlic

¼ cup dry white wine

1 teaspoon crumbled saffron threads

1 cup prepared mayonnaise, such as Hellmann's

2 tablespoons extra-virgin olive oil

Salt and freshly ground black pepper, to taste

FOR THE MUSSELS:

4 pounds mussels

1 tablespoon cornmeal

½ cup dry white wine

Salt and freshly ground pepper, to taste

FOR THE SALAD:

1 Granny Smith apple

1 large head frisée lettuce, tough outer leaves
    discarded, tender leaves separated,
    rinsed, and patted dry

1 cup diced red bell pepper (¼-inch dice)

3 scallions (white bulbs and 3 inches green), thinly sliced

½ small red onion, slivered lengthwise

3 tablespoons snipped fresh chives

Salt and freshly ground black pepper, to taste

2 tablespoons extra-virgin olive oil

2 tablespoons sherry vinegar

1. One day ahead, prepare the saffron mayonnaise: Preheat the oven to 350°F.

2. Remove most of the papery skin from the garlic cloves and trim off ¼ inch from each tip. Wrap the garlic cloves in a square of aluminum foil, and bake until they are very soft, 1 hour.

3. Meanwhile, combine the wine and saffron in a small saucepan and bring to a boil. Reduce the heat to low and simmer for 7 minutes to reduce by about half. Strain to remove the saffron threads. Set the liquid aside to cool to room temperature.

4. Place the mayonnaise in a small bowl. Whisk in the olive oil and 2 tablespoons of the reserved saffron wine. Season with salt and pepper. Squeeze the soft garlic from the cloves into the mayonnaise mixture, and whisk it in. Cover and refrigerate overnight.

5. The next day, prepare the mussels: First, scrub them in cold water. Remove any beards that might be attached. Then put them in a bowl, add cold water to cover, and stir in the cornmeal. Set them aside to soak for about 30 minutes. Then rinse them very well.

6. Fill a large pot with water to a depth of 2 inches. Add the wine and bring to a boil. Add the cleaned mussels, cover, and steam over medium heat, shaking the pot, until they open, 2 to 3 minutes. Drain, and set aside to cool. Discard any mussels that don't open.

7. When the mussels are cool enough to handle, remove them from the shells and place them in a bowl. Fold in ½ cup of the saffron mayonnaise.

8. Prepare the salad: Halve and core the apple, and cut it into ¼-inch dice (you want 1 cup diced apple). Place the diced apple in a large bowl and add the frisée, bell peppers, scallions, red onion, and 1 tablespoon of the chives. Season with salt and pepper. Add the olive oil and sherry vinegar, and toss. Divide the salad among six large salad plates. Spoon the mussels onto the center of each salad. Sprinkle with the remaining 2 tablespoons chives, and serve. ❧

SEASIDE SEAFOOD SALAD

SERVES 4 AS AN ENTREE, OR 8 AS A STARTER

this refreshing seafood salad is served at almost every outdoor trattoria on the coast of Italy, and each one has its own version. After spending two summers in Lerici, on the Italian Riviera, I was inspired to come up with my own. A chilled Orvieto or Pinot Grigio served alongside will transport you to Italy.

12 ounces cooked large shrimp, peeled,
    deveined, and halved crosswise
8 ounces cooked fresh lump crabmeat,
    picked over for any cartilage
8 ounces cooked fresh lobster meat,
    cut into ½-inch pieces
¼ cup finely diced carrot
¼ cup finely diced celery
1 tablespoon drained tiny capers
Salt and freshly ground black pepper, to taste
1 teaspoon finely minced seeded red or green
    jalapeño pepper
2 tablespoons chopped fresh flat-leaf
    parsley leaves

⅓ cup highest-quality extra-virgin olive oil
3 tablespoons fresh lemon juice

1. Place the shrimp, crabmeat, lobster, carrot, celery, and capers in a large bowl. Using a rubber spatula, gently fold the ingredients together, being careful not to break up the crab too much. Season with salt and pepper.

2. Add the jalapeño pepper and parsley. Carefully fold in the olive oil and lemon juice, tasting as you go. Adjust the seasonings as needed and serve immediately, or cover and refrigerate for up to 4 hours. ❧

TUNA BREAD SALAD

SERVES 6

Easy, light, and delicious—you can't ask more of a salad. I prefer imported tuna packed in oil to kick up the flavors, but if you're watching your calories, water-packed tuna will also give a tasty result. Not surprisingly, this is extra-delicious with summer tomatoes. The croutons add texture and contribute to the rustic look of this dynamic salad.

2 cups cubed French bread (½-inch pieces)

2 cans (each 6 ounces) tuna packed in oil, preferably Italian, drained

¼ small red onion, slivered lengthwise

2 ripe tomatoes, cut into ½-inch cubes

½ cup coarsely torn fresh basil leaves

2 tablespoons extra-virgin olive oil

1½ tablespoons red wine vinegar

Salt and freshly ground black pepper, to taste

1. Preheat the oven to 350°F.

2. Spread the bread cubes on a baking sheet and bake in the oven, tossing them once, until toasted, about 20 minutes. Set them aside.

3. Place the tuna in a bowl and break it apart into large chunks. (Don't mash it—just separate it into bite-size pieces.) Pull the onion slivers apart and add them to the tuna, along with the tomatoes, basil, oil, vinegar, and salt and pepper.

4. Just before serving, toss in the bread cubes. Divide the salad among six plates, and serve.

TUNA NIÇOISE CHOPPED SALAD

SERVES 6

Although a Niçoise salad is usually made with canned tuna, when made with fresh tuna, it takes on uptown airs that serve it very well. Accompany the salad with a platter laden with a selection of great French cheeses. Bon appétit!

1 tuna steak (1¼ pounds), cut 1 inch thick

2 tablespoons extra-virgin olive oil

2 tablespoons red wine vinegar

Coarse (kosher) salt and freshly ground black
     pepper, to taste

12 ounces green beans, trimmed

1 pound white boiling potatoes, peeled and cut
     into ½-inch cubes

⅓ cup coarsely chopped pitted Niçoise olives

2 tablespoons chopped fresh flat-leaf parsley leaves

½ cup Red Wine Vinaigrette (page 23)

4 hard-cooked eggs, coarsely chopped

6 to 8 anchovies, packed in oil

1. Place the tuna in a bowl and coat it with the oil and vinegar. Season with salt and pepper, and marinate for 15 minutes, turning the tuna once or twice.

2. Bring a medium-size saucepan of salted water to a boil, add the green beans, and cook until just tender, 3 to 4 minutes. Using a slotted spoon, transfer the beans to a colander and rinse under cold running water. Drain again, and set aside.

3. Add the potatoes to the same boiling water and cook until just tender, about 10 minutes. Drain, and set aside.

4. Heat a nonstick skillet over medium heat. Remove the tuna from the marinade and place it in the skillet. Sear, turning the tuna carefully with a spatula, until is lightly browned on the outside and pale pink on the inside, 5 minutes on the first side and 5 to 6 minutes on the second side. Transfer it to a plate and let it rest for 5 minutes.

5. Cut the tuna steak into 1-inch-thick slices across the grain, and then cut the slices into 1-inch cubes.

6. Cut the reserved green beans into ½-inch pieces and place them in a large bowl. Add the potatoes, olives, and 1 tablespoon of the chopped parsley. Season with salt and pepper. Toss with ¼ cup of the vinaigrette.

7. Arrange the beans and potatoes on a large oval, round, or rectangular platter. Arrange the cubes of tuna decoratively over the top, and sprinkle with the chopped egg.

8. Carefully rinse the anchovies, and pat them dry. Arrange them around the salad. Drizzle the salad with the remaining ¼ cup vinaigrette and sprinkle with the remaining 1 tablespoon chopped parsley. Then serve.

"...AN ELEGANT SALAD TO SERVE WITH AN ELEGANT MEAL..."

LEAFY SALADS

These days, a catalog of the leafy greens in a variety of sizes and shapes that are available in American markets could fill several pages. Each leaf has its own flavor, color, and texture, and when combined with other complementary greens and perhaps a few edible flowers, can make any number of delicious salads. For the past few years, there have even been packaged mixes in our markets that barely require washing, making leafy green salads so appealing and easy—no washing, no chopping—that large numbers of people now regularly eat salads who never did before.

Salad making is a fine balancing act. My Frisée and Apple Salad is a perfect example, in which a slightly bitter green works beautifully with the tart apple and a fruity vinaigrette. In another recipe, peppery watercress complements mild-flavored and elegant-textured mushrooms. A few years ago I might have said there was no place on today's table for iceberg lettuce, but that is no longer the case. With a wonderful crunch and a refreshing flavor, iceberg has gained new respect. I serve my iceberg in wedges topped with creamy, herbal, light Green Goddess Dressing, making it more refreshing still. Where there's good texture, with bite and crunch, and great color, there's a successful salad.

A REFINED LITTLE SALAD

SERVES 4

When you're looking for an elegant salad to serve with an elegant meal, this is the choice. The sight of two refined, buttery lettuces lightly dressed and flecked with fresh herbs tells your guests that you've made the selection yourself and didn't just dump a packaged salad mix into a bowl.

FOR THE SALAD GREENS:

2 heads Bibb lettuce, damaged outer leaves
    discarded

2 heads Boston lettuce, damaged outer
    leaves discarded

FOR THE VINAIGRETTE:

1 tablespoon Dijon mustard

2 tablespoons white wine vinegar

Salt and freshly ground black pepper,
    to taste

3 tablespoons extra-virgin olive oil

TO FINISH THE SALAD:

2 tablespoons finely minced shallots

2 tablespoons chopped fresh tarragon, chervil,
    or flat-leaf parsley leaves

1 tablespoon snipped fresh chives

Salt and freshly ground black pepper,
    to taste

1. Using a small sharp knife, remove the cores from the heads of lettuce. Separate the delicate leaves, discarding any bruised areas. Swish the lettuce in a large bowl of cold water; then rinse it under cold running water and drain well. Pat dry. Wrap the leaves in paper towels, then place them in a plastic bag, and refrigerate them in the crisper drawer for 4 to 6 hours.

2. Prepare the vinaigrette: Whisk the mustard, vinegar, and salt and pepper together in a small bowl. Whisking constantly, slowly drizzle in the olive oil; continue whisking until the dressing has thickened slightly. Set it aside.

3. Place the crisped lettuce leaves in a large salad bowl, and toss with the shallots, tarragon, and chives.

4. Just before serving, season the salad with salt and pepper, and toss it with the vinaigrette. Serve immediately.

ICEBERG WEDGES
WITH GREEN GODDESS DRESSING

SERVES 4

○

Iceberg lettuce has made a stunning comeback and is found on many sleek restaurant menus today—thick crisp wedges often accompanied by tomato wedges, red onion rings, and a blue cheese dressing. But you'll be serving this salad with a new Green Goddess Dressing, abounding in flavor from a bouquet of fresh herbs—chives, tarragon, and parsley (and with fewer calories if you use nonfat yogurt). Have it on hand to dollop on grilled chicken and fish as well. And if you're as big a fan of Green Goddess Dressing as I am, check out the variation on page 205, which includes a creamy avocado.

FOR THE GREEN GODDESS DRESSING
   (makes 3 cups):

1 cup Greek yogurt (nonfat if desired), drained

1 cup prepared mayonnaise, such as Hellmann's

6 canned or bottled anchovy fillets, drained,
      rinsed, patted dry, and minced

3 scallions (white bulbs and 3 inches green),
      finely minced

4 tablespoons snipped fresh chives

3 tablespoons chopped fresh flat-leaf parsley leaves

3 tablespoons chopped fresh tarragon leaves

1 tablespoon white wine vinegar

Salt and freshly ground black pepper, to taste

FOR THE SALAD:

1 head iceberg lettuce, trimmed, rinsed, drained,
      patted dry, and cut into 4 wedges

16 yellow and red pear tomatoes (mixed),
      halved lengthwise, for garnish

1. Prepare the Green Goddess Dressing: Combine the yogurt and mayonnaise in a bowl. Add the anchovies and scallions, and stir well. Stir in 3 tablespoons of the chives, along with the parsley, tarragon, and vinegar. Taste, and season with salt and pepper. Cover and refrigerate for up to 6 hours for the flavors to blend.

2. When you are ready to prepare the salad, place a wedge of iceberg lettuce in each of four shallow bowls. Pour ⅓ cup of the dressing over each wedge. Any extra salad dressing can be covered and refrigerated for 1 day.) Grind some pepper over the top, and sprinkle evenly with the remaining 1 tablespoon snipped chives. Scatter the tomatoes evenly around the wedges, and serve immediately. ❧

WATERCRESS AND MUSHROOM SALAD

SERVES 8

Watercress is so flavorful, it almost needs no dressing at all, but I love this Asian-style variation because it includes orange juice, which is light and refreshing. You could also use tangerine juice. The sweetness of the citrus complements the bitter greens. Removing the heavy watercress stems makes the salad easy to eat, and raw, thinly sliced mushrooms have a texture that works beautifully in combination with deeply colored greens.

FOR THE DRESSING (makes ¼ cup):

2 tablespoons fresh orange juice

2 teaspoons Dijon mustard

Salt and freshly ground black pepper, to taste

2 tablespoons extra-virgin olive oil

FOR THE SALAD:

2 bunches watercress, rinsed, tough stems removed,
   and patted dry

3 scallions (white bulbs and 3 inches green),
   thinly sliced on the diagonal

8 ounces white mushrooms

1 cup mung bean sprouts

Sea salt and freshly ground black pepper, to taste

1. Prepare the dressing: In a small bowl, whisk the orange juice, mustard, and salt and pepper together. Whisking constantly, drizzle in the oil; continue whisking until the dressing has thickened. Set it aside.

2. Place the watercress and scallions in a large bowl.

3. Wipe the mushroom caps clean with a damp paper towel. Trim the stems and thinly slice the mushrooms lengthwise. Add the mushrooms and the bean sprouts to the watercress.

4. Just before serving, season the salad with sea salt and black pepper. Toss with the reserved dressing, and serve immediately.

A NEW SALAD

There is such a wide variety of fresh head lettuces now available in markets, don't rely just on the bagged mixes—as good as they are—for your salad greens. Go ahead and create your own mixture. Buy a few heads—Boston, bibb, romaine, frisée, red leaf, Belgian endive—separate the leaves, then add in some arugula and fresh herbs, toss with a favorite vinaigrette or simply a squeeze of lime juice and some flaky salt, and enjoy. When you do it your way, you're sure to get the right amount of the greens you like best in your salad.

BELGIAN ENDIVE AND MACHE
WITH FROMAGE BLANC

SERVES 4

belgian endive, a member of the chicory family, is a winter green with a mildly bitter bite. It marries beautifully with mâche, also known as lamb's lettuce, a gently sweet small-leafed lettuce that is often sold with its roots still attached to a clump of earth. It's this lovely contrast that makes for such a delightful salad. I've dressed it sparingly and tossed in a few shallots for a crisp bite. To top off the greens, a dollop of fromage blanc—a delicate, fat-free, fresh creamy cheese, somewhat thicker than yogurt—creates a dressy finish.

FOR THE VINAIGRETTE:

2 teaspoons Dijon mustard

2 tablespoons white wine vinegar

Maldon (flaky) sea salt (see Note, page 66), to taste

Freshly ground black pepper, to taste

¼ cup walnut oil or extra-virgin olive oil

FOR THE SALAD:

4 Belgian endives, any bruised outer leaves discarded

3 cups (loosely packed) mâche leaves

¼ cup chopped fresh flat-leaf parsley leaves

2 tablespoons finely minced shallots

Maldon (flaky) sea salt, to taste

Freshly ground black pepper, to taste

½ cup fromage blanc

1. Prepare the vinaigrette: Whisk the mustard, vinegar, sea salt, and pepper together in a small bowl.

Whisking constantly, slowly drizzle in the oil; continue whisking until the dressing has thickened. Set it aside.

2. Just before serving, separate the endive leaves, rinse them under cold running water, and pat them thoroughly dry. Toss the endives, mâche, parsley, and shallots together in a large salad bowl. Season with sea salt and black pepper. Dress lightly with the vinaigrette, using just enough to coat the greens.

3. Divide the salad among four plates. Spoon a dollop of the fromage blanc onto the center of each one, and serve immediately.

NOTES:

+ Fromage blanc is available in cheese stores and specialty markets.

+ Any extra salad dressing can be covered and refrigerated; it will keep for 3 or 4 days. 🌿

A GREAT MIXED SALAD

SERVES 4

this salad—an assortment of greens, some tomatoes, chopped hard-cooked eggs, and croutons—is a sure bet. A simple red wine vinaigrette is all it needs. It's great with a steak and just right with roast chicken.

FOR THE SALAD GREENS:

6 cups assorted salad greens, such as Boston lettuce, mâche, and arugula

FOR THE CROUTONS:

1 cup cubed French bread
(day-old is fine; ½-inch cubes)

2 tablespoons olive oil

FOR THE VINAIGRETTE (makes ⅓ cup):

2 tablespoons red wine vinegar

1 tablespoon Dijon mustard

Salt and freshly ground black pepper,
to taste

3 tablespoons extra-virgin olive oil

TO FINISH THE SALAD:

½ cup (loosely packed) whole basil leaves,
coarsely torn

4 ripe plum tomatoes, each cut into 8 pieces

2 hard-cooked eggs, coarsely chopped

2 teaspoons finely minced garlic

Salt and freshly ground black pepper,
to taste

1. Prepare the greens: Swish the salad greens in a large bowl of cold water; then rinse them under cold running water and drain them well. Pat dry. Wrap the greens in paper towels, then place them in a plastic bag, and refrigerate them in the crisper drawer for 4 to 6 hours (this allows them to crisp up beautifully).

2. Preheat the oven to 350°F.

3. Prepare the croutons: Place the bread cubes in a bowl, sprinkle the olive oil over them, and toss. Then spread the cubes out in a single layer on a baking sheet and bake until they are golden brown, about 20 minutes. Set them aside to cool to room temperature.

4. Prepare the vinaigrette: Whisk the vinegar, mustard, and salt and pepper together in a small bowl. Whisking constantly, slowly drizzle in the olive oil; continue whisking until the dressing has thickened. Set it aside.

5. Just before serving, toss the crisped salad greens, basil, tomatoes, eggs, and garlic together in a large salad bowl. Season with salt and pepper, and toss with about ¼ cup of the vinaigrette.

6. Add the croutons to the salad, toss, and serve immediately. ❧

TEN CAESAR SALAD

SERVES 4

a universally popular salad, this mix of romaine lettuce, garlic, olive oil, lemon juice, egg, Parmesan cheese, and croutons doesn't have an unquestionably authentic derivation but it is generally recognized as the creation of an Italian immigrant named Caesar Cardini in Tijuana, Mexico (or maybe it was San Diego), on the Fourth of July weekend in 1924. Anchovies weren't part of the original recipe, but they are included in so many variations, it's surprising to learn that they weren't there at the beginning. I prefer a slightly milder dressing than those that go heavy on the anchovies. I find that rinsing them allows them to add their beguiling flavor, leaving the harsh salty bite behind. No Caesar salad is complete without an egg—and I don't mean hard-cooked. Traditionally it's raw, but I like mine coddled (and so did Signor Cardini), so I cook it for a minute.

FOR THE CROUTONS:

1½ cups cubed French bread (1-inch cubes)

2 tablespoons olive oil

Salt and freshly ground black pepper, to taste

FOR THE CAESAR DRESSING (makes ¾ cup):

¼ teaspoon coarse (kosher) salt

2 cloves garlic

About 4 canned or bottled anchovy fillets

2 teaspoons finely grated lemon zest

2 tablespoons fresh lemon juice

1 tablespoon red wine vinegar

1 tablespoon Dijon mustard

½ cup extra-virgin olive oil

Freshly ground black pepper, to taste

FOR THE SALAD:

1 large egg, at room temperature

2 romaine lettuce hearts, leaves separated, rinsed, and patted dry

2 to 3 tablespoons freshly grated Parmesan cheese

Salt and freshly ground black pepper, to taste

1. Preheat the oven to 350°F.

2. Prepare the croutons: Place the bread cubes in a bowl, and sprinkle the oil, salt, and pepper over them. Toss well. Spread the cubes out on a baking sheet and bake until golden brown, about 20 minutes. Set them aside.

3. Prepare the dressing: Sprinkle the coarse salt over the garlic cloves on a chopping board, and mash together to form a paste. Transfer the paste to a small bowl.

4. Rinse the anchovies, pat them dry, and mince them (you should have 1 tablespoon). Add the minced anchovies to the garlic paste, and whisk in the lemon zest, lemon juice, vinegar, and mustard. Whisking constantly, drizzle in the olive oil. Continue whisking until thickened. Season with black pepper to taste, and set aside.

5. When you are ready to serve the salad, bring a small saucepan of water to a boil. Add the egg and boil

for 1 minute. Drain, and set the egg aside. (When you crack the egg later, the yolk will be warm and slightly thickened and the white will be slightly runny.)

6. To assemble the salad, place the whole lettuce leaves in a large salad bowl. Toss with ¼ cup of the Caesar dressing. Break the egg into the salad and toss well. Sprinkle the cheese and the croutons over the salad, and toss well again. Taste, and then season with salt, if necessary, and pepper. Serve immediately.

NOTE: Cover and refrigerate the extra dressing; it will keep for 3 or 4 days. ❧

FRISEE AND APPLE SALAD

SERVES 4

When I serve a salad, I often add, as a surprise, something more than just the expected salad greens. Apples and carrots do the trick here. The use of basil as a salad herb is a Vietnamese influence, making the salad an especially nice complement to the Grilled Saigon Shrimp (page 221).

1 large or 2 small heads frisée lettuce

2 tablespoons fresh lemon juice

3 tablespoons extra-virgin olive oil

Freshly ground black pepper, to taste

1 Granny Smith apple, cored and cut into
    julienne strips

2 carrots, peeled and coarsely grated

2 tablespoons finely minced shallots

¼ cup (loosely packed) finely slivered fresh
    basil leaves

Salt, to taste

 4 full, short basil sprigs, for garnish

1. Separate the frisée leaves, discarding any coarse outer ones. Rinse the frisée in a bowl of cold water. Drain, and then shake it dry. Wrap it in paper towels, place them in a plastic bag, and refrigerate them in the crisper drawer for 4 to 6 hours.

2. Just before serving, whisk the lemon juice, olive oil, and pepper together in a large bowl. Add the apple and carrots, and toss well.

3. Add the frisée, shallots, and basil to the bowl and toss well, using tongs. Taste, and season with salt.

4. Divide the salad equally among four salad plates. Garnish each with a sprig of basil, and serve. ❧

GREEK-STYLE LUNCH SALAD

SERVES 2 FOR LUNCH, OR 4 AS A SIDE OR APPETIZER SALAD

there is something appealing about a crisp Greek salad. I think it's the way the feta cheese turns creamy once everything is tossed with the vinaigrette. A sliver of radicchio intensifies the colors, and parsley adds that garden-fresh flavor I love. Feta sold loose in brine is much better than the feta that's sold in a sealed package; you can find it in the cheese department of the supermarket or in cheese shops. Romaine hearts make a great salad green. Any extra dressing can be covered and refrigerated for 3 or 4 days.

FOR THE SALAD:

1 thin French baguette, cut into ½-inch-thick slices
    (2 cups)

2 tablespoons olive oil

2 romaine lettuce hearts

½ cup finely slivered inner radicchio leaves

½ cup diced hothouse (seedless) cucumber
    (¼-inch dice)

1 ripe tomato, cut into thin wedges; or 1 cup
    teardrop tomatoes, halved lengthwise

¼ cup thinly slivered red onion

4 ounces fresh feta cheese, cut into ½-inch cubes

2 tablespoons chopped fresh flat-leaf parsley leaves

FOR THE DRESSING:

2 tablespoons red wine vinegar

2 teaspoons Dijon mustard

Salt and freshly ground black pepper, to taste

3 tablespoons extra-virgin olive oil

TO FINISH:

Salt and freshly ground black pepper, to taste

Finely grated zest of 1 lemon

Juice of ½ lemon

1. Preheat the oven to 350°F.

2. Place the bread slices in a bowl, sprinkle the olive oil over them, and toss. Spread the slices out in a single layer on a baking sheet, and bake until golden brown, about 20 minutes. Set them aside.

3. Separate the romaine lettuce leaves, discarding any tough or bruised leaves. Rinse the leaves under cold running water, drain them well, and pat them dry. Tear the leaves into pieces.

4. Place the romaine in a large salad bowl, and add the radicchio, cucumber, tomato, onion, feta, and parsley.

5. Prepare the dressing: Whisk the vinegar, mustard, and salt and pepper together in a small bowl. Whisking constantly, slowly drizzle in the olive oil; continue whisking until the dressing has thickened slightly.

6. Just before serving, season the salad with salt and pepper, and drizzle it lightly with the dressing. Sprinkle the lemon zest and juice over the salad, and toss. Toss in the croutons. Serve immediately. ✿

BALTHAZAR
BEET AND ENDIVE SALAD

SERVES 6 TO 8

ee Hanson and Riad Nasr, chefs at New York's Balthazar and Pastis restaurants, created this stunning salad: As you toss it, the beets lend their magenta color to the pears and cheese with a dazzling effect.

FOR THE BEETS AND WALNUTS:

8 beets

1½ cups walnut halves

FOR THE DRESSING:

2 teaspoons Dijon mustard

¼ cup red wine vinegar

Salt and freshly ground black pepper, to taste

⅓ cup extra-virgin olive oil

TO FINISH THE SALAD:

4 Belgian endives

Juice of 1 lemon

2 ripe pears, preferably Anjou

Salt and freshly ground black pepper, to taste

¼ cup coarsely chopped fresh flat-leaf
    parsley leaves

6 ounces Roquefort cheese, broken into
    large pieces

1. Preheat the oven to 375°F.

2. Scrub the beets well. Trim off the stems and roots, leaving 1 inch of each. Wrap the beets individually in aluminum foil, place them on a baking sheet, and bake until tender, 1 to 1½ hours, depending on their size.

3. While the beets are cooking, spread the walnuts out in a single layer on a baking sheet and toast them in the same oven for 10 minutes. Remove them from the oven, chop coarsely, and set aside.

4. When the beets are tender, remove them from the oven, discard the foil, and allow them to cool a bit. Then slip off the skins, cut the beets into ½-inch cubes, and set them aside.

5. Prepare the dressing: Whisk the mustard, vinegar, and salt and pepper together in a small bowl. Whisking constantly, slowly drizzle in the olive oil; continue whisking until the dressing has thickened. Set it aside.

6. Cut the endives in half lengthwise, then crosswise, on the diagonal, into ½-inch pieces. Place them in a large bowl and drizzle with the lemon juice.

7. Peel, quarter, and core the pears. Thinly slice each quarter lengthwise. Place the slices in the bowl with the endives, and toss gently to coat with the lemon juice. Add the reserved beets and walnuts. Season with salt and pepper. Add the dressing and the parsley, and toss well. Gently fold in the Roquefort, and serve.

RUBY GRAPEFRUIT SALAD

SERVES 4

Not so long ago, a salad featuring both grapefruit and avocado seemed just pretty unusual. But that has certainly changed. Avocado's mild flavor and rich texture work beautifully with the grapefruit and frisée. Instead of tossing the avocado with the salad, I like to arrange it on top—that way, the avocado won't turn mushy. Chopped parsley or chives make a fresh-tasting garnish for this slightly bitter wintry salad. Cover and refrigerate the extra vinaigrette; it will keep for 3 to 4 days.

1 large head frisée lettuce, tough leaves discarded, rinsed and patted dry

2 ruby red grapefruits

2 teaspoons Dijon mustard

Salt and freshly ground black pepper, to taste

¼ cup olive oil

1 ripe (but not mushy) avocado, preferably Hass

2 scallions (white bulb and 3 inches of green), thinly sliced

2 tablespoons chopped flat-leaf parsley leaves

1. Separate the frisée leaves, discarding any coarse outer ones, and tear the larger leaves. Rinse the frisée in a bowl of cold water. Drain, and then shake it dry. Wrap it in paper towels, place them in a plastic bag, and refrigerate them in the crisper drawer for 4 to 6 hours.

2. Cut a thin slice off the top and bottom of each grapefruit. Place the grapefruit on a cut end, and using a sharp knife, carefully slice downward, removing the peel and all the white pith. Working over a bowl to catch all the juices, section the fruit from between the membranes, letting the sections and juice drop into the bowl. Squeeze all the juice from the grapefruit halves into the bowl. Set aside.

3. Prepare the vinaigrette: Transfer ¼ cup of the reserved grapefruit juice to a small bowl. Whisk in the mustard, and salt and pepper to taste. Whisking constantly, slowly drizzle in the olive oil; continue whisking until the vinaigrette has thickened slightly. Set it aside.

4. Cut the avocado in half and remove the pit. Using a teaspoon, scoop out spoonfuls of avocado and place them in a small bowl. Add 1 tablespoon of the reserved grapefruit juice and toss (this will prevent the avocado from discoloring).

5. Place the crisped frisée in a large bowl. Add the reserved grapefruit sections, scallions, and 1 tablespoon of the chopped parsley. Season with salt and pepper, and toss gently with 3 tablespoons of the vinaigrette. Arrange the avocado on top of the salad, sprinkle with the remaining 1 tablespoon chopped parsley, and serve.

"... SO DELICIOUS WHEN MADE WITH VEGETABLES FRESH FROM THE FARM STAND."

MIXED VEGETABLE SALADS

The summer farm stand: a riot of textures and color and flavors that go on and on. It's such a pleasure to shop at a local stand and come home with a selection of freshly picked vegetables, fruits, and herbs. I lay them out on my counter and think about what to make. When the green beans are pencil-thin, I mix them with chopped Kirby cukes and tomatoes, and toss in watermelon. Or I may roast some beets, and if fresh black figs are in season, I'll toss them with the beets, some Sherry Vinaigrette, and torn fresh mint leaves. And there's nothing like a late summer potato salad made from potatoes just out of the ground. There is no end to the creative license you can take with vegetables. In fact, I couldn't stop at 10 recipes for this chapter—so included are my top 11.

Vegetables combined are just a small example of the versatility that makes salads so appealing, so complex, and so varied today. Think of your creation as a painting, as Cézanne might paint a bowl or platter of fruit, adding color, a dab here or a taste there—salads as works of art. 🌿

ASIAN VEGETABLE SALAD

SERVES 4

I enjoyed these simple yet delicious vegetable ribbons at a restaurant in Beijing. When steamed and tossed with a little sesame oil, the vegetables' colors look beautiful on the plate and the flavors are unexpectedly bold. To stick with the theme, serve this salad with the flank steak on page 74.

½ hothouse (seedless) cucumber

1 carrot

1 rib celery, trimmed

1 red bell pepper

1 to 2 teaspoons toasted sesame oil

½ cup fresh mung bean sprouts

⅓ cup drained canned bamboo shoots

1 pinch Maldon (flaky) salt (see box, page 66),
    to taste

1. Peel the cucumber and the carrot, and cut them both into strips 3 inches long, ¼ inch wide, and ¼ inch thick. Cut the celery into strips the same size. Stem and seed the bell pepper, and cut it into strips the same size.

2. Bring water to a simmer in the bottom of a vegetable steamer. Place all the vegetable strips in the steamer basket, and steam until they are just cooked, 3 minutes.

3. Remove the vegetables from the steamer, pat them dry with paper towels, and transfer them to a bowl. Toss with the sesame oil. Add the bean sprouts and the bamboo shoots, and season with the flaky salt.

4. Transfer the salad to a serving bowl and serve immediately. Or cover and refrigerate it for up to 3 hours; bring to room temperature before serving. ✤

CHOPPED MIDDLE EASTERN SALAD

SERVES 4 TO 6

Serve this fresh and crispy Middle Eastern salad in the summer, when the tomatoes are in season, the cucumbers are garden-crisp, and mint has a peppery bite. Feta or soft goat cheese would be delicious served alongside, with warmed pita bread or toasted slices of peasant bread.

4 cups diced, seeded, peeled cucumbers
    (¼-inch dice)

2 cups diced ripe tomatoes (¼-inch dice)

4 scallions (white bulbs and 3 inches green),
    thinly sliced on the diagonal

¾ cup coarsely chopped fresh flat-leaf
    parsley leaves

½ cup coarsely chopped fresh mint leaves

3 tablespoons extra-virgin olive oil

2 tablespoons fresh lemon juice

Salt and freshly ground black pepper, to taste

Combine the cucumbers, tomatoes, scallions, parsley, and mint in a serving bowl. Just before serving, toss with the oil and lemon juice. Season with salt and pepper, and serve immediately. ❧

SPRING PEA SALAD

SERVES 8

The combination of these ingredients is so pleasing—the salad will complement your leg of lamb as well as a glazed salmon. Try to chop the celery and the pecans to the same size as the peas. The dried cherries add an unusual touch to the salad, making it especially flavorful.

2 cups fresh or frozen peas, thawed if frozen

4 ribs celery, finely diced

1 cup dried cherries

¾ cup chopped pecans

⅓ cup plus 1 tablespoon chopped fresh dill leaves

Salt and freshly ground black pepper,
    to taste

1 cup prepared mayonnaise, preferably
    Hellmann's

½ cup nonfat plain yogurt

1 fresh mint sprig, for garnish

1. If you are using fresh peas, bring a pot of lightly salted water to a boil. Add the peas and cook until tender, 2 to 3 minutes. Drain, refresh under cold running water, and pat dry with paper towels. If you are using thawed frozen peas, simply pat them dry.

2. Combine the peas, celery, cherries, pecans, and the ⅓ cup dill in a medium-size bowl. Season with salt and pepper.

3. Combine the mayonnaise and yogurt in a small bowl; gently fold this into the mixture, using a rubber spatula.

4. Transfer the salad to a decorative bowl and sprinkle with the remaining 1 tablespoon dill. Garnish with the mint sprig, and serve. ❧

WATERMELON CUBES, CUCUMBER, AND TOMATO SALAD

SERVES 4 TO 6

You may not think of teaming up tomatoes and cucumbers with sweet watermelon—but that's where I come in! During the summer, the combination is hard to beat. Be sure to seek out a high-quality feta cheese for the best results here—look for it at the cheese or deli counter sitting in a brine bath (it's usually better than the packaged variety).

4 cups cubed seeded watermelon (½-inch cubes)

2 cups diced seeded, peeled cucumber
    (½-inch cubes)

3 ripe tomatoes, seeded and cut into ½-inch pieces

Coarsely ground black pepper, to taste

3 tablespoons extra-virgin olive oil

6 ounces fresh feta cheese, cut into small cubes

½ cup plus 2 tablespoons fresh mint leaves,
    torn into coarse pieces

1. Combine the watermelon, cucumbers, and tomatoes in a large bowl. Sprinkle with pepper (do not salt as it would cause the fruit to give off too much water), and drizzle with the olive oil. Add the feta. Using a rubber spatula and working from underneath, fold the ingredients together gently.

2. Just before serving, toss in the ½ cup mint. Transfer the salad to a serving bowl, garnish with the remaining 2 tablespoons chopped mint, and serve.

HOW TO PEEL A TOMATO

Some recipes—for example, the cooked salad on page 269—call for peeled tomatoes. To peel them, set aside a large bowl filled with ice water. Bring a large pot of water to a boil. With a sharp paring knife, cut an X just through the skin on the bottom of each tomato. Drop the tomatoes, a few at a time, into the boiling water, and let them cook for 30 seconds. Using a slotted spoon, transfer the tomatoes to the ice water and let them cool. The skins will slip off easily. (If the tomatoes are to be cooked further, the ice bath is unnecessary.)

SUMMER GREEN BEAN, TOMATO, AND KIRBY CUKE SALAD

SERVES 6

This is a simple salad, but so delicious when made with vegetables fresh from the farm stand. The new beans need hardly any cooking. Kirby cucumbers have no wax coating and a great crunch, and with ripe tomatoes and fresh basil, all you need is the scallions for a bit of a kick.

1½ pounds tender green beans, stem ends
    snapped off

2 Kirby cucumbers, peeled, seeded if necessary,
    and cut into ½-inch pieces

1 large ripe tomato, halved lengthwise and
    cut into thin wedges

4 scallions (white bulbs and 3 inches green),
    thinly sliced on the diagonal

6 fresh basil leaves, thinly slivered

Salt and freshly ground black pepper, to taste

3 tablespoons Mustard Vinaigrette (recipe follows)

1. Bring a pot of lightly salted water to a boil over high heat. Add the green beans and cook until just tender, 2 to 3 minutes. Drain immediately into a colander and refresh under cold running water until cool. Pat the beans dry with paper towels, and place them in a large bowl. Add the cucumbers and tomato. Toss with the scallions and half of the basil.

2. Just before serving it, season the salad with salt and pepper, and dress it lightly with the vinaigrette. Sprinkle with the remaining basil. 🌿

MUSTARD VINAIGRETTE

MAKES ½ CUP

This vinaigrette, flavored and thickened with a generous amount of mustard, is perfect on a summer vegetable salad because it coats salad greens well. It's mellowed by a pinch of sugar and is great on assertive greens.

2 generous teaspoons Dijon mustard

2 tablespoons red wine vinegar

½ teaspoon sugar

Salt and freshly ground black pepper, to taste

¼ cup extra-virgin olive oil

Whisk the mustard, vinegar, sugar, and salt and pepper together in a small bowl. Whisking constantly, add the olive oil in a slow, steady stream, and continue whisking until thickened. Refrigerate any extra dressing, covered, for 3 to 4 days. 🌿

GARDEN GLORIES

SERVES 8

For a summer buffet, luncheon, or dinner extravaganza, nothing beats a spectacular platter of vegetables, fruits, and pickles creatively arranged and served with a delicious lemon mayonnaise. Have small plates nearby so that all your guests can help themselves to some of each vegetable and fruit, along with some egg.

FOR THE LEMON MAYONNAISE:

1 cup prepared mayonnaise, preferably Hellmann's

1 cup sour cream

Finely grated zest of 2 lemons

2 tablespoons fresh lemon juice

FOR THE SALAD:

8 small beets, stems and roots trimmed

8 medium-size red-skinned new potatoes, quartered

8 carrots, peeled and halved crosswise on the
    diagonal

1 head cauliflower, heavy stalks trimmed and
    discarded, broken into small florets

2 ripe avocados, preferably Hass

6 tablespoons fresh lemon juice
    (from 2 large lemons)

2 Granny Smith apples, cored

2 cups diced cantaloupe (½-inch dice)

4 hard-cooked eggs, halved lengthwise

1 cup diced dill pickles (½-inch dice)

Salt and freshly ground black pepper, to taste

Snipped fresh chives, for garnish

1. Prepare the Lemon Mayonnaise: Combine all the mayonnaise ingredients in a bowl, stir well, and refrigerate, covered, until ready to serve. (The mayonnaise can be made up to 1 day ahead.)

2. Prepare the salad: Bring a large pot of lightly salted water to a boil. Add the beets, cooking them until tender, about 45 minutes depending on size. Drain and reserve each vegetable separately. When the beets are cool enough to handle, peel and quarter them.

3. Meanwhile, bring another large pot of lightly salted water to a boil. Add the potatoes and cook until just tender, about 10 minutes. Remove them with a slotted spoon and drain them well. Set them aside. Using the same boiling water, repeat this process with the carrots, cooking until just tender, 8 to 10 minutes; then the cauliflower, cooking for 3 to 5 minutes.

4. Cut the avocados in half and remove the pits. Peel the halves and cut the flesh into ½-inch cubes. Toss the cubes in a small bowl with 2 tablespoons of the lemon juice. Cut the apples in half, and each half into ½-inch cubes. Toss the cubes in another small bowl with 2 tablespoons lemon juice.

5. Just before serving, arrange the vegetables, fruit, eggs, and pickles in groups on a large decorative platter. Sprinkle the remaining 2 tablespoons lemon juice over them, season with salt and pepper, and garnish with the fresh chives. Serve the Lemon Mayonnaise in a little dish alongside. 🌿

JOAN NATHAN'S COOKED TOMATO AND PEPPER SALAD

SERVES 6 (MAKES 3 CUPS)

Cookbook author Joan Nathan has gathered recipes from around the world to include in her books. I cooked with her one Passover, and we made this cooked salad (similar to an Israeli ratatouille) from her *Foods of Israel Today*. There is nothing like it! The preserved lemons brighten the flavors of the roasted peppers. Serve it with An Herb-Roasted Chicken (page 136), Lemon Herb-Roasted Chicken Drumsticks (page 149), or as a topping for turkey sausage.

2 red bell peppers

2 yellow bell peppers

¼ cup plus 1 tablespoon extra-virgin olive oil

3 pounds ripe tomatoes (about 6), peeled
   (see box, page 266), seeded, and diced

4 large cloves garlic, finely minced

1 teaspoon sugar

2 teaspoons sweet paprika

2 teaspoons salt, or to taste

Freshly ground black pepper, to taste

2 to 3 teaspoons chopped preserved lemon
   (rind only; see Sources, page 439), to taste

1. Position the broiler rack 3 inches from the heat source, and preheat the broiler.

2. Halve the bell peppers lengthwise. Remove the seeds and ribs, and place the halves on a baking sheet, skin side up. Place under the broiler and broil until the skins are well charred, 12 to 15 minutes. Remove the peppers from the oven, close them tightly in a plastic bag, and let them steam in the bag for 15 to 20 minutes. Then slip off and discard the skins. Cut the peppers into 1-inch pieces.

3. Heat the ¼ cup oil in a heavy skillet over low heat. Add the peppers, tomatoes, garlic, sugar, paprika, salt, and black pepper. Simmer, stirring occasionally and mashing the vegetables with a fork until the liquid begins to evaporate. Continue to cook until the salad thickens and has a saucelike consistency, 15 to 20 minutes.

4. Before serving, let cool to room temperature. (You can prepare the salad to this point up to 2 days ahead. Transfer it to a container, cover, and refrigerate. Remove it from the refrigerator 30 minutes before serving.)

5. Stir in the preserved lemon, transfer the salad to a pretty bowl, and drizzle with the remaining 1 tablespoon olive oil. ❧

MY ROASTED BEET AND FIG FANTASY

SERVES 4 TO 6

Sometimes foods of the same color work beautifully together. Here wine-red beets and purple figs are gently fused with a mellow Sherry Vinaigrette. The fresh mint garnish adds an amazing burst of energy to the deep magenta duo. Serve this salad with Roasted Rack of Pork (page 50), Seaside Seafood Salad (page 247), or Shrimp Curry (page 223).

4 beets, stems and roots trimmed to 1 inch, well scrubbed

8 ripe purple figs, stems snipped off, halved lengthwise

Salt and freshly ground black pepper, to taste

3 tablespoons Sherry Vinaigrette (recipe follows)

⅓ cup coarsely torn fresh mint leaves, for garnish

1. Preheat the oven to 350°F.

2. Wrap the beets individually in aluminum foil, place them on a baking sheet, and bake until tender, 1 to 1½ hours depending on their size. Remove the beets from the oven, remove the foil, and set them aside to cool a bit.

3. When the beets are cool enough to handle, slip the skins off and cut them into 1-inch pieces. Place the beets and the figs in a medium-size bowl.

4. Just before serving, season with salt and pepper, and toss gently with the vinaigrette. Place in a decorative serving bowl and sprinkle the mint over the top. Serve immediately. ❀

SHERRY VINAIGRETTE

MAKES ¾ CUP

When preparing a Sherry vinaigrette, the quality of the ingredients can make all the difference. For this one, I went for the best and chose L'Estornell Reserva, a popular smooth vinegar made from Spain's Palomino Fino, the grape of their fine sherries (see Sources, page 439). I combined the vinegar with a Portuguese extra-virgin olive oil, CARM (Casa Agricola Roboredo Madeira), produced from organically grown olives. The hand-milled olives have fine nuances of nuttiness and fresh apple, lending these qualities to a well-blended vinaigrette.

1 tablespoon Dijon mustard

¼ cup good-quality sherry vinegar

½ teaspoon sugar

Salt and freshly ground black pepper, to taste

⅓ cup extra-virgin olive oil, preferably Portuguese

1. Whisk the mustard, vinegar, sugar, and salt and pepper together in a small bowl. Whisking constantly, slowly drizzle in the olive oil. Continue whisking until the vinaigrette thickens. Adjust the seasonings as needed.

2. Store the dressing in a covered container in the refrigerator for up to 1 week. Use at room temperature, rewhisking before use. 🌿

STATE FAIR
POTATO SALAD

SERVES 6 TO 8

the late cookbook author Michael McLaughlin created this luscious potato salad and it deserves a blue ribbon! A drizzle of pickle juice over the warm potatoes gives them their initial kick while the eggs, buttermilk, and chopped pickles finish off the job. Every bite is pleasing. This salad could win out on any good Southern table. It's a must served alongside Michael's Cherry Cola–Glazed Spareribs (page 129).

3 pounds red-skinned potatoes, peeled and
    cut into 1-inch pieces
¼ cup sweet pickle juice (from the jar of pickles,
    see below)
¾ cup prepared mayonnaise, preferably Hellmann's
⅓ cup buttermilk
4 teaspoons Dijon mustard
1 teaspoon sugar
Freshly ground black pepper, to taste
½ cup diced red onion (¼-inch dice)
½ cup diced celery (¼-inch dice)
½ cup diced sweet pickles (¼-inch dice)
3 hard-cooked eggs, chopped
Coarse (kosher) salt, to taste

1. Bring a large pot of lightly salted water to a boil over high heat. Add the potatoes and cook until just tender, about 10 minutes. Drain, and transfer them to a large bowl. Drizzle the pickle juice over the warm potatoes and toss gently. Cool to room temperature.

2. Whisk the mayonnaise, buttermilk, mustard, sugar, and pepper together in a large bowl. Add the potatoes, onions, celery, and pickles. Using a rubber spatula, fold all together gently. Then fold in the eggs and season with salt. (This salad can be made up to 6 hours ahead of time. Cover and refrigerate; bring to room temperature before serving.) 🌿

PERUVIAN POTATO SALAD

SERVES 4 TO 6

I'm always on the lookout for a good potato salad and found a Peruvian-style one—which is warm and richly creamy—ironically in Violet Oon's *Singapore Family Cookbook*. While her recipe is delicious, I couldn't resist adapting it, making the sauce creamier and eliminating some of the spices. Enjoy this salad as an accompaniment to the strip steaks on page 67. Firm potatoes are called for, so stay away from russets and Yukon Golds.

1 small red onion, thinly sliced crosswise

Juice of ½ lemon

1 pound small red-skinned potatoes, scrubbed
   and halved (quartered if large)

4 ounces cream cheese, cut into cubes

¼ cup heavy (whipping) cream

2 teaspoons finely minced green jalapeño pepper

¼ teaspoon ground turmeric

Salt and freshly ground black pepper, to taste

2 heads romaine lettuce hearts, leaves separated,
   tough bottoms discarded, rinsed and
   patted dry, for serving

⅓ cup coarsely chopped pitted black olives, for garnish

2 tablespoons chopped fresh flat-leaf
   parsley leaves, for garnish

1. Combine the onion and lemon juice in a small bowl. Set aside.

2. Bring a pot of lightly salted water to a boil. Add the potatoes and cook until tender, about 10 minutes. Drain, and transfer them to a large bowl.

3. Combine the cream cheese, cream, jalapeño, turmeric, and salt to taste in a small heavy saucepan. Cook over low heat, stirring, until the mixture is smooth and thickened, about 8 minutes. Allow the mixture to cool slightly.

4. Toss the cream sauce with the potatoes. Season with salt and pepper.

5. Arrange the lettuce leaves on a serving platter. Spoon the potato salad onto the center of the platter, and scatter the reserved onion over the top. Sprinkle with the olives and chopped parsley, and serve.

LEMONY
ROASTED POTATO SALAD

SERVES 4 TO 6

Roasting baby potatoes at a high temperature results in a crispy skin and soft interior. Although lemon is not often thought of as a flavor accent for potatoes, it is standard in Greece and gives these a flashy finish, making them as delicious with steak as they are with Roasted Brined Chicken (page 137).

3 pounds baby white potatoes, halved crosswise

¼ cup extra-virgin olive oil

1½ teaspoons sea salt

⅛ teaspoon freshly ground black pepper

Finely grated zest of 1 lemon

2 tablespoons chopped fresh flat-leaf parsley

1. Preheat the oven to 350°F.

2. In a large bowl, toss the potatoes with the olive oil, salt, and pepper. Spread the potatoes in a single layer on two baking sheets. Bake for 2 hours, shaking the pans after 30 minutes and occasionally checking the potatoes and loosening from the pans with a metal spatula. After 2 hours, the potato skins will be crisp and the interiors soft.

3. Return the potatoes to the bowl and toss with the lemon zest and parsley. Adjust the seasonings as needed, and serve.

"SOME LIKE THEM SLENDER AND SOME LIKE THEM FAT AND SOME LIKE THEM IN THE MIDDLE."

SPRINGTIME ASPARAGUS

I adore asparagus, having long tended my own 60-foot bed. Every year, toward the end of March, I began circling around the edges, hoping to see some tips peeking up through the cold earth, but in the still-frigid weather this was not to be. Asparagus, after all, is the ultimate harbinger of spring. It sits all winter under the cold, often frozen earth, waiting for the exact right moment to send its shoots toward the sun.

When asparagus shoots do peek up, they can be anywhere from pencil-thin to thick, and ranging in colors, like the familiar green with its robust flavor, to purple-tinted, to white (if you grow them under mounds of soil to keep them away from the light). I like asparagus steamed and served hot, at room temperature, or chilled; pureed in soups; roasted; and grilled. It is great in salads, such as Asparagus, Shrimp, and Orange Salad, or with pasta—try Asparagus, Caviar, and Chopped Egg Spaghettini for a special springtime treat. For an elegant presentation of thick-stalked asparagus, peel the bottom 2 to 3 inches. 🌿

CREAMY WHITE
ASPARAGUS SOUP

SERVES 8

Cream of white asparagus soup—another one of life's luxuries. We see far fewer white asparagus in season than green, but when they're available, they're worth the indulgence. White asparagus are deprived of light by mounding soil over them as the tips emerge, so that they stay pure white as they grow. They're more frequently enjoyed in northern Europe than in America, but when properly prepared, white asparagus are quite delicious. My addition of leeks and parsnips enhances the flavor of the broth for the soup. A touch of cream finishes it all off.

1 large leek

1 tablespoon cider vinegar

2 tablespoons unsalted butter

2 tablespoons olive oil

1 onion, cut into ¼-inch dice

1 parsnip, peeled and cut into ½-inch dice

Salt and freshly ground black pepper, to taste

6 cups chicken or vegetable broth, preferably homemade (see pages 434 and 436)

2 pounds white asparagus, woody ends trimmed off, cut into 1-inch pieces

3 cups green asparagus tips (from about 3 bunches; see Note), for garnish

½ cup heavy (whipping) cream

2 tablespoons snipped fresh chives, for garnish

1. Trim off the root and all but 2 inches of green from the leek. Remove the tough outer leaves. Cut the leek in half lengthwise. Place it in a large bowl of water, add the vinegar, and let it soak for 30 minutes to remove any sand. Drain, rinse under cold water, drain again, and pat dry. Coarsely chop the leek.

2. Melt the butter in the oil in a large heavy pot over medium-low heat. Add the chopped leek, onion, and parsnip, and cook, stirring, until the vegetables have softened, 10 to 15 minutes. Season with salt and pepper.

3. Add the broth to the pot and bring to a boil over high heat. Then add the white asparagus, reduce the heat to low, partially cover, and simmer until the asparagus is tender, 30 minutes. Remove the pot from the heat and let the soup cool to room temperature.

4. While the soup is cooling, bring a medium-size saucepan of lightly salted water to a boil. Add the green asparagus tips and cook until just tender, 2 to 3 minutes. Drain, refresh under cold water, and drain again. Pat dry and set aside.

5. Puree the soup, in batches, in a food processor until it is very smooth. If the soup still seems stringy, pass it through a strainer into the pot. Otherwise, simply return the puree to the pot. Stir in the cream, and heat the soup through over low heat.

6. To serve, divide the soup among eight bowls. Garnish each portion equally with the reserved green asparagus tips and a sprinkling of chives. Serve immediately.

NOTE: When you are just using the asparagus tips, don't throw the stalks away. You can cut them into pieces, blanch them, and add them to blanched snap peas for a delicious vegetable side dish. Or you can add the blanched asparagus pieces to an omelet or scrambled eggs, or to chicken broth flavored with chopped dill.

GRILLED FRESH ASPARAGUS

SERVES 8

Most people steam or boil their asparagus, but just wait till you try it grilled and caramelized. Prepared this way, the natural sugars are released and the flavor intensifies. These stalks are fantastic.

2 pounds medium-size asparagus

⅓ cup extra-virgin olive oil

Coarse (kosher) salt and freshly ground black
    pepper, to taste

1 orange or lemon, halved crosswise

1½ tablespoons snipped fresh chives, for garnish

1. Preheat a barbecue grill to high heat.

2. Trim off 1 inch of the woody stem end of the asparagus spears. Place the asparagus in a large bowl, add the oil and salt and pepper, and toss.

3. Remove the asparagus from the bowl, reserving any oil left in the bowl. Grill the asparagus directly on the grill grate, turning them as they brown, 7 to 8 minutes. As the spears are grilled, transfer them to a plate.

4. Arrange the asparagus decoratively on a platter. Drizzle with any reserved oil and squeeze the orange over them. Sprinkle with the chives, and serve immediately.

ROASTED ASPARAGUS

SERVES 4

Roasting asparagus gives it a deep, rich flavor, which is especially welcome when you've had your fill of steamed asparagus during the height of asparagus season. Lemon brightens that flavor and parsley enlivens it as well. Coarse salt and fresh pepper also contribute.

1 pound medium-size asparagus, tough ends
    removed
2 tablespoons extra-virgin olive oil
Coarse (kosher) salt and freshly ground
    black pepper, to taste
1 tablespoon chopped fresh flat-leaf parsley leaves,
    for garnish
2 lemons, halved, for garnish

1. Position a rack in the center of the oven, and preheat the oven to 400°F.

2. Place the asparagus in a single layer in a roasting pan, all the spears facing in the same direction. Add the olive oil, season with salt and pepper, and toss to coat the spears.

3. Cover the pan with aluminum foil and roast for 10 minutes. Remove the foil and roast for another 10 minutes.

4. Transfer the asparagus to a serving dish, and sprinkle with the parsley. Serve with the lemon halves alongside, for squeezing.

ASPARAGUS MILANESE

SERVES 4

Whether you have these asparagus in Milan or in your own home, they're delicious—with the cheese melted over them, softened up with dabs of butter. Use thick asparagus for the most dramatic presentation. This dish is beautiful served with roast leg of lamb.

4 pounds thick asparagus, woody ends
    trimmed off
4 tablespoons (½ stick) unsalted butter

Coarse (kosher) salt and freshly ground black
    pepper, to taste
¼ cup freshly grated Parmigiano-Reggiano cheese

1. Preheat the oven to 350°F.

2. Bring a pot of salted water to a boil, add the asparagus, and cook until just tender, 3 minutes for large asparagus. Drain, and rinse under cold running water. Drain again and pat dry.

3. Butter an ovenproof baking dish that is large enough to hold the asparagus in a single layer, and arrange the asparagus in it. Dot the asparagus with the butter. Sprinkle with salt and pepper, and sprinkle evenly with the cheese.

4. Bake until the cheese melts, about 10 minutes. Serve immediately. ⚜

ASPARAGUS SALAD
ST. REMY

SERVES 4

When I visited the south of France I had the most marvelous lunch at Bistrot du Paradou, near Les Baux. The day I ate there, the house dish was cassoulet, preceded by this gorgeous asparagus salad—simple and divine. The salad arrived on a large oval dish with four large asparagus on one side and a small pile of salad greens on the opposite side. Both were simply dressed with olive oil and vinegar. Shaved Parmesan was gracefully arranged on top of the asparagus.

Large asparagus are most effective for this dish. Combining Bibb, Boston, and a touch of mesclun most closely evokes the garden-fresh salad on that platter. A light dressing is lovely on these greens.

FOR THE VINAIGRETTE:

2½ tablespoons red wine vinegar

Coarse (kosher) salt and freshly ground
    black pepper, to taste

¼ cup extra-virgin olive oil

1 large clove garlic, bruised (see box, page 82)

FOR THE SALAD:

2 heads Bibb lettuce, tough outer leaves discarded

2 heads Boston lettuce, tough outer leaves discarded

1 cup mesclun (mixed baby salad greens)

16 thick asparagus spears (about 2½ pounds),
    woody ends trimmed off

Coarse (kosher) salt and freshly ground black
    pepper, to taste

8 thin slices Parmigiano-Reggiano,
    (about 2½ x 2½ inches; about 2 ounces total)
    for garnish (see Note)

1. Prepare the vinaigrette: Whisk the vinegar, salt, and pepper together in a small bowl. Whisking constantly, slowly drizzle in the olive oil; continue whisking until the dressing thickens slightly. Add the garlic and set the dressing aside, covered, in the refrigerator for 2 hours.

2. Separate the Bibb and Boston lettuce leaves and rinse them in cold water. Drain and pat dry. Rinse the mesclun, drain, and pat dry. Wrap all the salad greens in kitchen towels and refrigerate until ready to use.

3. Fill a large wide bowl with ice water, and set it aside.

4. Using a vegetable peeler, peel the bottom 2 inches of each asparagus spear. Bring a large pot of salted water to a boil. Add the asparagus and cook until just tender, 2 to 3 minutes. Drain, and transfer the asparagus to the bowl of ice water to stop the cooking. When it has cooled, drain the asparagus and pat dry. (You can do this up to 3 hours ahead: wrap the asparagus in paper towels, put that in a plastic bag, and refrigerate it.)

5. Just before serving, assemble the salad: Remove the garlic from the vinaigrette. Place the asparagus in a large bowl. Season with salt and pepper, and toss lightly with half of the vinaigrette.

6. Place the salad greens in another bowl, and season with salt and pepper. Toss with the remaining vinaigrette. Arrange a handful of the greens in a pile on one side of each of four dinner plates. Arrange 4 asparagus spears on the other side of each plate. Top the asparagus with 2 overlapping slices of Parmesan cheese, arranging them just below the tips. Serve immediately.

NOTE: For this recipe, shave the slices for the garnish very thin with a vegetable peeler. ✿

ASPARAGUS SLIM AND ASPARAGUS THICK

Some like them slender and some like them fat and some like them somewhere in the middle. Whatever your preference, asparagus of any circumference are delicious fresh-picked and firm, with tight heads and a good, green color (or whatever color they're supposed to be). Usually, I don't peel asparagus, I just trim off the woody ends. Springtime is asparagus season and that's the time to enjoy them as often as possible. For most of my dishes, I call for medium-size asparagus. I find they are best in salads and for roasting. But in Asparagus Milanese and Asparagus Salad St. Remy, bold, thick stalks work best. Same great vegetable, but different effects.

ASPARAGUS
AND SNAP PEA SALAD

SERVES 8

When you're looking for the ideal springtime salad that marries beautifully with ham, lamb, or fish, or is a delectable light lunch on its own, there's nothing fresher or more welcoming than the two spring offerings of our gardens, tossed with a Lemon Vinaigrette. A sprinkling of dill, or chives if you prefer, adds the extra-special touch. The color of the chopped eggs matches the daffodils in your flowerbed.

2 pounds medium-size asparagus, tough stem ends
trimmed off, cut into 1-inch pieces

1½ pounds sugar snap peas, strings removed

Salt and freshly ground black pepper, to taste

¼ cup Lemon Vinaigrette (recipe follows)

2 tablespoons coarsely chopped fresh dill leaves or
snipped fresh chives

2 hard-cooked eggs, chopped, for garnish

1. Bring a large saucepan of salted water to a boil. Add the asparagus and cook until barely tender, 2 to 3 minutes. Using a slotted spoon, transfer the asparagus to a colander. Rinse under cold running water, and drain again. Pat the asparagus pieces dry with paper towels and transfer them to a large bowl.

2. Add the snap peas to the same pot of boiling water, and cook until crisp, about 2 minutes. Drain the snap peas, rinse them under cold running water, and drain again. Pat them dry with paper towels and add them to the bowl with the asparagus.

3. Season the vegetables with salt and pepper. Add the vinaigrette and the dill, and toss. Transfer the salad to a serving bowl, sprinkle with the chopped eggs, and serve.

LEMON VINAIGRETTE

MAKES ½ CUP

Lemon vinaigrette is so refreshing—the oils from the delicate zest highlight the flavor. A Microplane grater is the best tool to use for this purpose because it removes only the outer yellow skin and grates it very fine.

Finely grated zest of 1 lemon

¼ cup fresh lemon juice

1 tablespoon Dijon mustard

Salt and freshly ground black pepper, to taste

¼ cup extra-virgin olive oil, or to taste

Whisk the lemon zest, lemon juice, mustard, and salt and pepper together in a small bowl. While you continue whisking, slowly drizzle in the olive oil. Whisk until the vinaigrette has thickened. (The vinaigrette can be prepared up to 2 days in advance and stored in an airtight container in the refrigerator.) 🌺

ASPARAGUS, CAVIAR, AND CHOPPED EGG SPAGHETTINI

SERVES 4

When you are looking for a luncheon entrée or a light supper after the theater, this quick pasta dish fills the bill. Caviar has become extremely expensive these days, so I urge you to shop around: There are many new choices. Salmon caviar is excellent in this recipe, and the price is quite reasonable. For a splurge, of course, there are other choices available.

1½ pounds medium-size asparagus, woody ends
 trimmed off, cut into 1-inch lengths

1 tablespoon olive oil

12 ounces spaghettini

6 tablespoons (¾ stick) unsalted butter,
 cut into pieces at room temperature

Coarse (kosher) salt and freshly ground
 black pepper, to taste

4 scallions (white bulbs and 3 inches green),
 thinly sliced

4 hard-cooked eggs, coarsely chopped, for garnish

½ cup salmon caviar, for garnish

1. Bring a large saucepan of salted water to a boil. Add the asparagus and cook until just tender, 2 to 3 minutes. Drain, rinse under cold water, and pat dry. Set the asparagus aside.

2. Bring a large pot of salted water to a boil, and add the olive oil. Add the spaghettini and cook until just tender, about 9 minutes. Drain, and place it in a large bowl. Toss the hot pasta with the butter, and season it with salt and pepper. Add the reserved asparagus and the scallions, and toss well.

3. Divide the pasta among four shallow pasta bowls. Sprinkle the chopped egg evenly over the pasta, and then top each serving with a generous spoonful of the salmon caviar. Serve immediately.

ASPARAGUS, SHRIMP, AND ORANGE SALAD

SERVES 6

fresh asparagus combined with shrimp in a creamy, light, orange-flavored salad is just what is called for at a spring bridal shower or an anniversary luncheon. Fresh orange segments can be a delightful surprise when they appear in a salad. The citrus zest enhances the dressing, made ultra-delicious with crème fraîche. Radicchio leaves make divine little cups for this colorful salad.

FOR THE DRESSING:

¾ cup prepared mayonnaise, such as Hellmann's

¾ cup crème fraîche

3 tablespoons chopped fresh tarragon leaves,
    or 2 teaspoons dried

Finely grated zest of 2 oranges

Coarse (kosher) salt and freshly ground
    black pepper, to taste

FOR THE SHRIMP:

½ cup dry white wine

1 rib from the heart of the celery, with leaves

4 flat-leaf parsley sprigs

1½ pounds large shrimp, peeled and deveined

FOR THE SALAD:

1 pound medium-size asparagus, woody ends
    trimmed off, cut into 1-inch lengths

2 navel oranges, peeled and cut into segments
    (segments halved crosswise if they are
    very large)

1 tablespoon snipped fresh chives,
    for garnish

1. Prepare the dressing: Combine the mayonnaise and crème fraîche in a small bowl, and mix well. Stir in the tarragon, orange zest, and salt and pepper. Set aside. (The dressing can be made up to 6 hours before you use it.)

2. Prepare the shrimp: Fill a large pot halfway with water. Add the wine, celery, and parsley sprigs, and bring to a boil over high heat. Reduce the heat to medium-low, add the shrimp, and simmer until they are just cooked through, 2 to 3 minutes. Drain the shrimp and rinse them under cold running water to stop the cooking. Drain again and pat dry. Place them in a large bowl.

3. Bring a saucepan of salted water to a boil. Add the asparagus and cook until just tender, 2 to 3 minutes. Drain, rinse under cold running water, and drain again. Pat the asparagus dry, and add it to the shrimp. Add the orange segments and the dressing, and toss to combine.

4. Transfer the salad to a decorative bowl, sprinkle it with the chives, and serve.

ASPARAGUS, HAM, AND DILL QUICHE

SERVES 6 TO 8

O

In the 1970s, quiches were so prevalent that they began to seem somewhat ho-hum. But a properly made quiche is never boring. When asparagus is in season, this is the one to bake.

FOR THE CRUST:

1 ½ cups all-purpose flour

½ teaspoon salt

1 pinch sugar

5 tablespoons unsalted butter, chilled, cut into pieces

3 tablespoons solid vegetable shortening, chilled

¼ cup ice water

FOR THE FILLING:

4 tablespoons (½ stick) unsalted butter

¾ cup diced smoked ham (¼-inch dice)

½ cup diced onion (¼-inch dice)

1½ cups asparagus pieces, cut ½ inch long

FOR THE CUSTARD:

2 large eggs

2 large egg yolks

½ cup whole milk

½ cup heavy (whipping) cream

Salt and freshly ground black pepper, to taste

⅛ teaspoon ground nutmeg

2 dashes Tabasco sauce

2 tablespoons chopped fresh dill leaves or chives

FOR THE TOPPING:

½ cup coarsely grated Gruyère cheese

1. Prepare the crust: Place the flour, salt, and sugar in a food processor and process to combine. Add the butter and shortening, and process until the mixture resembles coarse sand. Add the ice water and process until the dough just forms a ball. Remove the ball of dough from the processor and flatten it slightly. Wrap it in plastic wrap and refrigerate it for at least 1 hour, or as long as 2 days.

2. Preheat the oven to 400°F.

3. Roll the dough out on a lightly floured surface to form a round that is about ⅛ inch thick and 11 inches in diameter. Transfer the round to a 9-inch glass or metal pie plate. Trim off the excess dough, leaving a 1-inch overhang. Turn the overhang under, and flute the edge decoratively. Use the tines of a fork to poke holes all over the bottom of the crust. Place two sheets of heavy-duty aluminum foil, one on top of the other, directly on the surface of the pie crust to weight it down. Bake the crust until it is light golden brown, about 15 minutes. Remove the foil, and continue baking to crisp the crust slightly, about 5 minutes. Set the crust aside.

4. Reduce the oven temperature to 375°F.

5. Prepare the filling: Melt the butter in a skillet over medium-low heat. Add the ham and onion, and sauté until the onion is partially softened, about 5 minutes. Add the asparagus and cook until the onion is translucent, another 5 minutes. Allow the filling to cool for about 10 minutes. Then spoon it into the prebaked crust.

6. Prepare the custard: Whisk all of the custard ingredients together in a bowl.

7. Pour the custard mixture over the filling in the crust, and sprinkle the cheese evenly over the top. Bake until the filling is set and the top is golden brown, about 30 minutes.

8. Let the quiche cool slightly on a wire rack. Serve it warm or at room temperature. 🌺

AN ASPARAGUS BRUNCH EGG SALAD

SERVES 4

At a leisurely brunch, surprise guests with this attractive egg salad, and present it alongside an elegant oval dish draped with smoked salmon or thinly sliced baked Virginia ham. Very thinly sliced black bread is the perfect choice for spreading. Freshly caught trout, fried and served with big wedges of lemon, adds the exclamation mark to super yum! Don't forget to put a jug of daffodils on the table.

1 pound medium-size asparagus

6 hard-cooked eggs, coarsely chopped

Salt and freshly ground black pepper, to taste

2 tablespoons coarsely chopped fresh dill leaves

⅓ cup prepared mayonnaise, such as Hellmann's

1 teaspoon Dijon mustard

1. Cut the tips from the asparagus (about 1 inch long); you should have ½ cup. (See Note, page 277.)

2. Bring a small pot of salted water to a boil. Add the asparagus tips and cook until they are just tender, 2 to 3 minutes. Drain, rinse under cold running water, and drain again. Pat the tips dry and set them aside.

3. Place the chopped eggs in a bowl and season them lightly with salt and pepper. Toss with the dill.

4. Combine the mayonnaise and the mustard in a small bowl, and fold this into the eggs. Then gently fold in the asparagus tips. Serve immediately, or cover and refrigerate for up to 4 hours before serving. 🌺

"BEANS HAVE GAINED NATIONWIDE RECOGNITON AS STARS IN THE KITCHEN."

BEANS AND LEGUMES

There's always been a place in our mealtime repertoire for beans and legumes. Wonderful Boston-style baked beans in the Northeast. Black-eyed peas in the South. Pinto beans or kidney beans in our Southwestern chilies. And as for legumes—well, for many of us, our legumes appeared as a scoop of boiled green peas or as split pea soup with plenty of homemade crispy croutons. All very tasty, but the selection has been limited. Not any more.

The dishes I've put together reflect the way more of us have been enjoying beans recently. In a spicy black bean soup redolent with the smoky flavor of bacon and finished with a swirl of sour cream. A Cajun-influenced red bean and rice dish filled with chunks of andouille sausage. A meatless chili chock-full of vegetables and featuring unusual painted pony beans. And Jerk Red Beans, packing heat from Scotch bonnet chiles and sweet relief from a dollop of Mango Salsa.

Lentils are my legume of choice and the two recipes I've included represent my love of the French way with their green lentilles du Puy—I've turned them into a tempting salad to serve with poultry—and the Indian way with theirs—a dal with plenty of fresh ginger. Simply delicious.

VELVETY
BLACK BEAN SOUP

SERVES 8

Jeremiah Tower, a great California chef, makes an elegant, smooth black bean soup with a sour cream swirl in the center. He serves his with a dollop of tomato salsa in the middle of the cream swirl. I'd suggest trying a pineapple, mango, or papaya salsa—about a scant tablespoon should do.

1 pound dried black turtle beans

1 onion, chopped

1 carrot, peeled and chopped

1 rib celery with leaves, chopped

6 cloves garlic, smashed

4 ounces slab bacon, or 1 ham hock, rinsed

2 or 3 fresh thyme sprigs

1 dried bay leaf

2 to 3 quarts chicken or vegetable broth, preferably
   homemade (see pages 434 and 436)

1 tablespoon ground cumin

1 tablespoon ancho chile powder (available in
   specialty food stores and some supermarkets)

Salt and freshly ground black pepper, to taste

½ cup sour cream

2 to 3 tablespoons milk

½ cup salsa, for garnish (optional, see page 365)

1. Pick over the beans, discarding any debris. Place them in a bowl, add cold water to cover by 2 inches, and soak overnight (or see How to Quick-Soak Dried Beans, page 291).

2. Drain the beans, rinse them well, and drain again. Place the beans in a large heavy pot. Add the onion, carrot, celery, garlic, bacon, thyme sprigs, and bay leaf. Pour in the broth, using enough to cover the ingredients. Bring to a boil, skimming off any foam that forms on the surface. Then reduce the heat to medium-low, partially cover the pot, and simmer, stirring occasionally, until the beans are tender, about 2 hours (adding more broth if the level of the liquid falls below the beans).

3. Remove the pot from the heat. Remove and discard the thyme sprigs and bay leaf. Place ½ cup of the beans, with some liquid, in a small bowl and add the cumin and ancho chile powder. Mix well, and stir this back into the pot.

4. Discard the bacon or ham hock and transfer the beans and liquid, in batches, to a blender or food processor and puree, adding as much extra broth as needed to achieve the consistency you desire. The soup should not be too thick. Return the soup to the pot and season it with salt and pepper to taste.

5. Combine the sour cream and the milk in a small bowl, and stir until smooth.

6. When you are ready to serve it, heat the soup through. Ladle the hot soup into shallow soup bowls. Swirl a tablespoon of the sour cream mixture in the center of each bowl, top with a spoonful of the salsa if desired, and serve immediately. 🌿

CHICKPEA STEW

SERVES 4

We are accustomed to using chickpeas as an ingredient in North African and Hispanic dishes, but here they are the feature attraction. (Canned chickpeas have great integrity and are readily available—it's not necessary to cook dried chickpeas for this recipe.) A dab of honey mellows the ingredients of this robust stew and pulls the flavors together.

2 tablespoons extra-virgin olive oil

1 red onion, cut into ¼-inch dice

2 tablespoons finely minced garlic

1 teaspoon ground cumin

2 cans (each 15 ounces) chickpeas (garbanzo beans), rinsed and drained

1 can (14 ounces) Italian plum tomatoes, chopped, with their juices

4 fresh thyme sprigs, or 1 teaspoon dried thyme leaves

1 teaspoon honey

1 teaspoon fresh lemon juice

1¾ cups chicken broth, preferably homemade (see page 434)

Salt and freshly ground black pepper, to taste

About 1⅓ cups couscous (optional)

½ cup chopped fresh flat-leaf parsley leaves

1. Heat the olive oil in a heavy saucepan over medium-low heat. Add the onion and cook, stirring occasionally, until it is almost completely wilted, 8 to 12 minutes. Add the garlic and cook for another 2 to 3 minutes. Stir in the cumin and cook to mellow the flavors, 2 minutes.

2. Add the chickpeas, tomatoes with their juices, thyme, honey, lemon juice, broth, and salt and pepper. Bring to a boil, skimming off any foam that forms on the surface. Then reduce the heat to medium and simmer, uncovered, until the sauce thickens slightly, 15 to 20 minutes.

3. Meanwhile, cook the couscous according to the package directions (you'll want about 4 cups cooked). Keep warm.

4. Taste the chickpea stew and adjust the seasonings as needed. Remove the thyme sprigs if using, and stir in the parsley. Spoon the couscous into four shallow bowls, top with chickpea stew, and serve immediately. 🌿

WHITE BEAN, GREEN BEAN, AND TUNA SALAD

SERVES 6

While canned beans are excellent for many dishes, I find that for this salad, it's worth taking the time to cook my own. The beans are firm and absorb the flavor of the vinaigrette while they are hot. The green beans, celery, and tuna make for a most delicious entrée. If you prefer a heartier flavor, substitute imported Italian canned tuna.

FOR THE WHITE BEANS:

8 ounces dried small white beans, pea beans, or cannellini beans picked over, debris discarded

1 onion, cut in half

1 carrot, peeled and cut in half

1 rib celery with leaves

2 flat-leaf parsley sprigs

1 clove garlic, bruised (see box, page 82)

1 dried bay leaf

Garlic Vinaigrette (recipe follows)

FOR THE SALAD:

8 ounces green beans, stem ends trimmed off, halved crosswise

1 cup grape tomatoes, halved lengthwise

½ cup diced celery (¼-inch dice)

⅓ cup pitted imported black olives or halved ripe California olives

¼ cup slivered red onion

1 can (6 ounces) white tuna packed in water, drained

3 tablespoons chopped fresh flat-leaf parsley leaves

Salt and freshly ground black pepper, to taste

Romaine, Boston lettuce, and radicchio leaves, for serving

1. Pick over the beans, discarding any debris. Place the beans in a large heavy pot, add cold water to cover by 2 inches, and set aside to soak overnight. (Or see How to Quick-Soak Dried Beans, facing page.)

2. Drain the beans, rinse them under cold running water, and drain again. Place them in a medium-size pot.

3. Add the onion, carrot, celery, parsley sprigs, garlic, and bay leaf to the beans. Add 8 cups water and bring to a boil. Then reduce the heat to medium and simmer, uncovered, until the beans are just tender but not mushy, 35 to 40 minutes.

4. Drain the beans, transfer them to a large bowl, and discard the vegetables and herbs. Toss the beans with the Garlic Vinaigrette. Set aside to cool to room temperature.

HOW TO QUICK-SOAK DRIED BEANS

Pick over the beans, discarding any debris. Place the beans in a large heavy pot, and add cold water to cover by 2 inches. Bring the water to a boil over medium-high heat and boil for 2 minutes. Then remove the pot from the heat, cover it, and set it aside for 1 hour.

Drain the beans, place them in a bowl, and rinse them in several changes of cold water. Drain again. The beans are now ready to cook in recipes.

5. Meanwhile, bring a saucepan of salted water to a boil. Add the green beans and cook until just tender, 3 to 4 minutes. Drain, and pat dry. Let the beans cool to room temperature.

6. Add the green beans, tomatoes, celery, olives, and red onion to the white beans. Break the tuna into chunks and add it to the bowl. Sprinkle with 2 tablespoons of the parsley, and season generously with salt and pepper. Use a large rubber spatula to fold all the ingredients together—gently, so the tuna doesn't break up.

7. Arrange the lettuce and radicchio leaves in a large shallow bowl or on a platter. Spoon the salad over the lettuce, sprinkle with the remaining 1 tablespoon parsley, and serve.

GARLIC VINAIGRETTE

MAKES ABOUT ½ CUP

there are times when we need just a small amount of a great vinaigrette for a particular salad. This delicious garlic vinaigrette does the trick.

 2 teaspoons Dijon mustard
 2 tablespoons red wine vinegar
 ½ teaspoon sugar
 Salt and freshly ground black pepper, to taste
 ⅓ cup extra-virgin olive oil
 2 cloves garlic, bruised (see box, page 82)

1. Place the mustard in a small bowl and whisk in the vinegar, sugar, and salt and pepper.

2. Still whisking, slowly drizzle in the olive oil. Continue whisking until the mixture thickens. Add the bruised garlic, and adjust the seasonings as needed. Cover and refrigerate overnight for the flavors to meld.

3. Remove and discard the garlic. Keep the vinaigrette, covered, in the refrigerator for up to 1 week. Bring it to room temperature before using.

SALAD OF GREEN FLAGEOLETS & ANDOUILLE SAUSAGE

SERVES 4 TO 6

O

I'm crazy about bean salads, and when made with French flageolets, they are really something extra-special. Flageolets are more delicate and slightly smaller than our great northern white bean; they're pale green and have the shape of an elongated kidney bean. Here I've combined them with spicy andouille sausage, red onions, and ripe tomato. To smooth the flavors, I've scooped in a ripe avocado. This is delicious for lunch or as a light supper.

FOR THE BEANS:

8 ounces dried flageolets picked over, debris discarded

1 onion, cut in half, each half studded with 2 whole cloves

1 rib celery with leaves, cut in half, plus extra celery leaves

2 cloves garlic, bruised (see box, page 82)

4 flat-leaf parsley sprigs

FOR THE SALAD:

5 tablespoons extra-virgin olive oil

2 andouille sausages (each 4 ounces)

2 tablespoons red wine vinegar

Salt and freshly ground black pepper, to taste

½ small red onion, slivered lengthwise

1 ripe tomato, halved lengthwise and cut into thin wedges

2 tablespoons chopped fresh flat-leaf parsley leaves

1 ripe avocado, preferably Hass

1. Pick over the beans, discarding any debris. Place the beans in a large heavy pot, add cold water to cover by 2 inches, and set aside to soak overnight. (Or see How to Quick-Soak Dried Beans, page 291.)

2. Return the beans to the pot and add the onion halves, celery, garlic, and parsley sprigs. Add water to cover, and bring to a boil. Reduce the heat and simmer, uncovered, until the beans are tender but not mushy, about 35 minutes.

3. While the beans are cooking, prepare the salad: Heat 2 tablespoons of the olive oil in a skillet over medium heat. Add the sausages and cook until they are lightly browned all over, about 10 minutes. Set them aside on a paper-towel-lined plate to drain. Then cut them into ½-inch-thick slices.

4. When the beans are tender, drain them and discard the onion halves, celery, garlic, and parsley sprigs. Transfer the beans to a large bowl.

5. In a small bowl, whisk the vinegar with the salt and pepper. Whisking constantly, slowly drizzle in the remaining 3 tablespoons olive oil, and continue whisking until slightly thickened. Toss this with the warm beans.

6. Add the sausages, onion, tomato, and parsley to the beans. Season with salt and pepper.

7. Just before serving, cut the avocado in half and remove the pit. Using a teaspoon, scoop out large pieces of avocado and add them to the salad. Toss lightly, and transfer the salad to a serving bowl. Serve immediately. ✣

RED BEANS AND ANDOUILLE SAUSAGE

SERVES 4

there's nothing like Cajun spices and the sexy heat of andouille sausages to spice up a pot of beans. Sausage king and cookbook author Bruce Aidells knows how to pull the flavors together, bringing us home to that Low Country cooking. His recipes are assertive, and his sausages are just the best!

3 tablespoons olive oil

Salt

1 cup long-grain converted rice

½ teaspoon ground cumin

¼ teaspoon sweet paprika

¼ teaspoon dried thyme leaves

¼ teaspoon dried oregano

2 andouille sausages (each about 4 ounces), cut into ½-inch pieces (see Sources, page 439)

1 small onion, cut into ¼-inch dice

2 ribs celery, cut into ¼-inch dice

1 teaspoon finely minced garlic

¼ cup diced bottled roasted red pepper or pimento (¼-inch dice)

1 can (15 ounces) dark red kidney beans, drained and rinsed

½ cup tomato sauce, homemade (see page 437) or prepared

½ cup low-sodium beef broth

¼ cup chopped fresh flat-leaf parsley leaves

Freshly ground black pepper, to taste

1. Bring 2¼ cups water to a boil in a large pot. Add 1 tablespoon of the oil and 1½ teaspoons salt. Stir in the rice. Reduce the heat to medium-low, cover the pot, and simmer until the rice is cooked and all the liquid has been absorbed, about 20 minutes.

2. While the rice is cooking, combine the cumin, paprika, thyme, and oregano in a small bowl, and stir well.

3. Heat the remaining 2 tablespoons olive oil in a large pot over medium-low heat. Add the sausages and cook, sprinkling them with the spice mixture, until they are lightly browned, 10 minutes. Add the onion, celery, and garlic, and cook until the onion has softened, 5 minutes.

4. Remove the rice from the heat and set it aside, covered.

5. Add the red pepper, beans, tomato sauce, and beef broth to the sausage mixture. Simmer, stirring occasionally, for 8 minutes. Stir in the parsley and cook for another 2 minutes. Season with salt and pepper.

6. Fluff the rice with a fork, and serve the beans and sausages over the hot rice. 🌿

SMALL WHITE BEANS
AND ITALIAN SAUSAGES

SERVES 6

White beans and sausages cooked up with sage and tomatoes, served in shallow pasta bowls with a wedge of crusty peasant bread alongside—it's Tuscany at its best. A Barolo is the perfect choice of wine. Follow with a bright peppery green salad, and then a buttery Italian Fontina served with ripe Bartlett or Anjou pears.

8 ounces dried small white beans

1 can (28 ounces) Italian peeled plum tomatoes, undrained

6 tablespoons extra-virgin olive oil

4 ounces slab bacon, rind removed, cut into ¼-inch pieces

2 large cloves garlic, bruised (see box, page 82)

3 sage sprigs

1 dried bay leaf

½ teaspoon crushed red pepper flakes

6 sweet Italian sausages

Salt and freshly ground black pepper, to taste

2 tablespoons chopped fresh flat-leaf parsley leaves

Crusty peasant bread, warmed, for serving

1. Pick over the beans, discarding any debris. Place the beans in a large heavy pot, add cold water to cover by 2 inches, and set aside to soak overnight. (Or see How to Quick-Soak Dried Beans, page 291.)

2. Drain the canned tomatoes, reserving the juices. Chop 4 of the tomatoes and set aside. Place the remaining tomatoes and all the juices in a food processor or blender, and puree. Set the puree aside.

3. Drain the beans, place them in a bowl, and rinse them in several changes of cold water. Drain again. Return the beans to the pot, and set it aside.

4. Heat 2 tablespoons of the olive oil in a nonstick skillet over medium-low heat. Add the bacon and cook, stirring occasionally, until it is golden brown, 6 to 7 minutes.

5. Using a slotted spoon, transfer the bacon to the bean pot. Add the garlic, sage sprigs, bay leaf, red pepper flakes, the reserved chopped tomatoes, and 6 cups cold water to the beans. Bring to a boil over high heat, skimming off any foam that forms on the surface. Reduce the heat to medium-low and simmer, uncovered, until the beans are tender but not mushy, about 40 minutes.

6. Drain the beans and set them aside.

7. Poke small holes in the sausages with a toothpick. Heat 2 tablespoons of the remaining olive oil in a large deep skillet over medium-high heat. Add the sausages and brown on all sides, 5 to 7 minutes. Remove all but 2 tablespoons of the fat from the skillet. Add the reserved pureed tomatoes and simmer over medium heat, shaking the skillet occasionally, for 5 minutes.

8. Add the drained beans to the skillet and season to taste with salt and pepper. Discard the bay leaf and the sage sprigs. Stir the remaining 2 tablespoons olive oil and the parsley into the bean mixture. Serve hot, in shallow bowls, with hot crusty bread alongside. 🌿

JERK RED BEANS
WITH MANGO SALSA

SERVES 6

take a pot full of beans and vegetables spiced with jerk flavors, serve them over rice and top with a juicy fresh mango salsa, and you've got something pretty special to add to your culinary repertoire. When I was creating this recipe, I couldn't stop eating it—and I usually only taste! A squeeze of fresh lime juice brightens all the flavors.

8 ounces dried red kidney beans

2 cups low-sodium chicken broth, preferably
    homemade (see page 434)

1½ cups drained canned Italian plum tomatoes,
    crushed

1 teaspoon Tabasco sauce

2 dried bay leaves

2 thyme sprigs

2 carrots, peeled, halved lengthwise, and
    cut into ½-inch pieces

2 ribs celery, halved lengthwise, and cut into
    ½-inch pieces

2 shallots, finely chopped

1 onion, chopped

1½ tablespoons minced garlic

1 tablespoon minced fresh ginger

1 teaspoon finely chopped fresh red or
    orange chile, such as Scotch bonnet or
    habanero

1 tablespoon dark or light brown sugar

1 teaspoon ground cinnamon

1 teaspoon ground nutmeg

¼ teaspoon ground allspice

1 ham hock

1 tablespoon olive oil

1½ teaspoons salt

1½ cups long-grain converted rice

Salt and freshly ground black pepper,
    to taste

4 scallions (white bulbs and 3 inches
    green), sliced on the diagonal,
    for garnish

Fresh Mango Salsa (page 369), for serving

1. Pick over the dried beans, discarding any debris. Place the beans in a bowl, add cold water to cover by 2 inches, and set aside to soak overnight. (Or see How to Quick-Soak Dried Beans, page 291.)

2. Drain the beans, place them in a bowl, and rinse them in several changes of water. Drain again, and set aside.

3. Preheat the oven to 350°F.

4. Combine the broth, tomatoes, Tabasco, bay leaves, thyme sprigs, and 1 cup water in a large flameproof casserole. Bring the mixture to a boil, and then remove the casserole from the heat.

5. Stir the beans into the hot mixture, and add the carrots, celery, shallots, onion, garlic, ginger, chile, brown sugar, cinnamon, nutmeg, and allspice. Tuck the ham hock into the center of the mixture. Cover the casserole, transfer it to the oven, and bake until the beans are almost tender, about 1½ hours.

6. Uncover the casserole and test the beans for doneness. Remove the ham hock, cut the meat from the bone, and stir the meat back into the casserole. Cover the casserole and cook until the beans are tender but not mushy, up to another 30 minutes.

7. Meanwhile, bring 3⅓ cups water to a boil in a large pot. Add the olive oil and the salt, and then stir in the rice. Reduce the heat to medium-low, cover the pot, and simmer until the rice is cooked and all the liquid has been absorbed, about 20 minutes. Remove the pot from the heat and set it aside, covered, for 5 minutes. Then fluff the rice with a fork.

8. When the beans are tender, remove and discard the bay leaves and thyme sprigs. Season the beans with salt and pepper.

9. Serve the beans over the rice in shallow bowls. Sprinkle the scallions over the top, and dollop each portion with some of the Fresh Mango Salsa.

ISLAND SEAFOOD CELEBRATION

Mussel and clams—and plenty of cold beer (how about Red Stripe)—make up an unusual and very tasty menu. Because the clams are part of a rice dish, you don't need to make extra for the jerk beans unless one of your guests is vegetarian. If this is the case, make the jerk beans with vegetable broth (page 436) instead of chicken broth and leave out the ham hock.

SAFFRON MUSSEL SALAD
PAGE 246

CLAMS, CHORIZO, AND RICE
PAGE 233

JERK RED BEANS
with Mango Salsa
FACING PAGE

PINEAPPLE SORBET
PAGE 431

PAINTED PONY BEAN CHILI

SERVES 8

hese unusual small beans are native to North America and are distinguished by a half-cream, half-brown coloration with a distinctive white eye. Because of their taste, look, and—of course—name, I thought they'd combine beautifully with chili spices and a rich blend of vegetables for a robust bean-and-vegetable chili. The garnishes make this a can't-miss meal.

FOR THE BEANS:

6 ounces dried painted pony beans or
    other small beans

1 onion, halved

1 rib celery with leaves

2 cloves garlic, crushed

3 flat-leaf parsley sprigs

2 tablespoons olive oil

FOR THE CHILI:

6 tablespoons olive oil

1 onion, cut into ¼-inch dice

1 tablespoon finely minced garlic

2 medium-size zucchini, trimmed and cut
    into ¼-inch dice

1 red bell pepper, stemmed, seeded, and
    cut into ¼-inch dice

1 teaspoon minced green jalapeño pepper

1 can (28 ounces) Italian plum tomatoes,
    chopped, with their juices

1½ pounds ripe fresh plum tomatoes,
    cut into ½-inch pieces

2 tablespoons chili powder

1 tablespoon ground cumin

1 tablespoon dried oregano

1 teaspoon fennel seeds

Salt and freshly ground black pepper, to taste

½ cup chopped fresh flat-leaf parsley leaves

2 cups long-grain converted rice

1 cup canned chickpeas (garbanzo beans),
    drained and rinsed

2 tablespoons fresh lemon juice

1 cup freshly grated Cheddar cheese, for
    garnish

4 scallions (white bulbs and 3 inches
    green), thinly sliced on the diagonal,
    for garnish

Greek yogurt or sour cream, for garnish

1. Prepare the beans: Pick over the painted pony beans, removing any debris. Rinse them under cold running water, and drain again. Place the beans in a bowl and add cold water to cover by 2 inches. Set aside to soak for 4 to 8 hours. Then drain, rinse well under cold water, and drain again. (Or see How to Quick-Soak Dried Beans, page 291.)

2. Place the painted pony beans, onion halves, celery, garlic, and parsley sprigs in a pot and add 6 cups water. Bring to a boil, skimming off any foam that forms on the surface. Reduce the heat to medium-low and simmer, uncovered, until the beans are tender but not mushy, 30 to 40 minutes depending on the size of the bean. Drain the beans and transfer them to a bowl, discarding the flavoring vegetables. Drizzle the olive oil over the beans, and set aside. (The beans can be cooked up to 6 hours ahead; if cooking ahead, store, covered, in the refrigerator.)

3. To make the chili, heat 4 tablespoons of the oil in a heavy pot over medium-low heat. Add the onion, garlic, zucchini, bell pepper, and jalapeño and cook, stirring, until the vegetables are just tender, about 10 minutes.

4. Add the canned tomatoes with their juices, the fresh tomatoes, chili powder, cumin, oregano, fennel seeds, salt and pepper, and the parsley. Cook over low heat, stirring occasionally, for 20 minutes.

5. Meanwhile, bring 4 cups water to a boil in a large pot. Add the remaining 2 tablespoons olive oil and 1½ teaspoons salt. Then stir in the rice. Reduce the heat to medium-low, cover the pot, and simmer until the rice is cooked and all the liquid has been absorbed, about 20 minutes. Remove the pot from the heat and set it aside, covered.

6. Stir 1 cup of the reserved painted pony beans, the chickpeas, and the lemon juice into the vegetable mixture. Cook for 5 minutes. Taste, and adjust the seasonings as needed.

7. Fluff the rice with a fork, and divide it among eight individual bowls. Spoon the chili over the rice. Garnish each bowl with the Cheddar, scallions, and a dollop of yogurt, and serve.

NOTE: This makes more than enough painted pony beans. Toss any extra beans with cooked corn kernels, chopped tomatoes, chopped cucumbers, and a vinaigrette for a nice side salad to serve with a burger. ❧

GREEN LENTIL SALAD

SERVES 6

Lentilles du Puy, the tiny, firm green lentils that come from the village of Le Puy-en-Velay in France's mountainous Auvergne region, are very different in appearance, color, and texture from the larger, softer brown lentils that we are more familiar with. I've turned these green lentils into a delicious salad, delightful to serve in the winter with poultry, roasted vegetables, and cheese. The trick here is not to overcook the lentils and to toss them in the vinaigrette while they're warm so they will absorb the flavor.

FOR THE LENTILS:

2 cups imported French green lentils
    (lentilles du Puy)
1 cup low-sodium chicken or vegetable broth,
    preferably homemade (see pages 434 and 436)
1 small onion, cut in half and stuck with
    3 whole cloves
2 cloves garlic, bruised (see box, page 82)
1 rib celery with leaves, halved crosswise,
    plus extra celery leaves
1 dried bay leaf

FOR THE SALAD:

2 carrots, peeled and cut into ¼-inch dice
¼ cup Red Wine Vinaigrette (page 23)
2 scallions (white bulbs and 3 inches green),
    thinly sliced
1 tablespoon chopped fresh tarragon leaves
2 tablespoons chopped fresh flat-leaf
    parsley leaves
Salt and freshly ground black pepper,
    to taste

1. Prepare the lentils: Pick over the lentils, discarding any debris. Place them in a strainer and rinse them under cold running water; drain. Transfer the lentils to a large heavy saucepan and add the broth, onion halves, garlic, celery, bay leaf, and 3 cups water. Bring to a boil, skimming off any foam that forms on the surface. Reduce the heat to low and simmer (do not boil), uncovered, until the lentils are just tender, about 25 minutes.

2. Meanwhile, bring a small pot of lightly salted water to a boil. Add the carrots and cook until they are just tender, 3 to 4 minutes. Drain, and set aside.

3. Prepare the salad: When the lentils are cooked, remove the pan from the heat. Discard the onion halves, garlic, celery, and bay leaf. Drain the lentils and transfer them to a bowl. While the lentils are still warm, toss them with the vinaigrette, making sure they are well coated with the dressing. Stir in the carrots, scallions, tarragon, and parsley. Season with salt and pepper, and serve at room temperature.

PINK LENTIL DAL
WITH FRESH GINGER

SERVES 4

My favorite Indian food in New York is created by the brilliant chefs at the restaurant Dévi. Here is one of their delicious dals, flavored intensely with a tempering oil made with cumin, fresh ginger, chiles, and garlic. (A dal is a dish of cooked legumes, most often flavored with spices that have been cooked in a hot oil.) Fresh cilantro brightens the dal just before serving. It's delicious served with Tandoori-Style Roast Chicken (page 142).

1 cup yellow (red) lentils

½ teaspoon ground turmeric

1 teaspoon salt, or to taste

2½ tablespoons canola oil

1¼ teaspoons cumin seeds, or ½ teaspoon
    ground cumin

1 whole dried red chile

1 tablespoon minced fresh ginger

1 teaspoon minced garlic

2 teaspoons finely minced fresh green serrano
    or jalapeño chile

¼ cup chopped fresh cilantro

Juice of ½ lemon

1. Pick over the lentils, discarding any debris. Rinse them under cold running water, and drain again. Combine the lentils, turmeric, salt, and 4 cups water in a large saucepan. Bring to a boil, skimming off any foam that forms on the surface. Reduce the heat to low, cover the pan, and simmer (do not boil) until the lentils are soft, about 20 minutes; if necessary, add more water while they are cooking. Taste, and add more salt if needed.

2. Ladle ½ cup of the lentils and some liquid into a small bowl and mash them with a spoon. Return the mashed lentils to the pan. (If you want a thicker dal, mash more lentils. If you prefer it thin, add more water.)

3. Prepare the tempering oil: Heat the canola oil and the cumin in a small skillet over medium heat. Add the dried chile, ginger, garlic, and green chile. Cook, stirring, until the garlic turns golden, 1 to 2 minutes. Remove the skillet from the heat and add 1 tablespoon cold water to stop the cooking.

4. Remove the dried chile and strain the tempering oil into the lentils, pressing down on the solids with the back of the spoon. Stir in half of the cilantro and all of the lemon juice. Simmer, uncovered, over medium-low heat for 5 minutes.

5. Transfer the dal to a serving bowl, garnish with the remaining cilantro, and serve at room temperature.

"...FLAVORS ARE HEIGHTENED BY THE ADDITION OF SWEET SUMMER CORN."

CORN

Taking a bite of corn is like taking a bite of summer. There is nothing sweeter and nothing more emblematic of the season. When fresh corn is plentiful, there's always a stick of butter waiting on my table and a large platter ready to hold the ears in a golden pyramid. I cover it with a linen napkin to keep the corn warm after cooking it in boiling salted and sugared water for no more than 2 minutes. Perfection.

Besides being delicious in its purest state, corn is ideal in chowders, creamed in creamed corn, and blended with cornmeal in Jalapeño Corn Bread and Blueberry Corn Muffins. Fresh corn also partners well with other summer vegetables, like tomatoes, green beans, and limas, resulting in a delicious Late Harvest Succotash. By this time we know that buying corn at a local farm stand is the next best thing to picking it yourself. It's best to eat corn right after it's picked, so don't let it sit around; cook it the same day that you buy it. Always buy corn in its husk. Be sure the husks are green and soft—the greener the husk, the fresher the corn—and tight to the cob. The tassels should be golden.

BLOND CORN AND VEGETABLE CHOWDER

SERVES 6

the availability of yellow tomatoes provided the germ of this idea: yellow tomatoes, yellow bell peppers, all blending with the season's delicious corn. What a sunny-looking chowder! A chiffonade of basil adds oomph just before serving.

2 tablespoons unsalted butter

2 tablespoons extra-virgin olive oil

2 cups chopped onions

2 tablespoons all-purpose flour

4 cups vegetable broth, preferably homemade
   (see page 436)

2 russet potatoes (each 8 ounces), peeled and
   cut into ¼-inch dice

1 cup half-and-half

4 cups fresh corn kernels
   (from about 8 ears of corn)

1 dash Tabasco sauce

Salt and freshly ground black pepper, to taste

1 large yellow bell pepper, stemmed, seeded,
   and cut into ¼-inch dice

4 scallions (white bulbs and 3 inches green), thinly sliced

1 large yellow tomato, cored, seeded,
   and cut into ¼-inch dice, for garnish

⅓ cup slivered, fresh basil leaves, for garnish

1. Melt the butter in the oil in a large pot over low heat.

2. Add the onions and cook, stirring occasionally, until wilted, about 10 minutes. Sprinkle with the flour and cook, stirring, for another 5 minutes.

3. Add the broth and potatoes. Raise the heat to medium, bring the broth to a boil, and cook until the potatoes are tender, about 8 minutes.

4. Add the half-and-half, corn, Tabasco, and salt and pepper. Cook, stirring occasionally, for 8 minutes. Then add the bell pepper and the scallions, adjust the seasonings as needed, and reduce the heat to low. Cook for another 5 minutes.

5. Serve immediately, garnished with the chopped tomato and the slivered basil. 🌿

SUMMER CORN CHOWDER

SERVES 8

This is another light corn chowder that captures three of my favorite flavors of summer: corn, tomatoes, and basil. I serve this creamy, pastel-colored soup in bright turquoise bowls for just a little extra hot-weather punch.

6 ears fresh sweet corn

6 cups chicken or vegetable broth, preferably homemade (see pages 434 and 436)

2 cloves garlic, bruised

1 russet potato, peeled and cut into ½-inch dice

2 cups whole milk

Salt and freshly ground black pepper, to taste

4 ounces slab bacon, rind removed, cut into ¼-inch dice (see Note)

2 tablespoons olive oil, if needed

1 onion, cut into ¼-inch dice

4 ripe tomatoes, seeded and cut into ¼-inch dice

¼ cup slivered fresh basil leaves

1. Use a sharp knife to strip the corn kernels off the cobs, cutting as close to the cobs as possible; you should have about 3 cups. Reserve the cobs and set the kernels aside.

2. Break the corncobs in half and place them in a heavy pot. Add the broth and garlic, and bring to a boil. Then reduce the heat to medium-low, partially cover the pot, and simmer to flavor the broth, about 10 minutes. Remove and discard the corncobs and the garlic cloves.

3. Stir the potato and half of the reserved corn kernels into the broth, and bring to a boil. Reduce the heat to medium, partially cover the pot, and simmer until the potato is tender, about 10 minutes. Remove the pot from the heat and let the chowder cool for 10 to 15 minutes.

4. Puree the soup, in batches, in a food processor and pour it into a large bowl. Add the milk and season with salt and pepper. Set it aside.

5. Cook the bacon in a large heavy pot over low heat, stirring occasionally, to render the fat, 6 to 7 minutes (add the 2 tablespoons olive oil if the bacon is lean). Add the onion and cook, stirring occasionally, until softened, about 10 minutes.

6. Pour the reserved pureed soup into the pot, stir in the remaining corn kernels, and simmer for 8 minutes. Adjust the seasonings as needed.

7. Just before serving, stir in the tomatoes and basil.

NOTE: If you want to make this a vegetarian soup, omit the bacon and cook the onion in 2 tablespoons olive oil.

FRESH CORN AND CRABMEAT SALAD

SERVES 4

Lump white crabmeat from the famously sweet Maryland blue crabs makes a particularly luscious salad. Of course the flavors are heightened by the addition of sweet summer corn. Chives and lemon zest add a bright touch. This makes an ideal starter for any spring or summer meal.

2 ears fresh sweet corn, shucked

8 ounces fresh lump crabmeat, picked over to remove all cartilage (do not break up the crab too much)

3 tablespoons snipped fresh chives

2 ripe plum tomatoes, seeded and cut into ¼-inch dice

Freshly ground black pepper, to taste

¼ cup sour cream

¼ cup prepared mayonnaise, such as Hellmann's

Finely grated zest of 1 lemon

Salt, to taste

4 medium-size whole Boston lettuce leaves, for serving

1. Bring a saucepan of salted water to a boil.

2. While the water is heating, use a sharp knife to strip the corn kernels off the cobs, cutting as close to the cobs as possible.

3. Cook the corn kernels in the boiling water until just tender, 2 to 3 minutes. Drain, run under cold water, and drain again. Pat dry, and transfer to a large bowl.

4. Add the crabmeat, 2 tablespoons of the chives, the tomatoes, and black pepper to the corn. Using a rubber spatula, gently combine the ingredients.

5. In another bowl, combine the sour cream, mayonnaise, and lemon zest. Using the rubber spatula, gently fold the dressing into the salad.

6. Just before serving, season the salad with salt. Place a lettuce leaf in the center of each of four salad plates. Spoon the crab salad into the lettuce leaves, and sprinkle the remaining 1 tablespoon chives over the salads. Serve immediately.

FARMERS' MARKET CORN SALAD

SERVES 4

Summer green beans are as tender as tiny French haricots verts and need just a few minutes' cooking for this salad. I use the slimmest, smallest beans I can find and keep them whole. They look beautiful mixed with the other vegetables. Make your vinaigrette before you shop, so all you have to do is fix the vegetables, toss, and serve.

4 ears fresh sweet corn, shucked

4 ounces slender fresh green beans, stem ends
    removed

1 cup diced, peeled, seeded cucumber (¼-inch dice)

2 medium-size ripe tomatoes, cut into ¼-inch dice

3 scallions (white bulbs and 3 inches green), thinly sliced

2 tablespoons chopped fresh flat-leaf parsley leaves

Coarse (kosher) salt and freshly ground
    black pepper, to taste

¼ cup Red Wine Vinaigrette (page 23)

1. Bring a saucepan of salted water to a boil.

2. While the water is heating, use a sharp knife to strip the corn kernels off the cobs, cutting as close to the cobs as possible; you should have 2 cups.

3. Cook the corn kernels in the boiling water until just tender, 2 to 3 minutes. Drain, run under cold water, and drain again. Pat dry and place in a large bowl.

4. Bring another saucepan of salted water to a boil, and add the green beans. Cook until just tender, about 3 minutes. Drain, run under cold water, and drain again. Pat dry and add to the corn. Toss in the cucumber, tomatoes, scallions, and parsley. (If you wish, you can refrigerate the mixture for up to 4 hours before serving. Remove it about 30 minutes before serving.)

5. Just before serving, season the salad with salt and pepper and toss it lightly with the vinaigrette. ❧

LATE HARVEST SUCCOTASH
WITH MOULARD DUCK BREASTS

SERVES 4

duck breasts decoratively fanned on fresh succotash is a colorful, appealing, and easy late summer–early autumn dish. The orange zest in the succotash carries over the classic French flavors of duck à l'orange, a dish many of us have feasted on in days past. Serve this with an Oregon Pinot Noir. Duck and pork are my favorite between-season meats, and an excellent pinot suits them well.

FOR THE SUCCOTASH:

1 cup fresh corn kernels (from about 2 ears of corn)

1 cup fresh slender green beans, stem ends trimmed, cut in half crosswise

2 tablespoons unsalted butter

2 tablespoons olive oil

1 cup diced onion (¼-inch dice)

1 cup frozen baby lima beans, thawed

½ cup diced red bell pepper (¼-inch dice)

¼ cup chicken or vegetable broth, preferably homemade (see pages 434 and 436)

2 tablespoons finely grated orange or tangerine zest

2 tablespoons chopped fresh tarragon leaves, or 1 to 2 teaspoons crushed dried

Salt and freshly ground black pepper, to taste

FOR THE DUCK:

1 whole boneless Moulard duck breast (about 2 pounds), halved lengthwise so that you have 2 breast halves

Salt and freshly ground black pepper, to taste

2 tablespoons chopped fresh flat-leaf parsley or fresh tarragon leaves, for garnish

1. Prepare the succotash: Bring a saucepan of salted water to a boil. Add the corn kernels and cook until just tender, 2 minutes. Drain, run under cold water, and drain again. Set aside.

2. Bring another saucepan of salted water to a boil, add the green beans, and cook until just tender, 3 minutes. Drain, run under cold water, and drain again. Set aside.

3. Melt the butter in the olive oil in a heavy pot over low heat. Add the onion and cook, stirring, until wilted, about 10 minutes.

4. Add the corn, green beans, lima beans, and bell pepper to the onion. Stir in the broth and the orange zest. Cook over low heat, stirring, to heat through, 5 minutes. Then stir in the tarragon, and season with salt and pepper. Set the succotash aside in the pot, loosely covered with aluminum foil.

5. Prepare the duck: Trim the fat from the duck breasts. Poke the skin all over with the tines of a fork (this will help to release the fat during cooking).

6. Heat a large nonstick skillet over medium heat. Add the duck breasts, skin side down, and cook until golden brown and crisp, 4 to 5 minutes. As the duck cooks, pour off the excess fat to prevent spattering.

7. Season the duck well with salt and pepper, turn it over, and cook until the meat is medium-rare, 5 to 7 minutes. Transfer the duck to a cutting board and let it rest for 10 minutes.

8. Meanwhile, reheat the succotash over low heat. Divide it among four dinner plates.

9. Carve the duck breasts diagonally into ¼-inch-thick slices, and fan them decoratively over the succotash. Sprinkle with the chopped parsley, and serve immediately. 🌿

CREAMED CORN

SERVES 8

There is something ethereal about creamed corn made with sweet summer corn—even with an hour of cooking. Perhaps the magic lies in the cream and the slow, steady simmer. Gilding the lily, I couldn't resist adding a dab of crème fraîche when the corn was off the stove. It lends a slight tang—excellent but purely optional. If you have any left over (who knows—you might), use it to make the Blueberry Corn Muffins on page 312.

10 ears fresh sweet corn, shucked

2 cups heavy (whipping) cream, plus more if necessary

2 tablespoons unsalted butter

2 teaspoons sugar

Salt and freshly ground black pepper, to taste

3 tablespoons crème fraîche (optional)

1. Using a sharp knife, strip the corn kernels off the cobs, cutting as close to the cobs as possible. Place the corn kernels in a large heavy pot. Using a soupspoon, scrape the milk from the cobs into the pot.

2. Stir in the cream, butter, sugar, and salt and pepper. Bring to a boil over high heat. Reduce the heat to medium-low, partially cover the pot, and simmer, stirring occasionally, for 30 minutes. Do not let the mixture boil; reduce the heat to low if necessary.

3. Remove the cover and cook, stirring occasionally, for another 30 minutes.

4. Remove the pot from the heat and let the corn cool slightly. Stir in the crème fraîche, if using, and serve immediately. 🌿

CONFETTI CORN PUDDING

MAKES NINE 3-INCH SQUARES

Corn pudding—both sweet and savory, with a touch of soufflé about it—is one of the best reasons for taking the kernels off the cob. Some corn puddings begin with small cubes of bacon, but this one is a vegetarian's delight. Bell peppers and chives add their flavors to the corn, and Tabasco sauce and mustard kick up the custard. Make it when fresh corn is in season. It's delicious served with grilled chicken or flank steak.

3 cups fresh corn kernels
    (from about 6 ears of corn)
2 tablespoons unsalted butter
1 tablespoon olive oil
1½ cups diced onions (¼-inch dice)
1 teaspoon sugar
⅓ cup diced red bell pepper
2 tablespoons snipped fresh chives
4 large eggs, lightly beaten
2 cups heavy (whipping) cream
1 teaspoon Dijon mustard
2 dashes Tabasco sauce
Salt and freshly ground black pepper, to taste
Boiling water, for the baking dish

1. Bring a pot of salted water to a boil, add the corn kernels, and cook until they are just tender, 2 minutes. Drain, run under cold water, and drain again. Set aside.

2. Melt the butter in the oil in a nonstick skillet over low heat. Add the onions and cook, stirring occa-sionally, until they are translucent, about 15 minutes. Sprinkle the sugar over the onions, and stir. Remove from the heat and set aside for 5 minutes.

3. Meanwhile, preheat the oven to 350°F.

4. Combine the onions, the reserved corn, the bell pepper, and the chives in a 9-x-9-x-2-inch baking dish.

5. Whisk the eggs, cream, mustard, Tabasco, and salt and pepper together in a bowl. Pour the cream mixture over the corn. Place the baking dish in a larger pan, and pour boiling water into the larger pan to reach about halfway up the sides of the baking dish. Carefully place it in the oven, and bake until the pudding is set and light gold, 1 hour.

6. Let the pudding rest for 10 minutes before cutting it into 3-inch squares. Serve hot.

GRILLED CORN
WITH CHIPOTLE BUTTER AND PARMESAN CHEESE

SERVES 4

Even the freshest corn can dry out when it is grilled, so I parboil my corn and then grill it—for the flavor—for just a few minutes. The chipotle chile powder adds a smoky touch here. This is where those cute little plastic corn holders come in handy! This recipe is easily doubled.

4 ears fresh sweet corn, shucked

4 tablespoons (½ stick) unsalted butter,
    at room temperature

1 teaspoon chipotle chile powder

Vegetable oil, for the grill

¼ cup olive oil

½ cup freshly grated Parmesan cheese

1. Preheat a barbecue grill to high heat.

2. While the grill is heating, bring a large pot of salted water to a boil. Add the ears of corn and cook for 2 minutes. Remove the corn and dry with a towel. Set aside.

3. Stir the butter and the chile powder together in a small bowl, and set it aside.

4. Oil the grill grate well, and spread the olive oil over the ears of corn. Arrange the corn on the grate and grill, turning the ears, until they have nice grill marks, about 3 minutes.

5. Transfer the ears of corn to a plate, and brush the chipotle butter over them. Sprinkle on the Parmesan cheese, and serve immediately. ✿

BLUEBERRY CORN MUFFINS

MAKES 12 MUFFINS

Cornmeal muffins are a favorite way to begin the day, and blueberries add a luscious juiciness to their coarse texture. In this version, creamed corn adds more wonderful moistness. Don't expect a high-domed muffin—cornmeal doesn't rise that much. These muffins are yummy, and when served warm, a pat of sweet butter brings them close to perfection.

¾ cup fresh blueberries

1 tablespoon plus ½ cup all-purpose flour

1½ cups yellow cornmeal

¼ cup sugar

1 tablespoon baking powder

½ teaspoon salt

2 large eggs, at room temperature

1 cup buttermilk

4 tablespoons (½ stick) unsalted butter, melted

¾ cup creamed corn, homemade (see page 309), frozen, or canned

1. Position a rack in the center of the oven, and preheat the oven to 350°F. Grease 12 regular muffin cups or line them with paper liners.

2. Toss the blueberries with the 1 tablespoon flour in a small bowl, and set aside.

3. Combine the cornmeal, remaining ½ cup flour, sugar, baking powder, and salt in a large bowl.

4. In another bowl, lightly whisk the eggs. Add the buttermilk and the melted butter to the eggs, whisking just to combine. Pour this mixture into the cornmeal mixture and stir with a spoon, just to combine. Stir in the creamed corn and the blueberries until just combined.

5. Spoon the batter into the prepared muffin cups, filling them three-quarters full. Bake until the muffins are a light golden brown and a toothpick inserted into the center of one comes out just clean, about 25 minutes.

6. Let the muffins cool in the pan on a wire rack for 15 minutes. Then unmold them and let them cool completely on the rack.

JALAPENO CORN BREAD

MAKES NINE 3-INCH SQUARES

I like my corn bread light and airy, so to achieve this effect, I don't overmix the batter. The addition of jalapeños gives the bread just the right bite. It's great served with a pot of butter and some good homemade chili or a nicely roasted chicken.

1 cup fresh corn kernels
    (from about 2 ears of corn)
1 cup yellow cornmeal
1 cup all-purpose flour
¼ cup sugar
1 tablespoon baking powder
1 teaspoon salt
1 large egg, at room temperature
1 cup whole milk
¼ cup canola oil
2 tablespoons finely minced seeded green
    jalapeño pepper

1. Preheat the oven to 400°F. Butter a 9-x-9-inch baking pan.

2. Bring a saucepan of salted water to a boil, add the corn kernels, and cook until they are just tender 2 minutes. Drain, run under cold water, and drain again. Pat dry, and set aside.

3. Combine the cornmeal, flour, sugar, baking powder, and salt in a bowl.

4. Lightly beat the egg in a mixing bowl. Whisk in the milk and the oil.

5. Stir the dry ingredients into the egg mixture until just combined—do not overmix. Stir in the reserved corn and the jalapeño pepper. Spoon the batter into the prepared baking pan.

6. Bake until the corn bread is light golden brown (it won't brown all over, or a lot) and a toothpick inserted in the center comes out just clean, 20 minutes.

7. Let the corn bread cool in the pan on a wire rack for 15 minutes. Then run a knife around the edges and unmold it onto a cutting board. Cut the corn bread into nine 3-inch squares. Serve hot, warm, or at room temperature.

"MODERN GRAIN DISHES TEMPT IN A WAY LIKE NEVER BEFORE."

GREAT GRAINS

It's an old idea that has shot to the top of the "gotta eat it" list: grains. These nutrient- and fiber-rich staples in so many ancient cuisines have now become bright stars in ours. Toss them with fresh vegetables, beans, fresh and dried fruits, herbs, and cheeses, then pull the combinations together with flavorful dressings. It's move over everything: We've got new centerpieces on our tables.

Grains are an easy escape from your day-to-day cooking rut, and they are readily available in supermarkets. The recipes included here use both whole grains and other old-time favorites. The variety is staggering; there's bulgur wheat (also called cracked wheat), and best known as the grain in the Middle East tabouleh; quinoa, a protein-rich flavorful grain from South America that I've tossed with herbs found in that continent's favorite sauce accompaniment to barbecued meats—chimichurri; and wheat berries, a chewy-textured grain that mixes well with pineapple, radicchio, and cucumber. Farro, popular in Italy, is now gaining recognition on the American table. I serve it tossed with scallions, tomato, and basil and crumbled fresh goat cheese. For tasty side dishes to include in traditional meals, try the Fluffy Grits Soufflé, a grand rendition of a Southern classic, or the Dress-Up Rice, made lively with herbs and lemon zest. 🔆

ITALIAN FARRO SALAD

SERVES 6

*f*arro, an Italian grain with a nutlike flavor, has become a delectable side dish in upscale Italian restaurants. Pleasantly chewy and packed with vitamins and minerals, farro was the standard grain of the Roman Legions, and from Rome spread throughout the Western world. It is a marvelous addition to our family of grains, and while I love to serve it warm with poultry and pork, it is perfect as a salad with tomatoes and goat cheese.

1 cup whole-grain farro (see Note)

Salt, to taste

¼ cup extra-virgin olive oil

1 tablespoon sherry vinegar

1 large ripe tomato, cut into ¼-inch dice

2 scallions (white bulbs and 3 inches green),
    thinly sliced on the diagonal

8 fresh basil leaves, slivered

Freshly ground black pepper, to taste

8 ounces fresh goat cheese

1. Combine the farro, 3 cups water, and the salt in a medium-size heavy pot. Bring to a boil, stir, reduce the heat to medium-low, and simmer (do not boil) until the farro is just tender but not mushy, about 15 minutes.

2. Drain the farro and run it under cold running water. Drain again. Transfer it to a baking sheet and spread it out to dry; leave it at room temperature, uncovered, for 20 to 25 minutes.

3. Whisk the oil and vinegar together in a large bowl. Add the farro and toss well to coat. Add the tomato, scallions, and basil. Season with salt and pepper, and toss well.

4. To serve, transfer the salad to a decorative bowl. Crumble the goat cheese around the edge of the salad, and serve.

NOTE: Farro looks a lot like barley and is sold in specialty food shops and many larger supermarkets. Look for farro that has been semi-pearled; it will be quicker cooking. If you buy farro that has not been pearled, you'll have to soak it in cold water overnight before proceeding with this recipe.

WHEAT BERRY SALAD
WITH PINEAPPLE AND CRANBERRIES

SERVES 10

Wheat berries have a wonderfully chewy texture, but they require a good overnight soak and an hour of cooking before they're ready to eat. This salad is worth the planning. I first tasted a wheat berry salad at Anna Pump's Loaves and Fishes—a favorite prepared-foods shop in Sagaponak, Long Island—and it inspired this one: ripe pineapple, cucumbers, and dried cranberries combined with this special grain. Pure magic.

1 cup wheat berries

½ teaspoon salt

½ hothouse (seedless) cucumber

1 cup diced ripe pineapple (¼-inch dice)

¾ cup dried cranberries

1 cup shredded tender radicchio leaves

3 tablespoons chopped fresh flat-leaf parsley

2 tablespoons olive oil

3 tablespoons fresh lemon juice

Salt and freshly ground black pepper, to taste

1. Place the wheat berries in a colander and rinse them under cold running water. Drain the wheat berries and transfer them to a bowl. Add cold water to cover by 2 inches, and set it aside to soak overnight.

2. Drain the wheat berries in a colander and rinse them well under cold running water. Transfer them to a large pot and add water to cover by 3 inches. Bring to a boil. Then reduce the heat and simmer, partially covered, until the wheat berries begin to soften, about 15 minutes.

3. Add the salt and cook, uncovered, until the wheat berries are tender, about 45 minutes; test them occasionally while they are cooking. Drain in a colander, and rinse thoroughly under cold running water. Drain the wheat berries well and spread them out on a baking sheet; let them dry for about 45 minutes.

4. Quarter the cucumber lengthwise (do not peel it) and thinly slice the quarters. You should have 1 cup cucumber pieces.

5. Place the wheat berries in a bowl and add the cucumbers, pineapple, and cranberries. Toss well with a fork. Toss in the radicchio and parsley. Add the oil, lemon juice, and salt and pepper, and fluff well with the fork. Let rest at room temperature for 20 minutes before serving. ✿

BUTTERNUT BARLEY RISOTTO

SERVES 6

Not so long ago, the market was limited to a few varieties of winter squash. Today it overflows with a wealth of them. Currently it's butternut squash that reigns in my kitchen. It is served in many fine restaurants, prepared in the most creative ways, from delicate purees to a filling for tiny ravioli. The dense orange flesh is not only delicious but also rich in complex carbohydrates, beta-carotene, dietary fiber, and potassium.

Here I've partnered the squash with barley, a mild grain that is most often identified as a basis for hearty soups like mushroom barley or beef and barley. Nowadays, it's finding a new place at the dinner table—in pilafs mixed with dried fruits, as well as in room-temperature salads mixed with bell peppers, chopped tomatoes, and cheese. Served hot, barley combined with butternut squash makes a comforting risotto-style dish. I love my risotto moist. If you do too, you may want to add a bit of extra broth.

1 butternut squash (about 1½ pounds),
    peeled, seeded, and cut into
    1½-inch pieces

3 tablespoons olive oil

1 onion, cut into ¼-inch dice

5 cups chicken or vegetable broth, preferably
    homemade (see pages 434 and 436),
    or more if needed

1 cinnamon stick (3 inches long)

1 cup diced seeded ripe plum tomatoes
    (¼-inch dice)

1 cup pearl barley, rinsed

4 tablespoons chopped fresh flat-leaf parsley

Salt and freshly ground black pepper,
    to taste

1. Bring a large pot of lightly salted water to a boil. Add the squash and cook until just tender, about 3 minutes. Drain, and set aside.

2. Heat the oil in a heavy pot over low heat. Add the onions and cook, stirring, until they are very tender, 10 to 15 minutes.

3. While the onions are cooking, pour the broth into a saucepan, add the cinnamon stick, and bring to a boil. Reduce the heat and simmer, partially covered, for 5 minutes. Discard the cinnamon stick and keep the broth hot.

4. Add the tomatoes to the onions and cook, stirring, for 2 minutes.

5. Stir the barley into the onion/tomato mixture, coating it well with the oil.

6. Raise the heat to medium and stir ½ cup of the hot broth into the barley mixture. Cook, stirring frequently, until it has been absorbed into the barley.

Continue this process, ½ cup at a time, making sure each addition of broth is absorbed before adding the next, until the barley is tender and most of the broth has been used, about 45 minutes.

7. Carefully fold in the reserved butternut squash, along with 2 tablespoons of the parsley. Cook to reheat the squash, about 1 minute. Season with salt and pepper.

8. Serve immediately in shallow bowls, garnished with the remaining 2 tablespoons parsley. 🌿

BRIGHT GREEN TABOULEH

MAKES 6 CUPS; SERVES 8 TO 10

I love the toothy texture of bulgur when it is sparked with lemon juice and tossed with the best of summer's farm stand tomatoes and crispy cucumbers, and for a mild onion flavor, scallions. I always go overboard with mint and parsley—I hope you will too. A tabouleh salad makes a good companion to Crown Roast of Lamb (page 56) and Lemon Herb–Roasted Chicken Drumsticks (page 149).

1 cup plus 2 tablespoons bulgur wheat

1 cup boiling water

2 tablespoons finely grated lemon zest
     (from 2 large lemons)

½ cup fresh lemon juice (from 3 large lemons)

⅓ cup extra-virgin olive oil

1 cup coarsely chopped fresh flat-leaf parsley leaves

1 cup coarsely chopped fresh mint leaves

4 scallions (white bulbs and 3 inches green),
     thinly sliced

1 tablespoon finely minced garlic

Salt and freshly ground black pepper, to taste

4 ripe plum tomatoes, seeded and cut into ¼-inch dice

1 cucumber, peeled, seeded, and cut into ¼-inch dice

1 fresh mint sprig, for garnish

1. Combine the bulgur wheat, boiling water, lemon zest and juice, and olive oil in a bowl. Mix well, cover, and refrigerate for 30 minutes.

2. Fluff the bulgur mixture with a fork. Add the parsley, mint, scallions, garlic, and salt and pepper. Toss well with the fork. Add the tomatoes and cucumbers, and toss again. Adjust the seasonings if necessary.

3. Let the salad stand, loosely covered, at room temperature for at least 30 minutes for the flavors to blend.

4. Garnish the salad with the mint sprig, and serve at room temperature. 🌿

CURRIED COUSCOUS SALAD

SERVES 4 TO 6

there is no easier grain salad to put together, and none that fits in a meal as well, as a vegetable couscous—enlivened with just the right spices, it's as comfortable with fried chicken as it is with grilled tuna. I add a few sweet currants as a foil to the hot pepper flakes. The colorful diced vegetables and the hit of spice give the somewhat shy couscous star power.

1 cup couscous

2 tablespoons extra-virgin olive oil

½ cup diced onion (¼-inch dice)

½ cup diced zucchini (¼-inch dice)

½ cup diced yellow squash (¼-inch dice)

⅓ cup diced red bell pepper (¼-inch dice)

2 teaspoons minced garlic

1 cup canned chickpeas (garbanzo beans),
      rinsed and drained

3 tablespoons dried currants

2 teaspoons curry powder

¼ teaspoon crushed red pepper flakes

Salt, to taste

2 tablespoons chopped fresh flat-leaf
      parsley leaves

1. Bring 1½ cups water to a boil in a medium-size saucepan. Remove the pan from the heat, stir in the couscous, cover, and let sit for 5 minutes. Then uncover the pan, fluff the grains with a fork, and set the pan aside, covered.

2. Heat the oil in a large skillet over medium-low heat. Add the onion, zucchini, squash, and bell pepper and cook, stirring, until softened, about 10 minutes. Add the garlic and cook for 2 minutes longer.

3. Reduce the heat to low and stir in the chickpeas, currants, curry powder, and red pepper flakes. Cook, stirring, for 2 to 3 minutes. Season with salt. Stir in the reserved couscous, 1 cup at a time, using a fork to fluff all the ingredients together. Toss in the parsley, and serve. ❧

QUINOA
WITH CHIMICHURRI HERBS

SERVES 4

Quinoa's delicate grains have an earthy, nutty flavor and a texture that's both chewy and crunchy. This important South American grain dates back to the early Inca civilization and today is considered all-important because it stands as a complete-protein grain. I decided it would be perfect embellished with familiar South American herbs and flavors such as oregano, parsley, jalapeño, and a touch of orange zest. Its pedigree makes quinoa (pronounced *keen*-wah) a natural to serve with hanger steaks or strip steaks.

1 cup quinoa

3 tablespoons extra-virgin olive oil

2 tablespoons white wine vinegar

3 tablespoons chopped fresh flat-leaf parsley
  leaves

3 tablespoons chopped fresh oregano leaves

2 teaspoons finely minced green jalapeño pepper

1 teaspoon finely minced garlic

Finely grated zest of 1 orange

Salt and freshly ground black pepper,
  to taste

2 scallions (white bulbs and 3 inches green),
  thinly sliced, for garnish

1. Combine the quinoa and 2 cups water in a medium-size saucepan and bring to a boil. Reduce the heat to a simmer, cover the pan, and cook until the liquid has been absorbed, 10 to 15 minutes. The grains should be soft and translucent, with the germ ring visible along the outside edge of each grain. Transfer the quinoa to a bowl.

2. Whisk the oil and vinegar together, and toss with the quinoa while it is still warm. Add the parsley, oregano, jalapeño, garlic, orange zest, and salt and pepper. Toss, using a fork to keep the grains fluffy. Sprinkle the scallions over the top, and serve at room temperature.

A NEW LOOK

For some people, grains still have an outdated "It's health food and boring" stigma attached to them. They shouldn't. Modern grain dishes tempt in a way like never before. Fresh herbs or vegetables and dried fruits complement a grain's chewy texture and incomparable flavor. Boring? I should say not. Served warm or at room temperature, these grains add excitement to a meal.

DRESS-UP RICE

SERVES 6

◯

Ilove rice but too often it's served as a plain little pile of grains alongside fish or chicken. Plain rice is perfect with Chinese food, but at other times I want my rice to have some personality. Cooking it in a flavored broth and fluffing it with fresh herbs and lemon zest gives a simple rice dish just the zip it needs. Serve this as an accompaniment to beef, poultry, or Dover sole.

3½ cups chicken or vegetable broth,
    preferably homemade (pages 434 and 436)
1 tablespoon unsalted butter
½ teaspoon salt
1½ cups long-grain white rice
½ cup chopped fresh dill leaves
¼ cup chopped fresh tarragon leaves
1 teaspoon finely grated lemon zest

1. Pour the broth into a heavy pot, add the butter and salt, and bring to a boil. Stir in the rice, reduce the heat to medium, cover the pot, and simmer until cooked through, about 20 minutes.

2. Fluff the rice with a fork, and stir in the dill, tarragon, and lemon zest. Adjust the seasonings as needed, and serve. ❧

AN ANYTIME PICNIC

When the day breaks sunny and warm, instead of the predicted rainy and cold, pack up the car and head out to the park or beach for a picnic lunch. Bring along a Provençal rosé and some mint iced tea.

A thermos of soup, easy-to-eat chicken drumsticks, some tasty rice served salad-style, and some fruit and sorbet add up to pure pleasure.

ROASTED CARROT GINGER SOUP
PAGE 43

DRESS-UP RICE
THIS PAGE

LEMON HERB–ROASTED CHICKEN DRUMSTICKS
PAGE 149

WATERMELON SLICES

RASPBERRY CASSIS SORBET
PAGE 427

MANGO SORBET
PAGE 430

KITCHEN RICE AND HAM

SERVES 6

*a*fter baking a special-occasion ham, you're sure to have leftovers. Use them to cook up a large pot of ham, rice, tomatoes, and peas, a dish that reminds me of Spanish rice, an old favorite. But this version is worth buying baked ham for. If you're an olive lover, add a few pitted green olives in the mix. Serve this with a wedge of a semi-firm Spanish cheese, such as Mahón, and some crusty bread. If it's a family dinner, sparkling white grape juice or apple juice is the ideal drink.

2 tablespoons extra-virgin olive oil

1 red onion, cut into ¼-inch dice

1 red bell pepper, stemmed, seeded, and
cut into ¼-inch dice

1½ cups diced celery (¼-inch dice)

1 tablespoon finely minced garlic

¼ teaspoon crushed saffron threads dissolved in
1 tablespoon water

1½ pounds baked ham, cut into ½-inch cubes
(1½ cups cubes)

1 can (28 ounces) plum tomatoes, chopped,
juices reserved

1 cup chicken broth, preferably homemade
(see page 434)

1½ cups long-grain white rice

½ cup frozen peas, thawed, at room temperature

⅓ cup chopped fresh flat-leaf parsley leaves

Salt and freshly ground black pepper, to taste

1. Heat the olive oil in a heavy pot over medium-low heat. Add the onion, bell pepper, and celery and cook, stirring occasionally, until softened, about 12 minutes. Add the garlic, dissolved saffron, and ham, and cook, stirring, for 5 minutes longer.

2. Add the tomatoes and chicken broth, and bring to a boil. Stir in the rice. Then reduce the heat to a simmer, cover, and cook until the rice is tender and the liquid has been absorbed, about 20 minutes.

3. Uncover the pot and fluff the rice with a fork. Stir in the peas and parsley, and season to taste with salt and pepper. Serve immediately.

PINEAPPLE GINGER RICE

SERVES 6 TO 8

When looking for a complementary rice for pork, salmon, or poultry, Pineapple Ginger Rice hits the spot with its moist, fruity sweetness. Fresh ripe pineapple has just the right sweetness and texture, but if you can't find a ripe one, canned pineapple does a fine job. Just be sure to drain it before stirring it into the rice.

2 tablespoons peanut oil

1 cup chopped onion

1 tablespoon minced garlic

1 tablespoon minced fresh ginger

1½ cups long-grain white rice

3½ cups chicken broth, preferably homemade
    (see page 434)

Salt and freshly ground black pepper, to taste

2 cups chopped fresh pineapple (about ½ pineapple),
    at room temperature

¼ cup chopped fresh cilantro leaves

1. Heat the oil in a heavy pot over low heat. Add the onions and cook, stirring, until almost softened, 7 minutes. Add the garlic and ginger, and cook for another 3 minutes.

2. Add the rice and stir to coat it well. Add the broth, season with salt and pepper, and bring to a boil over high heat. Reduce the heat to medium-low, cover the pot, and simmer until all of the liquid has been absorbed, 20 minutes.

3. Remove the pot from the heat and fluff the rice with a fork. Stir in the pineapple and cilantro, and serve immediately. 🌿

PICKING A PINEAPPLE

Quite a few of my recipes call for fresh pineapple. It's a fruit I love and like to use it in as many ways as possible. If you're a fan, but are intimidated by choosing a ripe pineapple, here are a few tips. By the way, don't bother pulling a leaf out of the top. Even if it comes out easily, it doesn't determine ripeness.

+ Since pineapples don't continue ripening after being picked, look for ones that are golden in color.

+ The pineapple should be firm, not soft.

+ Smell the fruit. It should have a pleasant pineapple smell.

+ Eat the fruit soon after you buy it. If you must hold it for a day or two, refrigerate it so it doesn't deteriorate.

FLUFFY GRITS SOUFFLE

SERVES 4 TO 5

○

I adore these grits: hot and fluffy, right out of the oven, crispy and golden on the top. They were inspired by a recipe of John Mariani's in his *Dictionary of American Food and Drink*. They don't take the dreaded hours of stirring, either. My one plea: Stay away from instant grits—do yourself a favor and buy a bag of whole stone-ground grits. For an extra-decadent brunch, serve them alongside soft scrambled eggs dolloped with crème fraîche.

1 cup whole milk

½ cup whole stone-ground grits

4 large eggs, separated

¼ cup freshly grated Parmesan cheese

2 dashes Tabasco sauce

Salt and freshly ground black pepper, to taste

1. Preheat the oven to 425°F. Lightly butter a 4-cup soufflé dish.

2. While the oven is heating, combine 1½ cups water and the milk in a heavy saucepan and warm the mixture over medium-low heat. Slowly stir or whisk in the grits (use a sturdy whisk), and continue stirring until smooth and thickened, about 15 minutes. Remove from the heat.

3. Lightly beat the egg yolks in a bowl. Gradually stir some of the hot grits into the egg yolks to temper them. Then stir the tempered egg yolks into the grits. Set aside to cool slightly.

4. Stir the Parmesan cheese, Tabasco sauce, and salt and pepper into the grits.

5. Place the egg whites in a bowl, add a pinch of salt, and beat until the whites are stiff but not dry. Using a rubber spatula, fold the whites into the grits until they are just combined. Do not overmix. Scrape the mixture into the prepared soufflé dish, and bake in the center of the oven until the soufflé rises and is lightly browned on top, 30 minutes. Serve immediately. 🌿

"...COMBINING COZINESS AND LUXURY WITH LUSCIOUS RESULTS."

MASHED POTATOES AND OTHER MASHES

When you think of comfort food, what do you think of first? I'm guessing mashed potatoes. Creamy with plenty of butter and milk—and with just enough little potato lumps to reassure that they're "real," not instant. Mashed potatoes is a side dish with main-dish clout. But that's just a start. What could be more dynamite than Lobster Mashed Potatoes with big chunks of lobster when you're really putting on the Ritz? Serve them with a steak for a modern—and unusual—take on "surf and turf." Match up Caramelized-Apple Mashed Potatoes with a crispy-skinned roast chicken. And don't overlook my favorite Brandade de Morue to slather on bread or to enjoy before a red meat entrée. Candied sweets mash up beautifully and are divine alongside Sunday Brisket or Filipino Pork Adobo. They accompany mild or savory dishes, so don't forget them!

But potatoes aren't the only food that tastes great mashed. There are other spectacular mashes, including a Lemon-Dill Parsnip Mash and a spicy butternut squash dish, great with pork or venison, that give potatoes a run for the money. ❧

SILKY MASHED POTATOES

SERVES 6

ashed potatoes take the blue ribbon as the premier comfort food. Today they're as at home served on fine china as they are on fun diner dishes. When it comes to mashed potatoes, there should be no stinting when it comes to butter and cream. I used half-and-half with these because they turn the potatoes all silky and smooth. I've infused the half-and-half with garlic for extra flavor, and stirred in fresh chives. These are divine with roast chicken, hanger steak (pages 136 and 73), and Lenny Schwartz's Market Street Meat Loaf (page 90).

2¾ to 3 pounds Yukon Gold potatoes, peeled
    and cut into 1-inch chunks (see Note)
Salt
1 cup half-and-half
4 large cloves garlic, bruised (see box, page 82)
8 tablespoons (1 stick) unsalted butter,
    at room temperature
Coarse (kosher) salt and freshly ground
    black pepper, to taste
1 tablespoon snipped fresh chives

1. Place the potatoes in a large heavy pot and add cold water to cover. Salt the water and bring to a boil over high heat. Reduce the heat to medium-low and simmer, partially covered, until the potatoes are very tender, about 20 minutes.

2. Meanwhile, combine the half-and-half and the garlic cloves in a small saucepan, and heat almost to the boiling point (but do not let it boil). Reduce

the heat to medium-low and simmer until the half-and-half is infused with the garlic flavor, 3 to 5 minutes. Discard the garlic and set the half-and-half aside.

3. Drain the potatoes well and return them to the pot. Place the pot over very low heat and shake it for about 1 minute to dry the potatoes.

4. Transfer the potatoes to a large bowl, and add the butter. Using a ricer, a potato masher, or a large fork, mash the potatoes with the butter. Stir in the hot half-and-half, and season generously with coarse salt and black pepper. Stir in the chives and serve immediately.

NOTE: When shopping for potatoes for mashing, choose Yukon Gold for a creamy-style or russets for a floury fluffy potato. Either will give you a good mashed potato consistency. 🌿

LOBSTER MASHED POTATOES

SERVES 6 TO 8

This dish will have your friends swooning—really! Big chunks of lobster peek through mounds of creamy potatoes, combining coziness and luxury with luscious results. Plenty of milk and butter lend the silky consistency that makes this the sexy recipe you'd expect, and lemon zest and chives highlight the lobster's flavor. Serve it with grilled or broiled steak.

2 live lobsters (each 1½ pounds), or 3 pounds
    lobster tails

2½ pounds russet potatoes, peeled and quartered

Salt to taste

1 cup whole milk, or more if needed, warmed

6 tablespoons (¾ stick) unsalted butter, or
    more if needed, at room temperature

Coarse (kosher) salt and freshly ground
    black pepper, to taste

Finely grated zest of 1 large lemon

2 tablespoons snipped fresh chives

1. Bring a large pot of salted water to a rolling boil. Holding the lobsters by the tail, plunge them head first into the boiling water (this will kill them instantly) and cover the pot. Once the water returns to a boil, cook the lobsters until they are bright red and cooked through, 8 to 10 minutes. Remove them from the pot and set them aside for 4 to 5 minutes. Then crack the lobsters and remove the meat from the tails and claws. Cut the meat into ½-inch pieces. Cover and set aside.

2. Place the potatoes in a large heavy saucepan and cover with cold water. Salt the water and bring to a boil over high heat. Then reduce the heat and simmer until tender, 20 to 25 minutes. Drain the potatoes and return them to the pot. Shake the pan over low heat for 10 seconds to dry them out.

3. Transfer the potatoes to a large bowl, and add the milk and butter. Using a ricer, potato masher, or fork, mash the potatoes, adding extra milk and/or butter if desired.

4. Season the potatoes generously with coarse salt and black pepper, and add the lemon zest. Gently fold in the lobster meat and the chives. Fluff with a fork, and serve immediately.

NOTE: To rewarm the potatoes, reheat them in a double boiler over simmering water. A microwave would toughen the lobster. ❧

WASABI MASHED POTATOES

SERVES 4 TO 6

ny form of mashed potatoes is irresistible, whether smothered in brisket and gravy, served alongside a perfectly roasted chicken, or mounded high with meat loaf. But when something a bit more sophisticated is called for, this wasabi-flavored mash is the way to go, especially when it's served with succulent Glazed Salmon Teriyaki (page 187).

2 pounds russet potatoes, peeled and quartered

Salt

6 tablespoons (¾ stick) unsalted butter

¾ cup half-and-half

2 teaspoons wasabi paste (see Note)

Coarse salt and freshly ground black pepper, to taste

1. Place the potatoes in a large heavy pot and add cold water to cover. Salt the water and bring to a boil over high heat. Reduce the heat to medium-low and simmer until the potatoes are very tender, 30 minutes.

2. Meanwhile, place the butter, half-and-half, and wasabi paste in a small saucepan, and stir, over low heat until the butter is melted. Keep warm.

3. When the potatoes are tender, drain them and then return them to the pot. Shake the pot over low heat to completely dry them, 10 seconds.

4. Transfer the potatoes to a large bowl. Using a ricer, a potato masher, or a fork, mash the potatoes. Add the half-and-half mixture and stir with a fork until fluffy. Season generously with coarse salt and black pepper. Serve immediately.

NOTE: I use S&B Japanese Horseradish—prepared wasabi in a tube—available at Asian groceries. I prefer this to powdered wasabi because it has a smoother flavor. I find powdered wasabi too harsh. ❧

CARAMELIZED-APPLE MASHED POTATOES

SERVES 6

the first time I enjoyed apple mashed potatoes was at a trendy New York restaurant called Barca 18. They were delicate, replete with sautéed apples. I just knew I had to develop my own version of the dish. I went all out and caramelized the apples before folding them into the potatoes. It's easy to do, and the sugar adds its mellow sweetness when it's combined with the rest of the ingredients. These are sublime when served with Roasted Brined Chicken (page 137). Be sure to pepper the potatoes well.

3 pounds Yukon Gold potatoes, peeled and
    cut into 1-inch chunks

Salt

3 tablespoons unsalted butter

2 Granny Smith or Golden Delicious apples,
    unpeeled, cut into ½-inch pieces

1 tablespoon sugar

1½ cups half-and-half

8 tablespoons (1 stick) unsalted butter,
    at room temperature

Coarse (kosher) salt and freshly ground black
    pepper, to taste

1. Place the potatoes in a large pot and add cold water to cover. Salt the water and bring to a boil over high heat. Reduce the heat to medium-low and simmer, partially covered, until the potatoes are very tender, about 20 minutes.

2. While the potatoes are cooking, prepare the apples: Melt the 3 tablespoons of butter in a large nonstick skillet over low heat. Add the apples and cook, stirring, until they have softened, about 10 minutes. Sprinkle the sugar over the apples and continue to cook, shaking the pan, until they are caramelized but not burned, 2 to 3 minutes. Set the apples aside.

3. Heat the half-and-half in a small saucepan over medium-low heat until bubbles just begin to form around the edges (do not let it boil). Set the pan aside.

4. Drain the potatoes well and return them to the pot. Place the pot over very low heat and shake it for about 1 minute to dry the potatoes well.

5. Transfer the potatoes to a bowl, and add the 8 tablespoons of butter. Using a ricer, a potato masher, or a large fork, mash the potatoes with the butter. Stir in the half-and-half, and season generously with coarse salt and black pepper. Fold in the reserved apples. Serve immediately. 🌿

BRANDADE DE MORUE

SERVES 6

ғrom the first taste of this heady mash of salt cod, garlic, crème fraîche, and potatoes, I was hooked on brandade. Served either as an appetizer on toasted peasant bread or at the table in small ramekins as an *amuse-bouche* with a glass of wine, it's a splendid start to the evening. Brandade is very rich, so be warned that a little goes a long way. This recipe, still my favorite, comes from my own *All Around the World Cookbook*. Note that you need to soak the salt cod overnight first.

1 pound salt cod (see Sources, page 439)

1 cup dry white wine

6 whole black peppercorns

1 bay leaf

1 pound Yukon Gold or other waxy potatoes,
    peeled and halved

Salt

½ cup extra-virgin olive oil

½ cup diced onion (¼-inch dice)

6 slices peasant bread, cut ½ inch thick,
    for serving

1 tablespoon finely minced garlic

1 cup crème fraîche

1 tablespoon chopped fresh thyme leaves

Freshly ground black pepper, to taste

1. One day ahead, prepare the salt cod: Cut the fish into large pieces and place them in a large bowl. Add cold water to cover, cover the bowl with plastic wrap, and soak overnight in the refrigerator, changing the water two or three times.

2. The next day, drain the salt cod, rinse it under cold water, and drain again.

3. Combine the wine, peppercorns, bay leaf, and 1 cup water in a large saucepan and bring to a boil. Reduce the heat, add the salt cod, and simmer until the fish is cooked through, about 10 minutes. Carefully remove the fish from the cooking liquid, and allow it to cool to room temperature.

4. When the fish has cooled, remove any bones and flake it into medium-size pieces. Set aside.

5. Place the potatoes in a medium-size saucepan and add cold water to cover. Salt the water and bring to a boil. Reduce the heat to medium-low and simmer, partially covered, until the potatoes are very tender, 20 to 25 minutes. Drain. While the potatoes are still warm, press them through a ricer or mash them in a bowl.

6. Heat the olive oil in a large nonstick skillet over medium-low heat. Add the onion and cook, stirring occasionally, until wilted, 15 minutes.

7. While the onion is cooking, toast the peasant bread and cut the slices in half.

8. Remove the skillet from the heat and add the garlic, crème fraîche, thyme, and pepper to the onion. Fold this mixture into the mashed potatoes. They should be moist and fluffy. Using a fork, gently stir in the flaked cod. Taste, and adjust the seasonings as needed.

9. Serve in a bowl, with toasted peasant bread alongside. ❧

MASHED CANDIED SWEETS

SERVES 8 TO 10

You may think that mini-marshmallows are silly, but my mother always loved to put them on sweet potatoes at Thanksgiving, and on they'll stay—that's *that*! They're fun and we're not too serious. Adding dark brown sugar and pure maple syrup to your candied sweets makes all the difference in the flavor—no "pancake syrup" here, please.

> 5 sweet potatoes (each about 8 ounces), peeled and cut into 1-inch pieces
> ¾ cup fresh orange juice (from 1 or 2 oranges)
> ½ cup pure maple syrup
> 3 tablespoons unsalted butter
> 1½ teaspoons ground ginger
> Salt, to taste
> 1 bag miniature marshmallows (optional)

1. Bring a large pot of salted water to a boil. Add the sweet potatoes and cook until they are very tender, about 15 minutes. Drain them well and transfer them to a large bowl. Add all the remaining ingredients except the marshmallows, and mash. (The potatoes can be prepared to this point a day ahead; cover and refrigerate. They may need a little longer in the oven if you put them in cold.)

2. Preheat the oven to 350°F.

3. Spoon the potatoes into an oven-to-table baking dish, and generously dot the surface with the marshmallows if desired. Bake until the marshmallows are somewhat melted and golden on top and the potatoes are warmed through, 15 to 20 minutes. Serve immediately. ❧

CURRY BUTTERNUT MASH

SERVES 6

butternut squash is a staple in my kitchen these days. It's readily available and its attractive sweet flavor and pleasant texture make it a perfect companion to roast turkey and rack of venison. It also peels easily and mashes like a dream.

2 butternut squash (each about 2 pounds),
    peeled, seeded, and cut into 2-inch cubes
4 tablespoons (½ stick) unsalted butter
2 tablespoons curry powder
2 tablespoons light or dark brown sugar
Salt and freshly ground black pepper, to taste

1. Bring a large pot of salted water to a boil. Add the squash and boil until it is very tender, about 20 minutes.

2. Meanwhile, combine the butter and the curry powder in a small saucepan over medium-low heat, and cook for 1 minute to mellow the flavor.

3. Drain the squash well and transfer it to a bowl. Add the butter mixture and the brown sugar to the squash, and mash until smooth (it's fine if it isn't completely smooth). Season with coarse salt and black pepper, and serve immediately.

NOTE: This dish can be prepared ahead, covered, and refrigerated. Reheat it, covered, in a 350°F oven for 15 to 20 minutes.

TRAVEL ON MY MIND MENU

When it's cold outside and the only traveling you'll be doing is to your kitchen, invite over a group of friends, cook up this menu—a delicious mix from all over—and plan your next vacation. Enjoy an Australian shiraz with this meal.

SHRIMP TOASTS
PAGE 217

FILIPINO PORK ADOBO
PAGE 88

CURRY BUTTERNUT MASH
THIS PAGE

ASIAN VEGETABLE SALAD
PAGE 264

OUR AMBROSIA
PAGE 409

GINGERSNAP BUTTERNUT MASH

SERVES 6 TO 8

a butternut squash is like a chameleon and is as well suited for the filling of a delicate Italian ravioli with a little fried sage as it is as a mash with the spices that make gingerbread so biting and delicious. I've gone heaviest on the ginger and lightest on the cloves, and you can't miss the taste of nutmeg, cinnamon, and allspice. The spices may darken the bright orange color of the squash, but they sure add explosions of flavor. Serve this mash with Roasted Loin of Venison (page 58) or with Tom Colicchio's Roasted Rack of Pork (page 50)—it complements stronger-tasting meats.

3 butternut squash (each about 1½ pounds),
    peeled, seeded, and cut into chunks
6 tablespoons (¾ stick) unsalted butter, cut into pieces
½ teaspoon ground ginger
¼ teaspoon ground cinnamon
¼ teaspoon ground nutmeg
¼ teaspoon ground allspice
⅛ teaspoon ground cloves
Salt and freshly ground black pepper, to taste

1. Bring a large pot of salted water to a boil. Add the squash. When the water returns to a boil, cook the squash until it is tender, about 20 minutes.

2. Meanwhile, place the butter pieces in a large bowl and sprinkle the ginger, cinnamon, nutmeg, allspice, and cloves over them.

3. Drain the squash well, and add it to the bowl. Toss well to melt the butter and distribute the spices. Mash the squash well with a fork, trying to make it as smooth as possible. Season well with salt and pepper. Serve immediately. ⚜

LEMON-DILL PARSNIP MASH

SERVES 4 TO 6

Okay, who still thinks of parsnips as some fuddy-duddy vegetable that's straight out of a Charles Dickens novel—maybe something the Cratchits might have served up with their goose in *A Christmas Carol?* Time to wake up and try this spectacular mash. In this recipe I've taken a winter vegetable and segued right into spring by adding lemon zest and juice and lovely fresh dill.

2 pounds parsnips, peeled

4 cups chicken broth (canned is fine)

Finely grated zest and juice of 1½ lemons

4 tablespoons (½ stick) unsalted butter

½ cup heavy (whipping) cream

2 tablespoons chopped fresh dill leaves

Salt and freshly ground black pepper, to taste

1. Cut the parsnips in half lengthwise and then in half crosswise. Place them in a large pot and add the broth, 4 cups water, and 1 tablespoon of the lemon juice. Bring to a boil. Then reduce the heat to medium and simmer until the parsnips are very tender, about 20 minutes.

2. While the parsnips are cooking, melt the butter in the cream in a small saucepan over low heat.

3. Drain the parsnips well, place them in a food processor, and puree, adding the cream mixture through the feed tube while the machine is running.

4. Transfer the pureed parsnips to a serving bowl. Add the lemon zest, the remaining lemon juice, and the dill. Season with salt and pepper. Serve immediately.

NOTE: This dish can be prepared up to 6 hours ahead, covered, and refrigerated. Reheat it, covered, in a 350°F oven for 15 to 20 minutes.

"MASHED" SWEET SHELL PEAS

SERVES 4

Peas and mint are harbingers of spring and are two of the earliest arrivals at the farm stand. Peas, lightly steamed and served with a little butter and chopped mint, are a favorite of mine, and I thought the combination would also work well mashed. When I tried mashing the peas with butter and cream, their skins put up some resistance, so it was off to the food processor for a perfect-tasting pea puree or "mash." Mashed shell peas are delicious served with leg of lamb or rack of lamb (see pages 55 and 57). I love them served along with roasted beets as well. This preparation is a very new take on this old friend.

1 teaspoon salt

1 teaspoon sugar

4 cups shelled fresh peas (about 4½ pounds
    in the pod; see Note)

4 tablespoons (½ stick) unsalted butter,
    at room temperature

¼ cup chicken or vegetable broth, preferably
    homemade (see pages 434 and 436)

¼ cup heavy (whipping) cream

3 tablespoons finely chopped fresh mint leaves

Salt and freshly ground black pepper,
    to taste

1. Add the salt and sugar to a large pot of water and bring to a boil. Add the peas and cook until tender, 3 to 4 minutes.

2. Drain the peas and place them in a bowl. Add the butter, broth, cream, and 2 tablespoons of the mint. Toss well, and season with salt and pepper.

3. Transfer the mixture to a food processor, and puree.

4. Spoon the puree into the top of a double boiler, set it over barely simmering water, and warm it through. Then transfer the puree to a serving bowl, sprinkle with the remaining 1 tablespoon chopped mint, and serve immediately.

NOTE: If fresh peas are unavailable, frozen peas do very nicely. Cook them according to the package directions. Then drain them and proceed with Step 2.

"SO MANY SHAPES, SO MUCH FUN."

PASTA PLUS

When I'm in the mood for noodles, it's difficult to choose a recipe because I've come to love the noodles of so many cultures. And with so much variation, to limit a chapter to 10 seems almost laughable. Italian pastas alone yield so many "bests" that moving on from them was difficult. However, Pad Thai makes a delicious appearance with its intoxicating flavors. Shrimp and fresh vegetables dress the rice sticks, and crisp bean sprouts add a little crunch for perfect mouth appeal. And I've included an easy and delicious summer soba noodle dish as well. Plus I've borrowed from a wonderful Jean-Georges Vongerichten rice noodle dish to create my Sesame Noodles. However, I make it with spaghettini (that pasta influence again!).

When I cook pasta, I'm usually drawn to Italian-style sauces. In summer I can't get enough of fresh tomato sauce with garlic and fresh herbs over any cooked noodles. I've gone traditional, too, and made a Bolognese for spaghetti. It's pretty straightforward—a rare approach for me—but so worth the effort.

I've used sea shells for my Italian tuna, tomatoes, and herbs because the shells work well with the fish. And for Andrew Engle's Mac and Cheese I chose penne, which catches all the creamy cheese sauce beautifully.

By the way, this chapter contains 11 recipes; sometimes 10 isn't enough. ❖

ANDREW ENGLE'S
MAC AND CHEESE

SERVES 8

No comfort food rates higher than creamy macaroni and cheese. Andrew Engle, chef at The Laundry in East Hampton on New York's Long Island, bakes up a beauty using three cheeses: Gruyère, sharp Cheddar, and mozzarella. If you're feeling sophisticated, then choose penne; if you're feeling nostalgic, use elbow macaroni. For a crusty, bubbly finish, bake this at a high heat for 20 minutes rather than the usual hour at a lower heat.

1 tablespoon olive oil

1 pound penne or elbow macaroni

6 tablespoons (¾ stick) unsalted butter

6 tablespoons all-purpose flour

4 cups whole milk, warmed

1½ cups (6 ounces) grated Gruyère cheese

1½ cups (6 ounces) grated sharp Cheddar
    cheese

1½ cups (6 ounces) grated mozzarella cheese

2 dashes Tabasco sauce

Salt and freshly ground black pepper,
    to taste

Sweet paprika, to taste

1. Bring a large pot of salted water to a boil. Add the olive oil, then the penne, and stir. Cook until al dente (just tender), 12 minutes. Drain, and return the penne to the pot. Cover, and set aside.

2. Preheat the oven to 400°F. Butter a 13-x-9-x-2-inch baking dish and set it aside.

3. Prepare the sauce: Melt the butter in a heavy-bottomed saucepan over low heat. Sprinkle in the flour, whisking constantly. Cook, stirring, for 3 minutes (do not let the mixture brown). While whisking, slowly add the warm milk. Continue to whisk until the mixture is smooth and thickened, 3 minutes. Remove from the heat.

4. Stir the three cheeses together in a mixing bowl. Set aside ¾ cup of the cheese mixture. Whisk the remaining cheese mixture, in small handfuls, into the sauce, whisking until it has melted completely and the sauce is smooth. If necessary, return the sauce to the heat. Season with the Tabasco, salt and pepper, and paprika. Fold the cooked penne into the sauce, coating it well.

5. Transfer the mixture to the prepared baking dish, and sprinkle the reserved ¾ cup cheese evenly over the top. Bake until the top is golden and crusty, about 25 minutes. Serve immediately.

CREAMY GOAT CHEESE BUTTERFLIES

SERVES 6

Every recipe repertoire needs a luxurious sauce that can be prepared ahead and that tastes as though it's been worked on for hours. Smoothing fresh goat cheese with a bit of cream cheese yields a velvety base for this sauce. The diced salami adds oomph to the dish and the lemon zest brings out all the flavors. Be generous with the black pepper.

1 cup (8 ounces) fresh goat cheese,
    at room temperature

½ cup cream cheese, at room temperature

4 tablespoons extra-virgin olive oil

1 cup diced soppressata salami (¼-inch dice;
    see Note)

¼ cup diced red onion (¼-inch dice)

2 teaspoons finely minced garlic

Finely grated zest of 1 lemon

3 tablespoons chopped fresh flat-leaf parsley
    leaves

Freshly ground black pepper, to taste

Salt, if needed, to taste

12 ounces farfalle (butterfly, or bow-tie, pasta)

1. Combine the goat cheese and cream cheese in a large bowl, and mix well. (If necessary, set the bowl over a pot of boiling water for 1 minute to soften the cheeses). Add 3 tablespoons of the olive oil along with the soppressata, onion, garlic, lemon zest, parsley, pepper, and salt (the goat cheese may be salty, so taste before you add salt). Set the sauce aside. (You can prepare and refrigerate the sauce several hours before you plan to serve it.)

2. Bring a large pot of salted water to a boil. Add the remaining 1 tablespoon olive oil to the water. Add the pasta and cook until al dente (just tender), about 12 minutes. Drain the pasta, reserving 1 cup of the cooking water.

3. Toss the hot pasta with the cheese sauce. The sauce may be quite thick; if so, drizzle in a bit of the reserved cooking water to thin it slightly. Serve immediately.

NOTE: Soppressata is a dry-cured pork salami that is subtly seasoned and somewhat rustic in appearance. If you can't find it, substitute Genoa or Milano salami. ❧

MY FAVORITE BEACH PASTA

SERVES 4

this has always been a favorite pasta of mine. It's brilliant in the summer, when tomatoes and basil are in their prime, and nowadays, with all the heirloom tomatoes that are available, you can throw in a kaleidoscope of colors. A touch of mint and a garnish of scallions add some crispness and bite. Make the sauce ahead and toss it with the pasta just before serving it for a delicious and easy August dinner at the beach.

4 large ripe tomatoes, cut into ½-inch dice

½ cup fresh basil leaves, slivered

¼ cup fresh mint leaves, coarsely chopped

8 ounces mozzarella cheese, cubed
(see Note)

2 teaspoons finely minced garlic

Freshly ground black pepper, to taste

½ cup plus 1 tablespoon extra-virgin olive oil

12 ounces linguine or spaghettini

Salt, to taste

2 scallions (white bulbs and 3 inches green),
thinly sliced, for garnish

1. Several hours before you plan to serve the pasta, combine the tomatoes, basil, mint, mozzarella, garlic, pepper, and the ½ cup olive oil in a large serving bowl. Toss to mix. Let sit to blend the flavors.

2. When you are ready to serve it, bring a large pot of salted water to a boil. Add the remaining 1 tablespoon olive oil. Add the pasta and cook until it is al dente (just tender), about 11 minutes. Drain the pasta well.

3. Add the hot linguine to the tomato mixture, and toss well. Season with salt, garnish with the scallions, and serve immediately.

NOTE: A soft melting cheese is just right for this pasta and that is why I like mozzarella. If possible, buy one that is freshly made, and prepare the dish on the day you bought the cheese. Other cheeses—a basil torta or a ripe brie or Camembert with the rind removed—are excellent as well. To remove the rind, firm up the cheese by placing it in the freezer for 30 minutes. Then cut off the rind. 🍀

PENNE
WITH SUNRISE ORANGE PEPPERS, GORGONZOLA, AND RADICCHIO

SERVES 6

There is a sweetness that emerges from bell peppers when they are wilted in good extra-virgin olive oil. In the summer, when delicate orange bells are at their most plentiful, treat friends to this dish, which is just made for patio entertaining. The sweet flavor of the bell peppers marries perfectly with the sweet Gorgonzola, and radicchio adds just the right bite to finish off the dish. Serve a crisp, lightly dressed arugula salad alongside.

¼ cup extra-virgin olive oil

2 cloves garlic, thinly sliced

2 onions, cut into ¼-inch dice

6 orange bell peppers, stemmed, seeded, and cut lengthwise into ¼-inch-wide strips

¾ cup dry white wine

Salt and freshly ground black pepper, to taste

12 ounces penne

8 ounces sweet Gorgonzola (Gorgonzola dolce)

¾ cup slivered tender radicchio leaves

½ cup torn fresh basil leaves, for garnish

1. Heat the olive oil in a saucepan over low heat. Add the garlic and cook for 2 minutes to soften; do not let it brown. Add the onions, raise the heat to medium-low, and cook, stirring, until wilted, 7 to 10 minutes.

2. Add the bell peppers and the wine, and cook, stirring, until the peppers are very soft, about 15 minutes. Season with salt and pepper.

3. While the peppers are cooking, bring a large pot of salted water to a boil over high heat. Add the penne and cook until tender, about 13 minutes. Drain the pasta and place it in a shallow serving bowl. Crumble the Gorgonzola over the hot pasta, and toss together until the cheese melts.

4. Add the pepper mixture and the radicchio to the pasta, and toss together well. Sprinkle with the basil and serve immediately. 🌿

PASTA SHELLS
WITH ITALIAN TUNA, TOMATOES, AND LEMON

SERVES 6

Pasta—so many shapes, so much fun. While this dish has no specific origin, each ingredient reminds me of Italy. Of course the flavors of summer tomatoes bring life to any dish. Scallions and the robust tuna, brightened by lemon juice, add lots of character. Each element contributes to a very interesting bowl of noodles. Served this with a rich Provençal Bandol or a Sicilian rosé, such as Regaleali.

12 ounces medium-size shell pasta

1 tablespoon plus ¾ cup extra-virgin olive oil

4 ripe tomatoes, cut into ½-inch dice

2 cans (each 6 ounces) imported tuna packed
    in olive oil, drained and broken into chunks

6 scallions (white bulbs and 3 inches green),
    thinly sliced

¼ cup thinly sliced cornichons

¼ cup chopped fresh flat-leaf parsley leaves

1 tablespoon drained tiny capers

Finely grated zest and juice of 1 lemon

Salt and freshly ground black pepper, to taste

2 hard-cooked eggs, coarsely chopped, for garnish

1. Bring a large pot of salted water to a boil. Add the 1 tablespoon olive oil. Add the pasta and cook until al dente (just tender), about 10 minutes.

2. While the pasta is cooking, combine the tomatoes, tuna, scallions, cornichons, parsley, capers, lemon zest and juice, and olive oil in a large shallow pasta bowl. Season with salt and pepper, and toss well.

3. Drain the pasta well and toss it with the tomato mixture. Just before serving, sprinkle the chopped eggs over the top. 🌿

RUSTIC RIGATONI

SERVES 6 TO 8

his rustic-style pasta dish has a robust flavor. The cheese adds a wonderful element, but be careful: it's slightly salty, which is why I use only pepper for seasoning. A Montepulciano or Chianti Classico would be my wine choice. Don't forget some bread and Italian Fontina or Taleggio cheese to serve at the table. A crisp salad is always welcome, as is a well-chosen charcuterie board.

FOR THE BEANS:

½ cup dried small white beans

1 small onion, halved

2 garlic cloves, bruised (see box, page 82)

1 rib celery, with leaves, cut in half

4 fresh flat-leaf parsley sprigs

FOR THE RIGATONI:

4 ripe plum tomatoes, seeded, each cut into
    8 pieces

1 tablespoon finely minced garlic

3 tablespoons torn fresh basil leaves

⅓ cup plus 1 tablespoon extra-virgin olive oil

4 tablespoons chopped fresh flat-leaf parsley leaves

12 ounces rigatoni

Freshly ground black pepper, to taste

6 ounces ricotta salata cheese

1. Prepare the beans: Pick over the beans, discarding any debris. Quick-soak them by placing them in a deep pot, adding water to cover by 2 inches, and bringing to a boil. Remove the pot from the heat, cover it, and set it aside for 1 hour.

2. Drain and rinse the beans, and place them in a heavy pot. Add the onion, garlic, celery, and parsley sprigs. Cover with 6 cups water. Bring to a boil, skimming off any foam that rises to the top. Reduce the heat and simmer, uncovered, until the beans are tender but not mushy, 35 to 40 minutes. Drain the beans in a colander, discarding the flavoring vegetables and herbs. Place them in a large bowl.

3. Add the tomatoes, garlic, basil, the ⅓ cup olive oil, and 2 tablespoons of the parsley to the beans, and toss well.

4. Prepare the pasta: Bring a large pot of salted water to a boil. Add the remaining 1 tablespoon olive oil. Add the rigatoni and cook until al dente (just tender), 13 to 14 minutes. Drain the pasta well, and add it to the beans and tomatoes. Toss well.

5. Transfer the pasta mixture to a large serving bowl. Grind the pepper over the top, then grate on the ricotta salata. Garnish with the remaining 2 tablespoons parsley and serve immediately.

SPAGHETTI BOLOGNESE

SERVES 6 TO 8

One of the best known Italian ragùs is Ragù Bolognese. A combination of beef and veal is traditional, but I prefer the flavor that comes from the addition of pork and use it in place of the veal. The choice is yours. Nutmeg, used gingerly, adds a distinctive flavor. My preference is barely a pinch.

3 tablespoons extra-virgin olive oil

4 ounces slab bacon, rind removed, cut into
    ¼-inch dice

1 onion, cut into ¼-inch dice

½ cup diced carrot (¼-inch dice)

½ cup diced celery (¼-inch dice)

8 ounces ground beef chuck

8 ounces ground pork or veal

½ cup dry white wine

1 can (28 ounces) Italian plum tomatoes,
    drained and chopped

2 tablespoons tomato paste

½ cup beef broth

1 pinch ground nutmeg, or more to taste

Salt and freshly ground black pepper, to taste

½ cup heavy (whipping) cream

12 ounces spaghetti

2 tablespoons chopped fresh flat-leaf parsley leaves,
    for garnish

Freshly grated Parmesan cheese, for serving

1. Heat 2 tablespoons of olive oil in a heavy pot over low heat. Add the bacon and cook, stirring occasionally, until lightly browned, 6 to 7 minutes.

2. Add the onion, carrot, and celery and continue to cook, stirring, until the vegetables are wilted, 5 to 8 minutes.

3. Raise the heat to medium, crumble in the ground beef and pork in small clumps, and cook, stirring, until the meat is browned and the liquid has evaporated, about 10 minutes.

4. Add the wine and cook, stirring, until it evaporates, about 5 minutes. Add the chopped tomatoes, tomato paste, beef broth, nutmeg, and salt and pepper. Bring the sauce to a boil. Then reduce the heat to medium-low, partially cover the pot, and simmer, stirring occasionally, until the flavors have blended, about 25 minutes.

5. Stir in the cream, reduce the heat to low, and cook, partially covered, for 20 minutes, uncovering the pot in the last 5 minutes. Taste, and adjust the seasonings.

6. Meanwhile, bring a large pot of salted water to a boil. Add the spaghetti and cook until it is al dente (just tender), 12 minutes. Drain the pasta, reserving some of the cooking water.

7. Toss the pasta with the sauce, adding some of the reserved cooking water if the sauce needs thinning. Transfer the mixture to a large pasta bowl, sprinkle with the chopped parsley, and serve. Pass the cheese!

SAFFRON ORZO

SERVES 6 AS A SIDE DISH

Orzo is such a pleasing "small" pasta—and just right to serve with many foods instead of rice because it is so much lighter. Here I've prepared it in a broth scented with saffron, making a delightful golden bed for veal or lamb.

8 cups chicken broth, preferably homemade
  (see page 434)
Salt, to taste
½ teaspoon crushed saffron threads
2 tablespoons olive oil
2 cups orzo
2 teaspoons chopped fresh flat-leaf parsley leaves
Freshly ground black pepper, to taste

1. Combine the chicken broth, salt, saffron, and 1 tablespoon of the oil in a medium-size pot and bring to a boil. Stir in the orzo, reduce the heat to a simmer, and cook, uncovered, until the orzo is just tender, about 9 minutes.

2. Drain the orzo and return it to the pot. Add the remaining 1 tablespoon oil and the parsley, and toss well. Season with salt and pepper. Serve hot.

A COMFY FALL MENU

It's late October, the weatherman says there's a chance of snow in the forecast, and everyone's looking for something to do. Divide up this menu and get them cooking. Hold the party at your place. Serve up a Vino Nobile di Montepulciano with the entrée and a vin santo with dessert.

JASON EPSTEIN'S CLAMS CASINO
PAGE 229

BRAISED OSSO BUCO WITH GREMOLATA
PAGE 84

SAFFRON ORZO
THIS PAGE

LAURIE'S LEMON SPICE CAKE
PAGE 397

SHRIMP AND VEGETABLE PAD THAI

SERVES 6

Pad Thai is kind of a "spokesman" for Thai cuisine. Its blend of flavors is easy to love and makes a safe—that is, non-fiery—introduction to a cuisine known for some potent (and delicious) heat. Pad Thai can be made with chicken, beef, or vegetables, but I prefer shrimp and vegetables in mine. When shopping for rice sticks (pad Thai), choose the medium width if they're available. They make the best dishes and the most attractive presentation.

8 ounces dried rice sticks (Thai rice noodles)

¼ cup Asian fish sauce

1 tablespoon rice vinegar

2 teaspoons soy sauce

6 tablespoons peanut oil

1 pound medium shrimp, peeled and deveined, rinsed and patted dry

1 onion, halved lengthwise and slivered

2 teaspoons finely minced garlic

⅔ cup julienned fresh snow peas

1 carrot, peeled and julienned

½ cup diced celery (¼-inch dice)

⅓ cup diced red bell pepper (¼-inch dice)

4 ounces mung bean sprouts (available at Asian grocery stores and some supermarkets)

2 scallions (white bulbs and 3 inches green), thinly sliced, for garnish

3 tablespoons finely chopped salted peanuts, for garnish

2 tablespoons chopped fresh cilantro, for garnish

1. Bring a large pot of water to a boil. Remove it from the heat and add the rice sticks. Let them soak, uncovered, for 5 minutes. Then drain in a colander.

2. Combine the fish sauce, rice vinegar, and soy sauce in a small bowl. Set it aside.

3. Heat 2 tablespoons of the peanut oil in a large skillet or a wok over medium heat. Add the shrimp and sauté until they are just cooked through, about 2 minutes per side. Transfer the shrimp to a plate and set it aside.

4. In the same skillet, heat the remaining 4 tablespoons oil over medium heat. Add the onion, garlic, snow peas, carrot, celery, and bell pepper. Cook, stirring, until the vegetables have softened, about 3 minutes. Add the reserved fish sauce mixture and the noodles, and toss well to combine. Toss in the reserved shrimp and the mung bean sprouts, and cook to heat through, 2 to 3 minutes.

5. Transfer the Pad Thai to a large serving platter. Sprinkle the scallions, peanuts, and cilantro over the top, and serve immediately in individual bowls.

SUMMER SOBA NOODLES
WITH A ZESTY DIPPING SAUCE

SERVES 2

𝑓rom the time I started enjoying Japanese food, these cold soba noodles—a favorite snack in Japan, where they are served in a bamboo basket over ice—have been a favorite of mine. The sauce is easy to put together and the buckwheat noodles are readily available. Just be sure to keep a jar of pickled ginger in your fridge for brightening the sauce, and you'll always have a fast, refreshing weeknight meal on hand.

FOR THE DIPPING SAUCE:

½ cup light soy sauce

1½ teaspoons toasted sesame oil

⅓ cup chopped scallions (white bulbs and
    3 inches green)

¼ cup pickled ginger, drained

FOR THE NOODLES:

1 package (3 bunches) soba noodles

1. Combine all the sauce ingredients in a bowl, stir in 2 tablespoons water, and set it aside for the flavors to meld, 15 minutes.

2. When you are ready to serve, divide the sauce between two small bowls for dipping.

3. Bring a large pot of salted water to a boil. Add the noodles and cook until al dente (just tender), about 6 minutes.

4. Drain the noodles and rinse them thoroughly under cold water. Drain again well. Serve the cold noodles in shallow pasta bowls, with the dipping sauce on the side. Be sure to pick up some of the ginger and scallions with each bite of noodles.

SESAME NOODLES
WITH APPLES AND CUCUMBERS

SERVES 6

this bright way to serve sesame noodles is inspired by Jean-Georges Vongerichten's delicious noodles at his former restaurant 66. He topped his rice noodles with a julienne of cucumbers and apples, which I found pure magic—refreshing and delightful. Here I toss up spaghettini with a richly flavored creamy sesame sauce and sprinkle the top with scallions, cucumbers, apples, peanuts, and a handful of radish or alfalfa sprouts for a final flourish.

FOR THE SESAME SAUCE:

⅓ cup soy sauce

¼ cup rice vinegar

1 tablespoon dark brown sugar

2 teaspoons minced peeled fresh ginger

1 teaspoon minced garlic

½ cup smooth peanut butter

¼ cup toasted sesame oil

3 tablespoons peanut oil

½ teaspoon chile oil, or more to taste

Salt and freshly ground black pepper,
    to taste

FOR THE NOODLES:

1 tablespoon olive oil

12 ounces spaghettini

Salt and freshly ground black pepper,
    to taste

FOR FINISHING:

1 Granny Smith apple, unpeeled, julienned,
    tossed with 1 tablespoon fresh lemon
    juice to prevent discoloration

BETTER IN A BOWL

These noodles are so good and fun to eat, I could have them for dinner three or four times a week. I love bowl and chopstick dining, so serve them up in wide, shallow bowls. There's enough depth for the noodles and sauce, and the apple and cucumber sticks have room to spread out. An ice cold beer completes the dish.

¾ hothouse (seedless) cucumber, peeled and
    julienned

4 scallions (white bulbs and 3 inches green),
    thinly sliced

3 tablespoons chopped salted peanuts

¼ cup tiny radish or alfalfa sprouts

1. One day ahead, prepare the sesame sauce: Place the soy sauce, vinegar, brown sugar, ginger, garlic, and peanut butter in a blender and process on high speed until smooth, 1 or 2 minutes.

2. Combine the sesame oil, peanut oil, and chile oil in a spouted measuring cup, and with the blender running, drizzle them into the sauce. Season to taste with salt and pepper. Cover, and refrigerate overnight to thicken.

3. Bring a large pot of salted water to a boil over high heat. Add the olive oil and the spaghettini, and cook until the noodles are al dente (just tender), 8 to 9 minutes. Drain, reserving some of the pasta cooking water. Place the noodles in a large bowl and toss with the sesame sauce, using the reserved cooking water to thin the sauce if necessary. Season with salt and pepper.

4. Transfer the noodles to a shallow pasta bowl. Drain the apple and sprinkle it evenly over the noodles, followed by the cucumber, scallions, peanuts, and sprouts. Serve immediately.

"MY ADVICE: GRAB 'EM WHILE YOU CAN."

TOMATOES

There's nothing better than the first juicy bite of summer's perfect ripe tomatoes. If you've ever picked one off the vine, warm and bright red and with that deep tomato smell, you're hooked. What our tomato gardeners strive for is taste, and now they've given it to us in a dazzling array of varieties. Not only do we have all our gorgeous ripe red summer tomatoes, but also Green Zebra, yellow Pineapple, Black Brandywine, and Cherokee Purple, to name just a few. Eat them straight—maybe with a sprinkling of salt—or turn them into soups, sauces, and, of course, salads.

My stack of thinly sliced heirloom tomatoes on a bed of rich, thick Russian Dressing may appear simple but it makes a stunning appetizer—and the color variety of the tomatoes will look spectacular on your table. Laurie's Delicious Tomato Pasta is a wow and a delightful way to use both red and yellow cherry tomatoes. Sliced, chopped, cooked, tossed, plain or dressed, when it's tomato time, they're always welcome in the kitchen.

Here's an important tip: If you must buy your tomatoes underripe, ripen them on the counter or windowsill, at room temperature. Don't put unripe tomatoes in the refrigerator; it prevents the flavors from developing. ❧

FRESH TOMATO SOUP

SERVES 8

a soup made from juicy tomatoes right off the vine rates high on my "I'm glad it's summer" meter. It is one of the treats that make summer eating so heavenly. This soup gives the others a run for their money. For many, a little basil is a must, but try using chives, as I do here, or tarragon for a change. The allspice adds richness, and the orange zest adds sweetness and bright flavor. Hot soup or cold, you'll fall in love—I promise.

2 tablespoons unsalted butter

2 tablespoons olive oil

1 cup chopped onion

1 tablespoon chopped garlic

Finely grated zest of 1 orange

¼ teaspoon ground allspice

3½ pounds ripe garden tomatoes, chopped

1 tablespoon tomato paste

1 teaspoon sugar

3 cups chicken or vegetable broth,
      preferably homemade (see pages
      434 and 436)

1½ cups heavy (whipping) cream

Salt and freshly ground black pepper,
      to taste

2 tablespoons snipped fresh chives,
      for garnish

1. Melt the butter in the oil in a heavy pot over low heat. Add the onion and cook, stirring occasionally, for 10 minutes. Add the garlic and cook until the onion is translucent, another 5 minutes. Sprinkle with the orange zest and the allspice, and cook for 1 minute longer.

2. Add the tomatoes, tomato paste, sugar, and broth, and bring to a boil. Reduce the heat to medium-low, partially cover the pot, and simmer, stirring occasionally, until the soup has thickened, about 30 minutes. Allow it to cool slightly.

3. Puree the soup, in batches, in a food processor or blender until it is completely smooth. Return the soup to the pot.

4. Stir in the cream, and season with salt and pepper. If you will be serving the soup cold, cover and refrigerate it for 4 to 6 hours. If you are serving it hot, reheat it gently, stirring, without boiling.

5. Sprinkle each portion with some of the snipped chives, and serve.

LUSH TOMATOES AND AVOCADOS

SERVES 4

Look for yellow, purple, or orange tomatoes to combine with your avocado. What a salad you'll have! Shallots add a great little kick.

2 large ripe tomatoes (each about 8 ounces), preferably heirloom

1½ tablespoons finely chopped shallots

2 tablespoons extra-virgin olive oil

Freshly ground black pepper, to taste

1 ripe avocado, preferably Hass, halved and pitted (do not peel)

1½ tablespoons fresh lemon juice

Salt, to taste

1 tablespoon chopped fresh flat-leaf parsley leaves, for garnish

1. Cut the tomatoes in half lengthwise, and then cut the halves into thin wedges. Arrange the tomatoes on a medium-size serving dish, and sprinkle 1 tablespoon of the shallots over them evenly. Drizzle with 1 tablespoon of the olive oil. Season lightly with pepper.

2. Use a teaspoon to remove small scoops of avocado from the avocado halves, and arrange the avocado scoops on top of the tomatoes and shallots. Sprinkle the lemon juice over the avocados. Then sprinkle the remaining 1 tablespoon olive oil and the remaining ½ tablespoon shallots over the salad. Season with salt and pepper, and garnish with the parsley. Serve immediately.

TOMATO TASTING

If you're fortunate enough to have a wide range of tomatoes available to you, I urge you to try them all. Cut them up in chunks, place each type on its own plate, sprinkle on a little flaky salt (or not), and taste. Soak up the leftover juices with slices of toasted baguette. What a delicious treat.

TOMATO BONANZA

SERVES 8

there's not much elaboration needed for a kaleidoscope of ripe heirloom tomatoes tossed together in a salad. No matter what the color—from Green Zebra to Black Brandywine to Pineapple with a dazzling orange starburst center—they all play with your taste buds like nothing you've ever eaten.

8 to 10 ripe tomatoes, preferably heirlooms, in mixed colors, shapes, and sizes

Salt and freshly ground black pepper, to taste

2 to 3 tablespoons extra-virgin olive oil

2 to 3 tablespoons red wine vinegar or fresh lemon juice

½ cup whole small fresh mint leaves, small fresh flat-leaf parsley leaves, or slivered fresh basil leaves, for garnish

1. Cut the tomatoes into different-size wedges, halves, and other assorted sizes and shapes. Place them in a large shallow serving bowl.

2. Shortly before serving, sprinkle with salt and pepper. Drizzle with the oil and vinegar.

3. Garnish with the mint, and serve.

STACK OF HEIRLOOM TOMATOES WITH RUSSIAN DRESSING

SERVES 4 TO 6

the new flush of heirloom tomatoes makes this appetizer salad possible—there's such a vast variety at local farm stands and at farmers' markets during tomato season. My advice: grab 'em while you can. For the stack of tomatoes, begin with a slice of the largest at the bottom and work up to the smallest. Try to vary the colors as much as possible—see the box on the facing page for some suggestions.

½ to ¾ cup Russian Dressing (recipe follows)
5 to 6 heirloom tomatoes, graduated in size,
    in different colors if possible, cut into
    ¼-inch-thick slices
1 tablespoon finely chopped or snipped fresh
    tarragon

1. Spoon 2 tablespoons of the Russian Dressing onto the center of each of four to six large salad plates. Spread it into a disk shape with the back of a spoon.

2. Place one of the largest tomato slices on top of the dressing on each of the plates. Continue stacking the tomato slices to achieve a pyramid shape, in alternating colors if possible. Sprinkle with the tarragon, and serve.

RUSSIAN DRESSING

MAKES 1⅓ CUPS

When I was doing some research on this dressing, I was surprised that the lore wasn't more exotic. The fact is that this deli sandwich spread has its roots in Eastern Europe and Russia, and when immigrants came to America, they simply brought it with them. I enrich the usual mayonnaise-and-ketchup mix with capers, tarragon, egg, and chili sauce. I find that this blend makes up for any exotic story that was left behind.

1 cup prepared mayonnaise, such as Hellmann's
¼ cup Heinz chili sauce
1 hard-cooked egg, minced
1 tablespoon drained tiny capers
2 tablespoons finely chopped fresh tarragon leaves
    or snipped fresh chives

Combine all the ingredients in a bowl. Use immediately or store, covered, in the refrigerator for up to 4 days.

TOMATO-BASIL RICE SALAD

SERVES 8

During the 1980s pasta salads were all the rage, and while they're still popular, they've taken a backseat to rice and vegetable salads—certainly on my table. Made with freshly cooked rice, this salad is an ideal buffet choice. Offer a simple entrée, a green salad, and you are set to go.

1 tablespoon olive oil

1½ teaspoons salt

2 cups long-grain converted rice

1 cup Red Wine Vinaigrette (page 23)

4 cups diced ripe tomatoes (½-inch dice)

1 cup (loosely packed) coarsely torn fresh
    basil leaves

Salt and freshly ground black pepper,
    to taste

1. Bring 4 cups of water to a boil in a large pot. Add the olive oil and the salt. Stir in the rice. Reduce the heat to medium-low, cover the pot, and simmer until the rice is cooked and all the liquid has been absorbed, about 20 minutes. Remove the pot from the heat and set it aside, covered, for 5 minutes. Then fluff the rice with a fork.

2. Place the warm rice in a large bowl and add the vinaigrette. Toss thoroughly with a fork to fluff the rice and coat it well. Let the rice cool to room temperature.

3. Add the tomatoes, basil, and salt and pepper, and toss again. Serve at room temperature in a decorative bowl.

TOMATO CARPACCIO

SERVES 4

A visit to Kendall Jackson's 2006 Heirloom Tomato Festival in Santa Rosa, California, inspired me to create this gorgeous dish from a huge ripe bright yellow Pineapple heirloom tomato. Any large tomatoes will do, but do look for nice ripe heirlooms. Sliced very thin and arranged so that the slices cover the plate completely, the tomatoes resemble carpaccio. The dish makes a sublime appetizer.

2 large heirloom tomatoes
    (about 1¼ pounds total)
2 tablespoons extra-virgin olive oil
Maldon (flaky) sea salt (see Note, page 66) or coarse
    (kosher) salt, to taste
Freshly ground black pepper, to taste
1 tablespoon drained tiny capers
Sliced olive or rosemary bread, toasted,
    for serving

1. Cut the tomatoes into very thin rounds. Spread the slices out on a large dinner or oval plate, overlapping slightly, so they cover the plate completely.

2. Drizzle the olive oil over the tomatoes. Just before serving, sprinkle the salt, pepper, and capers over them. Serve immediately, with the toasted bread alongside. 🌺

STUFFED TOMATOES

Tomatoes take to all types of stuffings and make impressive luncheon entrées. Choose ripe, firm tomatoes for stuffing. Slice off the top about ¼ inch down and a smaller piece off the bottom so that the tomato stands up straight. Use a teaspoon to hollow out the tomato leaving a ¼-inch-thick shell. Then use that spoon to scoop in a favorite salad. Here are some ideas for stuffings.

+ Egg salad mixed with plenty of chopped dill

+ Chicken salad with fresh tarragon

+ Ham salad with ditali pasta

+ Vegetable tuna salad mixed with diced celery and grated carrots

TOMATO-MOZZARELLA-BASIL SALAD

SERVES 4

Ripe tomatoes, fresh mozzarella, and fragrant basil: it's summer candy. Enhanced with a luscious Tomato Vinaigrette, this combination can't be beat.

3 ripe tomatoes in a variety of colors
   (red, yellow, orange), thinly sliced
1 fresh buffalo mozzarella (about 1 pound),
   cut crosswise into ¼-inch-thick slices
16 fresh basil leaves
¼ cup Tomato Vinaigrette (recipe follows)
Coarse (kosher) salt and freshly ground
   black pepper, to taste

1. Alternate the tomato and mozzarella slices, overlapping slightly, on a decorative platter. Tuck the basil leaves between the slices, pointing them in different directions for visual interest.

2. Just before serving, drizzle the Tomato Vinaigrette evenly over the slices. Sprinkle with salt and pepper, and serve. 🌿

TOMATO VINAIGRETTE

MAKES 1 CUP

This vinaigrette loves the tomato and absorbs the best of its sweet flavor. It's amazing how it raises a salad of tomatoes and mozzarella to an ethereal level.

1 large ripe tomato, seeded and
   cut into ¼-inch dice
½ teaspoon sugar
1 tablespoon finely minced shallots
½ teaspoon finely minced garlic
3 tablespoons red wine vinegar
3 tablespoons canned or bottled tomato juice
¼ cup extra-virgin olive oil
Salt and freshly ground black pepper, to taste

Place the tomato in a bowl and sprinkle with the sugar. Add the shallots and garlic. Stir in the vinegar and tomato juice. Whisk in the olive oil. Season with salt and pepper. Use right away for the best flavor. 🌿

LAURIE'S DELICIOUS TOMATO PASTA

SERVES 2

Laurie Griffith and I have worked together for years. Laurie is an excellent cook, and she knows how to cut to the chase. Case in point: this layered, balanced, and simple dish offers a luscious, elegant taste and texture. *Brava!* Serve it with a simple arugula salad.

4 tablespoons extra-virgin olive oil

3 cloves garlic, thinly sliced lengthwise

1 pinch crushed red pepper flakes

1 pound ripe plum tomatoes, cored and
    cut into ½-inch dice

1 teaspoon sugar

Salt and freshly ground black pepper, to taste

1 cup (loosely packed) torn fresh basil leaves

6 ounces spaghettini

1 tablespoon unsalted butter

Freshly grated Parmesan cheese, for serving

1. Heat 3 tablespoons of oil in a large skillet over medium-low heat. Add the garlic and cook, stirring occasionally, for 5 minutes. Add the red pepper flakes and continue cooking until the garlic is golden, about 5 minutes more.

2. Add the tomatoes, sugar, and salt and pepper. Raise the heat to medium and cook, stirring occasionally, until the sauce has thickened and a wooden spoon leaves a trail on the bottom of the skillet, 15 to 20 minutes. Stir in the basil and set aside.

3. Bring a large pot of salted water to a boil. Add the remaining tablespoon of olive oil. Add the spaghettini and cook until al dente (just tender), 8 to 9 minutes.

4. Drain the spaghettini well, and add it to the skillet containing the tomato sauce. Stir in the butter and cook over high heat, stirring constantly, so that some of the sauce is absorbed, 1 minute.

5. Serve the pasta and sauce in shallow pasta bowls, and pass the cheese.

ROASTED TINY RED AND YELLOW TOMATOES

SERVES 8

When you're looking for a colorful and easy accompaniment to either meat or fish, a quick roast of mini tomatoes in varying hues of red, yellow, and orange is a delicate and delicious choice. As the tomatoes caramelize, their flavors intensify.

1 pint (2 cups) red grape or pear tomatoes

1 pint (2 cups) yellow or orange pear or
    cherry tomatoes

2 tablespoons extra-virgin olive oil

1 teaspoon coarse (kosher) salt or sea salt

1 teaspoon coarsely ground black pepper

½ teaspoon sugar

2 tablespoons chopped fresh flat-leaf parsley leaves

1. Preheat the oven to 375°F.

2. Combine the tomatoes, oil, salt, pepper, and sugar in a bowl and gently toss together.

3. Arrange the coated tomatoes in a single layer on a rimmed baking sheet. Bake, shaking and turning the baking sheet once, until the tomatoes begin to caramelize, about 20 minutes (see Note). Remove and set aside for 5 to 6 minutes.

4. Using a spatula, carefully transfer the tomatoes to a serving plate. Sprinkle with the parsley, and serve immediately.

NOTE: The oven temperature at which I cooked these tomatoes, as well as the cooking time, were tricky to determine. I was looking for two things: for one, the tomatoes to retain their integrity, and for the other, for them to caramelize a little bit. Baking them at 375°F for 20 minutes worked well. Cook them an additional 5 minutes if you'd like the tomatoes more sugary.

VANILLA STEWED TOMATOES

SERVES 4

I am always enchanted by chef David Bouley's brilliant food. Once, when dining in his New York restaurant, Bouley, I ate some luscious tomatoes cooked with vanilla—and those tomatoes led me to this recipe. They're delicious with poultry, especially with Roasted Brined Chicken (page 137).

4 pounds ripe plum tomatoes

1 teaspoon sugar

1 vanilla bean, halved lengthwise

Salt and freshly ground black pepper,
    to taste

1. Peel, seed, and coarsely chop the tomatoes, catching all the juices in a bowl. (To peel tomatoes, see box, page 266.)

2. Place the chopped tomatoes in a nonreactive saucepan, and strain the juices into the pan. Add the sugar, and tuck the vanilla bean halves into the tomatoes.

3. Simmer the tomatoes, uncovered, stirring occasionally, over medium-low heat until the juices have reduced and the tomatoes are cooked through, about 45 minutes.

4. Remove the vanilla bean pieces, scrape the seeds from them, and return the seeds to the tomatoes. Season with salt and pepper. Let the tomatoes cool to room temperature. Then cover, and refrigerate for up to 2 days.

5. Bring the tomatoes to room temperature before serving, or warm them over low heat. Serve 2 generous spoonfuls in each of four small bowls or large ramekins.

"FRESH INGREDIENTS MAKE THE LIVELIEST, BEST-TASTING SALSAS."

SHEILA'S SALSAS

Colorful, and from south-of-the-border, salsa is a condiment that many of us north of the border have had our way with. I count myself an avid member of that group, having created some surprising combinations of favorite fruits and vegetables, resulting in spectacular results. To me, there's no more delicious or healthier eating than grilling a piece of lean poultry or fish and topping it with a Sparkling Pineapple Salsa laced with ginger and bell peppers, or perhaps a silky, slightly piquant Fresh Mango Salsa.

These new, delicious salsas are vibrant to taste and gorgeous to look at. My salsa experimentation over the past several years has cut across cultures. With tropical fruits and vegetables flourishing on the culinary scene, mangos, papayas, and jalapeños have nudged over the once familiar onion, tomato, bell pepper, and avocado salsa. Fresh limes and lime juice have remained. Watermelons, honeydews, and cantaloupes are also excellent salsa ingredients and mix well with tomatoes, onions, and chiles. Once you fall in love with making salsas and using them to top your meat and fish, you'll barely have a need for salads or vegetables on the same plate.

CHIMICHURRI SAUCE

MAKES ½ CUP

Chimichurri is probably not the first thing that comes to mind when you're considering salsas. But salsa translates as sauce and this chapter includes condiment sauces inspired by favorite flavors and pairings. Chimichurri is served alongside some of our most delicious steaks, at popular Argentinean steak houses. Pesto-like in consistency, this table sauce is classically made with parsley, vinegar, oil, garlic, and various seasonings. As usual, I've made a few changes, and I find the mellow results to be an ideal match with robust steaks, like a rare New York strip steak.

¼ cup chopped fresh mint leaves

¼ cup chopped fresh flat-leaf parsley leaves

1 to 2 teaspoons finely minced jalapeño,
    to taste

1 teaspoon finely minced garlic

1 teaspoon dried oregano

Salt and freshly ground black pepper,
    to taste

¼ cup sherry vinegar

⅓ cup extra-virgin olive oil

1. Combine the mint and parsley in a medium-size bowl. Add the jalapeño, garlic, oregano, and salt and pepper.

2. Stir in the vinegar. Then slowly whisk in the olive oil. Let rest at room temperature, loosely covered, for 2 to 3 hours for the flavors to blend.

3. Taste, and adjust the seasonings if needed. Use immediately, or store in an airtight container in the refrigerator for up to 1 week ❧

AN ANNIVERSARY DINNER

Help Mom and Dad or sister and brother-in-law or best friends celebrate a festive occasion with a blow-out dinner. Pop the Champagne and toast the happy twosome.

GRILLED SAIGON SHRIMP
PAGE 221

STRIP STEAKS
with Chimichurri Sauce
PAGE 67

QUINOA
with Chimichurri Herbs
PAGE 321

LUSH TOMATOES AND AVOCADOS
PAGE 355

AUNT SABELLA'S BLACK CHOCOLATE CAKE
with Fudge Icing
PAGE 378

FARM STAND CORN SALSA

MAKES 4 CUPS

fresh ingredients make the liveliest, best-tasting salsas. Corn, tomatoes, cucumbers, and cantaloupe(!) come together in a refreshing combination of flavors and textures. A dash of cumin, some lime juice, and a little oil pull it all together. Whether atop fish or in a taco, these new sauces add excitement and color to a dish!

2 cups fresh corn kernels (from 4 ears of corn)

2 cups diced seeded ripe tomatoes (¼-inch dice)

2 teaspoons finely minced green jalapeño pepper

3 scallions (white bulbs and 3 inches green),
    thinly sliced

1 tablespoon extra-virgin olive oil

2 tablespoons fresh lime juice

½ teaspoon ground cumin

½ cup diced seeded Kirby cucumber (¼-inch dice)

½ cup diced cantaloupe (¼-inch dice)

¼ cup chopped fresh mint leaves

Salt and freshly ground black pepper, to taste

1. Bring a saucepan of salted water to a boil, add the corn, and cook until just tender, 2 minutes. Drain, run under cold water, and drain again. Pat dry.

2. Combine the corn, tomatoes, jalapeño, scallions, olive oil, lime juice, and cumin in a medium-size bowl. Refrigerate, covered, for up to 6 hours.

3. Shortly before serving, toss in the cucumber, cantaloupe, and mint, and season with salt and pepper.

CORN AND MANGO SALSA

MAKES ABOUT 4 CUPS

Fresh corn kernels, cut straight from the cob, mixed with ripe tomatoes, sweet mango, spicy chile, and tart lime: another combination of vegetables and fruit that is ideal to top your grilled poultry, fish, and pork. Keep it simple: too much embellishment can result in a mushy, tasteless salsa. Strive for a clear, crisp relish.

1 cup fresh corn kernels (from 2 ears of corn)

1 ripe mango, peeled, pitted, and cut into ¼-inch dice (see box, this page)

4 ripe plum tomatoes, seeded and cut into ¼-inch dice

⅓ cup diced red onion (¼-inch dice)

Finely grated zest and juice of 1 lime

1 teaspoon finely minced garlic

1 teaspoon finely minced green jalapeño pepper

¼ cup chopped fresh basil leaves

1. Bring a saucepan of salted water to a boil, add the corn, and cook until just tender, 2 minutes. Drain, run under cold water, and drain again. Pat dry.

2. Combine the corn, mango, tomatoes, onion, lime zest and juice, garlic, and jalapeño pepper in a bowl. Cover, and refrigerate for up to 2 hours.

3. Just before serving, stir in the basil.

HOW TO PEEL A MANGO

There is a large flat seed, about ½ inch thick, in the center of a mango. To remove the flesh from this seed, it's easiest to cut the unpeeled fruit, lengthwise, top to stem end from each flat side of the seed. Then make evenly spaced crisscross slashes through the flesh without piercing the skin. Using both hands, gently bend back the edges of the fruit peel and push out the center flesh, which will separate the cut sections. Scrape them from the skin, and serve or prepare them further for salsas or salads.

FRESH MANGO SALSA

MAKES 2 CUPS

I love sweet, succulent fruit with a bite as a topping on savory beans, and there is nothing that suits jerk-flavored red beans (see page 296) better than this salsa. Here's a trick if your mango is not ripe: Place the mango and an apple in a paper bag. The natural gases from the apple will accelerate the ripening (although it will still take a day or two). If time is short, substitute a papaya for the mango.

2 ripe mangoes, peeled, pitted, and cut into
    ¼-inch dice (see box, facing page)

3 ripe plum tomatoes, seeded and cut into
    ¼-inch dice

¼ cup diced red onion (¼-inch dice)

2 teaspoons finely minced seeded green
    jalapeño pepper

2 teaspoons finely grated lime zest

Juice of 1 lime

1 tablespoon extra-virgin olive oil

⅓ cup plus 2 tablespoons chopped fresh cilantro or
    fresh flat-leaf parsley leaves

Salt and freshly ground black pepper, to taste

Combine all the ingredients, except the 2 tablespoons cilantro, in a bowl. Refrigerate, covered, for up to 4 hours. Just before serving, garnish with the remaining cilantro.

GREEN APPLE SALSA

MAKES 2 CUPS

this crisp salsa—with its four different green elements, each with a different texture and taste—is refreshing, crisp, and surprising as you eat it. It's more like a little salad than a sauce. The bright flavor of mint pops it at the end. It is delicious served spooned on tuna burgers and other fish and poultry. In case you're wondering, seedless cucumbers do, in fact, contain seeds, although they're smaller than the seeds in regular cukes. I like to remove them too.

1 Granny Smith apple, unpeeled

2 tablespoons fresh lemon juice

½ cup diced peeled, seeded hothouse (seedless) cucumber (¼-inch dice)

3 scallions (white bulbs and 3 inches green), thinly sliced on the diagonal

2 tablespoons chopped fresh mint leaves

Salt and freshly ground black pepper, to taste

1. Core the apple, cut it into ¼-inch dice, and toss it with the lemon juice in a bowl to prevent discoloration.

2. Drain the diced apple and place it in a bowl. Add the cucumber, scallions, and mint. Season with salt and pepper, and toss well. Serve immediately or store, covered, in the refrigerator for up to 1 day.

PINEAPPLE APPLE RAITA

MAKES 3 CUPS

a raita is a smooth Indian yogurt condiment that can be flavored with aromatics from cumin to garam masala. It can also be brightened with lime juice. Cucumber and tomato are often added. Raitas are refreshing to eat along with Indian dishes such as Tandoori-Style Roast Chicken (page 142), a favorite spicy curry, or Minty Lamb Kebabs (page 171) off the grill.

2 cups plain yogurt

Finely grated zest and juice of 1 lime

½ cup diced fresh pineapple (¼-inch dice)

1 ripe tomato, seeded and cut into ¼-inch
    dice

½ teaspoon ground cumin

1 tablespoon fresh lime juice

1 Granny Smith apple

2 tablespoons chopped fresh cilantro

1. Place the yogurt in a medium-size bowl. Stir in the lime zest and juice, pineapple, tomato, and cumin. Set aside.

2. Place the 1 tablespoon lime juice in a small bowl. Core and peel the apple, and then grate it into the bowl. Toss the grated apple with the lime juice. Fold the apple into the yogurt mixture. Then fold in the cilantro.

3. Refrigerate, covered, for up to 2 hours before serving. Stir before using. 🌿

SPARKLING
PINEAPPLE SALSA

MAKES 2 ½ CUPS

When I'm looking for a bright-tasting relish, nothing can beat the sweetness of ripe pineapple. Bell peppers, a little jalapeño, and lime juice add the kick of the Southwest. This is a burger-topper to go for—great for pork and poultry too!

2 cups diced fresh pineapple (½-inch dice)

¼ cup diced green bell pepper (¼-inch dice)

¼ cup diced orange bell pepper (¼-inch dice)

1 tablespoon chopped fresh mint leaves or
    fresh flat-leaf parsley leaves

1 teaspoon finely minced seeded green or red
    jalapeño pepper

2 teaspoons finely minced fresh ginger

1 tablespoon fresh lime juice

1 tablespoon sugar

Combine all the ingredients and mix well. Use immediately, or refrigerate, covered, for up to 4 hours.

TROPICAL SALSA

MAKES 3 ½ CUPS

lain grilled chicken breasts and fish fillets can be boring, right? Well, they are the perfect foils for this fresh fruit salsa, which is so good and light on the calories that you'll enjoy it even without an entrée to accompany it.

1 cup diced ripe papaya (¼-inch dice)

1 cup diced ripe mango (¼-inch dice)

1 cup diced ripe pineapple (¼-inch dice)

3 ripe plum tomatoes, cut into ¼-inch dice

¼ cup diced red onion (¼-inch dice)

1 tablespoon finely minced garlic

2 teaspoons finely minced green jalapeño pepper

Finely grated zest of 1 lime

Juice of ½ lime

1 tablespoon extra-virgin olive oil

Salt and freshly ground black pepper, to taste

2 tablespoons chopped fresh cilantro

1. Combine the papaya, mango, pineapple, tomatoes, red onion, garlic, jalapeño, lime zest, lime juice, and olive oil in a bowl. Stir well. Refrigerate, covered, for up to 1 hour before serving.

2. Shortly before serving, season with salt and pepper and toss with the cilantro.

WHOLE-CRANBERRY CHERRY SAUCE

SERVES 12

When cranberries are in season, I freeze a few bags so I can enjoy this cranberry sauce throughout the year. It's great served with a crown roast or rack of pork, game dishes, and of course Orange Spice Roasted Turkey (page 59). The combination of ruby port and orange juice blends the same delicious flavors found in England's traditional Cumberland sauce, a sweet and sour sauce served with cold meats and duck. Dried cherries add the sweet touch here.

1 pound fresh cranberries, picked over, rinsed, and drained

1 cup dried cherries

2 cups sugar

½ cup ruby port

½ cup fresh orange juice

Finely grated zest of 1 orange

1 tablespoon minced crystallized ginger

1. Combine all the ingredients in a heavy saucepan over medium heat, and cook until the cranberries pop open, about 10 minutes.

2. Skim the foam from the top with a metal spoon, and allow the mixture to cool to room temperature. Store in the refrigerator, covered, for up to 6 weeks; or freeze in a plastic container for up to 3 months (defrost it in the refrigerator).

TOMATO AND PICKLE TABLE SALSA

SERVES 4

I am always looking for something different to top a burger, and this salsa suits burgers really well. It contains favorite burger go-withs—tomatoes, onions, pickles—but when mixed up salsa-style, they feel brand new.

8 ripe plum tomatoes, seeded and cut into ¼-inch dice

½ cup diced yellow bell pepper (¼-inch dice)

¾ cup diced kosher baby dill pickles or gherkins (½-inch dice)

⅓ cup diced red onion (¼-inch dice)

2 thin scallions (white bulbs and 3 inches green), thinly sliced

3 tablespoons extra-virgin olive oil

2 tablespoons red wine vinegar

2 tablespoons chopped fresh flat-leaf parsley leaves

Salt, to taste

Combine all the ingredients, except the salt, in a bowl. Refrigerate, covered, for up to 2 hours. Just before serving, stir in salt to taste.

"WHEN YOU CAN'T IMPROVE ON PERFECTION, I SAY LEAVE WELL ENOUGH ALONE."

CHOCOLATE

Eve used an apple, but who knows what a bar of semisweet chocolate might have started! Few of us think of chocolate dispassionately. People are very specific about their chocolate choices: dark, semisweet, or milk chocolate. Milk chocolate is my favorite for straight eating; but for cooking and baking, I turn to the variety of available styles, depending on the intensity necessary for a particular recipe.

If you're crazy for chocolate, you'll adore the three-layer knockout Bittersweet Chocolate Cake with a luscious Chocolate Buttercream frosting. You might also become obsessed with Chocolate Cherry Bread Pudding over the holidays. But when you want to serve something so rich and fudgy it's practically a sin, go for the perfectly named Sinful Chocolate Tart. Very romantic.

When talking chocolate, it's not easy to pick an all-time favorite dessert. In the 1980s mine was The Very Best Chocolate Mousse, sold at The Silver Palate and served at every dinner party I gave. I still make it, but have added another dinner party *pièce de résistance*—Chocolate Soufflé. It really is meant for that very special occasion.

I truly believe that you can never have enough recipes for chocolate desserts. But these 10 recipes will get you started.

BITTERSWEET CHOCOLATE CAKE WITH CHOCOLATE BUTTERCREAM

SERVES 10

Now *this* is a chocolate cake! Three layers high and filled and frosted with a chocolate buttercream with a hint of coffee flavoring, eyes light up at the sight of it. And guests have been known to lick their fingers of any stray crumbs. Coating the pans with sugar gives the cake a nice crunchy coating.

1½ cups (3 sticks) unsalted butter, at room
    temperature, plus extra for greasing
    the pans
2¾ cups granulated sugar, plus extra for
    dusting the pans
2 cups all-purpose flour
1 cup good-quality unsweetened cocoa powder
1 teaspoon baking powder
½ teaspoon baking soda
1 teaspoon salt
5 large eggs, at room temperature
1 tablespoon pure vanilla extract
2 tablespoons brewed strong espresso
1½ cups buttermilk
Chocolate Buttercream (recipe follows)

1. Position a rack in the center of the oven and preheat the oven to 325°F. Generously butter the bottom and sides of three 8- or 9-inch cake pans. Dust the pans with granulated sugar and set them aside.

2. Sift the flour, cocoa powder, baking powder, baking soda, and salt together into a bowl. Set it aside.

3. Using an electric mixer on medium speed, cream the butter and sugar together in a bowl until the mixture is very fluffy, 5 minutes. With the mixer on low speed, add the eggs one at a time, beating well after each addition and frequently scraping down the sides of the bowl. Add the vanilla and espresso, and beat well.

4. With the mixer on low speed, add the flour mixture, one third at a time, alternating with the buttermilk and scraping down the sides of the bowl as needed. Mix on medium speed for 1 minute.

5. Pour the batter evenly into the prepared pans and bake until a wooden toothpick inserted in the center comes out clean, 35 to 40 minutes.

6. Cool the layer cakes in the pans on wire racks for 20 minutes. Then remove the layers from the pans and place them on the racks, bottom side up, to cool completely.

7. Place one cake layer, right side up, on a serving

plate. Spread one quarter of the buttercream over the top. Place the second layer on top, right side up, and spread another quarter of the buttercream over that. Top with the remaining layer, right side up. Frost the sides and top with the remaining buttercream. Store the cake in a cool place, loosely covered, for up to 3 days. ✤

CHOCOLATE BUTTERCREAM

MAKES 4 CUPS, ENOUGH TO FILL AND FROST A 9-INCH 3-LAYER CAKE

this buttercream is a pale mocha color, which complements the delectable Bittersweet Chocolate Cake beautifully. The flavor will remind you of the best of your childhood birthday parties.

> 9 ounces bittersweet or semisweet chocolate
> 1½ cups (3 sticks) unsalted butter, at room
>   temperature (very soft)
> 1 tablespoon milk
> 1 teaspoon pure vanilla extract
> 2 tablespoons strong brewed espresso
> About 2 cups sifted confectioners' sugar

1. Bring water to a simmer in the bottom of a double boiler or in a small saucepan. Place the chocolate in the top of the double boiler, or in a small heatproof bowl, and set it over the simmering water (do not let it touch the water). Heat the chocolate, stirring it occasionally with a wooden spoon, until it has melted. (Alternatively, melt the chocolate on high power in a microwave oven for 2 minutes.) Remove it from the heat and set it aside to cool.

2. While the chocolate is cooling, whip the butter with an electric mixer, scraping down the sides of the bowl occasionally, until it is very fluffy, 10 minutes.

3. Add the milk to the butter, and beat until smooth. Add the cooled melted chocolate and beat again. Then add the vanilla and espresso. Beat for 4 minutes, scraping down the sides of the bowl as necessary.

4. With the mixer on low speed, add the confectioners' sugar, using as much as needed to reach the desired consistency.

NOTE: Make the buttercream while the cake is cooling. It is best used right away, but it will keep for 3 to 4 hours. ✤

AUNT SABELLA'S
BLACK CHOCOLATE CAKE
WITH FUDGE ICING

MAKES ONE 8-INCH CAKE; SERVES 9 TO 12

this out-of-this-world chocolate cake comes from Clementine Paddleford's *How America Eats*. Often referred to as America's premier food editor, Paddleford wrote for the *New York Herald Tribune* as well as its Sunday supplement, *This Week* magazine, from the 1940s into the '60s. She traveled the country, sampling recipes from every state, in order to bring only the best to her readers. (By the way, the cake recipe is from Philadelphia and the icing from Washington.) What I love about this cake—besides its taste—is its size. It's baked in an 8-inch pan, which gives you perfect little brownie-like squares to serve.

FOR THE CAKE:

2 ounces unsweetened chocolate, chopped

1¼ cups sifted all-purpose flour

1 teaspoon salt

1 teaspoon baking soda

1 cup buttermilk

5 tablespoons unsalted butter, at room temperature, plus extra for greasing the pan

1 cup granulated sugar

2 large egg yolks, at room temperature

FOR THE ICING:

2¼ cups confectioners' sugar, sifted

5 tablespoons unsweetened cocoa powder

6 tablespoons (¾ stick) unsalted butter, melted

5 tablespoons hot freshly brewed coffee

1½ teaspoons pure vanilla extract

1. Position a rack in the center of the oven, and preheat the oven to 350°F. Butter an 8-inch square baking pan, and set it aside.

2. Prepare the cake: Bring water to a simmer in the bottom of a double boiler or in a small saucepan. Place the chocolate in the top of the double boiler, or in a small heatproof bowl, and set it over the simmering water (do not let it touch the water). Heat the chocolate, stirring it occasionally with a wooden spoon, until it has melted. Then remove it from the heat and set it aside to cool.

3. Sift the flour and salt together in a small bowl, and set it aside.

4. Stir the baking soda into the buttermilk in another small bowl, and set it aside.

5. With an electric mixer on medium speed, beat the butter and sugar together in a large mixing bowl until the mixture is light and fluffy, about 2 minutes. Then beat in the egg yolks, followed by the cooled melted chocolate, and beat until thoroughly combined.

6. Add one third of the flour mixture to the bowl, then one third of the buttermilk, beating well after each addition. Repeat twice, to use all of both mixtures.

7. Pour the batter into the prepared pan, and bake until a toothpick inserted in the center of the cake comes out clean, 40 to 50 minutes.

8. Let the cake cool completely in the pan on a wire rack. Then invert it onto a serving plate.

9. Prepare the icing: Sift the confectioners' sugar and cocoa powder together into a bowl. Stir in the melted butter, then the hot coffee, and then the vanilla, mixing well with a wooden spoon after each addition. Continue to stir until the icing is smooth.

10. Ice the top and sides of the cake. Cut the cake into squares, and serve. (Store the cake, loosely covered, in a cool place.) 🍀

CHOCOLATE BUTTER COOKIES

MAKES 68 COOKIES

two favorite flavors: chocolate and butter—delicious for cookies. You can prepare the dough for these cookies a day ahead and then slice and bake them when you're ready. They are splendid with a scoop of vanilla ice cream and heaven with a cup of cappuccino—or serve them with a bowl of sweetened whipped cream alongside for dunking or dolloping.

⅔ cup superfine sugar

½ cup Dutch-process cocoa powder, sifted

¼ teaspoon salt

1 cup (2 sticks) unsalted butter, at room
    temperature, plus extra for greasing the
    baking sheets

2 cups all-purpose flour

1. Combine the sugar, cocoa powder, and salt in a large bowl, and stir well.

2. Add the butter to the bowl, and using an electric mixer, cream the butter and the sugar mixture together until just combined. Do not overmix.

3. Using a wooden spoon or a rubber spatula, stir in the flour in two additions, blending until just combined.

4. Divide the dough in half. Place a sheet of wax paper on your work surface, place one of the halves on the paper, and form it into a log that is 8 to 9 inches long and about 1½ inches in diameter. Wrap the log in the paper, twisting the ends to enclose the dough. Repeat with the remaining half. Chill the dough logs in the refrigerator for at least 2 hours or as long as 2 days.

5. Preheat the oven to 350°F. Lightly butter two baking sheets.

6. Slice the dough into ¼-inch-thick rounds and arrange them, about 1 inch apart, on the prepared baking sheets. Re-refrigerate any remaining dough. Bake for 8 minutes.

7. Remove the baking sheets from the oven and let the cookies cool on the sheets for 10 minutes. Then transfer the cookies to a wire rack and let them cool completely. Repeat with the remaining dough.

8. Store the cookies in an airtight container for up to 10 days. 🍀

BROOKLYN BROWNIES

MAKES 9 BROWNIES

the scent of these yummy brownies wafted right through my television screen when I first saw Matt Lewis, proprietor of Baked, his Brooklyn bakery, prepare them. I couldn't wait to get to my oven. It was a Sunday afternoon when I wanted to make them and my corner grocery store didn't have any semisweet chocolate, so I bought some dark chocolate and milk chocolate candy bars and combined them to make up the 5 ounces needed for the recipe. The results were superb! Fudgy and slightly cakey, they are a delectable treat. Since then, I've made the brownies the way Matt intended and I suggest you do too. But if your store has only dark and milk chocolate bars, don't let that stop you.

¾ cup all-purpose flour

1 tablespoon best-quality unsweetened
    cocoa powder, preferably Valrhona

¼ teaspoon salt

8 tablespoons (1 stick) unsalted butter,
    plus extra for greasing the pan

¾ teaspoon instant espresso powder

5 ounces semisweet chocolate, finely chopped

¾ cup granulated sugar

¼ cup (packed) light brown sugar

3 large eggs, at room temperature

1 teaspoon pure vanilla extract

¾ cup (4½ ounces) semisweet chocolate chips
    (optional)

1. Preheat the oven to 350°F. Butter an 8-inch square baking pan. Line the pan with wax or parchment paper, and butter the paper.

2. Sift the flour, cocoa powder, and salt together in a medium-size bowl. Set it aside.

3. Combine the butter and espresso powder in a large heavy saucepan. Place the pan over low heat and stir until the butter has melted. Add the chocolate, and stir constantly until the mixture is smooth, about 2 minutes. Remove the pan from the heat and add both sugars, stirring until well combined.

4. Add the eggs, one at a time, to the chocolate mixture. Then add the vanilla and continue stirring until it is well incorporated and the mixture no longer appears grainy.

5. Gradually add the flour mixture to the batter, stirring until just combined. Stir in the chocolate chips, if using.

6. Scrape the batter into the prepared baking pan. Smooth the top with a spatula or the back of a wooden spoon. Bake until a toothpick inserted in the center comes out with a few moist crumbs, 28 to 30 minutes. Be sure not to overbake the brownie.

7. Let the brownie cool completely in the pan on a wire rack. Then carefully remove it from the pan, peel off the wax paper, and cut it into 9 squares. (Store the brownies, covered with wax paper, in a tightly covered tin in a cool, dry place for up to 1 week.)

THE VERY BEST
CHOCOLATE MOUSSE

SERVES 8

When you can't improve on perfection, I say leave well enough alone. Everyone I've made this for thinks it is the best chocolate mousse they've ever tasted. My friend Don Forst was kind enough to share his recipe with me back in the early '80s for our Silver Palate store. It was the most successful dessert we had in the shop. At home I serve it garnished with whipped cream or crème fraîche and a light sprinkling of chocolate shavings.

1½ pounds semisweet chocolate chips

½ cup brewed espresso

½ cup Grand Marnier

4 large egg yolks (see Notes)

2 cups heavy (whipping) cream, chilled

¼ cup sugar

8 large egg whites

Pinch of salt

½ teaspoon pure vanilla extract

Chocolate shavings, for garnish (see Notes)

1. Place the chocolate chips in a heavy saucepan and melt them, stirring constantly, over very low heat. Off the heat, add the espresso and then stir in the Grand Marnier. Let the mixture cool to room temperature.

2. Add the egg yolks, one at a time, to the cooled chocolate mixture, beating thoroughly after each addition. Set it aside.

3. Whip 1 cup of the cream in a large bowl until thickened. Gradually add the sugar, beating until the cream is thickened but not overwhipped.

4. Combine the egg whites and the salt in a large bowl, and beat with an electric mixer until they form stiff peaks. Gently fold the egg whites into the whipped cream.

5. Stir about one third of the egg white mixture into the chocolate mixture, mixing it in thoroughly. Then, using a large rubber spatula, scrape the remaining egg white mixture over the chocolate base and gently fold them together.

6. Spoon the mousse into individual dessert cups or into a serving bowl, and refrigerate until set, 2 hours.

7. At serving time, whip the remaining 1 cup cream until thickened. Add the vanilla and whip until soft peaks form. Top each serving of mousse with a dollop of the whipped cream and a sprinkling of chocolate shavings.

NOTES:

- The eggs in this mousse are uncooked, so use only the freshest eggs and be sure they've been kept refrigerated.
- To make chocolate shavings, just pull a vegetable peeler along a large chilled bar of chocolate. Keep the shavings on wax paper in a cool place until you are ready to use them. 🍀

SCHRAFFT'S HOT FUDGE SAUCE

MAKES ABOUT 2 CUPS

When I was a little girl and my mother and I came to New York City to shop, we never missed the opportunity to lunch at Schrafft's on Fifth Avenue. We always splurged on their hot fudge sundae for dessert. The sauce uses both melted chocolate and cocoa powder, resulting in a full-bodied fudgy sauce. Schrafft's is long gone, but that wonderful fudge sauce lives on. We owe a debt of gratitude to food journalist Florence Fabricant, who tracked down the luscious recipe for Richard Sax, who put it in his book *Classic Home Desserts*. Thanks to them, I can share it with you.

¼ cup best-quality unsweetened cocoa powder

½ cup sugar

1 pinch salt

½ cup whole milk

1 cup heavy (whipping) cream

1 cup light corn syrup

3 ounces best-quality semisweet chocolate
    (such as Scharffen Berger, Callebaut, or
    Valrhona)

Few drops of cider vinegar

2 tablespoons unsalted butter, cut into thin slices

1 teaspoon pure vanilla extract

1. Whisk the cocoa powder, sugar, salt, and milk together in a heavy saucepan until the mixture forms a smooth paste. Place the pan over medium heat and stir in the cream, corn syrup, 2 ounces of the chocolate, and the vinegar. Bring the mixture to a boil, whisking or stirring frequently, and cook until the sauce reaches 220° to 225°F on a candy thermometer, about 8 minutes.

2. Remove the pan from the heat. Whisk in the butter, vanilla, and the remaining 1 ounce chocolate, stirring until the sauce is smooth. Set it aside for a few minutes before serving.

NOTE: This sauce keeps well. Store it, in a tightly covered jar or container, in the refrigerator for 3 weeks or longer. Rewarm it before serving, either by spooning a little into a small skillet or by heating the entire jar, uncovered, in a microwave oven. You can also place the jar in a saucepan of cold water and slowly bring it to a bare simmer. 🍂

CHOCOLATE CHERRY BREAD PUDDING

SERVES 12

You may have tasted many bread puddings during your culinary adventures, but I guarantee you've never tasted one quite as scrumptious as this. While I've used French bread rather than an eggy brioche, you are welcome to try the brioche—different, but equally successful. Because of the chocolate, I prefer to serve the hot pudding with whipped cream or crème fraîche, or with vanilla or eggnog ice cream, rather than with a whiskey sauce.

1 large loaf French bread, cut into 1-inch-thick slices

4 tablespoons (½ stick) unsalted butter, melted

1 quart whole milk

8 ounces (1 cup) semisweet chocolate chips

1 tablespoon unsalted butter, for greasing the pan

4 large eggs, at room temperature

1½ cups sugar

2 tablespoons pure vanilla extract

1 cup dried tart cherries

1 cup heavy (whipping) cream, whipped, or
    1 cup crème fraîche, for serving

2 ounces semisweet chocolate shavings
    (see Note, page 382), for garnish

1. Position a rack 4 inches from the heat source, and preheat the broiler.

2. Arrange the bread slices on a baking sheet and toast them under the broiler until lightly browned, 1 to 2 minutes per side. Set them aside to cool.

3. When the toasted bread has cooled, tear it into 1½-inch pieces and place them in a large bowl. Drizzle the melted butter over the bread, and toss well.

4. Pour the milk into a heavy saucepan, add the chocolate chips, and heat over low heat, stirring often, until the chocolate has melted. Allow the mixture to cool slightly, about 10 minutes. Then pour the chocolate mixture over the bread, making sure all the pieces are coated. Let it sit, tossing it occasionally, for 1 hour.

5. Position a rack in the center of the oven, and preheat the oven to 325°F. Butter a 13-x-9-x-2-inch baking dish with the butter. Set the dish aside.

6. Combine the eggs, sugar, and vanilla in a medium-size bowl, and whisk well. Add the egg mixture and the dried cherries to the soaked bread, and fold the mixture together with a large rubber spatula.

7. Transfer the mixture to the prepared baking dish, and bake until the pudding is set, about 1 hour and 10 minutes.

8. To serve, cut the pudding into 12 rectangular pieces, and place each one on a dessert dish. Dollop each serving with whipped cream, and sprinkle with chocolate shavings. ✣

CHOCOLATE SOUFFLES

SERVES 6

O

Individual chocolate soufflés are a celebration unto themselves, especially when you don't have too many other last-minute preparations to take care of. There's a handy trick here to make it easier if you're serving them for company: Preparing the chocolate mixture ahead and keeping it warm in a thermos allows you to avoid being absent from your guests for too long. Just serve a cheese course while you excuse yourself to whip up the egg whites.

> 5 ounces good-quality bittersweet or semisweet chocolate, coarsely chopped
>
> ½ cup heavy (whipping) cream
>
> 3 large egg yolks, at room temperature
>
> 1 teaspoon pure vanilla extract
>
> Butter, for greasing the ramekins
>
> 5 large egg whites, at room temperature
>
> ¼ cup granulated sugar, plus extra for dusting the ramekins
>
> Confectioners' sugar, for garnish

1. Place the chocolate and the cream in a saucepan over low heat and cook, stirring, until the chocolate has melted and the mixture is smooth and incorporated, about 5 minutes. Let the mixture cool for 5 minutes.

2. Whisk the egg yolks, one at a time, into the chocolate mixture. Then whisk in the vanilla. Pour the mixture into a wide-mouthed thermos to keep it warm. This can be done as much as 4 hours ahead, if desired.

3. Shortly before you sit down to dinner, position a rack in the center of the oven and preheat to 425°F.

4. At the same time, generously butter six ⅔-cup ramekins, and chill them in the freezer for 20 minutes. Then butter the ramekins again and dust them all over with granulated sugar. Hold them in the refrigerator while you eat dinner.

5. When you are ready to bake the soufflés, use an electric mixer to beat the egg whites in a medium-size bowl until stiff peaks form. Add the sugar and continue beating until the whites are glossy and firm.

6. Pour the reserved chocolate mixture—which should be lukewarm—into a large bowl. Stir one fourth of the egg whites into the chocolate mixture. Using a rubber spatula, gently fold in the remaining egg whites until they are just combined.

7. Divide the soufflé mixture among the prepared ramekins, filling them to the top. Smooth the tops and run a finger around the inside edge (the top ⅓ inch) of each ramekin so it is completely clean (this will encourage the soufflé to rise).

8. Place the ramekins on a baking sheet and bake until the soufflés are puffed and set around the edges, about 6 minutes. Dust with confectioners' sugar, and serve. 🪷

SINFUL CHOCOLATE TART

SERVES 8 TO 10

this fudgy pie is filled with an incredibly rich chocolate ganache. Serve a dollop of crème fraîche alongside each wedge of tart to cut the richness. Since chocolate is the star here, use only the best quality; Valrhona and Scharffen Berger are two good brands.

FOR THE TART CRUST:

8 tablespoons (1 stick) unsalted butter, chilled,
    cut into cubes

½ cup confectioners' sugar

½ cup almond flour (see Note)

⅓ cup plus 1¼ cups all-purpose flour

1 large egg, lightly beaten

½ teaspoon pure vanilla extract

½ teaspoon salt

FOR THE CHOCOLATE GANACHE FILLING:

12 ounces good-quality bittersweet or semisweet
    chocolate, chopped (chips or pastilles can be used)

1¼ cups heavy (whipping) cream

1 tablespoon light corn syrup

1 tablespoon unsalted butter

FOR SERVING:

8 ounces crème fraîche

1. Prepare the tart crust: Using an electric mixer, beat the butter, confectioners' sugar, almond flour, the ⅓ cup all-purpose flour, and the egg and vanilla in a bowl, scraping down the sides of the bowl as needed, until well combined, about 2 minutes. Add the remaining 1¼ cups flour and the salt, and mix until just blended. Form the dough into a thick disk. Wrap it in plastic wrap and refrigerate it for at least 2 hours or as long as 2 days. Or, for faster chilling, place the wrapped dough in the freezer for 30 minutes.

2. Preheat the oven to 350°F.

3. Remove the dough from the refrigerator and roll it out on a lightly floured work surface to form an 11-inch round, about ¼ inch thick. Fit the dough into a 9-inch tart pan with a removable bottom, and trim off the overhang.

4. Bake the tart crust until it is golden brown, about 15 minutes. Place the pan on a wire rack and allow the crust to cool. When the crust is cool enough to handle, carefully remove it from the sides of the pan and place the crust on a decorative plate. Set it aside.

5. Prepare the ganache filling: Place the chocolate in a medium-size bowl, and set it aside.

6. Combine the cream, corn syrup, and butter in a saucepan over medium heat and bring just to a boil, stirring to combine. Immediately pour this over the reserved chocolate, and cover the bowl with plastic

wrap. Let it stand for 1 minute, and then stir to combine. Re-cover the bowl, let it stand for 1 minute longer, and then stir again. Set the ganache aside to cool for about 15 minutes.

7. Pour the ganache mixture into the tart crust. Let it sit at room temperature until it is thickened and set, 2 to 4 hours; or chill it in the refrigerator for 2 hours.

8. Cut the tart into thin wedges and serve, with the crème fraîche alongside.

NOTE: If you cannot find almond flour, you can make it yourself: Place 1 cup sliced or slivered blanched almonds and 1 tablespoon cornstarch in a food processor, and process until very fine. Use as directed. ❧

RASPBERRY CHOCOLATE TRUFFLES

MAKES 20 PIECES

While they may seem a little old-fashioned, nobody ever refuses a chocolate truffle. They grace the finest chocolate shops, and now they'll be gracing your table. Chambord, a French black raspberry liqueur, is the perfect flavor to combine with chocolate for these delectable after-dinner treats.

2 tablespoons heavy (whipping) cream
1 tablespoon whole milk
1½ tablespoons sugar
4½ ounces best-quality semisweet chocolate,
    broken into pieces
1 tablespoon Chambord
About ¼ cup best-quality unsweetened cocoa powder

1. Place the cream, milk, and sugar in a small heavy saucepan. Stir, and bring slowly to a boil over medium-low heat. Remove the pan from the heat, add the chocolate, and stir until it has melted completely.

2. Add the Chambord and stir until the mixture is perfectly smooth. Using a rubber spatula, scrape it into a shallow bowl. Refrigerate the mixture until it has thickened to the consistency of thick cake icing, about 50 minutes.

3. Place the cocoa powder in a shallow bowl.

4. Remove the chocolate mixture from the refrigerator. Using a teaspoon, scoop it out and shape it into 1-inch balls. Roll the balls in the cocoa powder, and place them on a plate. Store the truffles, loosely covered with foil, in the refrigerator until serving time. ❧

"...WORTHY OF A CUT-CRYSTAL CAKE STAND..."

HOMEMADE CAKES AND TEA CAKES

A cake, beautifully frosted and perched high on a cut-glass cake stand—is there a dessert more glamorous and tempting? Cakes are synonymous with celebrations and not just birthdays—all special occasions deserve a made-from-scratch cake. There are all kinds of cakes to show off with. Bundts and loaf cakes and single layers and more—whether you're impressing your boss, welcoming friends and family, or honoring a retiring coworker, freshly baked cakes make you look good.

On the hit parade are chocolate cakes—of course—but you'll find those in the Chocolate chapter (page 375). Here vying for a top spot are a moist and delicious carrot cake, a spectacular strawberry shortcake, a gorgeous coconut cake, a creamy but light ricotta cheesecake, my friend Laura Donnelly's toffee date cake—plus five more favorites.

The cakes included are not hard to bake and the results are worth the effort. Your family will thank you, your friends will thank you, and your boss will definitely give you a raise. They're that good! 🌿

COCONUT LAYER CAKE

SERVES 10 TO 12

In my opinion, there is nothing yummier than a coconut cake. This light and fluffy version is close to perfection, and it's my choice for my birthday cake this year. Of course, there will be only one pink candle in the center!

FOR THE CAKE:

8 tablespoons (1 stick) unsalted butter, at room temperature, plus extra for greasing the pans

All-purpose or cake flour for dusting the pans

1½ cups granulated sugar

2 large eggs, at room temperature

1 teaspoon pure vanilla extract

2¼ cups cake flour

1 tablespoon baking powder

½ teaspoon salt

1 cup buttermilk

1½ cups (about 6 ounces) shredded sweetened coconut, finely chopped

FOR THE FROSTING:

8 ounces cream cheese, at room temperature

6 tablespoons unsalted butter, at room temperature

1 teaspoon pure vanilla extract

3 cups confectioners' sugar, sifted

1½ cups (about 6 ounces) shredded sweetened coconut

1. Position a rack in the center of the oven, and preheat the oven to 350°F. Butter the bottoms and sides of two 9-inch round cake pans. Line the bottoms with rounds of wax or parchment paper, and butter the paper. Dust the bottoms and sides of the pans with flour, tapping out any excess.

2. Prepare the cake: Using an electric mixer on medium speed, cream the butter in a large bowl until it is light and creamy, 2 minutes. Add the sugar and beat until the mixture is light, 4 minutes. Then add the eggs, one at a time, beating well after each addition. Stir in the vanilla.

3. Sift the cake flour, baking powder, and salt together into another bowl. Add one third of the flour mixture to the butter mixture, beating on low speed until it is incorporated. Add half of the buttermilk and beat until incorporated, scraping down the sides of the bowl. Repeat with another third of the flour, followed by the remaining buttermilk. Add the remaining flour, scrape down the sides of the bowl, and beat on medium speed until well incorporated. Beat in the shredded coconut until combined.

4. Scrape the batter evenly into the prepared pans, and bake until a wooden toothpick inserted in the center of a layer comes out clean, 25 minutes.

5. Let the layers cool in the pans on a wire rack for 10 minutes. Then invert the layers onto the wire rack, carefully peel off the paper, and let them cool completely.

6. Prepare the frosting: Place the cream cheese, butter, and vanilla in a large bowl and beat until smooth and well blended, 2 minutes. Add the confectioners' sugar and beat on low speed until the frosting is smooth.

7. To assemble the cake, place a cake layer, right side up (level it off with a serrated knife if it is uneven), on a serving plate. Spread it with one third of the frosting. Top with the remaining layer, right side up. Frost the sides and top of the cake with the remaining frosting. Using your hands, press about ¾ cup of the coconut onto the sides of the cake, and then sprinkle the remaining coconut evenly over the top. (This cake is best served at room temperature; stored in an airtight container, it will keep for up to 3 days at room temperature or for 5 to 6 days in the refrigerator.)

NOTE: If you are an avid cake baker, it's worth investing in a cake stand and a plastic or glass cake cover to fit over your cakes in order to store them properly.

VANILLA

Vanilla intoxicates. It's no longer simply relegated to the dessert pantry, where it does its mighty magic; now we coax those tiny black seeds into sweet melted butter to poach lobsters and roast pork loins in a vanilla-scented sauce. A dab of vanilla oil behind each ear is my aphrodisiac of choice.

The vanilla plant, with its vines reaching over 100 feet, produces a pale yellow orchid. When it is pollinated, it develops pods, or beans, that contain hundreds of black seeds. Once the beans are dried in the sun and cured, they acquire the distinctive aroma we know as vanilla.

Vanilla beans are an extremely valuable commodity, and there are always booms and busts when dealing in commodities. Of course weather is a prime factor, supply and demand another. One region thrives, another not. Mexico booms one year, Madagascar may not, or Indonesia may be offering better prices. Today's high-quality vanilla beans are at an all-time high, demanding as much as $500 per kilogram. They are so valuable, it is often necessary for growers to hire guards to watch over their crops.

While we covet a vanilla bean, most of us are apt to reach for pure vanilla extract in our cooking. To make the extract, the dried beans are slivered into small pieces and a mixture of warm water and alcohol is percolated through them several times (imagine a large urn of coffee). This process intensifies the flavor. The liquid is strained, aged, and bottled. The vanilla extract can be aged in oak barrels for up to 10 years.

When shopping for vanilla for your cakes and cooking, remember, you want pure vanilla extract. Please, no imitation vanilla flavoring in your food.

BIG STRAWBERRY SHORTCAKE

SERVES 8 TO 10

his is a spectacular dessert—a must when local berries are in season. The texture is somewhere between a pound cake and a classic layer cake. Assembly is easy, if you don't eat it all while making it!

FOR THE CAKE:

1 cup (2 sticks) unsalted butter, plus extra
    for greasing the pans

2 cups all-purpose flour, sifted, plus extra
    for dusting the pans

2 cups sugar

2 teaspoons finely grated orange zest

3 tablespoons fresh orange juice

5 large eggs, at room temperature

FOR THE FILLING:

2 pints ripe strawberries, lightly rinsed,
    patted dry, and hulled

3 tablespoons sugar

2 cups heavy (whipping) cream

1 teaspoon pure vanilla extract

1. Position a rack in the center of the oven, and preheat the oven to 350°F. Butter the bottom and sides of two 9-inch round cake pans. Line the bottoms with rounds of wax or parchment paper, and butter the paper. Dust the bottoms and sides of the pans with flour, tapping out any excess. Set the pans aside.

2. Prepare the cake: Using an electric mixer, cream the butter until it is pale yellow, about 2 minutes.

Add the sugar and beat until the mixture is light and fluffy, about 2 minutes. Add the flour and mix until just blended. Add the orange zest and juice. Add the eggs, one at a time, beating well after each addition.

3. Scrape the batter evenly into the prepared cake pans. Bake until a wooden toothpick inserted in the center comes out clean, 25 minutes.

4. Allow the cake layers to cool in the pans on a wire rack for about 20 minutes. Then invert the layers onto the wire rack, carefully peel off the wax paper, and let them cool completely. (The cake layers can be baked 1 day ahead. Wrap them in aluminum foil and refrigerate them.)

5. About 4 hours before serving, prepare the filling: Set aside the 12 best strawberries for garnish. Quarter the remaining strawberries and toss them in a bowl with 2 tablespoons of the sugar. Cover and refrigerate for 4 hours for the juices to form.

6. About 2 hours before serving, combine the cream, vanilla, and the remaining 1 tablespoon sugar in a bowl, and whip until it holds soft peaks.

7. Place a cake layer, right side up (level it off with serrated knife if it is uneven), on a pedestal cake stand. Spoon half of the quartered strawberries over the cake. Spread half of the whipped cream over the strawberries. Cover with the remaining cake layer. Spoon the remaining quartered strawberries over the cake, and then cover with the remaining whipped cream. Arrange the whole berries decoratively on top.

8. Serve the cake immediately, or keep it in the refrigerator for up to 4 hours before serving. It's best eaten right away. ❧

BERTA'S
CARROT TEA CAKE

SERVES 12

My mother's carrot cake is so moist and flavorful that it has appeared, in different forms, in each one of my cookbooks. This book will be no different. When we first opened the Silver Palate shop, she delivered a carrot cake every week. This loaf cake version is easy to slice, and I love to serve it with tea—I'd recommend an orange pekoe. A scoop of vanilla ice cream is delicious as well.

FOR THE CAKE:

Butter, for greasing the pan

2 cups all-purpose flour

2 teaspoons baking soda

2 teaspoons ground cinnamon

3 large eggs, at room temperature

1 cup corn or canola oil

1 tablespoon pure vanilla extract

1½ cups granulated sugar

½ cup (packed) dark brown sugar

1½ cups (packed) grated fresh carrots
    (about 6 carrots)

1 cup coarsely chopped walnuts

1 cup shredded sweetened coconut

¾ cup drained canned crushed pineapple

FOR THE CREAM CHEESE FROSTING:

4 ounces cream cheese, at room temperature

2 tablespoons unsalted butter, at room
    temperature

2 teaspoons finely grated orange zest

½ teaspoon fresh orange juice

2½ cups confectioners' sugar, sifted

1. Position a rack in the center of the oven, and preheat the oven to 350°F. Butter a 9-x-5-x-2¾-inch loaf pan. Line the bottom of the pan with wax paper, and butter the paper. Set the pan aside.

2. Prepare the cake: Sift the flour, baking soda, and cinnamon together into a medium-size bowl.

3. Beat the eggs lightly in a mixing bowl. Add the oil, vanilla, granulated sugar, and brown sugar. Using an electric mixer, beat on high speed until the mixture is very smooth, 5 minutes. Add the flour mixture and mix until just combined. Then stir in the carrots, walnuts, coconut, and pineapple until just combined.

4. Scrape the batter into the prepared loaf pan. Tap the pan on the counter to level the batter. Bake until a toothpick inserted in the center comes out just clean, about 1¼ hours.

5. Let the cake cool in the pan on a wire rack for 10 minutes. Then invert the cake onto a plate, remove the wax paper, and set it, right side up, on the wire rack to cool completely.

6. Prepare the cream cheese frosting: Using an electric mixer, cream the cream cheese and butter together in a bowl until the mixture is fluffy, 4 minutes. Mix in the orange zest and juice. Slowly add 2¼ cups of the confectioners' sugar, beating until fully incorporated, about 3 minutes.

7. Place the cooled loaf on a cake plate, and spread the frosting over just the top. Dust the top of the cake with the remaining ¼ cup confectioners' sugar. Cut it into slices for serving. (Stored in an airtight container, the cake will keep for 2 days at room temperature or for 1 week in the fridge.)

CINNAMON

Beguiling cinnamon is at home on everyone's spice rack. Recipes both sweet and savory depend on its fragrant flavor. In the United States, most of what we call cinnamon is actually a closely related spice called cassia. Two varieties are especially highly regarded.

KORINTJI, OR INDONESIAN CINNAMON, has a warm, delicate flavor. It comes from small young trees with a very thin bark that emits a mild citrusy flavor, making it a most pleasant aromatic. This cinnamon grows in western Sumatra.

SAIGON CINNAMON is highly coveted and the most richly flavored cinnamon available—you can find the ground version in the spice aisle of your supermarket. This Vietnamese cinnamon is cultivated mostly on small farms. The prize cinnamon is from the thickest bark on the lowest three feet of the trees.

Korintji cinnamon, with its delicate flavor, is best for baking, while Saigon cinnamon, with its robust flavor, is best for stews such as curries, couscous, and Greek dishes. It stands out in rubs and marinades.

If you see it at your local spice shop, give true cinnamon, sometimes called Ceylon cinnamon, a try. It has a milder flavor and a paler tan color.

CHOCOLATE ORANGE TEA CAKE

SERVES 8 TO 10

Chocolate and orange have an affinity for each other, and no cake shows it off better than this moist tea cake. It's lovely served at teatime—or after dinner, topped with mango sorbet.

FOR THE CAKE:

1 cup all-purpose flour

½ cup unsweetened cocoa powder, plus extra
    for dusting the loaf pan

½ teaspoon ground cinnamon

½ teaspoon baking powder

¼ teaspoon baking soda

½ teaspoon salt

¾ cup (1½ sticks) unsalted butter, at room
    temperature, plus extra for greasing the
    loaf pan

⅔ cup (packed) dark brown sugar

⅔ cup granulated sugar

2 large eggs, at room temperature

1 tablespoon pure vanilla extract

¾ cup buttermilk

Finely grated zest of 1 orange

FOR THE CINNAMON WHIPPED CREAM:

1 cup heavy (whipping) cream

2 tablespoons granulated sugar

¼ teaspoon ground cinnamon

¼ teaspoon pure vanilla extract

1. Position a rack in the center of the oven, and preheat the oven to 325°F. Lightly butter a 9-x-5-x-2¾-inch loaf pan. Line the bottom of the pan with a piece of waxed or parchment paper, and butter the paper. Dust the bottom and sides of the pan with cocoa powder, tapping out any excess.

2. Prepare the cake: Sift the flour, cocoa powder, cinnamon, baking powder, baking soda, and salt together into a medium-size bowl.

3. Place the butter, brown sugar, and granulated sugar in a large bowl and cream with an electric mixer until the mixture is light and fluffy, about 5 minutes. Add the eggs, one at a time, beating well after each addition. Add the vanilla.

4. With the mixer on low speed, add the flour mixture in thirds, alternating with the buttermilk and scraping down the sides of the bowl as needed; mix until well combined. Then mix in the orange zest.

5. Scrape the batter into the prepared loaf pan, and bake until a wooden toothpick inserted in the center comes out clean, about 1 hour.

6. Let the loaf cool in the pan on a wire rack for 10 minutes. Then run a knife around the edges of the pan to loosen the cake, remove it from the pan, and place it, right side up, on the wire rack to cool.

7. Prepare the cinnamon whipped cream: Using an electric mixer on medium speed, beat the cream in a large bowl until it becomes frothy. Add the sugar, cinnamon, and vanilla, and continue beating until the cream holds soft peaks. Do not overbeat.

8. Serve the cake slightly warm, dolloped with the whipped cream. (Well wrapped, this cake will keep for 3 days at room temperature or for 5 days in the fridge.) ❧

MARBLE CAKE

SERVES 8 TO 10

According to Jean Anderson's *American Century Cookbook*, marble cakes began to appear in the United States after the Civil War. The dark part was usually colored with molasses or a mixture of spices. Chocolate marble cakes are a twentieth-century invention. This one is like a pound cake—fairly dense and tightly crumbed. The chocolate is mild, not fudgy, and balances with the vanilla for the perfect any-occasion cake.

8 tablespoons (1 stick) unsalted butter, at room
    temperature, plus extra for greasing the pan

2¼ cups all-purpose flour, plus extra for dusting the pan

1 tablespoon baking powder

½ teaspoon salt

1¼ cups sugar

3 large eggs, at room temperature

1 teaspoon pure vanilla extract

½ cup whole milk

½ cup sour cream

4 ounces semisweet chocolate, melted and cooled

1. Position a rack in the center of the oven, and preheat the oven to 350°F. Butter a 9-x-5-x-2¾-inch loaf pan. Line the bottom of the pan with parchment or wax paper, and butter the paper. Lightly flour the pan, shaking out the excess.

2. Prepare the batter: Sift the flour, baking powder, and salt together into a bowl.

3. Using an electric mixer, cream the butter in a large bowl for 3 minutes. Add the sugar and beat until the mixture is light and fluffy, 3 minutes. Add the eggs, one at a time, beating well after each addition. Beat in the vanilla.

4. Add the flour mixture in thirds, alternating with the milk and sour cream (start and end with the dry ingredients), mixing just enough to combine the ingredients after each addition.

5. Scrape half of the batter into another bowl and add the melted chocolate to it. Mix just until combined.

6. Place alternating spoonfuls of the two batters in the prepared loaf pan until both are used up. Drag a knife lengthwise through the batter in three evenly spaced lines, all going the same direction. Then drag the knife lengthwise in the opposite direction, making two lines between the first lines. Don't overdo it or you will lose the marble effect.

7. Bake the cake until a wooden toothpick inserted in the center comes out clean, about 1 hour.

8. Let the loaf cool in the pan on a wire rack for 10 minutes. Then run a knife around the edges of the pan to loosen the cake, remove it from the pan, peel off the paper, and place it, right side up, on a wire rack to cool completely. (Well wrapped, the cake will keep for 4 days at room temperature or up to 6 days in the refrigerator.)

LAURIE'S
LEMON SPICE CAKE

SERVES 12

Gingerbread is an American favorite with a great warm-from-the-oven aroma. When Laurie set out to make this cake, she was looking for a subtler version of gingerbread, using a few of the hallmark spices: ginger, nutmeg, and cinnamon. And she succeeded—baked in a Bundt pan, the results turned out to be a delicate, sophisticated cake, infused with a complementary lemon glaze. It is much lighter on the spices than gingerbread, and the lemon zest freshens it up, making it spring-y, not winter-y. This is worthy of a cut-crystal cake stand and a scoop of creamy Key Lime Ice Cream (page 423).

1½ cups (3 sticks) unsalted butter, at room
    temperature, plus extra for greasing the pan

3 cups all-purpose flour, plus extra for dusting the pan

1½ teaspoons baking powder

1½ teaspoons salt

1½ teaspoons ground nutmeg

1½ teaspoons ground coriander

¾ teaspoon ground cinnamon

¾ teaspoon ground cloves

¾ teaspoon ground ginger

2⅔ cups (packed) dark brown sugar

3 large eggs, at room temperature

1 tablespoon finely grated lemon zest

2 teaspoons pure vanilla extract

1½ cups sour cream

FOR THE GLAZE:

¾ cup confectioners' sugar

1 tablespoon fresh lemon juice, or more
    as needed

1. Position a rack in the center of the oven, and preheat the oven to 350°F. Butter a 12-cup Bundt pan. Dust the pan with flour, tapping out any excess. Set the pan aside.

2. Whisk the flour, baking powder, salt, and all the spices together in a bowl. Set aside.

3. Using an electric mixer, cream the butter and brown sugar in a large bowl until the mixture is light and fluffy, about 5 minutes. With the mixer on low speed, add the eggs, one at a time, beating for 1 minute after each addition. Mix in the lemon zest, vanilla, and sour cream until combined.

4. With the mixer on low speed, add the dry ingredients gradually and mix until just combined, scraping down the sides of the bowl.

5. Scrape the batter into the prepared Bundt pan and bake until a wooden toothpick inserted in the center comes out clean, 55 minutes to 1 hour.

6. Let the cake cool in the pan on a wire rack for 20 minutes. Then unmold the cake, set it on the rack, and let it cool to room temperature.

7. Meanwhile, prepare the glaze: Combine the confectioners' sugar and the lemon juice in a small bowl. You want the mixture to fall easily from a spoon, so if it is too thick, slowly add more lemon juice, drop by drop.

8. Place the cake, still on the wire rack, on a baking sheet. Using a spoon, drizzle the glaze decoratively over the cake so that it drips down the sides. When the glaze has set, transfer the cake to a serving platter.

9. This cake is best served at room temperature. (Well wrapped, it will keep for up to 4 days at room temperature and 5 to 6 days in the refrigerator. It will keep in the freezer for up to 1 month.) ✤

CINNAMON RAISIN CAKE

SERVES 12

I have always loved cinnamon toast with lots of butter and extra cinnamon sugar—but then there are few who don't. So, I thought, why not a luscious Bundt cake with the same flavors?

1 cup (2 sticks) unsalted butter, at room
    temperature, plus extra for greasing the pan
3½ cups plus 1 tablespoon all-purpose flour,
    plus extra for dusting the pan
1 tablespoon baking powder
1 teaspoon salt
2½ cups granulated sugar
4 large eggs, at room temperature
1 teaspoon pure vanilla extract
1 cup sour cream
1 cup raisins
2 tablespoons ground cinnamon
Confectioners' sugar, for serving

1. Position a rack in the center of the oven, and preheat the oven to 350°F. Butter a 12-cup Bundt pan. Lightly flour the pan, shaking out any excess.

2. Prepare the batter: Sift the 3½ cups flour, the baking powder, and the salt together into a bowl.

3. Using an electric mixer, cream the butter in a large bowl for 3 minutes. Add 2 cups of the sugar and beat until light and fluffy, 3 minutes. Add the eggs, one at a time, beating well after each addition. Beat in the vanilla.

4. Add the flour mixture in thirds, alternating with the sour cream (start and end with the dry ingredients), mixing just enough to combine after each addition.

5. In a small bowl, toss the raisins with the remaining 1 tablespoon flour. Add them to the batter and mix until just combined.

6. In another small bowl, combine the cinnamon and the remaining ½ cup sugar.

7. Spread one third of the batter evenly in the prepared Bundt pan. Sprinkle half of the cinnamon sugar over the batter. Spread half of the remaining batter evenly in the pan. Sprinkle it evenly with the remaining cinnamon sugar. Spread the remaining batter evenly on top. Using a knife, make a zigzag pattern through the dough to marbleize the cinnamon sugar. Don't overdo it or there will be no pattern.

8. Bake the cake until a wooden toothpick inserted in the center comes out clean, about 1 hour.

9. Let the cake cool in the pan on a wire rack for 15 minutes. Then run a knife gently around the edges to loosen the cake, invert and remove it from the pan, and place it, right side up, on the rack to cool completely.

10. Just before serving, sprinkle the confectioners' sugar over the cake. (The cake will keep, well wrapped, for up to 6 days in the refrigerator.) 🌸

LAURA'S STICKY
TOFFEE DATE CAKE

SERVES 8

Iaura Donnelly was the pastry goddess of the great Laundry restaurant in East Hampton for years. Her Sticky Toffee Date Cake is renowned—I've been eating and loving it for ages. Laura was kind enough to share her recipe.

FOR THE CAKE:

8 tablespoons (1 stick) unsalted butter, at room temperature, plus extra for greasing the pan

8 ounces pitted dried dates, chopped

1 teaspoon baking soda

5 tablespoons granulated sugar

2 large eggs, at room temperature

½ teaspoon pure vanilla extract

1¼ cups all-purpose flour

½ teaspoon salt

1¾ tablespoons baking powder

FOR THE SAUCE:

1 cup (2 sticks) unsalted butter

½ cup heavy (whipping) cream

1 cup (packed) dark or light brown sugar

1 teaspoon pure vanilla extract

Vanilla ice cream or whipped cream, for serving

1. Position a rack in the center of the oven, and preheat the oven to 350°F. Butter the bottom and sides of a 9-inch round cake pan. Set the pan aside.

2. Place the chopped dates in a small saucepan, add 1 cup water, and bring to a boil over medium-high heat. Then reduce the heat to medium-low and simmer for 3 minutes. Stir in the baking soda (the mixture will bubble up slightly). Set the pan aside to cool.

3. Using an electric mixer, cream the butter and sugar together in a large bowl until the mixture is light and fluffy, about 4 minutes. With the mixer on low speed, add the eggs, one at a time, mixing well after each addition. Scrape down the sides of the bowl. Add the vanilla and mix to combine.

4. Add the flour and salt, and mix to combine. Stir in the dates, including any liquid, and then stir in the baking powder.

5. Scrape the batter into the prepared cake pan, and bake until a wooden toothpick inserted in the center comes out clean, 30 to 35 minutes. Do not overbake or the cake will be dry.

6. Let the cake cool in the pan on a wire rack for 10 minutes. Then remove the cake from the pan, and place it on a plate.

7. While the cake is cooling, prepare the sauce: Combine all the sauce ingredients in a small saucepan. Place the pan over medium-low heat and cook, stirring, until the butter has melted and the sauce is smooth, 2 to 3 minutes. Raise the heat slightly, and simmer until the sauce thickens slightly, 3 minutes. Let the sauce cool for about 5 minutes.

8. Using a skewer, poke holes all over the surface of the cake. Pour the sauce over the cake while both are still warm.

9. Serve the cake warm, with ice cream or whipped cream on top.

NOTES:

+ Laura says this cake freezes very well: Cool the cake completely, cut it into wedges, and then freeze the wedges individually, well wrapped, for up to 2 months. A slice can then be thawed and reheated.

+ The cake can be reheated in a 350°F oven for 10 minutes.

BILL YOSSES'S
VANILLA CAKE

SERVES 8

Bill Yosses—one of our cherished master bakers, now the chief baker at the White House—creates some of the most original cakes and tarts I have ever tasted. His vanilla cake is just one example of his creativity.

Although Bill has always loved chocolate, he feels that vanilla has never gotten its due, and that such an extraordinary flavor should take center stage. The chunks of white chocolate baked into the center of these individual cakes form a divinely creamy center.

The batter is prepared a day ahead and refrigerated overnight, so plan accordingly.

7 tablespoons unsalted butter

10 ounces good-quality white chocolate

5 large eggs, at room temperature, separated

3 vanilla beans, split lengthwise, seeds scraped out and reserved (see Notes)

⅓ cup all-purpose flour

1 pinch cream of tartar

⅓ cup granulated sugar

Butter or vegetable cooking spray, for greasing the molds

Confectioners' sugar, for garnish

Vanilla ice cream, for serving

1. The day before you plan to serve the cake, prepare the batter: Combine the butter and 7 ounces of the white chocolate in the top of a double boiler, and set it over simmering water. When the butter and white chocolate have melted, remove the pan from the heat and stir until smooth. Transfer the mixture to a large mixing bowl and let it cool for 5 minutes.

2. Whisk the egg yolks and vanilla seeds into the white chocolate mixture. Sift the flour over the mixture, and blend it in with a wooden spoon. Set it aside.

3. Place the egg whites in a large bowl, add the cream of tartar, and beat with an electric mixer on low speed until foamy. Increase the speed to high and gradually add the sugar. Continue beating until the egg whites are shiny and stiff, 5 to 7 minutes.

4. Using a large rubber spatula, fold the egg whites into the white chocolate mixture until smooth and combined. Cover the bowl with plastic wrap, and refrigerate overnight.

5. The next day, position a rack in the center of the oven and preheat the oven to 375°F. Butter, or coat generously with vegetable cooking spray, eight individual 4-ounce aluminum cupcake-shaped molds (see Notes). Cut small parchment or wax paper rounds to fit in the bottom of the molds, and place them in the molds. Have eight dessert plates ready for when the cakes come out of the oven.

6. Break the remaining 3 ounces white chocolate into ½-inch pieces. Set them aside.

7. Spoon the batter into the prepared molds, filling them three-quarters full. Insert the chocolate pieces into the center of the batter, dividing them evenly and covering them with the batter. Smooth the surface with the back of a spoon.

8. Place the filled molds on a baking sheet, evenly spaced so the heat will circulate well. Bake until the cakes are golden brown and give some resistance when pressed (they should feel like a filled balloon), 12 to 14 minutes.

9. Remove the molds from the oven, and run the tip of a paring knife carefully around the edge to loosen the cakes. Tap each mold gently on a work surface to loosen the cake, and then invert it onto a plate, tapping the mold gently if it doesn't lift right off. Remove the parchment paper.

10. Sprinkle the cakes with confectioners' sugar, and serve with vanilla ice cream.

NOTES:

+ The 4-ounce aluminum molds can be found in good kitchen supply shops. They measure 1¾ inches tall, 2½ inches diameter across the top, and 2 inches in diameter across the bottom. Similarly sized ramekins could also be used—or you could even cut apart a disposable cupcake pan to make individual molds.

+ Don't throw away those scraped-out vanilla beans! Place them in a large jar, add 4 to 6 cups granulated sugar, cover the jar, and let it sit for 3 weeks to create vanilla sugar. As you use the sugar, keep adding more to the jar. The beans will keep indefinitely.

FRESH LEMON
RICOTTA CHEESECAKE

SERVES 16

This cheesecake is creamy, but light and fluffy, thanks to the delicate fresh ricotta cheese. Spoon some fresh strawberry sauce (page 412) over the cake when the berries are in season.

FOR THE CAKE:

Unsalted butter for greasing the pan

⅓ cup fresh bread crumbs (see Note, page 91)

1 pound fresh ricotta cheese (from the cheese
    counter or store, not from the dairy case)

1 pound cream cheese, at room temperature

6 large eggs, at room temperature

1 cup sugar

1½ teaspoons pure vanilla extract

1 tablespoon finely grated lemon zest

FOR THE TOPPING:

1½ cups sour cream

¼ cup sugar

1 teaspoon pure vanilla extract

1 tablespoon finely grated lemon zest

1. Position a rack in the center of the oven, and preheat the oven to 350°F. Lightly butter the bottom and sides of a 9-inch springform pan. Coat the pan with the bread crumbs, shaking out the excess. Set the pan aside.

2. Strain the ricotta into a large mixing bowl, using the back of a spoon to push it through the strainer. Add the cream cheese to the bowl, and beat with an electric mixer on medium speed until smooth, about 5 minutes. Add the eggs, one at a time, beating well after each addition. Add the sugar, vanilla, and lemon zest, and beat until smooth, about 3 minutes.

3. Place the prepared springform pan on a baking sheet. Pour the cheesecake mixture into the pan, and bake until the cake is set and the top is beginning to brown, about 1 hour. (To test, shake the springform pan slightly: if the cake jiggles, it isn't set yet.) Reduce the heat to 300°F and bake until the top is light golden brown, 15 minutes.

4. Meanwhile, combine all the topping ingredients in a bowl, and mix well.

5. Remove the cheesecake from the oven, leaving the heat on. Carefully spread the topping over the cheesecake. Return the cheesecake to the oven and bake until the topping is set, 20 minutes.

6. Let the cheesecake cool completely in the pan on a wire rack. (Do not remove the springform sides.) When it has cooled, cover it with plastic wrap and refrigerate it for 4 hours or as long as overnight.

7. Run a knife around the rim of the pan to loosen the cake. Remove the springform sides, and transfer the cheesecake to a decorative plate. Refrigerate it until you are ready to serve it. Refrigerate any leftovers. ❧

"EASY, SIMPLE, SIMPLY DELICIOUS . . ."

FRUIT DESSERTS

Fruit, fresh and perfectly ripe, needs no help when it comes to enjoying it. Still, whenever I think of a fruit dessert, the first thing that comes to my mind is pies, hot out of the oven, their luscious aromas wafting around the house. In the fall, there are apple pies made with a variety of apples tossed up in a fragrant mix of cinnamon, nutmeg, and sugar. When the apricot season arrives in summer, a sumptuous French-style Fresh Apricot-Almond Tart is a must. So, too, is an outrageously delicious Peach Blueberry Pie, especially with a lattice top crust and all the baked fruit juices oozing in and out of it. When the local strawberries are in season, Strawberries-and-Cream Tart is another beauty.

While we're in summer, a Summer Berry Crisp combines blackberries, blueberries, and raspberries, their fresh sweet juices touched up with a little sugar and cinnamon. The crisp topping complements the hot juicy fruit. It's a scrumptious dessert served with whipped cream or vanilla ice cream.

Cold Cherry Borscht and Blueberry Fool on a Berry Fruit Salad—even a new take on an old Southern favorite, ambrosia—are easy to prepare and give fruit the center stage it deserves. ❧

COLD CHERRY BORSCHT

SERVES 4

O

I've always been a big fan of beet borscht, so after recently enjoying a big bowl of cherries in season, I thought, why not blend them with a fruity wine to create a rich dessert soup that's reminiscent of its vegetable counterpart? The play of sweet and sour brings out the best of the fruit's natural flavors. Just a dollop of crème fraîche tops the soup off.

3 pounds fresh Bing cherries, unpitted,
    stems removed

3 cups Beaujolais wine

1 teaspoon salt, or more to taste

Juice of 2 lemons

3 tablespoons sugar

½ cup crème fraîche, for garnish

4 mint sprigs, for garnish

4 small lavender sprigs, for garnish
    (optional)

1. Reserve 4 of the best cherries for garnish. Place the remaining cherries in a medium-size heavy nonreactive pot.

2. Add the wine, salt, and 3 cups water, and bring to a boil. Then reduce the heat to medium-low, partially cover the pot, and simmer for 30 minutes, skimming off any foam that forms on the surface. As they cook, mash the cherries down a bit to release the juice.

3. Remove the pot from the heat and drain the cherries through a strainer set over a large bowl, pressing down on them with the back of a spoon to extract all the juices. Discard the strained cherries. Return the juices to the pot, and add the lemon juice and sugar. Heat the juices over medium-low heat to dissolve the sugar, about 2 minutes. Taste the soup to see if the right balance of sweet and sour is achieved, and adjust the flavor as needed.

4. Let cool to room temperature, then transfer the soup to a container, cover, and refrigerate for at least 6 hours or overnight.

5. When you are ready to serve the dessert, pit the reserved 4 cherries and halve them lengthwise. Ladle the cold borscht into four bowls. Garnish each portion with 2 cherry halves, a dollop of crème fraîche, a mint sprig, and a lavender sprig if desired. ✤

SUMMER FRUIT SALAD

SERVES 4

There's an amazing moment in June and July when all the summer fruits are ripe. That's the time to make this extraordinary salad—which might seem simple, but the particular flavors, colors, shapes, and sizes are combined in a very special kaleidoscope of nature's best. Raspberries are delicate, so add them just before serving.

8 chunks ripe cantaloupe (1-inch pieces)

8 chunks honeydew melon (1-inch pieces)

2 navel oranges, peeled, each cut crosswise into
   8 thin slices

6 ripe strawberries, lightly rinsed, hulled, and
   halved lengthwise

12 chunks ripe fresh pineapple (1-inch pieces)

4 thin slices peeled kiwi

4 to 6 chunks ripe papaya (1-inch pieces)

14 blueberries, lightly rinsed and patted dry

8 blackberries, lightly rinsed and patted dry

10 raspberries, lightly rinsed and patted dry

2 tablespoons chopped fresh mint leaves

1. Combine all the fruit except the raspberries in a large bowl.

2. Fifteen minutes before serving, gently fold in the raspberries, and then toss with the mint.

3. Serve the fruit salad in small glass bowls.

SOMETHING SPECIAL

Fruit salads featuring summer fruits are always inviting, but if the occasion is really special, serve this one in red wine glasses with a small scoop of Pineapple Sorbet (page 431) on top. Add a fresh mint sprig to each serving.

BLUEBERRY FOOL
ON A BERRY FRUIT SALAD

SERVES 6

the word *fool* was at one time synonymous with *trifle*, meaning a thing of little consequence. Evidently a dessert of whipped cream folded with pureed cooked fruit was considered a mere trifle. Not in my book! I've always thought that a fool is one of the most satisfying desserts in the world, and this one, made with blueberries, is thoroughly memorable. I've gently folded the lightly cooked, chilled blueberries into the cream so that they create a marbleized effect. The fool is spooned over a midnight-blue blueberry and blackberry salad. A midsummer evening's dream . . .

FOR THE BLUEBERRY FOOL (makes 1 quart):

1 pint (2 cups) fresh blueberries, lightly rinsed
    and patted dry

¼ cup plus 3 tablespoons sugar

1½ cups heavy (whipping) cream

1 teaspoon pure vanilla extract

½ cup crème fraîche

FOR THE BERRY FRUIT SALAD:

1 pint (2 cups) fresh blueberries, lightly rinsed
    and patted dry

1 pint (2 cups) fresh blackberries, lightly rinsed
    and patted dry

2 tablespoons fresh lemon juice

2 tablespoons sugar

2 tablespoons chopped fresh mint leaves

FOR THE GARNISH:

6 full mint sprigs

1. Prepare the Blueberry Fool: Place 1 cup of the blueberries and the ¼ cup sugar in a saucepan over medium-low heat, and cook, stirring occasionally, until the sugar has dissolved and the berries have softened, about 10 minutes. Transfer the berries to a bowl, and let them cool completely. (To speed the process, chill the berries in the refrigerator for 20 minutes, or for 5 minutes in the freezer.)

2. Combine the cooled cooked berries with the remaining 1 cup uncooked blueberries. Set aside.

3. Combine the cream, the remaining 3 tablespoons sugar, and the vanilla in a large bowl. Whip with an electric mixer until the cream holds soft peaks. Add the crème fraîche and continue beating just until it is combined and the mixture again holds soft peaks.

4. Using a large rubber spatula, gently fold the blueberry mixture into the whipped cream. Do not overmix—you want to create a marbleized effect. Refrigerate, loosely covered, for up to 2 hours before serving.

5. While the fool is chilling, prepare the Berry Fruit Salad: Combine the blueberries, blackberries, lemon juice, and sugar in a bowl. Let it rest for 2 hours at room temperature for the juices to develop. Shortly before serving, toss the berry mixture with the chopped mint.

6. To serve, spoon about ½ cup of the fruit salad into each of six dessert bowls, and top with a generous portion of the fool. Garnish each portion with a mint sprig. 🌿

OUR AMBROSIA

SERVES 8

from the Greek *ambrotos*, "ambrosia," meaning "immortal," refers to the food of the ancient gods, thought to bestow immortality. It's more commonly known in the South as a dessert. Made from a combination of canned mandarin oranges, pineapple, marshmallows, coconut, pecans or walnuts, and sour cream, it's one of those buffet table entries that is both beloved and laughed at (usually by the same people who pile a big mound on their plates). While I enjoy the original, I've updated ambrosia, combining many delicious fresh fruits in a creamy salad to serve on its own or over a slice of pound cake. Eating it may not make you immortal, but it sure will make you glad to be alive.

2 bananas

2 tablespoons fresh lemon juice

1 cup red seedless grapes, halved crosswise

1 cup diced ripe pineapple (¼-inch dice)

1 cup diced ripe cantaloupe (¼-inch dice)

1 cup diced hulled ripe strawberries (¼-inch dice)

2 kiwis, peeled and cut into ¼ inch dice

½ cup chopped fresh mint leaves

½ cup sour cream

1 tablespoon fresh orange juice

1 tablespoon sugar

1. Slice the bananas in half lengthwise, and then slice them crosswise. Combine the banana slices with the lemon juice in a bowl, and toss (this will prevent the bananas from discoloring).

2. Combine the grapes, pineapple, cantaloupe, strawberries, kiwis, the bananas with any lemon juice, and all but 1 tablespoon of the mint in a large bowl.

3. In a separate bowl, combine the sour cream, orange juice, and sugar. Add this dressing to the fruit, and use a rubber spatula to gently fold it in. For the best texture and vibrant colors, do not overmix.

4. Serve the ambrosia in pretty glass bowls, sprinkled with the reserved 1 tablespoon chopped mint. 🌿

STRAWBERRIES-AND-CREAM TART

SERVES 6 TO 8

When local berries are in season, there's nothing better than strawberries and cream, and this is the ideal way to combine them in an elegant tart. The berries stand at attention, glazed to a high sheen with strawberry jam. The tart looks and tastes best the day it is made.

FOR THE CRUST:

1½ cups all-purpose flour

1 tablespoon sugar

1 teaspoon salt

10 tablespoons (1¼ sticks) unsalted butter, chilled, cut into small squares

¼ cup ice water, or more as needed

FOR THE PASTRY CREAM FILLING:

⅓ cup sugar

1 tablespoon all-purpose flour

1 tablespoon cornstarch

1 pinch salt

2 large egg yolks

1 cup heavy (whipping) cream

½ cup whole milk

2 teaspoon pure vanilla extract

1 tablespoon unsalted butter

¼ cup crème fraîche

FOR THE BERRY TOPPING:

4 cups ripe strawberries (preferably small berries), lightly rinsed, hulled, and patted dry

¼ cup strained strawberry preserves

1. Prepare the crust: Combine the flour, sugar, and salt in a food processor, and pulse to mix. Add the butter and pulse until the mixture resembles a coarse meal. With the machine running, trickle the ¼ cup ice water through the feed tube, processing just until the dough gathers together. (If the dough seems dry, add up to 1 tablespoon more water, ½ teaspoon at a time.) Flatten the dough with the palm of your hand to form a thick disk. Wrap the disk in plastic wrap, and refrigerate it for at least 1 hour or as long as 2 days.

2. Remove the dough from the refrigerator. Roll it out on a lightly floured work surface to form a round that is 12 inches in diameter and ⅛ inch thick. Work quickly, as the dough can become sticky. Using a spatula to help lift the dough, fold the round loosely in half, and then into quarters. Gently transfer it to a 10-inch tart pan with removable bottom, centering the corner of the dough in the center of the pan. Unfold the dough and press it lightly into the pan. If the dough should tear, just press it gently together. Trim the edges so that the dough is even with the rim of the pan. Chill in the refrigerator for 30 minutes.

3. Preheat the oven to 350°F.

4. Remove the tart pan from the refrigerator. Press a double layer of heavy-duty aluminum foil into the tart shell and bake until it is set, 15 minutes. Remove the foil and continue baking until it is golden brown, 15 minutes. Let the crust cool completely on a wire rack.

5. Meanwhile, prepare the cream filling: Combine the sugar, flour, cornstarch, and salt in a saucepan.

6. Whisk the egg yolks, ½ cup of the cream, and the milk together in a small bowl. Then whisk this mixture into the dry ingredients until smooth. Place the saucepan over medium heat and cook, whisking constantly, until the mixture is thick and is starting to boil, about 10 minutes. Continue to cook for 1 minute, whisking constantly. The mixture should be thick and smooth. Remove the pan from the heat, and press the cream through a strainer into a bowl. Stir in the vanilla and the butter. Place a piece of plastic wrap directly on the surface (to prevent a skin from forming), and refrigerate until completely cooled, about 20 minutes.

7. When the pastry cream is completely cooled, whisk it well to fluff it up.

8. In another bowl, whip the remaining ½ cup cream until it holds stiff peaks. Whisk in the crème fraîche. Then whisk this cream mixture into the pastry cream until just combined. Spread 1¼ cups of the filling over the bottom of the cooled tart shell.

9. To complete the tart, cover the surface with a single layer of strawberries, all standing on their stem ends.

10. To glaze the tart, place the strained strawberry preserves and 1 tablespoon water in a saucepan over medium heat and stir until thinned, 2 minutes. Use a pastry brush to gently brush the glaze over the strawberries. Refrigerate until ready to serve. ❧

YES, THERE ARE 11 RECIPES HERE

It's not that I can't count, it's that sometimes I can't limit myself. When considering the recipes for this chapter, I found myself spending too much time trying to decide which ones to eliminate. I finally got the total down to 11 and thought, well, an occasional bonus recipe is a very good thing. In this case, it's the Fresh Strawberry Sauce on page 412. It's so easy to prepare, and one like it may already be in your repertoire—but if it isn't, do add it. You'll find it a wonderful way to enjoy fresh berries.

FRESH
STRAWBERRY SAUCE

MAKES 1½ CUPS

Easy, simple, simply delicious—when strawberries are at their peak, this sauce is a must. It dresses up strawberry ice cream, strawberry shortcake, Fresh Lemon Ricotta Cheesecake (page 403), pancakes, and waffles. Just about everything tastes better with a spoonful of strawberry sauce.

1 pint (2 cups) ripe strawberries, lightly rinsed and patted dry
1 tablespoon fresh lemon juice
1 tablespoon sugar

Hull the strawberries and cut them into ½-inch pieces. Place them in a bowl, and toss with the lemon juice and sugar. Let them rest for 2 hours for the juices to develop. Then cover and refrigerate for up to 4 hours before using.

FRESH
APRICOT-ALMOND TART

SERVES 8 TO 10

Fresh apricots have such a fleeting season, so when they're in, I like to enjoy them in as many ways as possible. The almond-sprinkled crust in this tart brings out the rich apricot flavor. As the tart bakes, it develops a light "burn" from the sugar dusting, which is luscious-looking and -tasting. A small scoop of vanilla ice cream or dollop of crème fraîche is perfect for serving with this tart.

FOR THE PASTRY:
2 cups all-purpose flour
8 tablespoons (1 stick) unsalted butter, chilled, cut into small pieces

1 tablespoon sugar
½ teaspoon salt
1 large egg yolk
⅓ cup ice water

½ cup whole blanched almonds

6 tablespoons sugar

2 tablespoons all-purpose flour

2 pounds small ripe apricots,
    halved and pitted

4 tablespoons (½ stick) unsalted butter,
    cut into small pieces

½ cup apricot jam or apple jelly

1 tablespoon amaretto

1. Prepare the pastry: Combine the flour, butter, sugar, and salt in a food processor and process until the mixture resembles coarse meal. Add the egg yolk and ice water, and process until the dough just comes together. Wrap the dough in plastic wrap and refrigerate it for 1 hour.

2. Position a rack in the center of the oven, and preheat the oven to 400°F.

3. Prepare the filling: Combine the almonds, 4 tablespoons of the sugar, and the flour in a food processor and process until the mixture is a powder. Set it aside.

4. Roll the dough out on a lightly floured surface to form a large rectangle, ⅛ inch thick. Transfer the dough to a baking sheet. Sprinkle the almond mixture over the dough, leaving a 1-inch border all around.

5. Arrange the apricot halves, cut side down, in rows over the almond mixture. Fold the border of the dough up, pressing and pinching it together to make a nice rim. Dot the apricots with the butter, and sprinkle the remaining 2 tablespoons sugar over them.

6. Bake until the apricot juices are bubbling and the crust is golden, about 1 hour. (If the apricots start to burn, tent the tart loosely with aluminum foil.)

7. Meanwhile, combine the apricot jam and the amaretto in a small saucepan over low heat, and heat until warmed. (Or warm them on low power in a microwave oven.)

8. As soon as the tart comes out of the oven, brush the jam-amaretto mixture over it. Let the tart cool slightly. Serve warm.

NOTE: You can make this tart up to 1 day in advance. Cover it with aluminum foil and keep it at room temperature. If you wish to reheat it before serving, remove the foil and warm the tart in a preheated 350°F oven for 15 minutes.

LAURIE'S BEST APPLE PIE

SERVES 8

this fruit pie is extraordinary—a delicious crust and a marvelous mix of apples. Choose from Jonathan, Granny Smith, Pippin, Ida Red, and Rhode Island Greening apples. You want an apple that is not too watery and that has an assertive flavor. The spicing here is just right—it complements without being overpowering. Yummy!

FOR THE CRUST:

3 cups all-purpose flour

1 tablespoon sugar

1½ teaspoons salt

12 tablespoons (1½ sticks) unsalted butter, chilled, cut into small pieces

8 tablespoons solid vegetable shortening, chilled

4 to 5 tablespoons ice water

Butter, for greasing the pie plate

FOR THE FILLING:

10 tablespoons sugar

1½ tablespoons cornstarch

½ teaspoon ground cinnamon

1 pinch ground nutmeg

¼ teaspoon salt

Finely grated zest of 1 lemon

2½ pounds apples (mixed varieties; about 5 large), peeled, cored, and cut into ¼-inch-thick slices

1 large egg white, lightly beaten

2 tablespoons unsalted butter, cut into small pieces

TO FINISH THE TOP:

About 2 tablespoons heavy (whipping) cream

2 tablespoons sugar

1. Prepare the crust: Place the flour, sugar, and salt in a food processor and pulse the machine on and off to combine. Add the butter and shortening, and process until the mixture resembles a coarse meal. Do not overprocess. Gradually add the ice water through the feed tube, pulsing the machine once or twice between additions, until the dough holds together. Divide the dough in half, and form each half into a disk. Wrap the disks of dough in plastic wrap, and refrigerate for at least 1 hour or as long as 2 days.

2. Butter a 9-inch glass pie plate. Remove 1 dough disk from the refrigerator. Roll it out on a lightly floured work surface to form a round that is ⅛ inch thick and 2 inches larger than the pie plate. Using a spatula and working quickly so the dough doesn't become sticky, lift the dough, fold it loosely in half, and then fold it into quarters. Gently transfer it to the pie plate, centering the corner of the dough in the center of the pie plate. Unfold the dough and press it lightly into the pie plate to fit. If the dough should tear, just press it lightly together. Trim the dough, leaving a 1-inch overhang. Place the pie plate in the refrigerator.

3. Line a baking sheet with wax paper. Remove the other dough disk from the refrigerator and roll it out the same way, forming a round that is 2 inches wider than the pie plate. Trim off the uneven edges. Transfer the round (which will be the top crust) to the prepared baking sheet. Roll out the scraps and use a knife to cut out six leaf shapes, each 3 inches long and 1 inch wide, to decorate the pie. Place them on the baking sheet as well. Cover with another sheet of wax paper, and place in the refrigerator.

4. Position a rack in the center of the oven, and preheat the oven to 425°F.

5. Prepare the filling: Combine the sugar, cornstarch, cinnamon, nutmeg, salt, and lemon zest in a large bowl. Add the apples and toss well.

6. Brush the egg white lightly all over the bottom crust (this will prevent the crust from getting soggy).

Mound the apples in the bottom crust, and dot with the butter.

7. Carefully transfer the top crust to the pie, covering the apples. Trim the overhang to 1 inch. Use a little water to moisten the edges of the top and bottom crusts where they meet, press them together lightly, and turn them under. Crimp the edges decoratively.

8. Brush the cream all over the surface of the pie. Arrange the pastry leaves evenly around the circumference. Brush cream over the leaves as well. Cut a small slit in the dough between each pair of leaves, and cut a ¾-inch round out of the center. Sprinkle the 2 tablespoons sugar over the surface of the pie.

9. Place the pie plate on a rimmed baking sheet and bake for 15 minutes. Reduce the heat to 375°F and bake until the crust is golden and the juices are bubbling, about 1 hour. (If the top is getting too brown, tent the pie with aluminum foil after about 30 minutes.)

10. Let the pie cool on a wire rack before serving it slightly warm or at room temperature.

PEACH BLUEBERRY PIE

SERVES 8

My friend Emma Feigenbaum, who cooked with me for this book, says that when it comes to a pie filling, the combination of peaches and blueberries is her favorite, and with very good reason. Peach season—the height of ripe, juicy summer fruits—collides happily with blueberry season in this pie. A bit of brown sugar adds a caramel flavor. This could take the blue ribbon as your best summer pie.

FOR THE CRUST:

3 cups all-purpose flour

1 tablespoon granulated sugar

1½ teaspoons salt

12 tablespoons (1½ sticks) unsalted butter, chilled, cut into small pieces

8 tablespoons solid vegetable shortening, chilled

4 to 5 tablespoons ice water

Butter, for greasing the pie plate

FOR THE FILLING:

3 to 3½ pounds ripe peaches

1 tablespoon fresh lemon juice

1 cup fresh blueberries, lightly rinsed and patted dry

1 tablespoon pure vanilla extract

½ cup granulated sugar

⅓ cup (packed) light brown sugar

5 tablespoons all-purpose flour

1 large egg white, lightly beaten

2 tablespoons unsalted butter, cut into small pieces

TO FINISH THE TOP:

2 tablespoons heavy (whipping) cream

2 tablespoons granulated sugar

1. Prepare the crust: Place the flour, sugar, and salt in a food processor and pulse the machine on and off to combine. Add the butter and shortening, and process until the mixture resembles a coarse meal. Do not overprocess. Gradually add the ice water through the feed tube, pulsing the machine once or twice between additions of water, until the dough holds together. Divide the dough in half, and form each half into a disk. Wrap the disks of dough in plastic wrap, and refrigerate for at least 1 hour or as long as 2 days.

2. Butter a 9-inch glass pie plate. Remove 1 dough disk from the refrigerator. Roll it out on a lightly floured work surface to form a round that is ⅛ inch thick and 2 inches larger than the pie plate. Using a spatula and working quickly so the dough doesn't become sticky, lift the dough, fold it loosely in half, and then fold it into quarters. Gently transfer it to the pie plate, centering the corner of the dough in the center of the pie plate. Unfold the dough and press it lightly into the pie plate to fit. If the dough should tear, just press it lightly together. Trim the dough, leaving a 1-inch overhang. Place the pie plate in the refrigerator.

3. Line a baking sheet with wax paper. Remove the other dough disk from the refrigerator and roll it out the same way, forming a round that is 2 inches wider than the pie plate. Transfer the round to the prepared baking sheet. Cover it with another sheet of wax paper, and place in the refrigerator.

4. Position a rack in the center of the oven, and preheat the oven to 425°F.

5. Prepare the filling: Bring a large pot of water to a boil.

6. Using a paring knife, cut an X in the bottom of each peach. Drop the peaches into the boiling water and leave them for 1 minute. Then transfer them to a large bowl. When they are cool enough to handle, slip off the skins. Cut the peaches into ¾-inch-thick wedges and place them in a large bowl. Add the lemon juice (to prevent discoloring) and toss.

7. Add the blueberries, vanilla, granulated sugar, brown sugar, and the flour to the peaches, and toss well to combine.

8. Brush the egg white lightly all over the bottom crust (this will prevent the crust from getting soggy). Spoon the filling into the bottom crust and dot with the butter.

9. Remove the top crust from the refrigerator, and cut it into ¾-inch-wide strips. Arrange the strips in a lattice design over the filling. Trim the overhangs to 1 inch. Use a little water to moisten the edges of the strips where they meet the bottom crust, press the strips and crust together lightly, and turn them under. Crimp the edges decoratively.

10. Brush the cream over the lattice and the rim. Sprinkle the 2 tablespoons sugar over the surface.

11. Place the pie plate on a rimmed baking sheet and bake for 15 minutes. Reduce the heat to 375°F and bake until the lattice is golden and the juices are bubbling, 50 to 60 minutes. (If the lattice is getting too brown, tent the pie with aluminum foil after about 30 minutes.)

12. Let the pie cool on a wire rack before serving it slightly warm or at room temperature.

SUMMER BERRY CRISP

SERVES 6

fruit crisps, all hot and bubbly, can't be beat. The combination of blueberries, raspberries, and blackberries, spiked with a pinch of cinnamon, is stunning, and the crunchy top, with its oaty texture, is a great foil for the berries. A scoop of whipped cream or vanilla ice cream is essential with this very summery dessert.

Butter, for greasing the pie plate

2 cups fresh blueberries, lightly rinsed and patted dry

2 cups fresh blackberries, lightly rinsed and patted dry

2 cups fresh raspberries, lightly rinsed and patted dry

¼ cup granulated sugar

¼ cup all-purpose flour

¼ teaspoon ground cinnamon

FOR THE CRISP TOPPING:

1 cup rolled oats

½ cup all-purpose flour

½ cup (packed) light brown sugar

½ cup granulated sugar

1 pinch salt

8 tablespoons (1 stick) unsalted butter, chilled, cut into small pieces

FOR SERVING:

Whipped cream or vanilla ice cream

1. Position a rack in the center of the oven, and preheat the oven to 350°F. Butter a 9-inch glass pie plate.

2. Place all the berries in a large bowl. Combine the sugar, flour, and cinnamon in a small bowl, stir together well, and then gently toss the mixture with the berries. Transfer the berry mixture to the prepared pie plate, and set it aside.

3. Prepare the crisp topping: Combine the oats, flour, brown sugar, granulated sugar, and salt in a bowl, and stir well. Using a pastry blender or two knives, work in the butter until the mixture resembles a coarse meal. Sprinkle the topping evenly over the berries.

4. Place the pie plate on a baking sheet, and bake until the fruit is bubbling and the topping is golden brown, about 1 hour.

5. Allow the crisp to cool slightly on a wire rack. Serve it in dessert bowls, topped with whipped cream or vanilla ice cream. 🌿

BANANA UPSIDE-DOWN CAKE

SERVES 8

Whenever I eat at Craft, Tom Colicchio's New York City restaurant, I know I can expect perfectly prepared food, and this crackly banana cake created by pastry chef Karen DeMasco is a caramelized dream of a dessert.

3 small to medium-size ripe bananas

2 cups sugar

4 tablespoons (½ stick) unsalted butter

1½ cups all-purpose flour

2 teaspoons baking powder

½ teaspoon coarse (kosher) salt

½ cup clarified butter (see Note, page 196)

2 large eggs, at room temperature

½ cup buttermilk

2 teaspoons pure vanilla extract

1. Position a rack in the center of the oven, and preheat the oven to 325°F.

2. Cut the bananas in half lengthwise, and then cut each piece in half crosswise. Set them aside.

3. Combine 1 cup of the sugar with about 2 tablespoons water (enough so that the mixture looks like damp sand) in a saucepan. Melt the sugar over high heat, swirling the pan occasionally, until it turns a dark amber, about 6 minutes (watch closely; once it gets going, it goes fast). Add the butter and stir to combine. Then immediately pour the mixture into an 8-inch cake pan, and set it aside for 3 to 5 minutes to allow the caramel to set.

4. Arrange the bananas, cut side down, in a single layer on top of the caramel.

5. Sift the flour, baking powder, and salt together into a bowl, and set aside.

6. Using the whisk attachment in an electric mixer, combine the remaining 1 cup sugar with the clarified butter. With the mixer on low speed, add the eggs, one at a time, beating after each addition. Add the buttermilk and vanilla. Add the flour mixture in three batches, beating well after each addition. Pour the batter over the bananas.

7. Bake until the cake is beginning to pull away from the sides of the pan and springs back when touched with a finger, about 50 minutes.

8. Allow the cake to cool in the pan for 5 minutes. Then invert it onto a platter, and serve warm or at room temperature. ❧

"...REMINISCENT OF THE DAYS OF ICE-CREAM PARLORS."

ICE CREAMS AND SORBETS

There is one thing that comes to mind whenever I think of ice cream: the Good Humor man who used to come down my street every night about 6:30 P.M. when I was a child. I'm sure I'm not the only one to remember the bells ringing on the truck, announcing its arrival. We kids would line up on the curb desperately hoping the truck wouldn't run out of our choice by the time it was our turn.

Love for ice cream doesn't fade when you reach adulthood. And nowadays, creative chefs and ice-cream artisans are making and selling the most glorious ice creams in flavors we'd never have thought of years ago. This chapter includes traditional choices like fresh summery strawberry and cool mint chocolate chip, and delicious new choices like burnt orange and Key lime.

Adulthood also brings with it an appreciation of the lighter icy dessert—sorbet—and the mix of flavors here (blueberry, green apple, raspberry cassis, to name a few) will keep your ice-cream maker churning away.

Have an ice-cream sundae party on the porch: Make plenty of ice cream ahead of time, and take it out of the freezer shortly before serving. Get out some old-fashioned ice-cream dishes, and start scooping up the sundaes! 🌺

BILL GROSS'S BURNT ORANGE ICE CREAM

MAKES 5 CUPS

bill Gross, who was executive sous chef at Café Gray in New York City, was kind enough to create this recipe for me—and it is simply delicious. The technique is fascinating, but it does require some careful watching while the sugar caramelizes. The oranges are prepared two days ahead, and the ice cream one day ahead—and the waiting is well worth it!

FOR THE ORANGES:

2½ cups granulated sugar

4 tablespoons (½ stick) unsalted butter,
    at room temperature

2 large navel oranges (each about 6 ounces)

FOR THE ICE CREAM:

3 cups heavy (whipping) cream

⅔ cup half-and-half

Seeds scraped from 1 vanilla bean (see Note,
    page 402), or 1 tablespoon pure vanilla extract

2 large egg yolks

1. One day ahead, prepare the oranges: Position a rack in the center of the oven, and preheat the oven to 450°F.

2. Place ½ cup of the sugar on a plate. Rub the butter over the oranges, then roll them in the sugar.

3. Pour the unused sugar from the plate into an 8-inch square baking pan, and shake it around to cover the bottom of the pan. Place the oranges in the pan and bake, moving them around once to break up any unmelted sugar, until they start to color and some of the sugar in the pan starts to melt, 15 to 20 minutes.

4. Remove the pan from the oven (leaving the oven on), and using tongs and a sharp knife, carefully quarter the oranges. Place the quarters, skin side up, in the baking pan and bake until the peel is dark brown, about 35 minutes. Let the orange quarters cool slightly.

5. Remove the peel from 4 of the browned quarters, discarding the pulp. Leave the other 4 quarters intact.

6. Combine the orange peel, the 4 intact quarters, the sugar from the pan, and the remaining 2 cups sugar in a food processor, and puree. Strain the puree into a container, cover it, and refrigerate for at least 8 hours.

7. The next day, prepare the ice cream mixture: Place the orange puree in a saucepan over medium-low heat, and bring it to a simmer.

8. While the orange puree is heating, whisk the cream, half-and-half, vanilla seeds, and egg yolks together in a large bowl. Then, whisking constantly, slowly add the hot orange puree. Let the mixture cool to room temperature, and then refrigerate it until it is cold, 3 to 4 hours.

9. Freeze the mixture in an ice-cream maker according to the manufacturer's instructions.

10. Transfer the ice cream to a container, cover, and store in the freezer until ready to serve. ❧

KEY LIME ICE CREAM

MAKES 1½ QUARTS

If you thought Key lime pie was good, just wait until you taste this ice cream. It's the real McCoy, creamy and smooth, and bottled Key lime juice does the trick if you can't get fresh. Fresh lime zest adds a nice intensity of flavor. For absolute perfection, drizzle a little Schrafft's Hot Fudge Sauce (page 383) over this ice cream.

2 cups half-and-half

2 cups heavy (whipping) cream

6 large egg yolks

½ cup sugar

½ cup fresh or bottled Key lime juice
   (see Sources, page 439)

1 tablespoon finely grated lime zest

1. Combine the half-and-half and the heavy cream in a saucepan over medium-low heat, and heat to just below the boiling point.

2. Meanwhile, combine the egg yolks and the sugar in a bowl, and whisk until lemon-colored, about 2 minutes.

3. Remove the saucepan from the heat. Whisking constantly, slowly pour 1 cup of the hot cream mixture into the egg yolks, and continue whisking until smooth. Then, whisking constantly, slowly pour the egg mixture back into the cream mixture and whisk until smooth. Whisk in the Key lime juice. Cook over medium heat, stirring constantly, until the mixture coats the back of the spoon, 6 to 8 minutes. Do not let the mixture boil.

4. Strain the mixture through a fine-mesh strainer into a bowl, and stir in the lime zest. Let it cool to room temperature.

5. Freeze the mixture in an ice-cream maker according to the manufacturer's instructions. Transfer the ice cream to a container, cover, and store in the freezer until ready to serve. ❧

MINT CHOCOLATE CHIP ICE CREAM

MAKES 1 QUART

mint chocolate chip ice cream is wonderfully refreshing and a perfect way to use all that yummy fresh mint in your garden. I add a few drops of green food coloring just to tint the ice cream an icy green, but you don't have too. Delicious.

2 cups half-and-half

2 cups heavy (whipping) cream

2 large bunches fresh mint (6 to 8 ounces total), rinsed, and patted dry

6 large egg yolks

¾ cup sugar

4 drops green food coloring (optional)

1 cup semisweet chocolate chips or coarsely chopped semisweet chocolate

1. Combine the half-and-half and the heavy cream in a saucepan over medium-high heat, and bring to a simmer. Remove the pan from the heat and add the mint, using a wooden spoon to push the leaves and stems under the cream and press on them a bit. Let the mixture sit, occasionally using the spoon to press on the leaves and stems, until the cream is infused with the flavor of the mint, 30 to 45 minutes (preferably 45).

2. Pour the cream through a fine-mesh strainer into a bowl to remove the mint, and return the strained cream to the saucepan. Bring it to a simmer over medium-low heat. Discard the mint.

3. Meanwhile, combine the egg yolks and the sugar in a bowl and whisk until lemon-colored, about 2 minutes.

4. Remove the saucepan from the heat. Whisking constantly, slowly pour 1 cup of the hot cream into the egg yolks, and continue whisking until smooth. Then, whisking constantly, slowly pour the egg mixture back into the cream mixture and whisk until smooth. Cook over medium heat, stirring constantly, until the mixture coats the back of the spoon, 6 to 8 minutes. Do not let the mixture boil.

5. Strain the mixture through a fine-mesh sieve into a bowl, and let it cool to room temperature. Stir in the green food coloring, if desired.

6. Following the manufacturer's instructions, partially freeze the mixture in an ice-cream maker. Just before the mixture has finished freezing, stir in the chocolate chips. Finish the freezing. Then transfer the ice cream to a container, cover, and store in the freezer until ready to serve. ✿

MOCHA ICE CREAM

MAKES 5 CUPS

Yum! This sophisticated espresso-and-chocolate ice cream combines two complementary flavors to produce a very grown-up dessert. It's a perfect ending to a meal of Braised Osso Buco (page 84). Serve it in parfait dishes with dollops of whipped cream.

2 cups half-and-half

3 tablespoons ground espresso beans
    (medium grind)

2 cups heavy (whipping) cream

8 large egg yolks

1 cup sugar

½ cup unsweetened cocoa powder

1. Heat 1 cup of the half-and-half in a small saucepan over medium heat to just below the boiling point. Remove the pan from the heat, stir in the coffee grounds, and set aside for 1 hour.

2. Line a strainer with a doubled piece of cheesecloth or a coffee filter, and strain the coffee mixture into a medium-size saucepan. Add the remaining 1 cup half-and-half and the cream, place it over medium heat, and heat it to just below the boiling point.

3. While the mixture is heating, combine the egg yolks and the sugar in a bowl, and whisk until lemon-colored, about 1½ minutes.

4. Remove the saucepan from the heat. Whisking constantly, slowly pour 1 cup of the hot cream mixture into the egg yolks, and continue whisking until smooth. Then, whisking constantly, slowly pour the egg mixture back into the cream mixture and whisk until smooth.

5. Place the cocoa powder in a bowl, and whisk 1 cup of the hot cream mixture into it to make a smooth paste. Whisk the chocolate paste back into the cream mixture until well mixed. Cook over medium heat, stirring constantly, until the mixture coats the back of a spoon, about 5 minutes. Do not let the mixture boil.

6. Strain the mixture through a fine-mesh sieve into a bowl, and let it cool to room temperature.

7. Freeze the mixture in an ice-cream maker according to the manufacturer's instructions. Then transfer the ice cream to a container, cover it, and store in the freezer until ready to serve.

STRAWBERRY ICE CREAM

MAKES 1 QUART

Old-fashioned homemade strawberry ice cream has a wonderful nostalgic feel to it—reminiscent of the days of ice-cream parlors. Soaking the sliced berries in sugar syrup keeps them from freezing in the ice-cream machine, making the ice cream both creamy and fruity. Scoop it into freshly made waffle cones (if you can find them at a local ice-cream store) or atop freshly baked waffles.

1 cup sugar

2 cups strawberries, rinsed, hulled, and coarsely sliced

2 cups heavy (whipping) cream

1 cup whole milk

2 large egg yolks

2 teaspoons pure vanilla extract

1. Make a sugar syrup: Combine ½ cup of the sugar with ½ cup water in a small saucepan and bring it to a boil over medium heat. Reduce the heat and simmer until the sugar dissolves, about 5 minutes. Let the syrup cool slightly.

2. Place 1 cup of the strawberries in a bowl and stir in ¼ cup of the warm sugar syrup. Let soak for 15 minutes.

3. Meanwhile, puree the remaining 1 cup strawberries in a food processor or blender. Set the puree aside.

4. Combine the cream and the milk in a saucepan over medium heat and heat, stirring frequently, until the mixture is hot but not boiling, about 8 minutes. Remove the pan from the heat.

5. Place the egg yolks, the remaining ½ cup sugar, and the vanilla in a small bowl and whisk to mix. Whisking constantly, slowly pour in 1 cup of the hot milk mixture and continue whisking until smooth. Then slowly pour the egg mixture back into the hot milk mixture in the saucepan, whisking constantly until well combined. Place the saucepan over medium-low heat and stir the mixture constantly until the mixture is thick enough to coat the back of a spoon, 6 to 8 minutes.

6. Strain the mixture through a fine-mesh sieve into a bowl, and let it cool completely.

7. Drain the strawberries soaking in syrup, and stir the berries into the cooled ice cream mixture. Stir in the pureed strawberries. Refrigerate until cold.

8. Freeze in an ice-cream maker according to the manufacturer's instructions. Transfer the ice cream to a container, cover, and store in the freezer until ready to serve. ❧

RASPBERRY CASSIS SORBET

MAKES 5 CUPS

Raspberries make a very elegant sorbet on their own, but cassis, made from black currants, is what makes this one special—it adds such depth of flavor and color. If you're a fan of raspberries, this is the sorbet for you. Serve it alongside Mango Sorbet (page 430).

2 packages (each 12 ounces) frozen raspberries
  (without syrup), thawed
¼ cup Sugar Syrup (page 8)
1 tablespoon fresh lemon juice
¼ cup crème de cassis

1. Combine the raspberries, sugar syrup, and lemon juice in a food processor. Add the crème de cassis and process to combine.

2. Freeze the mixture in an ice-cream maker according to the manufacturer's instructions. Then transfer it to a container, cover, and store in the freezer until ready to serve. 🌸

CREME DE CASSIS

Crème de Cassis is a sweet liqueur originally from Burgundy that is made from black currants crushed in alcohol with sugar added. Dijon is where some of the best cassis is made. If you've had a bottle in your liquor cabinet for the last decade (you bought it when kir—that white wine and cassis aperitif—was super popular), it's probably time to buy a fresh one, which will reward you with its flavor. And do add a bit to white wine—a traditional kir is still delicious.

BLUEBERRY SORBET

MAKES 1 ½ QUARTS

bryan Miller and Bill Yosses were kind enough to share their tempting recipe for blueberry sorbet with me; it appears in their book *Desserts for Dummies*. When it's blueberry season, there's nothing quite like a scoop of this sorbet atop Peach Blueberry Pie (page 416) or underneath Blueberry Fool (page 408). Bryan and Bill have captured the very essence of the berry in an easy-to-make dessert.

8 cups fresh blueberries, rinsed and
    patted dry
¾ cup sugar
¼ cup fresh lemon juice

1. Place the blueberries in a blender or food processor, and puree them. Transfer the puree to a medium-size saucepan.

2. Add the sugar, lemon juice, and ½ cup water to the puree, and bring to a boil. Remove the pan from the heat, and strain the mixture through a fine-mesh sieve into a bowl. Set it aside to cool.

3. Freeze the mixture in an ice-cream maker according to the manufacturer's instructions. Transfer the sorbet to a container, cover, and store in the freezer until ready to serve.

GREEN APPLE SORBET

MAKES 1 QUART

This refreshing pale green sorbet is delightful after a robust autumn dinner. Granny Smith apples have a crisp bite, and I love them for their palate-cleansing quality. Serve the sorbet in small wineglasses or delicate cut-glass bowls, garnished with a sprig of mint.

3 Granny Smith apples (1½ pounds)
2 tablespoons fresh lemon juice
1½ cups Sugar Syrup (page 8)
Mint sprigs, for garnish

1. Core the apples and cut them into thin slices (do not peel them). Place the slices in a bowl, and toss with the lemon juice.

2. Combine the sugar syrup with 1 cup water in a medium-size saucepan, and bring to a boil. Remove the pan from the heat and add the apple slices. Stir well to coat them with the syrup. Push the slices under the syrup as much as possible, and set the pan aside for 30 minutes.

3. Transfer the apples and syrup to a food processor or blender, and puree. Strain the puree through a fine-mesh strainer into a bowl, using the back of a spoon to press it through the strainer. Let the puree cool to room temperature.

4. Freeze the mixture in an ice-cream maker according to the manufacturer's instructions. Transfer the sorbet to a container, cover, and store in the freezer until ready to serve.

5. Spoon the sorbet into serving glasses or bowls, garnish each with a mint sprig, and serve.

MANGO SORBET

MAKES 1 QUART

his smooth, creamy sorbet partners well with the Raspberry Cassis and Green Apple sorbets (pages 427 and 429). Serve all three together in small glass bowls and you'll be reminded of a Gauguin painting! Be sure the mangoes are very ripe.

3 ripe mangoes (each 1 pound)

3 tablespoons fresh lemon juice

1 cup Sugar Syrup (page 8)

1. Peel and pit the mangoes (see box, page 368). Cut the fruit into chunks, place them in a food processor, and puree. Strain the puree through a fine-mesh sieve into a bowl, pressing on it with the back of a wooden spoon to remove any fibers.

2. Place 3 cups of the puree in a bowl. Stir in the lemon juice and the sugar syrup.

3. Freeze the mixture in an ice-cream maker according to the manufacturer's instructions. Transfer the sorbet to a container, cover, and store in the freezer until ready to serve. ♣

PINEAPPLE SORBET

MAKES 5 CUPS

a ripe fresh pineapple makes a surprisingly delicious sorbet. I serve this sweet pale lemon-colored confection alongside a royal-blue Blueberry Sorbet (page 428) for a dazzling visual and taste sensation. It also goes well with the fruit salad on page 407. Garnish each serving with a lavish mint sprig.

1 ripe pineapple (about 4 pounds)

1 tablespoon fresh lemon juice

1 cup Sugar Syrup (page 8)

Mint sprigs, for garnish

1. Peel and core the pineapple, and cut it into 1-inch cubes; you should have 1¾ pounds of cubes. Place the cubes in a food processor and process until the puree is lemon-colored and frothy, about 3 minutes. Strain the puree through a fine-mesh sieve into a bowl to remove any peel or fibers, using a spatula to press it through the strainer as necessary; you should now have 3½ cups of puree.

2. Combine the pineapple puree, lemon juice, and sugar syrup in a bowl and mix well.

3. Freeze the mixture in an ice-cream maker according to the manufacturer's instructions. Then transfer the sorbet to a container, cover it, and store in the freezer until ready to serve.

4. Spoon the sorbet into bowls or wineglasses, and garnish each with a mint sprig. ❧

BASICS

SOURCES

CONVERSIONS

INDEX

BASICS

Here to help you get your recipes off to a good start are a few pantry favorites—those recipes that are called for over and over again as ingredients in other recipes. Some tasty broths, a basic tomato sauce, instructions on roasting garlic and peppers—get these right and you can't go wrong.

ROASTED GARLIC

MAKES 1 HEAD

It's amazing how uncooked garlic is transformed from a hard sharp clove to a soft sweet puree when it's roasted. It takes just an hour and it's so easy to do. Roasted garlic became all the rage a few years ago, when chic restaurants were offering sweet roasted garlic to spread on thick toasted croutons.

1 head garlic
1 to 2 tablespoons olive oil
½ teaspoon dried thyme leaves
Salt and freshly ground black pepper, to taste

1. Preheat the oven to 350°F.

2. Remove the papery exterior from the garlic, but do not separate or peel the cloves. Cut a ¼-inch slice off the top of the head.

3. Place the garlic in an ovenproof ramekin. Drizzle the oil over it, and then sprinkle with the thyme, salt, and pepper. Cover the ramekin with aluminum foil and bake the garlic until it is soft, about 1 hour.

4. Let cool for a few minutes, then squeeze the soft roasted garlic out of the cloves, and use as directed.

BASIC CHICKEN BROTH

MAKES 3 QUARTS

there's nothing like homemade chicken broth. I like to punch up the flavor by adding a few extra wings to my soup chicken or stewing hen. My mom always included parsnips and fresh dill. All these flavors plus slow simmering result in a delicious broth. Try not to boil the broth as it cooks, because boiling will cloud the end result. Slow and steady is the key. Partially cover the pot so your broth doesn't cook away. You'll be using a tough chicken—usually excellent for soup but not very good for eating—but try the meat before you discard it. It might be fine for a little chicken salad.

1 soup chicken or stewing hen
    (5½ to 6 pounds), cut into 6 pieces,
    plus extra wings (optional)
1 large onion, unpeeled
4 whole cloves
2 celery ribs with leaves, cut into chunks
2 carrots, unpeeled, cut into chunks
2 parsnips, unpeeled, cut into chunks
1 large leek (white bulb and 2 inches green),
    trimmed, halved lengthwise, and well washed
4 cloves garlic, unpeeled, lightly crushed
2 plum tomatoes, halved and seeded
6 dill sprigs
6 flat-leaf parsley sprigs
6 whole black peppercorns
2 tablespoons coarse (kosher) salt

1. Remove the giblets from the chicken and reserve them for another use. Rinse the chicken and wings and trim off any excess fat. Place the chicken and extra wings, if using, in a large soup pot.

2. Stud the onion with the cloves, add it to the soup pot, and then add all the remaining ingredients. Pour in 12 cups of water.

3. Bring the water to a boil over high heat, skimming off any foam that forms on the surface. Reduce the heat to medium, partially cover the pot, and simmer until the chicken is cooked through, about 1½ hours.

4. Remove the chicken pieces from the pot (set them aside if you want to use the meat). Discard the large vegetables. Carefully strain the broth through a fine-mesh sieve into a bowl. Taste, and adjust the seasonings as needed. Let the broth cool to room temperature. If it is not for immediate use, transfer the cooled broth to a storage container, cover it, and refrigerate it until the layer of fat has solidified on top, 4 hours or overnight. Remove the fat before using.

NOTE: Refrigerated, the broth will keep for up to 3 days; frozen, for up to 3 months. ❧

BEEF BROTH

MAKES ABOUT 6 CUPS

These days it seems to be a great luxury to have homemade beef broth on hand—but it's not at all difficult to make. Roasting the bones and vegetables first results in a darker and richer-tasting broth.

4 onions, unpeeled

4 celery ribs with leaves

4 carrots, unpeeled

4 tomatoes

3 parsnips, unpeeled

3 leeks (white bulb and 3 inches green), halved
    lengthwise and well washed

4 cloves garlic, unpeeled, lightly crushed

3 pounds soup beef with bones

3 pounds beef bones

8 whole black peppercorns

4 whole cloves

4 large thyme sprigs

1 bay leaf

Coarse (kosher) salt, to taste

1. Preheat the oven to 450°F.

2. Rinse and coarsely chop the onions, celery, carrots, tomatoes, parsnips, and leeks. Place them in a flameproof roasting pan, add the garlic, and arrange the meat and bones on top. Roast, uncovered, for 1 hour.

3. Transfer all the meat, bones, and vegetables to a very large soup pot.

4. Pour 4 cups water into the roasting pan and bring it to a hard boil over high heat, scraping up any brown bits in the bottom of the pan. Pour this into the soup pot, and add another 12 cups water.

5. Add the peppercorns, cloves, thyme sprigs, and bay leaf to the pot. Bring to a boil over high heat, skimming off any foam that forms on the surface. Then reduce the heat to medium-low, partially cover the pot, and simmer for 2 hours.

6. Partially uncover the pot and simmer for 30 minutes. Add salt to taste, and simmer for another 30 minutes to reduce the liquid and concentrate the flavors.

7. Remove the meat and bones. Strain the broth through a sieve into a large bowl. Discard the solids. Then line the sieve with a double thickness of dampened cheesecloth and strain the broth again. Allow it to cool to room temperature.

8. If the broth is to be used immediately, allow the fat to rise to the surface, then degrease the broth thoroughly by skimming off the fat with a metal spoon or by pouring the broth through a gravy separator. If it is not for immediate use, transfer the cooled broth to a storage container, cover it, and refrigerate it until the layer of fat has solidified on top, 4 hours or overnight. Remove the fat before using.

NOTE: Refrigerated, the broth will keep for up to 2 days; frozen, for up to 3 months. ✤

VEGETABLE BROTH

MAKES ABOUT 6 CUPS

homemade vegetable broth comes in very handy these days, with so many star vegetable dishes calling for vegetable broth in place of chicken broth. The goal is to achieve a deep, rich flavor. So instead of placing the vegetables directly in my soup pot, I sauté them to bring out some caramelization, adding flavor to the finished broth. Each vegetable contributes: mushrooms add earthy flavor while the parsnips add sweetness. Try not to let the broth boil—it'll turn cloudy.

1 onion

3 whole cloves

2 tablespoons olive oil

2 celery ribs with leaves, cut into large chunks

2 carrots, unpeeled, rinsed and cut into large chunks

2 leeks (white bulb and 3 inches green), trimmed, halved lengthwise, well rinsed, and cut into large chunks

1 parsnip, unpeeled, rinsed and cut into large chunks

4 cloves garlic, lightly crushed

2 ripe plum tomatoes, quartered and seeded

4 white mushrooms, wiped clean and cut in half

1 new potato, unpeeled, rinsed and cut in half

6 flat-leaf parsley sprigs, stems lightly crushed

4 dill sprigs

1 bay leaf

4 whole black peppercorns

2 teaspoons coarse (kosher) salt

1. Stud the onion with the cloves.

2. Heat the oil in a large heavy pot over medium-low heat. Add the onion, celery, carrots, and leeks and cook, stirring, until slightly caramelized, about 15 minutes.

3. Add 10 cups water to the pot, and then add all the remaining ingredients. Bring to a boil over high heat. Reduce the heat to medium-low, partially cover the pot, and simmer for 1 hour.

4. Uncover the pot and simmer for 30 minutes more to reduce the liquid and concentrate the flavors. Taste, and adjust the seasonings as needed.

5. Strain the broth through a colander into a large bowl, pressing down on the vegetables with the back of a spoon to extract all the broth. Allow the broth to cool to room temperature.

6. Use the broth immediately, or transfer it to an airtight container and refrigerate it.

NOTES: Refrigerated, the broth will keep for up to 4 days; frozen, for up to 3 months. This recipe is easily doubled. ❧

BASIC TOMATO SAUCE

MAKES 8 CUPS

It is important to have a very good basic tomato sauce in your culinary repertoire, to toss over some pasta for an easy dinner or to use in other sauces. This one can be made all-year-round and either used right away or frozen so you'll always have some on hand.

4 cans (each 28 ounces) peeled Italian plum
    tomatoes, undrained

⅓ cup extra-virgin olive oil

4 cloves garlic, bruised

½ cup dry red wine

½ cup (packed) coarsely torn fresh basil leaves

½ cup chopped fresh flat-leaf parsley leaves

2 teaspoons dried oregano

2 teaspoons sugar

¼ teaspoon crushed red pepper flakes

Salt and freshly ground black pepper, to taste

1. Drain the tomatoes, reserving the juices. Measure out and set aside 2½ cups of the juices. Coarsely chop the tomatoes, and set them aside.

2. Heat the oil in a large heavy pot over low heat. Add the garlic and cook until slightly colored, about 5 minutes.

3. Remove the pot from the heat, and use a slotted spoon to remove the garlic from the oil; discard the garlic. Add the chopped tomatoes and 1½ cups of the reserved juices to the pot. Stir in the wine.

4. Return the pot to the heat and stir in the basil, parsley, oregano, sugar, red pepper flakes, and salt and pepper. Simmer, uncovered, stirring occasionally, for 30 minutes. Do not let it boil.

5. Taste, and adjust the seasonings as needed. If the sauce is too thick, thin it with some of the reserved tomato juices.

6. Serve immediately, or cool to room temperature, cover, and store in the refrigerator for up to 2 days. This sauce freezes well for up to 2 months. ❧

ROASTED
BELL PEPPERS

Roasting peppers takes more care and attention than I had thought in the past. I find that if they get too charred, it ruins the texture, so I keep the peppers farther away from the heat nowadays to achieve a slow, even char. After the peppers steam, the skins are easy to peel off.

Red, green, yellow, or orange bell peppers,
    cut in half lengthwise, stemmed,
    and seeded
Extra-virgin olive oil, if storing

1. Position a rack about 7 inches from the heat source, and preheat the broiler. Line a baking sheet with aluminum foil.

2. Flatten each pepper half slightly with the palm of your hand. Lay the peppers, skin side up, in a single layer on the prepared baking sheet. Broil until the skins are charred (but not too crisp), 12 to 15 minutes.

3. Transfer the peppers to a plastic or paper bag, close it, and let them steam in the bag for 15 to 20 minutes.

4. Slip off the charred skins and use the peppers as directed in the recipe. Or if you are storing them, drizzle the peppers lightly with olive oil, place them in an airtight container, and refrigerate for up to 10 days. 🌿

HOW TO COOK AN ARTICHOKE

Bring a large pot of lightly salted water to a boil, or bring water to a boil in the bottom of a pot fitted with a vegetable steamer.

Remove the tough outer leaves from the bottom of the artichoke. Snip the tips off the remaining leaves, slice off 1½ inches of the top of the artichoke, and then slice off the stem. Sit the artichokes right side up in the boiling water or the vegetable steamer and boil or steam until the leaves are tender, about 40 minutes. Remove the artichokes from the pot or steamer and drain them, if necessary, upside down on a rack set in a pan.

To reach the artichoke heart, remove the outer leaves (eat the soft bottoms of each leaf dipped in sauce or in melted butter mixed with lemon juice), then twist out the inner leaves and use a teaspoon to scrape out the fuzzy choke; discard the choke. Now the heart is ready to enjoy dipped in a little sauce.

SOURCES

In this age of big, savvy supermarkets, most of the ingredients included in this cookbook are not difficult to find. A few might still be a bit harder to locate, however, and the Internet is a good resource for store locators and online purchases. Below is a little extra help, should you need it.

AIDELLS SAUSAGE (used in Red Beans and Andouille Sausages, page 293): Available in supermarkets all over the country but if you can't find them, go to www.aidells.com. The website has a store locator by city, town, village—you name it. If that fails, you can order online.

CARM GRANDE ESCOLHA EXTRA-VIRGIN OLIVE OIL (used in Sherry Vinaigrette, page 270): Available in local fine food shops. It's imported by Forever Cheese and is available through its website, www .forevercheese.com. It is also available at Dean & DeLuca, www.deandeluca.com.

L'ESTORNELL RESERVA SHERRY VINEGAR (used in Sherry Vinaigrette, page 270): If you can't find it locally, it's easy to order online at www.amazon.com.

KEY LIME JUICE (used in Key Lime Ice Cream, page 423): Most fine food stores carry Key lime juice. In the unlikely case that you cannot find it, a popular brand is Nellie & Joe's Famous Key West Lime Juice. There is a store locator on their site, www.keylimejuice.com, or you can order directly from them, although there may be a minimum purchase.

MOULARD DUCK LEGS (used in Tom Valenti's Braised Duck in Red Wine and Tomatoes, page 160): If you can't find them at your local butcher, they are available from D'Artagnan, Inc., www.dartagnan.com or (800) 327-8246.

PANKO (Japanese bread crumbs, used in Tuna Burger Extravaganza, page 117): Now sold in many supermarkets and fine food stores. If you can't find them in your area, several varieties are at www.amazon.com.

POMEGRANATE JUICE (used in Pomegranate Coupe de Champagne, page 7): Made by POM, pomegranate juice is available in the refrigerated juice or salad section of grocery stores. If you can't find it, go to www.pomwonderful.com for a store locator.

PRESERVED LEMONS (used in Joan Nathan's Cooked Tomato and Pepper Salad, page 269): Can be mail-ordered from Mustapha's Moroccan, www.mustaphas.com, or by phone, (800) 481-4590.

ROSE WATER (used in Vodka Rose, page 9): Indian and other ethnic markets carry rose water, but if you can't find it, go to www.Kalustyans.com. They carry a full line of Indian products.

SALT COD (used in Brandade de Morue, page 332): Can usually be found in ethnic markets or ordered through your local fish shop. If you have trouble, it's amazing what you can find at www.amazon.com—even salt cod.

WASABI PASTE (used in Wasabi Mashed Potatoes, page 330): If you can't find a brand locally, S&B Prepared Wasabi in a Tube is available at www.yesshopnow.com.

CONVERSIONS

TABLESPOONS AND OUNCES TO GRAMS

(U.S. CUSTOMARY SYSTEM)   **(METRIC SYSTEM)**

1 pinch = less than ⅛ teaspoon (dry)	0.50 grams
1 dash = 3 drops to ¼ teaspoon (liquid)	1.25 grams
1 teaspoon (liquid)	5.00 grams
3 teaspoons = 1 tablespoon = ½ ounce	14.30 grams
2 tablespoons = 1 ounce	28.35 grams
4 tablespoons = 2 ounces = ¼ cup	56.70 grams
8 tablespoons = 4 ounces = ¼ cup (1 stick of butter)	113.40 grams
8 tablespoons (flour) = about 2 ounces	72.00 grams
16 tablespoons = 8 ounces = 1 cup = ½ pound	226.80 grams
32 tablespoons = 16 ounces = 2 cups = 1 pound	453.60 grams or 0.4536 kilogram
64 tablespoons = 32 ounces = 1 quart = 2 pounds	907.00 grams or 0.9070 kilogram
1 quart = (roughly 1 liter)	

TEMPERATURES: °FAHRENHEIT (F) TO °CELSIUS (C)

−10°F = −23.3°C (freezer storage)		300°F = 148.8°C	
0°F = −17.7°C		325°F = 162.8°C	
32°F = 0°C (water freezes)		350°F = 177°C (baking)	
50°F = 10°C		375°F = 190.5°C	
68°F = 20°C (room temperature)		400°F = 204.4°C (hot oven)	
100°F = 37.7°C		425°F = 218.3°C	
150°F = 65.5°C		450°F = 232°C (very hot oven)	
205°F = 96.1°C (water simmers)		475°F = 246.1°C	
212°F = 100°C (water boils)		500°F = 260°C (broiling)	

CONVERSION FACTORS

ounces to grams: multiply ounce figure by 28.3 to get number of grams

grams to ounces: multiply gram figure by 0.0353 to get number of ounces

pounds to grams: multiply pound figure by 453.59 to get number of grams

pounds to kilograms: multiply pound figure by 0.45 to get number of kilograms

ounces to milliliters: multiply ounce figure by 30 to get number of milliliters

cups to liters: multiply cup figure by 0.24 to get number of liters

Fahrenheit to Celsius: subtract 32 from the Fahrenheit figure, multiply by 5, then divide by 9 to get Celsius figure

Celsius to Fahrenheit: multiply Celsius figure by 9, divide by 5, then add 32 to get Fahrenheit figure

inches to centimeters: multiply inch figure by 2.54 to get number of centimeters

centimeters to inches: multiply centimeter figure by 0.39 to get number of inches

INDEX